The Armies of the Caliphs

'. . . this is an extraordinarily rich and original book. It forces a reassessment of the early Islamic conquests from standpoints that have hitherto been totally ignored or undervalued.'

Professor Carole Hillenbrand, University of Edinburgh

During the mediaeval period, the Middle East was a battleground in which the Umayyad and the 'Abbasid Caliphs fought for dominance of an empire that stretched from Spain to the borders of India. *The Armies of the Caliphs* is the first major study of the relationship between army and society in the early Islamic period, and reveals the pivotal role of the military in politics.

Over the key period of 600–945, the Muslims developed a salaried, semi-professional army, dependent on the state for its livelihood. In this extraordinary survey, Kennedy shows how the army began to influence and eventually dominate the political system, and reflects on how the involvement of the military in Middle-Eastern politics today has its origins in this period.

Through an examination of recruitment, payment, weaponry and fortifications in the armies, *The Armies of the Caliphs* offers the most comprehensive view to date of how the early Muslim Empire grew to control so many people. Using Arabic chronicles, surviving documents, and archaeological evidence, this book analyses the military and the face of battle, and offers a timely reassessment of the early Islamic State.

Hugh Kennedy is Professor of Middle Eastern History at the University of St Andrews. His major publications include *The Early 'Abbasid Caliphate* (1980), *The Prophet and the Age of the Caliphs* (1986), *Crusader Castles* (1994) and *Muslim Spain and Portugal* (1996).

Warfare and History
General Editor
Jeremy Black
Professor of History, University of Exeter

Air Power in the Age of Total War
John Buckley

The Armies of the Caliphs: Military and Society in the Early Islamic State
Hugh Kennedy

The Balkan Wars, 1912–1913: Prelude to the First World War
Richard C. Hall

English Warfare, 1511–1642
Mark Charles Fissel

European and Native American Warfare, 1675–1815
Armstrong Starkey

European Warfare, 1660–1815
Jeremy Black

The First Punic War
J. F. Lazenby

Frontiersmen: Warfare in Africa Since 1950
Anthony Clayton

German Armies: War and German Politics, 1648–1806
Peter H. Wilson

The Great War 1914–1918
Spencer C. Tucker

Israel's Wars, 1947–1993
Ahron Bregman

The Korean War: No Victors, no Vanquished
Stanley Sandler

Modern Chinese Warfare, 1795–1989
Bruce A. Elleman

Modern Insurgencies and Counter-insurgencies: Guerillas and their Opponents since 1750
Ian F. W. Beckett

Naval Warfare, 1815–1914
Lawrence Sondhaus

Ottoman Warfare, 1500–1700
Rhoads Murphey

Seapower and Naval Warfare, 1650–1830
Richard Harding

The Soviet Military Experience
Roger R. Reese

Vietnam
Spencer C. Tucker

The War for Independence and the Transformation of American Society
Harry M. Ward

Warfare and Society in Europe, 1792–1914
Geoffrey Wawro

Warfare at Sea, 1500–1650
Jan Glete

Warfare in Atlantic Africa, 1500–1800: Maritime Conflicts and the Transformation of Europe
John K. Thornton

Warfare, State and Society in the Byzantine World, 565–1204
John Haldon

War in the Early Modern World, 1450–1815
Jeremy Black

Wars of Imperial Conquest in Africa, 1830–1914
Bruce Vandervort

Western Warfare in the Age of the Crusades, 1000–1300
John France

The Armies of the Caliphs

Military and Society in the Early Islamic State

Hugh Kennedy

Routledge
Taylor & Francis Group
LONDON AND NEW YORK

First published 2001
by Routledge
2 Park Square, Milton Park, Abingdon, Oxon, OX14 4RN

Simultaneously published in the USA and Canada
by Routledge
605 Third Avenue, New York, NY 10017

Routledge is an imprint of the Taylor & Francis Group, an informa business

Typeset in Jaghbub by BOOK NOW Ltd

British Library Cataloguing in Publication Data
A catalogue record for this book is available from the British Library

Library of Congress Cataloging in Publication Data
has been applied for

ISBN 13: 978-0-415-25093-1 (pbk)
ISBN 13: 978-0-415-25092-4 (hbk)

This book is dedicated to my son James, who is always interested in soldiers and battles

Contents

List of maps

Acknowledgements

It is a pleasure to acknowledge and thank many people and institutions who have helped me in this work. I am extremely grateful to the British Academy for giving me a Research Readership which gave me time and freedom from teaching and administration without which this research could not have been completed. I am also grateful to the University of St Andrews and colleagues in the Department of Mediaeval History and Arabic studies for support and comments.

I am grateful to David Cannadine for inviting me to speak to the Anglo-American conference of historians in London in the summer of 2000 and to put my ideas before an audience of general historians. I would like to thank John Haldon and all the other participants at the Late Antiquity and Early Islam Colloquium held at Birmingham in 1999, which gave me the opportunity to share my idea with a number of colleagues, and from which I learned much. I am also grateful to David Wasserstein for an invitation to his conference on 'Islamic Elites' in Tel Aviv in 1998, another very fruitful and enjoyable sharing of views.

I owe a particular debt of gratitude to Patricia Crone who took the trouble to read parts of this work and whose unrivalled knowledge of the sources for the Umayyad period and sharp critical appreciation were of great value to me. I have benefited from fruitful and enjoyable discussion at Princeton with Patricia, Chase Robinson and Harry Bone. I am also very grateful to Michael Bates who took the time to discuss early Islamic coinage and wider aspects of the history of the period and provided me with many important insights. The help these scholars have given me does not mean that they will agree with everything I have written, still less do they bear any responsibility for the errors which undoubtedly remain.

I am grateful to Jeremy Black for commissioning this book in the *Warfare and History* series and I hope its presence there will encourage some historians of other areas to look into the history of the early mediaeval Middle East. I would also like to thank Victoria Peters, Senior Editor at Routledge, for all her help.

On a more personal note, I would like to thank Helen and Robert Irwin for unfailing support and hospitality in London, my children Xana, Katharine, Alice and James and above all my wife Hilary for their encouragement, understanding and love.

Hugh Kennedy
St Andrews, 2001

List of abbreviations

BSOAS	*Bulletin of the School of Oriental and African Studies*
EI2	*Encyclopaedia of Islam* (New edition, Leiden, 1960)
IJMES	*International Journal of Middle East Studies*
JAOS	*Journal of the American Oriental Society*
JESHO	*Journal of the Economic and Social History of the Orient*
JNES	*Journal of Near Eastern Studies*
JRAS	*Journal of the Royal Asiatic Society*
JSAI	*Jerusalem Studies in Arabic and Islam*
JSS	*Journal of Semitic Studies*
LAEI	*Studies in Late Antiquity and Early Islam, The Byzantine and Islamic Near East*: i, *Problems in the Literary Source Material*, eds A. Cameron and L. I. Conrad (Princeton, 1992); ii, *Land Use and Settlement Patterns*, eds G. R. D. King and A. Cameron (Princeton, 1994); iii, *States, Resources and Armies*, ed. A. Cameron (Princeton, 1995).

For abbreviations of primary sources used in the notes, see the Bibliography of Primary Sources on pages 211–13.

A note on the use of Arabic sources

This study of the military in the early Islamic world is based on the great narrative sources compiled by authors of the third/ninth and fourth/tenth centuries, like al-Balādhurī and, above all, al-Ṭabarī.[1] It was they who edited and republished earlier collections of narratives and transmitted the texts in the form in which they have come down to us. This is not the place to review once again the arguments surrounding the veracity and usefulness of these collections but it is necessary to make some comments on the way I have approached and used this material. There can be no doubt that this historical writing, in all its richness and variety, forms one of the great monuments of world historiography. It does, however, have its distinct characteristics and these must inevitably influence the approach and conclusions of the modern scholar.

The early Islamic historians are more interested in individuals and groups of individuals rather than institutions. They do not discuss the army as a corporate body but rather how different people performed when fighting with or against each other. Nor do they systematically discuss institutions like the *dīwān* or methods of payment.[2] Rather we are given anecdotes about individual disputes about payments, or how much a certain person or group received on a certain occasion. This in turn makes the writing of the history heavily prosopographical. Some readers of this book will no doubt share some of E. M. Forster's anguish when reading the translation of the Baburnama: 'Those awful Oriental names! They welter from start to finish. Sometimes twenty new ones occur on a page and never recur.'[3] Yet these names are essential for understanding the development of the military. Take the institution of the *shurṭa* (military police), for example. The existence of this body is attested from early Umayyad times but in no place are we told of its functions or composition. In order to understand what this group did, we have to collect examples of the *shurṭa* in action and the names of its commanders at different times.[4] In this way we can establish, or at least suggest, that the *shurṭa* of the Umayyad Caliphs was indeed a body whose membership was fairly continuous from one Caliph to the next, rather than simply the chosen bodyguard of the individual ruler. The continuity of the names of the commanders points to the continuity of the institution. We can also show that the commanders of the *shurṭa* in important cities like Basra, Kūfa and Fusṭāṭ (old Cairo) were chosen by the Umayyad governors from the local élites, so demonstrating their role as mediators between these élites and the authority of the Caliph and his representative. But no source says this explicitly, only the prosopography reveals it. Or, again, we find constant references to the *quwwād* (military commanders) in the early 'Abbasid period, but no source discusses and explains the recruitment and duties of a *qā'id*: we can investigate this only by taking the biographies of individual *quwwād* and trying to extrapolate from them what the nature and functions of the office were.

There is marked contrast in this respect with the sources available to John Haldon when writing the volume on the Byzantine army which is the counterpart of this book.[5] He had at his disposal works like the *De Administrando Imperii* of the Emperor Constantine Porphyrogenitus which, as its name implies, discusses institutions of administration and occasionally mentions individuals who played an important role. By contrast, it is the prosopography which drives this account of early Muslim military practice and it is examples, rather than explanation or prescription, which form the raw materials of the research. Nor can I emulate Rhoads Murphey, in his volume on Ottoman warfare in this series,[6] in discussing the commissariat, the calorific value of the diets of soldiers and all the other details of operations and movements which the Ottoman documentation reveals. This is not because I feel they are unimportant, simply that the nature of the sources means that the information is entirely lacking.

Another feature of the Arabic sources is the strength of the narrative material. We have full, sometimes vivid, exciting and moving accounts of military operations and battles. I have tried in this work to do some justice to this material, either in summary or direct quotation. At certain points, I have decided to concentrate on key encounters which are well reported in the texts and to use them as illustrations of what John Keegan refers to as the 'face of battle' at various periods. I make no apology for this, though it runs against the grain of much sober and scientific historiography of recent years. If we are to investigate the military and society, we have to try to understand what went on in battles and how they were remembered and recorded.

A particular problem attaches to the numbers of soldiers in armies mentioned in the chronicles. Some critics may feel that all numbers mentioned in early mediaeval sources are likely to be wildly exaggerated, or at least formulaic and unreliable.[7] They may be surprised that I have taken these as a basis for discussion on numerous occasions. I believe, however, that there are good reasons for doing so. The first test is that in many cases the numbers presented are plausible in the context of the historical record: vastly exaggerated numbers of the sort sometimes encountered in, say, Western accounts of the Crusades, are rare. Clearly this is not by itself a very convincing reason for trusting them, but it at least means that in many cases they are not unreasonably large or small.

A more compelling justification for accepting some numbers as a general guide given is that troops were counted and their numbers recorded at the time. Certainly from the reign of 'Abd al-Malik onwards, soldiers had their names recorded in the *dīwān* and payments were made to them. For example, when Abū Muslim heard that a group of soldiers under Muḥriz b. Ibrāhim had assembled to support him, he ordered a clerk *(kātib)* to be sent to count them and enter their names in a book; he found that there were exactly 804.[8] The method of payment must have meant that soldiers were regularly counted. The numbers must have been known, therefore, to the clerks who recorded the names and made the payments, to the commanders who led them and presumably, by extension, to many of the soldiers themselves. It would not be surprising if such well-known information found its way into the historical record along with other details of the military expeditions.

Some contemporaries were very skilled in estimating numbers as suggested by the following anecdote: the time is shortly after the defeat of the Umayyad Caliph Marwān II by the ʿAbbasid ʿAbd Allāh b. ʿAlī in 132/750 at the battle of Tell Kushāf, which meant the end of Umayyad power. The speaker is Abū Mūsā b. Muṣʿab of Mosul, who had been one of Marwān's secretaries.

> When Marwān was defeated and ʿAbd Allāh b. ʿAlī triumphed over the people of Syria, I asked for an amnesty and he gave it to me. One day I was sitting with him and he was reclining when the conversation turned to Marwān and his defeat . He [ʿAbd Allāh] said to me, 'Were you present at the battle?' and I answered, 'Yes, may God glorify the Amir.' So he went on, 'Tell me about it' and I replied, 'On the day, he [Marwān] asked me to guess the number of the enemy.' I replied, 'I am secretary, not a military man.' He then looked to left and right and said to me, 'They are 12,000 strong.' ʿAbd Allāh sat bolt upright and said, 'God damn him! There were 12,000 men in the *dīwān* that day!'[9]

This is not to say that all numbers should be trusted implicitly. Sometimes contradictory numbers are recorded. There seems to be a suspiciously high incidence of armies of 4000 in the Umayyad period, perhaps the number here represents a formula for a small to medium-sized force. Furthermore, it would be unwise to put much reliance on estimates of the numbers in armies before the establishment of the *dīwān*. This is particularly true of the numbers quoted for the armies of the Islamic conquests which must have been no more than estimates. Estimates of non-Muslim armies, notably the Byzantines and Sasanians, or of volunteers or rebels whose names were not recorded in a *dīwān* must be treated with scepticism. It is also important to be cautious in cases where there is an obvious reason to exaggerate for propaganda reasons, as when a small army of Muslims defeats a much larger number of Byzantines, or a smaller army of ʿAbbasid troops fights a much larger number of Umayyad supporters, but such contrasts are unusual in the sources.

In general, then, and I believe with due caution, the numbers quoted in the texts for regular soldiers, that is to say soldiers whose names were recorded in a *dīwān*, will be accepted as an approximate indication of the actual numbers.[10]

Another methodological problem is provided by the patchiness of the sources. Some conflicts are covered in great detail, others apparently just as important, get only a cursory mention. Are the military campaigns on which we are best informed typical or exceptional? We can only try to extrapolate intelligently from the examples we have.

The accounts preserved in the works of such scholars as al-Balādhurī and al-Ṭabarī are very varied in quality. Many of them take the form of narratives which purport to be (and in many cases probably are) first-hand accounts. While these are likely to be partial and are always partisan, they contain much incidental information about tactics and equipment which is likely to be fairly reliable. For the purposes of this study, the important aspect is not so much that they reflect exactly what happened in one particular incident or conflict, but rather that they show what happened in warfare at that time and how such warfare was perceived by the participants.

The richness of the narrative accounts does not always reflect the wider importance of the conflicts, since it is based more on the survival of material than on conscious editorial decision. Thus we know very little about the course of some battles which radically affected the history of the Islamic world, the battle of Marj Rāhiṭ in 65/684 which led to the accession of the Marwanid branch of the Umayyad family, for example, or the battle of Rayy in 195/811 which led to al-Ma'mūn's victory over his brother al-Amīn. We know the names of the main participants and the final outcome, but not what happened in the turmoil and why one side won and another lost.

Surprisingly we have very little detailed information on the campaigns of the Muslims against the Byzantines. It might be thought that these campaigns, which were the focus of the military activities of Umayyad and 'Abbasid Caliphs and which occurred comparatively close to the seats of power, would have given rise to an extensive historiography in praise of rulers and the Muslim armies. In fact, we have little more than notes of raids and their outcomes.

In contrast to these bald narratives, we have much richer accounts of other conflicts. This is principally owing to the efforts of two early compilers whose work al-Ṭabarī was able to call and incorporate, Abū Mikhnaf and al-Madā'inī. Abū Mikhnaf Lūṭ b. Yaḥyā al-Azdī (d. 157/774) was descended from a companion of 'Alī's and was based in Iraq.[11] He is recorded as having written a large number of books and pamphlets at least some of which were used by al-Ṭabarī. From the point of view of military history, the most important of these are probably the works entitled 'Sulaymān b. Ṣurad and 'Ayn al-Warda' and 'Shabīb al-Ḥarūrī and Ṣāliḥ b. Musarrah'. The first of these is the account of the attempt of an army of pious Kufans to avenge the murder of al-Husayn by marching on Syria in 65/684 while the second describes the daring exploits of two Khārijī leaders and the attempts of the governor al-Ḥajjāj to defeat them. Other works preserve the details of civil wars among the Iraqis and struggles with other Khārijīs. In many cases, the compiler would have been in a position to speak with eye-witnesses or participants. Abū Mikhnaf's purpose was largely commemorative rather than military, but the writing is often clear and vivid with a fine eye for the detail of military encounters.

'Alī b. Muḥammad al-Madā'inī (d. *c*. 235/850) wrote extensively, among other subjects, on the history of Khurāsān, especially of the long conflicts between the invading Muslims and the Turks and Soghdians of Transoxania. Perhaps because he was further than Abū Mikhnaf in both time and distance from the scenes he describes, his accounts of battles are more impressionistic but he has preserved much interesting material, with the result that we know vastly more about the warfare in Central Asia than we do of the warfare against the Byzantines.

The sources for the history of warfare in the early 'Abbasid period are, curiously, less revealing than those of the Umayyad period. In general, the sources used by al-Ṭabarī are much more fragmented, lacking the sustained narratives of the earlier period. There is certainly nothing to compare with Abū Mikhnaf's descriptions of battles in Iraq or even al-Madā'inī's narratives of the conquests in Transoxania. The extended narratives we do have, notably 'Umar b. Shabba's account of the rebellion of Muḥammad al-Nafs al-Zākiyya and his brother Ibrāhīm in Madīna and Basra in 145/762–3,[12] are more concerned with the religious and political discourse than with details of the military encounters. It is only in the accounts of the campaigns of Khāzim b. Khuzayma, the most successful of the early 'Abbasid generals, against the Khārijītes and Ustādhsīs, that we get a real feel for battle.[13] In the Umayyad period, we know little about the life of the court but a good deal about military activities. In the early 'Abbasid period, the position is reversed, the court becomes the focus of interest and campaigns, even major campaigns involving the Caliph himself, like Hārūn's raids on the Byzantine Empire, are treated in such a cursory fashion that we cannot form any real impression of the warfare involved.

The accounts of the civil war which followed the death of Hārūn al-Rashīd in 193/809 provide more details of military activity though, as already mentioned, the crucial battle outside Rayy in 195/811 is reported in such vague and abbreviated terms that it is impossible to understand the course of the conflict. By contrast, the blockade of Baghdad which followed produced some of the most vivid narratives of siege warfare and hand-to-hand fighting encountered anywhere in early Arabic literature.

In the third/ninth century, a new genre of narrative appears. In contrast to early Islamic accounts with their use of multiple, parallel and sometimes contradictory *akhbār* (short stories), these are essentially linear narratives, carefully detailing the course of military campaigns. These narratives also provide detailed descriptions of organisation and equipment. Such narratives appear in the accounts of al-Mu'taṣim's campaign against Amorion in 233/838 and in the more extended narratives of the campaigns against Bābak in Azerbayjān (219–22/834–7). Even more striking is the long and meticulous account of the campaigns of al-Muwaffaq and al-Mu'taḍid against the Zanj rebels in southern Iraq (266–70/879–83) ascribed to Muḥammad b. al-Ḥasan b. Sahl, known as Shaylama. Whether the much more developed military organisation described in these accounts represents a real change in the nature of early Islamic armies, or simply a changing style of reporting, or both, remains problematic.

The early Islamic historical sources both inform and tantalise us. Their priorities are not our priorities, at least as concerns this study. We often have to tease nuggets of information from incidental detail and there are many questions we cannot hope to answer. The shape of this book is necessarily restricted by the nature of the sources on which it depends.

Notes

1 For overviews of the early Islamic historiographical tradition, see A. A. Durī, *The Rise of Historical Writing Among The Arabs*, trans. L. I. Conrad (Princeton, 1983) and T. Khalidi, *Arabic Historical Thought in the Classical Period* (Cambridge, 1994). The reliability of the early Muslim tradition has been vigorously challenged, notably in P. Crone and M. Cook, *Hagarism: The Making of the Islamic World* (Cambridge, 1977) and P. Crone, *Meccan Trade and the Rise of Islam* (Princeton, 1987). A more nuanced critique, stressing the formulaic elements in many of the accounts of the Muslim conquests can be found in A. Noth and L. I. Conrad, *The Early Arabic Historical Tradition: A Source Critical Study*, trans. M. Bohles (Princeton, 1994). For the current state of the debate, and a more positive view of the early tradition, see F. M. Donner, *Narratives of Islamic Origins: The Beginnings of Islamic Historical Writing* (Princeton, 1998).

2 The *Kitāb al-Kharāj* of Qudāma b. Ja'far (d. *c.* 320/932), written right at the end of the period, is an exception and survives only in part and tells us little about the structure of the army.

3 E. M. Forster, 'The Emperor Babur', in *Abinger Harvest*, quoted in W. H. Thackston (trans.), *The Baburnama* (Oxford, 1996), 17.

4 See pp. 13–14.

5 J. Haldon, *Warfare, State and Society in the Byzantine World, 565–1204* (London, 1999).

6 R. Murphey, *Ottoman Warfare, 1500–1700* (London, 1999).

7 For this point of view, see L. I. Conrad, 'Seven and the *tasbī'*: On the Implications of Numerical Symbolism for the Study of Medieval Islamic History', *JESHO*, 31 (1988), 42–73. Conrad's arguments are not, I believe, incompatible with my position.

8 Ṭa., ii, 1957.

9 al-Azdī, 126–7.

10 For further discussion, see pp. 19–21.

11 On his sources and work, see U. Sezgin, *Abū Mihnaf... Ein betrag zu Historiographie der umaiyadischen Zeit* (Leiden, 1971). Despite the full and scholarly treatment, Sezgin almost ignores Abū Mikhnaf's family connections and his position among the *ashrāf* of Kūfa.

12 Extensive extracts from this account can be found in Ṭa., iii, 143–318 and al-Iṣfahānī, Abū'l-Faraj, *Maqātil al-Ṭālibiyīn*, ed. A. Saqr (Cairo, 1949), 232–99, 315–86.

13 See pp. 100–03.

Maps

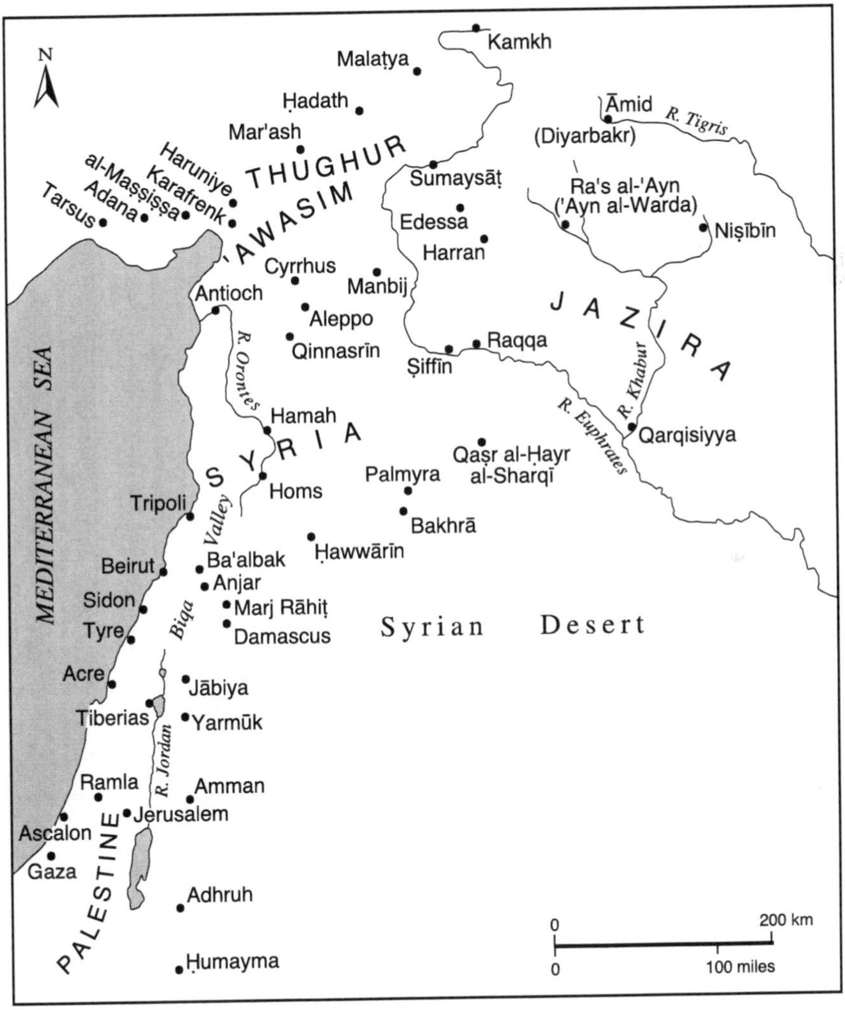

Map 1 Syria, Palestine and the Western Jazīra

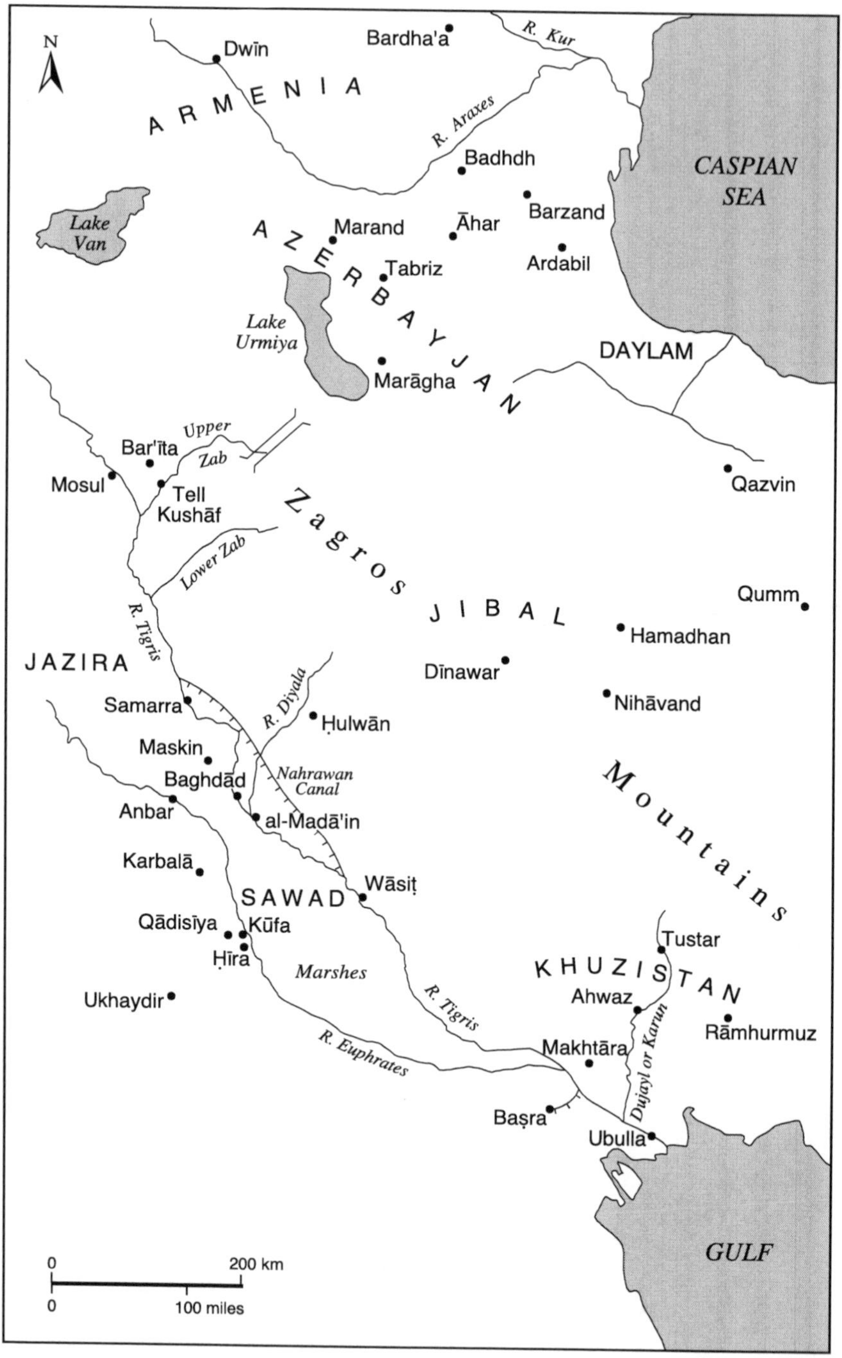

Map 2 Iraq and Western Iran

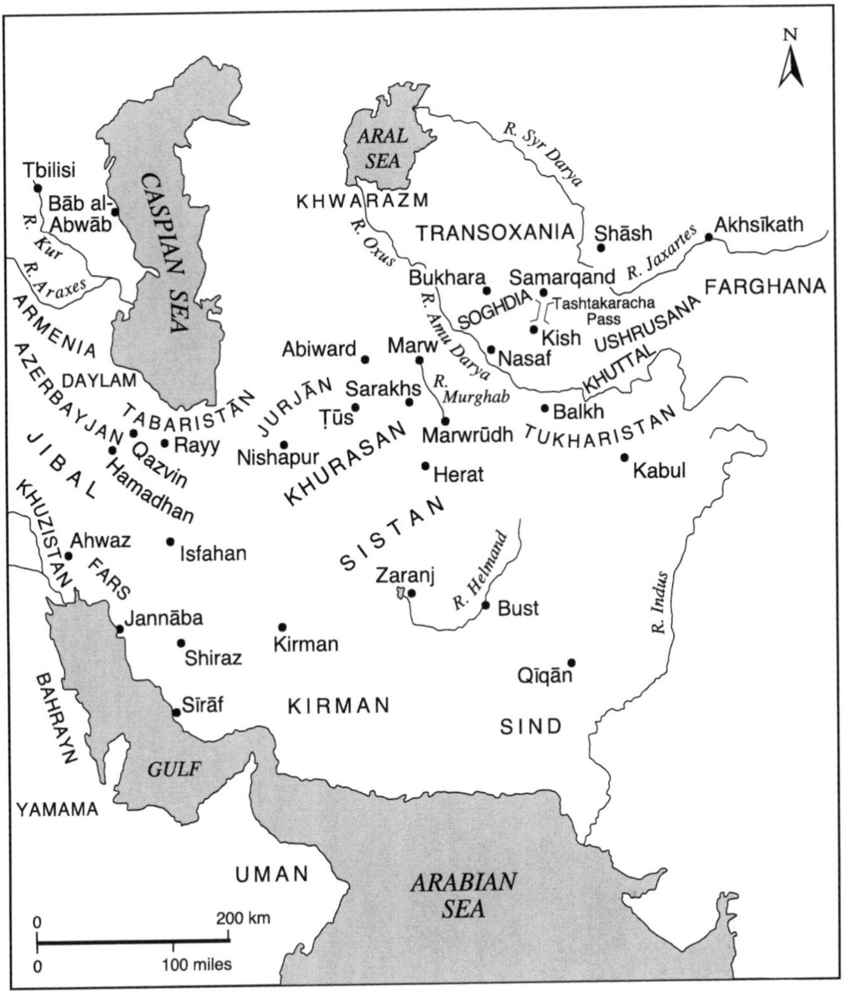

Map 3 Iran and Central Asia

CHAPTER ONE

The conquests and after: Muslim armies, 11–64/632–83

Before the conquests

The armies of the first Caliphs were formed in the Prophet's lifetime and during the spectacular conquests which followed his death in 11/632. Most of the men who joined the armies of the conquests were of bedouin origin.[1] Raiding and fighting, as well as defending themselves against the raids of others, were an integral part of their lives, as both the poems and narratives of the *Jāhiliya* and information about modern bedouin societies makes clear.[2] This meant that most adult males had experience of military activity and some practice and even skill in riding, using spears and swords and archery. Hunting, too, provided training in such skills. Compared with the farmers and citizens of the settled areas of the Near East, they were a military population.

They did not, however, form armies. An army, as an identifiable unit in society, can exist only if there are sections of society which are in effect non-military or civilian. In the bedouin tribe, this was not the case: with few marginal exceptions, all adult males were fighters and all females and children the families and dependants of fighters. Only after the conquests and settlements did there develop the social specialisation which meant that the army formed a discrete group.

The military forces lacked any system of remuneration, fighting as they did for booty, honour or self-defence. Nor did they have any structure of command with coercive powers. There were certainly tribal nobles, the *ashrāf* (sing., *sharīf*), who owed their status to descent and their own abilities, but they were obeyed only voluntarily. The individual bedouin tent preserved its own autonomy, just as it provided its own subsistence and the warrior his own weapons. Social identity, formal training, provided equipment and payment, all characteristics of a true army, were foreign to this society.

How far this changed in the first years of Islam, the lifetime of the Prophet, is very difficult to tell.[3] The latest authority on the subject[4] stresses the extent to which our sources on the practice of the Prophet in military affairs, as elsewhere, have been shaped by later legal discussion. We can probably assume that Muḥammad's own unique position meant that his orders were accepted more readily than those of other contemporaries. There is some evidence that the nascent Muslim community did, on occasion, supply weapons and food to allow its more indigent members to join in campaigns.[5] There is no sign, however, of a structure of command, of military units other than the tribe, or of regular payment. We should be very wary of burdening this fluid and expanding community with a developed military system on the basis of later evidence of doubtful historicity.

The armies of the conquests

The great Muslim conquests in the decade which followed the death of the Prophet Muḥammad in 11/632 were among the most dramatic and far-reaching in history. By 20/641, all the lands of the Fertile Crescent, Iraq, Syria and Palestine and Egypt had been conquered. By 30/650 much of Iran had been subdued as well. The lands which were taken in these swift campaigns were to remain under Muslim rule, with only limited exceptions, right down to the present day.

This massive change has not given rise to the wealth of speculation and argument which can be found, for example, in the historiography of the fall of the Roman Empire in the West.[6] There is no doubt that there were important long-term factors, such as the effects of plague and military exhaustion and political instability in the Byzantine and Sasanian Empires, but the immediate cause for the Muslim conquests was the military victories of Muslim armies over their rivals, most famously the Battles of Yarmūk in Syria and al-Qādisiya in Iraq, both probably in 15/636, when the military power of the Byzantine and Sasanian Empires was shattered. The indications, such as they are, suggest that the Muslim armies were less numerous and probably less well equipped than their opponents. If the battles of Yarmūk and al-Qādisiya had been decisive victories for the Byzantines and Sasanians, and the Muslim armies had been slaughtered and scattered, it is unlikely that the Islamic conquests would ever have occurred.

To understand the conquests, it is important to keep the military history centre stage. However, this is less easy than might be supposed and the amount of scholarly discussion devoted to the military reasons for the triumph of Islam is very small. This is not because there are no sources; indeed almost the opposite is true.[7] While Byzantine and Persian writers have little enough to say on the subject,[8] the Arabic texts purporting to describe the events run to thousands of pages, packed with names and apparently eye-witness accounts. These accounts present almost insuperable problems to the military historian. For them, victory was the result of God's will, the valour of individuals and groups and the cowardice, pride or foolishness of their enemies. As explanations for the great events of the seventh century these are at best partial. This is not to say that the Muslims were not brave and that the conviction that they were doing Allah's will was not significant: it clearly was. But their opponents also had firm ideological commitments and there is no reason to assume that individuals were likely to be any less brave. Despite the great mass of words, the full explanation for Muslim victory still eludes us.

Muslim historians of the Umayyad and early 'Abbasid period would naturally tend to imagine the armies of the conquests in the context of armies of their own time, in the same way as Western mediaeval painters dressed figures from the classical past in the armour of their own period. They might well assume that the early Muslim troops were drawn up in lines of battle and that they were divided into units of ten, organised by *'arīfs*[9] for some administrative purposes, as were soldiers in their own day. This unwitting anachronism could impose a false sense of organisation and method on military manoeuvres which were, in reality, much more chaotic.

Furthermore, the short stories (*akhbār*) which form the basis of the Arabic accounts are clearly not as reliable as they claim to be. Often there are totally contradictory accounts of the same event. Many of the details turn out to be *topoi*, formulaic accounts which can be transferred from one conquest to another. The tellers of these tales often had good reason to claim that certain individuals in certain tribes participated or were martyred in certain conflicts. It was not only a question of tribal or personal honour; it was a question of serious money. When the conquests were over, those who had participated in great battles like al-Qādisiya in 636, which led to the conquest of Iraq, were entitled to much higher wages than those who had not. There was an immediate and compelling need to establish, truly or falsely, that named people fought in particular campaigns.

Other issues emerged to cloud the picture with later polemic. Robinson[10] has shown how accounts of the conquest of Khuzistan were heavily influenced by later debates about the rights to the proceeds of the taxation (*fay'*) of this rich area. If it had been conquered by the Basrans alone, then the revenues belonged to them but if Kufan forces had been involved, then the revenues should be divided. This meant that the issue was one of pressing concern as long as the concept of *fay'* remained the basis for the distribution of revenues (probably until the late Umayyad period in this area), and it was precisely during this period that the traditions which have come down to us concerning this conquest were first elaborated and recorded.

This is not to say that the accounts were all fabrications. Obviously the Muslim conquests did occur and it is clear beyond reasonable doubt that the main battles happened where they did (though the exact chronology is much more problematic). We can assume, too, that some of the individuals and groups mentioned did in fact take part in the campaigns to which they are ascribed and that some of the incidents did actually occur. The trouble is that it is very difficult to tell which. This in turn means that it would be quite unsafe for the historian to search these accounts for examples of Muslim strategy, tactics, composition of armies or even of the weapons they carried. The account of the armies of the conquests can never be more than a suggestive prologue to the discussion of the armies of the Caliphs.

Despite the problems of the source material, Donner has proposed some tentative conclusions about the organisation and equipment of the Muslim armies at this time. The secret of Muslim success did not lie in overwhelming numerical superiority, though the very high numbers given for their Byzantine and Sasanian opponents should be treated with complete scepticism. Numbers for the Muslim army at the battle of Yarmūk in Syria range between 20 000 and 40 000, with most estimates tending towards the lower end.[11] The numbers given for their enemies range as high as a quarter of a million, figures which should not be taken literally, but which do suggest that they were at least as numerous as the Muslims.[12] For the Muslim army at al-Qādisiya in Iraq, Donner suggests a figure of 6000–12 000 or fewer.[13] The army operating in southern Iraq in the first phase of the conquests, seems to have been no more than 2000–4000.[14] Hinds suggests 2000–3000 in the earliest Arab expeditions to Fārs, a force that proved too small to penetrate much beyond the coastal plain.[15] The forces with which 'Amr b. al-'Āṣ took Egypt are said to have numbered 15 500 at the most.[16] These totals are approximate but not entirely unreasonable. Numbers soon increased and there can be no doubt that in the years immediately following these victories, the original Muslim armies were joined by large numbers of tribesmen from Arabia and the Fertile Crescent who wanted a share of the action.

The Muslim sources suggest that the Caliphs in Madīna exercised a considerable degree of control over the armies of the conquests.[17] Communications between the capital and the front lines in Syria and Iraq may not have taken much more than a week each way and Donner concludes that 'Operational co-ordination of a broadly conceived strategy for the Islamic conquests by the Caliphs in Madīna certainly seems to have been feasible given the prevailing communications of the day.'[18] The sources give us examples of the despatch of armies from one from to another and, perhaps most convincingly, the removal of governors who had achieved the conquests and their replacement by the Caliph's own men, as when 'Uthmān dismissed the conqueror of Egypt, 'Amr b. al-'Āṣ, and replaced him by his own foster-brother. Nonetheless, the sources clearly have a tendency to explain events in terms of the Caliph's will and decree and we should be wary of attributing too much weight to his word or letter.

The Muslim troops were definitely an army, not a tribal migration. They consisted overwhelmingly of adult males, without families or flocks and herds.[19] Migration of tribes followed the conquests, after the military victories had been won. The weapons[20] they used were the sword and the spear. They had archers and some of them probably wore chain mail and iron helmets. They were both infantry and cavalry but the distinction was blurred: the cavalry often fought on foot while the infantry were transported to meet the enemy on horses and camels. Their mounts enabled them to travel more quickly to the scene of battle and conduct reconnaissance expeditions.[21] Camels were used largely for transport. In short, they enjoyed no identifiable technological advantage over their enemies but may have been more mobile, especially in the semi-desert and pasture lands. This mobility allowed them to strike where they wished and to retreat to safety and regroup when necessary.

From an early stage in the conquests the Arabs were joined by groups of non-Arab troops. The most famous of these were several units of élite Sasanian troops who defected to the conquerors during the course of the conquests of Iraq.[22] As early as the battle of al-Qādisiya, 4000 of the 'Army of the king of kings' (*jund shāhānshāh*) are said to have defected to the Muslims; in exchange they demanded to be allowed to settle where they liked, to become affiliated to an Arab group of their choice and be paid salaries.[23] There were 4000 foot soldiers from Daylam, in northern Iran, who joined the Muslims, converted to Islam and became allies of the Banū Tamīm. They, and other Persians who joined the Muslims at this early stage, were known as the *Ḥamrā'* (red people) and had their own mosque in Kūfa and are said[24] to have received the same pay (2000 *dirhams*) as those who had fought at al-Qādisiya. At the battle of Ṣiffīn, 'Ali's Kufan forces are said to have included some 8000 *mawālī* (clients) and slaves (*'abīd, mamālik*), all presumably non-Arabs, out of total force of some 70 000.[25]

There were also the famous Asāwira,[26] Persian élite troops commanded by one of Yazdgard's senior commanders, known to the Arab sources as Siyāh al-Uswārī. They had joined the Muslims at the time of the conquests of southern Iraq and agreed to convert to Islam and fight alongside the Muslims against their fellow Iranians. In exchange, they were given the highest level of pay, a place to settle in Basra and a quasi-genealogical position as a sub-group the tribe of Tamīm, and were immediately despatched to help the Muslim armies in the siege of Tustar. In 64/683–4 they were engaged in the civil wars between the tribes in Basra: they were commanded by one Māh Afrīdhūn (an obviously Persian name) and spoke Persian. Their numbers are given as 400 or 500, but whether this was the total number or refers only to those under the command of Māh Afrīdhūn is not clear.[27] They distinguished themselves as archers who never wasted a shot.[28] Their example was followed by other groups of Sasanian soldiers originating from Sind, the Sayābija, Zuṭṭ and Indighār who joined the Muslims and were settled in Basra;[29] they continued to be an element in the Muslim army of Iraq until it was effectively demilitarised in the early second/eighth century.[30] Non-Arabs seem to have formed part of 'Amr b. al-'Āṣ' army during the invasion of Egypt. The traditions are confused, but there seem to have been both Greeks and Persians involved and both groups were given areas to settle in the newly founded garrison city of Fusṭāṭ.[31] Such groups of renegades may have been important in stiffening the Muslim armies and introducing new military techniques, and their role is likely to have been underplayed in the Arabic sources.

The Arabs seem to have fought in tribal units, each following its own banner (*liwā, rāya*). However, we are also told that they were drawn up in lines of battle (*ṣufūf*) with the classic formation of centre (*qalb* = heart), right wing (*maymana*) and left wing (*maysara*), implying some supra-tribal organisation, but this may be no more than a projection back of later practice. According to some accounts, Sa'd b. Abī Waqqāṣ, the Muslim commander at the battle of al-Qādisiya had some sort of command structure with the Amīr appointing leaders of various units and the division of soldiers into units of ten.[32] Here again, however, this may be no more than a later rationalisation.

The most detailed reconstruction we have of one of the major battles of the conquests is Kaegi's account[33] of the Battle of the Yarmūk, which is itself based on Caetani's account. It benefits from the fact that the battlefield was visited both by Caetani and Kaegi and that the topography is clear and marked by definable features, notably the steep-sided valley of the Yarmūk itself. This account has the Muslim army manoeuvring with considerable confidence and consciously preparing a trap for their enemy, aided perhaps by more familiarity with the terrain and the passive support of the local people whom the Byzantines had antagonised. One of the Muslim commanders, Khālid b. al-Walīd succeeded in driving a wedge between the Byzantine cavalry and infantry and trapping much of the Byzantine army between ravines, into which they were driven and destroyed. The reconstruction is ingenious and may well be correct in its broad outlines, but the Arabic texts need to be used selectively to give so clear a picture.

The accounts of the conquest of Shushtar in Khuzistan, which the Arabic sources refer to as Tustar, provides an interesting example of the taking of a fortified and well-defended citadel.[34] The Arabic sources are extensive but, as usual, full of contradictions and uncertainties. However in this case, a Syriac source[35] composed soon after the events gives a well-informed account which is completely independent of the Arabic tradition. The Syriac account is short and linear, rather than a series of competing narratives in the early Islamic mode. The Muslim attack was led by Abū Mūsā al-Ash'arī and resisted by the local Sasanian commander, Hormizdān the Mede. Faced by this attack, Hormizdān sued for peace and a truce was arranged and the Persians agreed to pay tribute. After two years Hormizdān felt strong enough to refuse to pay and executed the two Christian churchmen who had acted as intermediaries. This led to Muslim assaults on his two main cities, Sūs and Shushtar. Sus fell to direct assault after a few days but Shushtar was well-fortified and held out for two years. In the end it fell by treachery when a man whose house was on the city walls agreed, in exchange for a third of the tribute, to open tunnels so that the Muslims could enter. The Syriac account is also supported by the surviving topography of Shushtar, notably the strongly fortified site and the rivers and tunnels.[36] If this account is compared with the much longer Muslim narratives, some interesting conclusions can be draw. All the important features of the Syriac narrative can be found in one or more of the Arabic accounts. However, none of the Arabic accounts contains all of the material found in the Syriac and they all contain extraneous material. Without the Syriac, we would have no idea which of the various Arabic traditions was closest to being a factual account of what occurred at Shushtar. In addition to confirming the broad outlines of the campaign, the account also shows the difficulties that the Muslims had when faced with well-defended fortified sites.

Morale and mobility may be the main reasons for Muslim military success at the time of the conquests. Certainly there is no evidence that overwhelming numbers or new technologies were responsible. It is also clear that, while Muslim armies were collected and sent to certain fronts, military administration was very simple. Men fought for their religion, the prospect of booty and because their friends and fellow tribesmen were also doing it. They were not paid salaries, nor were their names recorded in registers. The regimentation of these forces into organised and established armies was the work of the decades which followed the initial military successes.

The settlement of the conquerors

In the immediate aftermath of their victories, it seems there was some confusion about what should be done with the conquered lands. Traditionally, the Arabs had taken booty, either animals or portable wealth, which could be simply divided up between them. With the conquests they had acquired farm lands, orchards, grazing, villages, cities and monasteries. Not only that, but they had acquired domination over a vast number of people, many of whom would have been resentful and eager to throw off the authority of the Muslims. Then there were outside enemies, most notably the Byzantines, who could and did try to combine with elements in the local population to undermine Muslim rule.

The response of the Caliph 'Umar b. al-Khaṭṭāb (13–23/634–44) in Madīna is said to have been to instruct that the Muslims should be settled in garrison cities (*amṣār*, sing. *miṣr*) rather than be dispersed through the countryside.[37] This would enable them to maintain their military control and discourage them from becoming assimilated and losing their religious and ethnic identity. Two such *amṣār* were founded in Iraq, at Kūfa, south of Baghdad and Basra at the head of the Gulf. In Egypt a *miṣr* was established at Fusṭāṭ. In Syria a *miṣr* is said to have been founded at Jābiya, south west of Damascus, but it never thrived and the Muslim settlers in Syria were dispersed in the existing towns and rural settlements.[38]

Within the *amṣār* the tribesmen were settled, or settled themselves, next to their kinsmen. The fighting men of these cities were known as the *muqātila*. In the earliest phases, the people of Kūfa were divided into 'Sevenths', grouping members of smaller tribes together,[39] but tribal identities remained strong and tribal leaders very influential. It was probably at this time, too, that the first mechanisms for paying pensions and salaries to the conquerors and their families were developed.[40]

The military in the first civil war

The first civil war (*fitna*) began with the murder of the Caliph 'Uthmān at the end of 35/June 656.[41] 'Alī b. Abī Ṭālib, the Prophet's cousin and son-in-law, was widely accepted as his natural successor but there was considerable opposition from those who were angry, or claimed to be angry, that he had not done more to defend 'Uthmān or punish his murderers. Among these were two veteran companions of the Prophet, Ṭalḥa and al-Zubayr, who joined with Muḥammad's wife 'Ā'isha and moved to Basra to mount an open defiance. 'Alī left Madīna and moved to Iraq to oppose them. Here he forged a link with the people of Kūfa, including men like Mālik al-Ashtar who had been prominent among the assailants of 'Uthmān. In a conflict known as the Battle of the Camel, 'Alī and his supporters decisively defeated his opponents and both Ṭalḥa and al-Zubayr were killed.

More effective opposition was offered by the governor of Syria, Mu'āwiya b. Abī Sufyān, a relative of the dead Caliph, who now took up his cause. 'Alī mobilised an Iraqi army which confronted Mu'āwiya and his Syrian supporters at Ṣiffīn on the Euphrates. After some intermittent fighting, the two leaders agree to arbitration and the armies returned to their homelands. A number of 'Alī's supporters became disillusioned with his apparent lack of firmness and left his army to form armed bands of rebels in the countryside and deserts of Iraq. Known as Khārijīs (Arabic pl., Khawārij), they considered themselves the only true Muslims with a duty to attack and a right to slaughter supporters of 'Alī and Mu'āwiya alike. Meanwhile, the arbitration decided nothing but shortly afterwards 'Alī was assassinated in Kūfa in 40/661 and Mu'āwiya moved swiftly to take over Iraq and the whole of the Caliphate.

The Muslim sources give us very extensive accounts of the military operations involved but, as usual, there is a vast amount of information about individuals and their doings and sayings, but only fragmentary information about the raising and management of armies. There are extensive accounts of the two main confrontation, the battles of the Camel and Ṣiffīn.[42] Ṣiffīn, in fact gave rise to a whole library of historical literature, including the surviving monograph, the 'Battle of Ṣiffīn', by Naṣr b. Muzāḥim al-Minqarī.[43]

The armies of the first civil war remained very much tribal armies in the sense that they were recruited and were led and fought mostly in tribal groups. When 'Alī was trying to raise an army from Kūfa to fight the Khārijīs in the aftermath of the Battle of Ṣiffīn, 'he assembled the leaders [*ru'ūs*] of the "sevenths", the leaders of the tribes [*qabā'il*] and the prominent men [*wujūh*]' and tried to persuade them to supply an army; 'I ask the head of each tribe [*qawm*]', he is said to have demanded, 'to write down for me what fighting men [*muqātila*], sons of fighting men who have reached fighting age and slaves, he has in his tribe [*'ashīra*] and their *mawālī*'. A number of important leaders agreed.

> Then the chiefs of the tribes wrote down the names of those who were under them and presented them to 'Alī and ordered that their sons and slaves and *mawālī* should go out with them and that none of them should lag behind. They presented to 'Alī 40,000 *muqātila* and 17,000 of their sons who had reached the right age and 8,000 clients and slaves. They said, 'Commander of the Faithful, as for those fighting men with us and their sons who have reached manhood and can fight, we have put before you those who are strong and resolute and we have ordered them to depart with us. But there are also non fighting men [*ḍu'afā*], and they are on our estates and doing other useful things'.[44]

The passage is very interesting. It shows the importance of tribal chiefs, clearly, but it also points to an absence of military bureaucracy or command structure: 'Alī raises his army by negotiation with the *ru'ūs*. There is no mention of lists of men available (*dīwāns*), nor of the officials known as *'arīfs*[45] and of the groups of ten they were supposed to organise. Taken at face value, the description suggests that the leaders were expected to be literate and make their own records, though in practice they probably used secretaries. There is a marked contrast with what happened at the same time in Basra, where is governor, 'Abd Allāh b. al-'Abbās attempted to order the *muqātila* of Basra to join the army. Despite threats only 3200 men out of an estimated 60 000 actually assembled.[46]

The influence of tribal loyalties is important throughout the first *fitna*. At Ṣiffīn the Arabs were assembled and commanded by their tribal leaders, fought under their tribal banners and used their tribal war cries, most of which probably dated back to the wars of the pre-Islamic Jāhiliya.[47] Having said that, however, regional loyalties cut across tribal ones in a decisive fashion. When making his dispositions for battle, 'Alī is said to have ordered his men to take on their fellow tribesmen

> When he knew who the Syrian tribes were, he said to the Azd [on his own side] 'take care of the Azd for me', and to the Khath'am, 'Take care of the Khath'am for me'. He asked each tribe [*qabīla*] among the men of Iraq to take care of its counterpart among the Syrians, and if there was a tribe of which there were none in Syria he would assign it against another of whom there were members among the Syrian but not among the Iraqis.[48]

The struggle at Ṣiffīn was essentially between the people (*ahl*) of Syria and the people of Iraq. Many, if not all, tribes had groups fighting for both Syria and Iraq. This meant that on occasion they might avoid fighting their fellow tribesmen on the other side or intercede for them if they were captured but, in general, regional loyalties proved stronger than tribal ones.

As well as the tribal groups we also hear of the *qurrā'*.[49] There is a general consensus that the word means (Qur'an) readers or reciters, and Hinds has argued that it refers to individuals who were early participants in the conquests but who had since lost status to the tribal leaders and the governor appointed by 'Uthmān. They are an interesting group, partly because they apparently abandoned their tribal identities, which had not brought them much status, and adopted a separate, 'para-tribal' identity. Though only numbering a few hundred,[50] they were a key element in 'Alī's army and some of them later became the nucleus of the Kharijite movement. There are also said to have been 4000 Syrian *qurrā'*,[51] but it is not clear that they had a separate identity.

Our understanding of the techniques and technology of warfare at the time of the first *fitna* is based on the battle narratives. Often these give us little more than rhetorical generalisations about how fighting was actually done but in the case of the Battle of Ṣiffīn, and especially the battle for the water which constitutes the military episode on which we are best informed, we have the first of the great battle narratives of Abū Mikhnaf which provide so much of the detail about military encounters in the Umayyad period. Whether these give us an accurate account of what happened at Ṣiffīn is, of course debatable, but they do reflect the conditions of warfare in the Umayyad period when they were elaborated.

Two things seem clear from the accounts. The first is that the serious and decisive fighting was done on foot. In a highly rhetorical speech, 'Alī is said to have urged his men to 'accustom yourselves to dismounting to fight, assaulting and being assaulted, individual combat, contention, fighting with swords and staves, wresting, biting and grappling'.[52] When battle was joined the Iraqi horsemen failed to make any headway against 'Amr b. al-'Āṣ's men until they were reinforced by foot soldiers.[53] Tribesmen from 'Akk are said to have performed what became the classic Syrian tactical manoeuvre when they knelt down to resist an Iraqi attack,[54] and at a critical stage in the encounter, just before the Syrians appealed for arbitration, Mālik al-Ashtar dismounted and sent away his horse so that he could fight on foot and clinch the day.[55]

The importance of foot soldiers is emphasised in the account Abū Mikhnaf gives of the encounter between the forces of 'Alī and the Khārijīs after he returned to Iraq. The Khārijīs, who numbered about 2800 by this stage, began the battle:

> they marched against 'Alī, who sent forward his cavalry in front of the foot soldiers and arranged his men in two lines behind the horsemen, placing the archers (*murāmiya*) in front of the first line.
>
> 'Alī said to his men, 'Hold back from them until they attack you – and the majority of them are on foot – they are bound to be tired when they get to you while you will be repulsing them and defending against them' . . .
>
> 'Alī's horsemen were in front of his infantry but the horsemen of the Muslims ['Alī's followers] did not hold firm against the attack and split into two groups, one on the right and one on the left, and the Khārijīs advanced on the infantry. 'Alī's archers confronted them with their arrows (*nabl*), while the horsemen from both the left and the right turned on them and the footmen rushed at them with spears and swords. By God, they wasted no time in killing the Khārijīs. Then Ḥamza b. Sinān, the leader of the cavalry of the Khārijīs, when he saw the destruction, called to his men, 'Dismount', and they began to do so but they had not taken up positions before . . . horsemen came at them from the direction of 'Alī. They were slain in a short time.[56]

This passage demonstrates the second point, the importance of archers in battle. The Battle of the Camel seems to have been characterised by fierce exchanges of arrows and the howda where 'Ā'isha was seated on the eponymous camel was said to have looked like a hedgehog.[57] The battle for the water at Ṣiffīn opened with a barrage of arrows from each side before they moved on the spears and finally swords.[58]

Later battles show some of the same characteristics. Archers played a major role in the martyrdom of al-Ḥusayn b. 'Alī at Karbalā in 61/680 and the skills and discipline of the Syrian infantry and archers at the battle of Ḥarrā' outside Madīna in 64/683 played a decisive role in the victory of the Umayyad forces.[59]

The battle narratives of the first *fitna* show warfare largely conducted between armies of footmen fighting with bows, spears and swords. Horses were used to bring men to the battle-field and cavalry could be used for scouting or turning a flank or engaging other cavalry, but they could not win a battle against well-prepared and disciplined infantry.

The conflict at Ṣiffīn also brings into focus the careers of two military commanders. Mālik b. al-Ḥārith al-Nakh'ī known as al-Ashtar[60] (the man with the inverted eyelid) was one of those who had joined the conquest of Iraq in the early stages and fought to maintain their status. He came to the fore in 33/653–4 when he began a brawl at the court of the governor of Kūfa, Sa'īd b. al-'Āṣ, in protest at what he saw as the Caliph 'Uthmān's unwarranted interference in the affairs of the province. After this, he was briefly deported to Syria but was soon back in Kūfa where he led the 3000 or so *qurrā'* who effectively took over the Sawad in opposition to the governor. He joined the Kūfans who marched on Madīna to demand redress from 'Uthmān and was generally held, rightly or wrongly, to have been involved in the Caliph's murder. When 'Alī became Caliph, al-Ashtar emerged as his most vigorous military supporter and he urged his master to mount a military expedition against Mu'āwiya in Syria. A large man with an unkempt beard,[61] his presence was an inspiration to many of 'Alī's men at Ṣiffīn, at one point saving the army from fleeing in panic,[62] but he was unable to prevent the arbitration agreement and 'Alī's subsequent retreat to Iraq. After this, the Caliph sent him to Egypt to try to prevent conquest of that country by the Umayyads but he was killed, apparently by poison, before he could reach it.

'Amr b. Sufyān al-Sulamī, known as Abū'l-A'war (the one-eyed) had been prominent in the early Syrian conquests.[63] Though originally opposed to Muḥammad, he is said to have commanded one of the squadrons at the Battle of Yarmūk and to have participated in the conquest of Baysan and Tiberias. He led the *ahl al-Shām* in the attack on Amorion in 23/644.[64] He seems to have been closely associated with 'Amr b. al-'Āṣ, who appointed him as his deputy in al-Urdunn.[65] He is known to have been a partisan of 'Uthmān and one story says that he was the messenger who carried the fatal letter from the Caliph to his governor of Egypt which convinced the dissidents that 'Uthmān had betrayed them.[66] At Ṣiffīn he was in command of Mu'āwiya's advance guard[67] and it was he who prevented 'Alī's men reaching the water they so desperately wanted: '[he] had lined up horsemen and foot soldiers by [the water source] and placed archers in front of his men. He had formed a row with spears and shields and helmets on their heads.'[68] After the truce, he was one of the signatories of the arbitration agreement between Mu'āwiya and 'Alī and later supported his patron 'Amr b. al-'Āṣ in conquering Egypt for the Umayyads.[69] He is last heard of in 51/671 in an honoured position at Mu'āwiya's court.[70]

Although both men made their careers in the early phases of the Muslim conquests, their fates could hardly have been more different. The sources draw a contrast in personalities: when the two armies first met at Ṣiffīn, al-Ashtar, in his flamboyant, swaggering style, challenged Abū'l-A'war to single combat. The

Syrian was far too cautious to be drawn, criticising his opponent's lack of sense and bad judgement in being involved in the murder of 'Uthmān and claiming that he was liable for the dead Caliph's blood.[71] It is debatable how much weight should be given to individual anecdotes. However, the contrast may go further than the personalities: al-Ashtar comes across as a larger-than-life individual, exhorting and leading small and undisciplined groups of 'Alī's supporters, Abū'l-A'war as the cautious leader of a disciplined and well-equipped body of soldiers. It was a contrast to be repeated in many subsequent encounters between Syrians and Iraqis.

The reigns of Mu'āwiya and Yazīd b. Mu'āwiya (41–64/661–83)

As often in periods of comparative peace, we have little information about the organisation of the military in Mu'āwiya's long reign. The Caliph seems to have been largely content to allow the system of local *muqātila* in the various areas to continue in existence and he does not seem to have made any attempt to expand the role of the Syrian armies beyond the boundaries of the province. In his short political testament to his son, he is made to advise that he should look after the Syrians, 'for they are your retinue [*biṭāna*] and the ones you can trust.[72] If you are attacked by an enemy, be victorious with them but when. When you have attained your objective with them, return the people of Syria to their own lands, because if they stay in another country, they will change character.'[73] The *muqātila* of each area were more or less autonomous, under the leadership of the local governor. They were expected to form armies to defend the Muslims against internal dissidence and external attack and to live off the taxation collected in their own areas. Instead of a centralised army, provincial governors remained responsible for the *muqātila* and the *dīwān*s in their own areas.

Mu'āwiya made moves to strengthen the coastal defences of Syria against the real threat of Byzantine raids. Since Arabs were reluctant to settle in the coastal cities, he moved Persians (Furs) from Baalbak, Ḥoms and Antioch (presumably men who had been left behind by the retreating Persian armies in 628) and Asāwira from Kūfa and Basra to help the defences of the coastal areas of Syria and Lebanon against the Byzantines.[74]

Mu'āwiya's reign also saw major Muslim campaigns against Byzantium by land and sea, especially the four-year Arab blockade of the city of Constantinople by a fleet based at Cyzicus, across the Sea of Marmara.[75] Unfortunately, beyond the names of the commanders of the expeditions, which are often confused, we have almost no information about the composition and activities of the Muslim forces. Worse still, Conrad has demonstrated that almost all the information which the Arabic sources offer is so confused as to be valueless. The Muslim armies in Mu'āwiya's time must have been been effectively organised and led, but we have no means of knowing how this was done, or how they fought.

Shurṭa and *ḥaras*

Mu'āwiya's reign saw the development of the *shurṭa* and the *ḥaras* into established institutions. There are scattered references to the *shurṭa* (or more commonly to the plural *shuraṭ*) from the reign of 'Uthmān onwards. Originally the term probably meant simply 'choice troops',[76] but it soon developed by usage to mean police or security forces. In 33/653–4 the governor of Kūfa, Sa'īd b. al-'Āṣ is said to have had a *ṣāḥib al-shurṭa*, 'Abd al-Raḥman al-Asadī, who is possibly the first known holder of this office in Islamic history.[77] 'Alī had Qays b. Sa'd in charge of his *shuraṭ* after his return from Ṣiffīn[78] and Mu'āwiya ordered that a *ḥaras* (guard) and *shurṭa* should be with him day and night after the failed assassination attempt of 40/661.[79] The names of the commanders of the Caliph's *shurṭa* are listed, and seem to have been mostly Arab tribesmen. The commanders of the guard (*aṣḥāb al-ḥaras*), by contrast, usually seem to have been non-Arab *mawlā*s (freedmen).[80]

In the reign of Mu'āwiya we get the clearest evidence of the development of the *shurṭa* in the context of events in Iraq. 'Abd Allāh b. 'Āmir, who was appointed governor of Basra in 41/661–2, is said to have had a *shurṭa*. Under al-Mughīra b. Shu'ba in Kūfa they began to assume recognisably police and security functions, as in 43/663 when they surrounded the house of a Khārijī leader and arrested him and his fellow conspirators.[81] After his appointment as governor of Basra in 45/665–6, Ziyād b. Abī Sufyān established a *shurṭa* of 4000 men which was responsible for law and order and enforcing a strict curfew.[82] It was the *shurṭa* who undertook the politically sensitive arrest of Ḥujr b.'Adī in 51/671–2[83] and the *shurṭa*, under its commander, Ḥuṣayn b.Tamīm played a leading role in the death of al-Ḥusayn b.'Alī at Karbalā in 61/680.[84] 'Ubayd Allāh b. Ziyād had *shuraṭī*s armed with swords in his audiences, and the thirty members of the *shurṭa* he had with him in his palace in Kūfa in 60/680 enabled him to hold off the Shi'ite followers of Muslim b.'Aqīl while he created a diversion.[85] When the bandit 'Ubayd Allah b. al-Ḥurr, anxious to free his wife, launched a surprise attack on the prison in Kūfa with axes and grappling irons, it was the *shurṭa* which attempted to prevent him.[86] They also had a ceremonial role as the governor's escort and Ziyād established the protocol of the leader of the *shurṭa* carrying a ceremonial spear, the *ḥarba*, before him. They were certainly armed with swords but the characteristic weapon was the stave (*'amūd*) which they would used to quell civil disturbances.[87] The commander of the *shurṭa*, who was always an Arab tribesman, was sometimes called the *amīr al-shurṭa* in the beginning[88] but the usage *ṣāḥib al-shurṭa* soon became generally established. Ziyād also recruited a guard (*ḥaras*) of 500 men who were stationed (*rābiṭa*) in the mosque.[89]

By the end of Mu'āwiya's reign, the *shurṭa* and the *ḥaras* had emerged as the two main military/police units. They became an essential part of the apparatus of Islamic government. The commander of the Caliph's police and the guards (*ṣāḥib al-shurṭa*, *ṣāḥib al-ḥaras*) was one of the major offices of state in both Umayyad and early 'Abbasid times. Each major provincial capital also had its own *shurṭa*, with a *ṣāḥib* appointed by the governor, usually from among the local notables. It is probably true to say that they were the only full-time, permanent troops regularly available to Caliphs and governors.

Conclusion

The successes of the Muslim armies in the 630s and 640s were both spectacularly swift and astonishingly enduring. However, it is frustratingly difficult to examine and describe the armies which accomplished these immense military achievements. The nature of the sources makes it well nigh impossible for us to come to any firm conclusions about the reasons for the military successes of the early Islamic armies. They seem to have been no more numerous nor better equipped than their enemies and their only discernible advantages seem to be those of mobility and morale. After the conquest, the Muslim armies remained essentially tribal in structure and the armies of the conquests were settled in and supported from the provinces they had conquered. From an early stage, non-Arabs were incorporated into the forces, although they remained very much a minority. Mechanisms for payment and administration of the military seem to have remained very simple but, at least in Iraq and Egypt, bureaucracies were developed which listed troops and provided them with payments in both cash and kind.

Notes

1 See F. M. Donner, *The Early Islamic Conquests* (Princeton, 1981), 11–49 for an overview of pre-Islamic Arabia.

2 For introductions to modern bedouin society, see A. Musil, *The Manners and Customs of the Rwala Bedouin* (New York, 1928b); D. P. Cole, *Nomads of the Nomads: the Āl Murrah Bedouin of the Empty Quarter* (Chicago, 1975); W. Lancaster, *The Rwala Bedouin Today* (Cambridge, 1981); J. S. Jabbur, *The Bedouins and the Desert*, trans. L. I. Conrad (Albany, 1995).

3 See Donner, *The Early Islamic Conquests*, 51–90.

4 E. Landau-Tasseron, 'Features of the Pre-Conquest Muslim Army in the Time of Muḥammad', *LAEI*, iii (1995), 299–336.

5 Landau-Tasseron, 'Features', 324–34.

6 The best account is Donner, *The Early Islamic Conquests*; on the conquest of Egypt (not discussed by Donner), see A. J. Butler, *The Arab Conquest of Egypt*, 2nd edn, P. M. Fraser (Oxford, 1978); W. E. Kaegi, 'Egypt on the Eve of the Muslim Conquest', in C. F. Petry (ed.), *The Cambridge History of Egypt*, i (Cambridge, 1998), 34–61.

7 For the fundamental discussion of the problems posed by the early Muslim sources for the conquests, see A. Noth and L. I. Conrad, *The Early Arabic Historical Tradition: A Source Critical Study*, trans. M. Bonner (Princeton, 1994). For detailed studies of the narratives of individual conquests, see G. M. Hinds, 'The First Arab Conquests in Fārs', *Iran*, 22 (1984), 39–53 republished in G. M. Hinds, *Studies in Early Islamic History*, ed. G. R. Hawting (Princeton, 1996), 199–231; L. I. Conrad, 'The Conquest of Arwād: A Source Critical Study in the Historiography of the Medieval Near East', *LAEI*, i (1992), 317–401; C. F. Robinson, 'The Conquest of Khuzistan: A Historio-

graphical Reassessment', in L. I. Conrad (ed.), *History and Historiography in Early Islamic Times* (Princeton, 1998), 1–44.

8 For non-Arab accounts, see A. Palmer, *The Seventh Century in West-Syrian Chronicles* (Liverpool, 1993); R. Hoyland, *Seeing Islam as Others Saw It: A Survey and Evaluation of Christian, Jewish and Zoroastrian Writings* (Princeton, 1997). See also now Sebeos, *The Armenian History attributed to Sebeos*, trans. R. W. Thomson with historical commentary by J. Howard-Johnston with T. Greenwood, 2 vols (Liverpool, 1999).

9 See p. 22.

10 Robinson, 'The Conquest of Khuzistan'.

11 Donner, *The Early Islamic Conquests*, 133, 135, 221.

12 W. Kaegi, *Byzantium and the Early Islamic Conquests* (Cambridge, 1992), 131, considers it unlikely that the Byzantine army at the Yarmūk numbered more than 15 000–20 000.

13 Donner, *The Early Islamic Conquests*, 205–9, 221.

14 Donner, *The Early Islamic Conquests*, 213, 217, 221.

15 Hinds, *Studies*, 218, 231.

16 K. Morimoto, 'The Dīwāns as Registers of the Arab Stipendiaries in Early Islamic Egypt', in R. Curiel and R. Gyselen (eds), *Itinéraires d'Orient: Hommages à Claude Cahen* (Bures-sur-Yvette, 1994), 353–65, p. 354.

17 The issue of Caliphal control over the armies of the conquests is discussed in F. M. Donner, 'Centralized Authority and Military Autonomy in the Early Muslim Conquests', *LAEI*, iii (1995), 337–60.

18 Donner, 'Centralized Authority', 347.

19 Donner, *The Early Islamic Conquests*, 221–6; for a discussion of early military organization keeping close to the Muslim sources, see F. M. Donner, 'The Growth of Military Institutions in the Early Caliphate and their Relation to Civilian Authority', *Al-Qantara*, xiv (1991), 311–26.

20 For military equipment, see pp. 173–8.

21 For the mobility of the Muslims and the use of mobility in warfare, see D. R. Hill, 'The Role of the Camel and the Horse in the Early Arab Conquests', in V. J. Parry and M. E. Yapp (eds), *War, Technology, and Society in the Middle East* (Oxford, 1975), 32–43 which, despite the author's somewhat cavalier attitude to the sources, makes some interesting observations.

22 For further discussion, see Morony, *Iraq after the Muslim Conquest* (Princeton, 1984), 197–8; the traditions about these troops have been collected and discussed in I. Hasson, 'Les *mawālī* dans l'armée musulman sous les premiers Umayyades', *JSAI*, 14 (1991), 176–213, pp. 185–91. Traditions concerning these Persian troops are somewhat confused and it is not always clear if they refer to the same or different units, or exactly when they defected. Many Muslims of Persian origin would have been keen to prove that their compatriots played a part in the early conquests. However, there is no reason to doubt the main point, that units of the Sasanian army did join the Muslims at an early stage.

23 Bal., *Futūḥ*, 280.

24 By Sayf b. 'Umar, Ṭa., i, 2261.

25 Ṭa., i, 3371–2.

26 On the Asāwira, see Bal., *Futūḥ*, 372–4; Ṭa., i, 2562–3, see also *Encyclopaedia Iranica* sv. Asāvera (C. E. Bosworth); D. Ayalon, 'Preliminary Remarks on the Mamlūk Institution in Islam', in V. J. Parry and M. E. Yapp (eds), *War, Technology, and Society in the Middle East*, 44–58, pp. 44–7; Morony, *Iraq*, 198, 207–8; K. Athāmina, 'Non-Arab Regiments and Private Militias during the Umayyad Period', *Arabica*, 40 (1998), 347–75. Despite the original use of the word to describe cavalry, it is clear that they fought primarily as archers in Iraq. For a broader view, stressing (and perhaps

exaggerating) the role of these troops as bearers of Iranian culture, see M. Zakeri, *Sasanid Soldiers in Early Muslim Society: The Origins of 'Ayyaran and Futuwwa* (Wiesbaden, 1995).

27 Ṭa., ii, 452, 454.

28 Ṭa., ii, 454; Bal., *Futūḥ*, 375.

29 Bal., *Futūḥ*, 375; see p. 7.

30 Bal., *Futūḥ*, 374.

31 Ibn 'Abd al-Ḥakam, *Futūḥ Miṣr*, ed. C. Torrey (New Haven, 1922), 129; Hasson, 'Les mawāli', 192–3.

32 Donner, *The Early Islamic Conquests*, 202–9.

33 Kaegi, *Byzantium and the Early Islamic Conquests*, 112–46.

34 This discussion is based on Robinson, 'The Conquest of Khuzistan'.

35 The relevant section is translated in Robinson, 'The Conquest of Khuzistan', 6–9.

36 Robinson does not mention or discuss the archaeological evidence but see S. Matheson, *Persia: an Archaeological Guide* (London, 1972), 159–61; see also Ṭa., trans. Juynboll, Appendix A.

37 For the settlement of Basra and Kūfa, see Donner, *The Early Islamic Conquests*, 226–37; Morony, *Iraq*, 239–50, 598–9; specifically on Kūfa, see H. Djait, *Al-Kūfa: naissance de la ville islamique* (Paris, 1982); on Syria, see Donner, *The Early Islamic Conquests*, 245–50; on Fusṭāṭ, see W. Kubiak, *Al-Fusṭāṭ: Its Foundation and Early Urban Development* (Warsaw, 1982, Cairo, 1987).

38 Donner, *The Early Islamic Conquests*, 245–50.

39 Donner, *The Early Islamic Conquests*, 235 and Morony, *Iraq*, 243 list the constituent elements of the 'Sevenths'.

40 See pp. 59–73.

41 For the events of the first *fitna*, see J. Wellhausen, *The Arab Kingdom and its Fall* (trans. M. Weir, Calcutta, 1927, repr. Beirut, 1963), 75–112; G. R. Hawting, *The First Dynasty of Islam* (London, 1986), 24–33; H. Kennedy, *The Prophet and the Age of the Caliphates: The Islamic Near East from the Sixth to the Eleventh Century* (London, 1986), 75–81.

42 On which see E. L. Petersen, *'Alī and Mu'āwiya in the Early Arabic Tradition* (Copenhagen, 1964); U. Sezgin, *Abū Mihnaf . . . ein betrag zu Historiographie der Umaiyadischen zeit* (Leiden, 1971), 123–45; Hinds, 'The Banners and Battle Cries of the Arabs at Ṣiffīn', *Al-Abhath*, 4 (1971), 3–42; Hinds, 'The Ṣiffīn Arbitration Agreement', *JSS*, 17 (1972), 93–129.

43 al-Minqarī, *Waq'at Ṣiffīn*, ed. M. A. Harun (Beirut, 1990).

44 Ṭa., i, 3371–2. The translation is based on Tabari trans., xvii (Hawting), 121–2 with modifications.

45 See p. 22.

46 Ṭa., i, 3370–1.

47 Hinds, 'The Banners and Battle Cries', pp. 60–7.

48 Ṭa., i, 3287 trans., 34.

49 For Qurrā', see G. M. Hinds 'Kūfan Political Alignments and their Background in the Mid-Seventh Century AD', *IJMES*, 2 (1971) 346–67, pp. 358–60, 363–6.

50 Ṭa., i, 3298.

51 Ṭa., i, 3312.

52 Ṭa., i, 3282–3 trans. (Hawting), 33. Despite the rhetoric, it is clear that hand-to-hand combat on foot is being described.

53 Ṭa., i, 3284–5.

54 Ṭa., i, 3300.

55 Ṭa., i, 3328.

56 Ṭa., i, 3381, trans. (Hawting), 131 slightly abbreviated.

57 Ṭa., i, 3191, 3212, 3214–15.

58 Ṭa., i, 3265.
59 Ṭa., ii, 345, 414–17.
60 For his career and importance, see Hinds, 'Kūfan Political Alignments', 357–64; also G. M. Hinds, 'The Murder of the Caliph 'Uthmān', *IJMES*, 3 (1972), 450–69, pp. 459–61.
61 Ṭa., i, 3297.
62 Ṭa., i, 3294.
63 For his life, see L. I. Conrad 'The Conquest of Arwād', 361–2.
64 Ibn 'Abd al-Ḥakam, 108. On this attack, see W. Kaegi, 'The First Arab Expedition against Amorium', *Byzantine and Modern Greek Studies*, 3 (1977), 19–22.
65 Ṭa., i, 2398.
66 Ṭa., i, 2984.
67 al-Minqarī, 156–7.
68 Ṭa., i, 3268.
69 al- Kindī, *Wulāt*, 29.
70 Ṭa., ii, 139.
71 Ṭa., ii, 3263–4; al-Minqarī, 154–5; Ibn A'tham, ii, 490–3.
72 *'aybatak*, see Lane sv.
73 Ṭa., ii, 197.
74 Bal., *Futūḥ*, 117. Two different traditions are presented: it is not clear whether the Persians were moved to or from Antioch but it is clear that Persians (*Furs*) were settled in these areas, see Hasson, 'Les *mawālī*',197–8.
75 For a general account, see J. F. Haldon, *Byzantium in the Seventh Century* (Cambridge, 1990), 63–4. For the problems with the Arabic sources, see Conrad, 'The Conquest of Arwād'.
76 See Lane, sv.
77 Ṭa., i, 2916.
78 Ṭa., i, 3392.
79 Ṭa., i, 3365.
80 Ṭa., ii, 197, 205; Ibn Khayyāṭ, 227.
81 Ṭa., ii, 28–9; cf. P. Crone, *Slaves on Horseback (*Cambridge, 1980), 248 n. 474 where it is argued that the *shurṭa* was 'not the urban police force but rather the military division which fought in the vicinity of the caliph, prince or general in battle under the leadership of a commander who was responsible for discipline, the hearing of complaints, the meting out of punishments and the *'amr al-'askar* in general'. In fact the *shurṭa* seems to have fulfilled a dual role in the field army and the city.
82 Bal., *Ansāb*, iva, 171, 188.
83 Ṭa., ii, 117–20.
84 Ṭa., ii, 288–9, 303, 341–2.
85 Ṭa., ii, 230, 255–6.
86 Bal., *Ansāb*, v, 293.
87 Ṭa., ii, 119–20.
88 Ṭa., ii, 117, 118; Crone, *Slaves on Horseback*, 248, n. 474.
89 Ṭa., ii, 77–9; Bal., *Ansāb*, iva, 192.

CHAPTER TWO

The armies of the Marwanid period, 64–132/683–750: recruitment, leadership and tactics[1]

The civil wars which followed the death of the Caliph Yazīd I in 64/683 mark a decisive step in the development of the Islamic state. By the time of his death, the Caliph ʿAbd al-Malik (65–86/685–705) had created an army, largely recruited from the Syrians (*ahl al-Shām*), which was a distinct and largely professional force. It was the instrument of his authority, and that of his Marwanid successors, over the rest of the peoples of the Caliphate, Muslim and non-Muslim alike. In a real sense, his reign sees the emergence of an army, as opposed to a society which could be mobilised for war.

In 64/683 this was all still in the future. At this time there was still no hard and fast division between soldier and civilian. Many, probably the majority, of men who served in the armies of the Caliphate, and who were paid for doing so, were essentially part-time soldiers, called up or volunteering for a particular campaign and being paid off at the end. And some soldiers were more part-time than others: some would serve on a military campaign only once in a lifetime, others would serve every year and be constantly available to be called up.

There was no one 'Umayyad army' but rather a number of different armies at different times. The most important of these was the Syrian army, the *ahl al-Shām*, constantly referred to in the sources. These certainly formed the underpinning of the Umayyad regime but were by no means the only military force. The army of Iraq – or, more precisely, the armies of Basra and Kūfa – were employed in the early decades of Marwanid rule, but increasingly phased out as they proved unreliable or incompetent. As long as they existed, however, they retained their separate identities – that is, Basrans did not serve in the army of Kūfa, nor did Syrians. In contrast to the Syrians, the armies of Kūfa and Basra served only in Iraq, though elements of them were despatched to Khurāsān or Sistan on occasion.

The army of Khurāsān was, so to speak, the offspring of the armies of Kūfa and Basra which, by dint of serving in this troubled frontier province, acquired its own identity (or, rather, identities since it remained bitterly divided by tribal rivalries).

In the last decades of Umayyad rule, some Syrian soldiers were also sent to Khurāsān, further complicating the local rivalries.

The position was different again in Egypt. Despite Coptic rebellions in the later Umayyad period, Egypt was comparatively peaceful.[2] The local Egyptian *jund* was small and largely composed of the conquerors of the country and their descendants. In fact the army was a small, hereditary ruling class, very few outsiders made their way into it and Egyptian soldiers never served in other areas of the Caliphate (except North Africa and Spain). And because it was large enough to keep the peace in Egypt, more or less, but too small to be the basis for rebellion, it was largely undisturbed by the wider currents of change in the Caliphate.

Overall numbers

The Muslim fighting men were the mainstay of the early Islamic state. They provided its armies and consumed most of its resources. It is important, therefore, to try to make some estimate of the overall numbers involved. However, it is impossible to give an accurate figure for the number of *muqātila* (fighting men) registered in the *dīwāns* of the Muslim world at the beginning of the Marwanid period. This is not because the sources do not provide figures; on the contrary, we are given figures on many occasions. The problem is rather that the figures often contradict each other and many seem to be formulaic round numbers rather than real assessments. Nor is there a clear relationship between the overall figures for men and their families enrolled in the *dīwāns*, and the numbers who could actually be recruited for military action. As a rule of thumb, I would like to suggest that the figures given in the sources may well be out by a factor of two, but unlikely to be out by a factor of 10: that is, a figure of 40 000 may represent 20 000 or 60 000 but is unlikely to represent 4000 or 400 000. Clearly, this is not a very satisfactory basis on which to work but, in the absence of reliable statistics, it is the best we have and it may be possible to suggest some tentative conclusions.

In the early Umayyad period, large numbers of troops are said to have had their names recorded in the *dīwāns*. Al-Balādhurī records that the man in charge of the *dīwān* of the Arab troops at the end of the Umayyad period had looked back to see how many *muqātila* there had been in Basra and Kūfa in the time of the governor b. Ziyād b. Abī Sufyān (d. 53/673). For Basra he found 80 000 with 120 000 in their families and for Kūfa, 60 000 and 80 000 in their families.[3] We are given a number of figures for the *dīwān* of Basra, reported to show how the governor, Ziyād, or his son 'Ubayd Allāh, had increased the numbers during their period of office. Ziyād is said to have increased the numbers from 40 000 to 80 000 and the offspring from 80 000 to 120 000.[4] In 64/684 the governor of Iraq, 'Ubayd Allāh b. Ziyād, is said to have claimed that he had increased the number of *muqātila* in the *dīwān* of Basra from 70 000 to 80 000 men and the number of dependants from 90 000 to 140 000, though he was wanting to talk the numbers up to show his beneficence to the people of the city.[5] In 24/645, at the beginning of 'Uthmān's

Caliphate, there were said to have been 40 000 *muqātila* in Kūfa, of whom 10 000 went on campaign every year.[6] Later when al-Ḥajjāj tried to mobilise all the *muqātila* of Kūfa against the Khārijīs, he had 40 000 and an additional 10 000 young men who wanted to join up.[7]

These apparently precise figures present serious problems of interpretation. The contexts are mostly rhetorical (the achievements of Ziyād and his son) rather than bureaucratic. Furthermore the numbers, even in reports of the same speech, are varied and suspiciously rounded. There is a strong possibility that they are no more than the same rhetorical device recycled. If however, we take a leap of faith and accept that they may represent some sort of historical reality, then we could suggest that the number of *muqātila* whose names were registered in the *dīwān* of Basra increased during the reign of Mu'āwiya and may have reached about 80 000 by the death of Yazīd I in 64/683. The numbers in Kūfa seem to have been rather smaller, perhaps three-quarters of those in Basra. All in all, when the Caliph Mu'āwiya, on his deathbed, told his son that there were 100 000 swords in Iraq which might be unsheathed against him, he was probably not exaggerating.[8]

The same considerations apply to the numbers given for other areas. In 96/715 there were said to have been 47 000 soldiers in Khurāsān.[9] In 112/730–1, the inexperienced governor of Khurāsān, al-Junayd b. 'Abd al-Raḥmān was warned that he should not invade Transoxania with less than 50 000 men.[10] Total numbers from Syria are more difficult to estimate, but it is unlikely that they were many fewer than in Iraq. There were also a smaller number, perhaps 40 000 at the most, in Egypt.[11]

Occasionally we find mentions of very large numbers of troops engaged in individual campaigns. Yazīd b. al-Muhallab is said to have led 100 000 *muqātila* apart from slave soldiers and volunteers on his campaign in Jurjān in 98/716–7,[12] but it is likely that presence of a charismatic commander and the promise of the spiritual and material rewards of the Holy War encouraged mass participation. Very large figures are also mentioned in the civil wars in Syria at the end of the Umayyad Caliphate. At the Battle of 'Ain al-Jarr between the forces of Marwān b. Muḥammad and Sulaymān b. Hishām in 127/744, Sulaymān is said to have had 120 000 horsemen and Marwān 80 000. The lines of battle stretched right across the Biqa valley.[13] However, there is no indication that these were all regular troops and the figures probably reflect the very high degree of mobilisation in the Syrian Arab population at the time.

If we were to suggest that in *c*. 80/700 there were about 100 000 *muqātila* in the *dīwāns* of Iraq, about the same in Syria,[14] 50 000 in Khurāsān and western Iran, and another 40 000 in Egypt, the Hijaz and other areas, this would give a global figure of between 250 000 and 300 000 troops enrolled in the registers. This, of course, does not mean that anything like this number could actually be raised to go on campaign. The sources from Iraq make it clear that it was often difficult to persuade even a small fraction of the men registered to turn out, especially if the fighting was both unprofitable and dangerous, as against the Khārijīs. With the effective demilitarisation of the Iraqi towns after 82/701, numbers in Iraq declined steeply, with some being transferred to Khurāsān. In contrast, numbers of Syrian soldiers probably increased to provide garrisons in Iraq and troops to serve in North Africa.

These totals might usefully be compared with numbers in the late Roman armies.[15] The one source who gives an overall figure for the late Roman army is Agathias, who says that Justinian reduced the numbers from 654 000 to 150 000. The purpose of citing these figures is polemical and the contrast is certainly exaggerated. Some of the difference may well be created by the distinction between the mobile field forces (*comitatenses*) and the *limitanei* attached to certain areas. The *limitanei* may, or may not, have been abolished by Justinian. Jones estimated the eastern mobile army at 104 000[16] while the revisionist MacMullen suggests 93 000. Whitby accepts a figure of around 150 000.[17] To these should be added the *limitanei*, and if this is done MacMullen suggests 400 000.[18] These large numbers, of course, include *limitanei* who were part-time or potential soldiers, but so, of course, were many of the *muqātila*.The figures would suggest that the 300 000 I propose for the number of Muslim *muqātila* is not absurdly large. Late Roman expeditionary forces of up 30 000 are recorded in the sixth century while the army of 52 000 assembled for the Persian war in 503 is described by Procopius as beyond comparison with earlier and later armies.[19] Again, these numbers are not entirely out of line with those given for Muslim expeditions.

Numbers for the Byzantine armies of the eighth, ninth and tenth centuries vary significantly. Generally accepted figures, based largely on the reports of Arab geographers, suggest a standing army of up to 120 000.[20] However, Whittow has suggested that this total is much too high and that 10 000 cavalry and 20 000 infantry may be nearer the mark.[21] As in the case of the numbers in Muslim armies, part of the discrepancy may be the result of confusion between potential numbers of soldiers and the effective numbers who could actually be put in the field.

The structure of command

Modern armies are divided into discrete sub-divisions (regiments, companies, etc.) and have precise command structures. Soldiers have ranks and some are more senior than others. It is also generally the case that men rise through the ranks by way of promotion so that generals started their careers at the bottom of the officer hierarchy. None of these things were true of early Islamic armies. Men were appointed to command armies for many different reasons: they were loyal to the regime, they could recruit followers and attract men to their service, they could organise the collection and payment of revenues and they were effective and knowledgeable commanders in battle. There are a few instances of men, al-Muhallab b. Abī Ṣufra is perhaps the best example, who seem to have risen from comparatively modest backgrounds by demonstrating their competence as commanders – in al-Muhallab's case, against the Khārijīs. In the main, however, it is unhelpful to think of a hierarchy, of generals, or of an officer class.

In the early Umayyad period, many military commanders were chosen from the tribal *ashrāf* (nobility) and no doubt used their position to recruit troops and secure their loyalty.[22] The government also interfered in the choice of tribal chiefs and to move the *ri'āsa* (headship) from one family to another. In this way, the tribal *ashrāf* were half-way to becoming government appointed commanders.[23] There was a growing tendency, especially after the revolt of Ibn al-Ash'ath, for command to be entrusted to men of more modest social origins and the development of a cadre of professional commanders, precursors of the *quwwād* of the early Abbasid period.[24]

Apart from commanders, we hear of officials called *'arīf* (pl., *'urafā'*). According to one account, they were first introduced by Ziyād b. Abī Sufyān when he was governing Iraq for Mu'āwiya.[25] These are said to have been in charge of ten or fifteen men[26] and it is tempting to think of them as sort of sergeants or junior officers. In fact this is misleading. The *'urafā'* were in charge of assembling and paying the men but not of leading them in battle.[27] 'Ubayd Allāh b. Ziyād forced all the *'urafā* of Kūfa to list any subversives they knew of and to declare that there were no enemies of the Caliph or wanted men in their *'urāfa*s: if they failed to do this they would be exiled.[28] In this case the *'arīf*s were effectively being treated as a sort of military police.The *'urafā'* do not seem to have been chosen from the tribal élite and indeed they may have been employed precisely to restrict the authority of the *ashrāf*.[29] In 75/694–5 when al-Ḥajjāj was trying to force the unwilling army of Kūfa to join al-Muhallab in his campaign against the Khārijīs, he ordered the *'urafā'* to take their men to the front and return with receipts to confirm that they had done so, suggesting that they were not remaining with their men during the fighting.[30] On another occasion, the *'urafā'* and the men in charge of the dīwān (*aṣḥāb al-dawāwīn)* were responsible for raising, but not leading, men to fight the Khārijīs.[31] When Qutayba b. Muslim was planning his attack on Samarqand in 93/711–12, he ordered the *'urafā'* to choose the bravest men for the assault, but there is no evidence that they led them into battle.[32] The Umayyad governor of Kūfa, al-Ḥakam b. al-Ṣalt, faced with the rebellion of Zayd b. 'Alī, summoned the *'urafā'*, and well as the police (*shuraṭ*), and lesser officials known as the *manākib*, to arrange the campaign against the rebels. Given the number of descriptions of battle which survive from this period, it is surprising that we do not hear more of the *'urafā'* and it is particularly striking that we hardly know the name of a single individual among them.[33]

We also hear of an official called the *'āriḍ* (pl., *'urāḍ*) whose function it was to count the numbers of troops leaving Basra to join the campaign against the Khārijīs and make sure that all the men were at their battle-stations.[34] They also decided who was fit to fight and have their names recorded in the *dīwān*.[35]

Commanders seem to have made their dispositions at the time of battle. Typically commanders would appoint men they could trust over the left wing, the right wing or the cavalry and the infantry but these seem to have been one-off appointments for that particular conflict rather than permanent posts. We also hear of rebel leaders appointing substitutes who would take their place if they were killed in battle. Sulaymān b. Ṣurad is said to have appointed no less than six men to succeed him one after the other when he confronted the Umayyad armies: as usual in such stories, we are told that only the sixth lived to lead the few survivors to safety.[36]

In general, there is no evidence of an organised military hierarchy in the Marwanid period. Typically, command structures were fluid and temporary and, as we shall see, when battle was joined, the real unit of action was the small group fighting by its banner rather than more established large-scale structures.

The course of battle

When al-Ḥārith b. Abī Rabī'a addressed his men before they left to fight the Khārijīs in 68/687–8, he described what battle was all about: 'The first part of fighting is the shooting of arrows, then the pointing of spears, then the thrusting of them to left and right and then the drawing of swords. That's all there is to it.'[37] Al-Ḥārith's observations seem to reflect the reality of many conflicts. After initial skirmishing between cavalry, the decisive encounters were between foot soldiers, fighting first with long spears and later at close quarters with drawn swords.

Armies were conventionally drawn up for battle in lines (*ṣufūf*). These were composed of a centre (*qalb*, lit. heart) and a right wing, *maymana*, and a left wing, *maysara*. The *muqaddima* (vanguard) would lead the advance and the *sāqa* would defend the rear and collect up any stragglers. Every officer (*qā'id*) should know his men and each man must know his position in the line *(markaz)* and the banners and flags (*bunūd, a'lām, rāyāt*) under which he serves. Then the whole army should advance on the enemy as a single unit.[38] Such at least was the theory but the practice must have varied very much according to circumstances.

Al-Harthamī describes three different forms of line. The first is the straight line, which is the best. The second is the Crescent (*hilālī*), with the wings advanced and the centre further back. This leaves the two wings exposed and the commander should send a squadron (*kardūs*) of horse to protect each one. The third is the Curved (*ma'ṭūf*) with the centre advanced and the wings behind. This is the worst and should be employed only in cases of dire necessity. In this case two *kardūs*es should be stationed to support the centre.[39]

We have a good description of Ibrāhīm b. al-Ashtar, the most talented commander Kūfa produced during the Marwanid period, making preparations for his encounter with the Umayyad forces led by 'Ubayd Allāh b. Ziyād.[40] The two armies met up at Bār'īta on the Khāzir river east of Mosul in 67/686–7. A disaffected member of Ibn Ziyād's army advised Ibrāhīm not to delay but fight the next day. He spent a sleepless night and in the grey early dawn he arranged his squadrons (*katā'ib*)[41] and his commanders. He appointed commanders to the left and right wings, the horse and the foot and appointed someone to hold his banner. He led the men in prayer and then sent to commanders to their post, keeping the cavalry close to him because he had only a few of them. Then he led his men on foot to the top of a hill whence he could look down on the enemy, who had not yet begun to stir. Ibrāhīm called for his horse and rode up and down the line talking to each of the standard bearers, since he knew they would play a crucial part in the battle. Then he addressed the men, stressing the righteousness of their cause.

By this time Ibn Ziyād's forces were advancing on them, wing against wing. At first things went badly for the Kūfans and a number of banner-holders were killed but Ibn al-Ashtar rallied them, fighting the enemy with his sword and urging his banner-holder forward. 'We walked toward them', one of his men later recalled, 'and when we were near them we fought briefly with spears and then turned to swords and maces and struck blows at each other for a large part of the day'. In the end Ibn al-Ashtar's men were victorious and the hated Ibn Ziyād lay dead on the field. We cannot be certain of the cause of victory but it looks as if Ibrahīm's careful preparations played their part.

There were other ways of arranging an army. 'Attāb b. Warqā fighting the Khārijīs in Iraq in 77/696–7 arranged his cavalry on the left and right wings and the infantry in the centre in three ranks (*ṣufūf*), a rank with swords, a rank with spears and a rank of archers while 'Attāb himself commanded sitting on a carpet in the centre.[42] In the event, however, his careful preparations availed him nothing and he and his forces were ridden down by the Khārijīs.

Commanders usually stationed themselves at the centre. Curiously, they often chose to command sitting down, either on a carpet, like the unfortunate 'Attāb, or on a chair. Al-Ḥajjāj commanded the Syrians from a chair which had to be moved forward as the troops advanced.[43] Yazīd b. al-Muhallab in Khurāsān commanded his troops sitting in a chair, perhaps because his armour was too heavy (400 *ratl*s, about 80lb) for him to be able to mount a horse.[44] Qutayba b. Muslim sat to direct the Muslim attack on Bukhārā in 90/708.[45] The reasons for this apparently relaxed attitude to command are not clear. It may reflect Sasanian practice but it may also have been practical, in that a stationary commander is much easier for his subordinates to find than one who is dashing all over the battlefield.

A purely cavalry force could be arranged in squadrons (*katā'ib*) to give more flexibility. Zufar b. al-Ḥārith advised Sulaymān b. Ṣurad to do this when he faced a larger Umayyad army which consisted of both horse and foot.[46] At the end of the Umayyad period, we find Marwān II breaking up his conventional line of battle (*ṣaff*) and dispersing his men in small units (*kardūs*, pl. *karādīs*)[47] to fight the Khārijīs more effectively. The Khārijīs responded by adopting the same formation.[48]

After battle had been joined at close quarters, it was difficult for any commander to have much control over the course of events. In the hand-to-hand fighting it was the small groups gathered around their banners which were the real fighting unit, men from the same tribe or locality who knew each other and were prepared to die with each other.[49] Such was the small group huddled together their banner who Marwān b. al-Ḥakam encountered at the Battle of Marj Rāhit and who assured him that they had seen angels fighting on his side.[50] In the battles of the Kūfans against Ibn Ziyād at 'Ayn al-Warda and Bār'īta, banners played a crucial role in providing a focus for the troops.

Battles might begin with cavalry engagements but they often became infantry struggles as time went on. One of the most characteristic features of warfare at this time was the practice of dismounting to engage the enemy more effectively. When Ibn al-Ashtar was leading his men to take over Kūfa in the name of al-Mukhtār in 66/ 686–6, he ordered them to dismount and advance with drawn swords.[51] The next year when Muṣʻab b. al-Zubayr was leading his men to attack al-Mukhtār in Kūfa, he dismounted and advanced with a bow on his shoulder: later he is seen kneeling to fire arrows and rally his men,[52] while his opponent al-Mukhtār also dismounted and fought on foot.[53]

When the government forces were in danger of being overwhelmed by the Khārijī cavalry in an encounter in the northern Jazīra in 76/695, they chose to fight on foot: 'Their two commanders dismounted', one of the Khārijīs later recalled, 'and ordered most of their men to dismount as well. Then we could no longer do as we wished with them. When we attacked them, their infantry met us with spears (*rimāḥ*) and their archers rained arrows on us, their cavalry charging us all the while. We fought them until evening when darkness finally separated us.'[54] The Khārijīs subsequently left under cover of darkness.

This tactic, the use of the infantry spear-wall to defeat a cavalry charge, became common practice in warfare of the Marwanid period. It was especially effective against the daring cavalry attacks of the Khārijīs. In another encounter between the Khārijīs led by Shabīb b. Yazīd, both groups dismounted to fight more effectively on foot.[55] In the final climactic battle for the control of Kūfa between Shabīb and the Umayyad forces commanded by al-Ḥajjāj in person, al-Ḥajjāj gave his men strict instructions: 'Lower your eyes, get down on your knees and meet the enemy with the points of your spears.' The Syrians obeyed their orders, remaining kneeling pointing their spear at the enemy and looking 'like a field of black stones' until the enemy were almost on them. Then they rose and thrust with their spears, advancing steadily against the enemy and Kūfa was saved for the Umayyads.[56] The most striking example of the effectiveness of these tactics, however, comes from the time of the fall of the Umayyad Caliphate, at the Battle of Tell Kushāf when the 'Abbasid troops under 'Abd Allāh b.'Alī used exactly these tactics to defeat Marwān II's army.[57]

In a different environment, Syrian military tactics were put to the test in the street fighting in Kūfa at the time of the rebellion of Zayd b. 'Alī in 122/740. At one point the Syrian cavalry were told to dismount and fight on foot because 'in a narrow place, cavalry can't do anything against foot soldiers'. The next day the Syrian cavalry were worsted by Zayd's supporters and the Umayyad cause was saved only by the Bukhāriya and Qīqānīya foot archers who were sent as reinforcements. It was they who inflicted the wound which killed Zayd and led directly to the collapse of the rebellion.[58]

These details are important in accounting for the victories of the Syrian armies in Iraq and the success of fairly small numbers of Syrian troops in maintaining the Umayyad hold over this rich but potentially troublesome area (though Syrians were by no means the only troops to use these techniques). The ability of Syrian troops to obey orders, to maintain their discipline, kneeling with their spears in the face of an oncoming cavalry charge, is a sign of training and professionalism. It was this discipline and training which gave them the advantage over their enthusiastic but disorganised enemies. We see here the beginnings of a really professional standing army.

The khandaq and its uses

The word *khandaq* (from Persian, *kanda*) was used to describe a ditch or trench dug for defensive purposes. The Prophet himself had dug such a trench to defend Madīna against the attack of the Meccans, so the device carried an ideological message as well as a practical one: good Muslims were those who were sheltered by the *khandaq*. In early Islamic warfare, the word *khandaq* denotes everything from a hastily dug obstacle to a marching camp, roughly rectangular in shape with two or four gates and possibly towers as well. The walls were of earth and stones, not masonary, and the ramparts might be defended with shields or *ḥasak*, a term which means either thorn-scrub or metal caltrops. It seems that *khandaq*s were often dug by the soldiers themselves but some forces were accompanied by professional sappers (*fa'ala*) for this purpose.[59]

The *khandaq* came into its own during government campaigns against the guerrilla bands of the Khārijīs. Al-Muhallab b. Abī Ṣufra was the great pioneer of this sort of warfare. 'When al-Muhallab camped with his men, he constructed a *khandaq*, posted lookouts, sent out scouts and placed sentries. the men remained in their battle lines, the men with their banners and in their Fifths. Men were appointed to guard the gates of the *khandaq*'.[60] Julius Caesar would have been proud of him, and the Khārijīs were certainly unable to take his men by surprise.

Wise commanders in the war against the Khārijīs followed al-Muhallab's example. Al-Jazl b. Sa'īd, for example, leading the men of Kūfa against the Khārijīs in 76/695–6 'always marched in formation [*'alā tabī'atin*] and always made a *khandaq* for himself when he halted', with the result that the Khārijī leader Shabīb became impatient and decided to launch a night attack. He divided his small forces (just 160 men) into four groups to attack al-Jazl's camp on each side. The encountered a party of scouts and drove them back to the *khandaq*, hoping to follow them into the fortification. The defenders, however, refused to let their comrades in and showered the Khārijīs with arrows until they were forced to restreat. Another assault the next night was no more successful.[61] The *khandaq* described here was obviously a well-defended quadrilateral enclosure. In the early 'Abbasid period, Khāzim b. Khuzayma was repeatedly to prove the value of the *khandaq* in the defeat of highly mobile enemies.[62]

Some *khandaq*s were clearly quite substantial structures. The *khandaq* Muṣ'ab b. al-Zubayr built near Maskin when he was trying to defend himself against 'Abd al-Malik's troops was still to be seen in al-Balādhurī's time, more than a century and a half later, and it was still known as Khirbat (ruin) Muṣ'ab.[63] On the other hand, the *khandaq*s al-Junayd ordered his commanders to dig in the heat of battle at the Day of the Pass in 112/731 must have been no more than hastily dug trenches.[64]

'Abd al-Ḥamīd al-Kātib, writing at the end of the Umayyad period, gives instructions for the construction of a *khandaq*. After the baggage has been set down and the army has been assigned its places to stay, before any tents are set up. Each officer (*qā'id*) should be assigned a section of ground which he is to dig a trench (*khandaq*). It should be defended by *ḥasak* (either thorns or artificial caltrops). There are to be two gates each to be defended by an officer and a hundred men.[65]

A tale of two battles

To examine the realities of warfare, we can look at accounts of two very different battles fought in the Umayyad period, both chosen because we have particularly full accounts of them which enable us to trace the course of battle in some detail.

The first of these is the battle fought at Ra's al-'Ayn in northern Syria in Jumādā I, 65/early January 685.[66] The background to the conflict was the killing of al-Ḥusayn, grandson of the Prophet, at Karbalā on 10 Muḥarram, 64/7 September 683 on the orders of the then Umayyad governor of Iraq, 'Ubayd Allāh b. Ziyād. Many people in Kūfa were sadly aware that they had failed to aid al-Ḥusayn in his hour of need and with the collapse of the Umayyad regime in Iraq after the death of the Caliph Yazīd b. Mu'āwiya and the flight of Ibn Ziyād to Syria, they determined to revenge al-Ḥusayn and atone for their own sins. The leadership was assumed by one Sulaymān b. Ṣurad.

Sulaymān left Kūfa in Rabī' II/November 684 and camped at Nukhayla, a short way from the city. He was disappointed to find that of the 16 000 who had pledged that they would join him, only some 4000 appeared. After a certain amount of persuading, another 1000 eventually turned up. Sulaymān claimed he was not discouraged since he knew that he and his small band were doing God's will while the rest had fallen away. After paying their respects to the tomb of al-Ḥusayn in a display of penitence and grief which may the earliest example of tomb-veneration in Islam, they moved off up the Euphrates valley.

When they arrived at Qarqisīya, they found that it was held by Zufar b. al-Ḥārith al-Kilābī. Qarqisīya was the old Roman frontier post of Circesium and its walls, now completely ruined, were then clearly still in good repair. Zufar had come there after the defeat of the Qays-Muḍar at the Battle of Marj Rāhiṭ and had gathered the remnants of the Qays under his leadership. He would not have been displeased to see Umayyad authority challenged but was not prepared to join a venture which he must have known was doomed to failure. After Sulaymān sent an envoy to him, Zufar established a market so that the army could buy provisions. He wished them well but did not allow them inside the walls.

He is also said to have given Sulaymān advice which is perhaps the nearest we have to a work of military instruction from this period. The wily and experienced Zufar is shown telling the naive and untried Sulaymān how to conduct warfare:[67]

> The enemy [the Umayyads] has left Raqqa. If you rush to 'Ayn al-Warda ahead of them and put the town at your back, then the district, the water supply and the food will be in your hands and you will have security in the region between your town and ours [i.e. the steppe land between Ra's al-'Ayn and Qarqisīya]. Move your camp this instant to 'Ayn al-Warda. The enemy is marching as an army [i.e. at the pace of the foot-soldiers], but you have horses and, by God, I have rarely seen a group of horses more noble than they. Get them ready immediately and I hope you will get there before them and beat them to 'Ayn al-Warda. Do not fight them, firing arrows at them and thrusting at them in an open space for they outnumber you and you cannot be sure that you will not be surrounded. Do not stand still, firing at them and thrusting at them for you have nothing like their manpower, and if you leave yourselves open to them, it will not be long before they overwhelm you. And do not form a line [*ṣuff*] when they confront you for I see no foot soldiers with you but you are all horsemen, while the enemy is coming at you with foot and horse. Their cavalry will protect their infantry and their infantry their cavalry, but you have no footmen to defend your cavalry. So meet them with small units [*katā'ib*] and detachments [*manāqib*] of cavalry and distribute them between the right and left wings of the enemy. Place one cavalry squadron alongside another so that if one is attacked, the other can dismount and support the first with horses and men. When a squadron wants to be mounted it can and when it wants to dismount it can. But if you fight in one line and the enemy's men advance on you and you are forced out of the line, it will be broken and that means defeat.

Zufar was stressing the importance of access to supplies, a flexible order of battle and the interdependence of cavalry and infantry: it is not clear that Sulaymān acted on much of his advice.

The army then moved on up the Khabur valley and camped, as Zufar had advised, to the west of 'Ayn al-Warda. Here they had five days rest before the Syrians arrived. The Syrian forces were greatly superior in numbers, being about 20 000 in all, but command was divided between Ḥuṣayn b. Numayr, the senior commander, and Ibn Dhī'l-Kalā', who maintained he had an independent command. The first encounter between a squadron of Sulaymān's men and Ibn Dhī'l-Kalā' went in favour of the Iraqis, but Ibn Ziyād united the command under Ḥuṣayn and the superior numbers of the Syrians began to tell. On the third day of conflict, Sulaymān saw that his men were being driven back and ordered them to dismount and break the sheaths of their swords and advance on foot. Ḥuṣayn sent in reinforcements, including foot archers (the Iraqis do not seem to have had any archers) and Sulaymān's men were surrounded. Sulaymān was soon killed and the banner, which was the centre of resistance, was passed down the chain of command. By now the battle was being fought out on foot with swords and hand-to-hand conflict.[68] The Iraqis were soon in serious trouble and the banner had passed to the last in the chain of command originally nominated by Sulaymān,

Rifāʻa b. Shaddād, and it was he who gathered the survivors and led them to safety under cover of night, first to Qarqisīya, where Zufar offered them sympathy and medical help, and then to Kūfa.

The account of the battle is full of rhetorical flourishes, brave words and spoken in the heat of action and we are told of many who chose to die in a just cause rather than return home. We are also given the point of view of Syrians who resented being called infidels by the Iraqi rebels.[69] Despite these elements, we can see the general outline of the conflict. Cavalry were used to make first contact and in the initial stages. As battle grew fiercer and more intense, it was fought out on foot with swords. Archers were used at crucial moments. The banners were a key element in maintaining cohesion and morale in the confusion of a closely fought conflict.

The other conflict to be considered in detail, is the so-called Battle of the Pass (*Yawm al-shiʻb*), probably fought in 112–3/731 and described in some detail in al-Tabarī's history.[70] This account is basically the account in al-Madā'inī's *Futūḥ Khurāsān*, probably compiled about a century after the events described on the basis of earlier accounts. Al-Madā'inī's account is more impressionistic than Abū Mikhnaf's and the tone is very different, the accent is on heroic achievement, and the blunders of the Muslim commander Junayd, rather than of pious resignation.

In 112/731 the new governor of Khurāsān, Junayd b. ʻAbd al-Raḥmān was faced by a major rebellion in Transoxania, led by the Khāqān of the Turgesh Turks and supported by Ghūrak, the local Soghdian ruler of Samarqand. The Muslim governor of Samarqand, Sawra b. al-Ḥurr, was cut off in the city and wrote asking for help. Despite the warnings of advisers who urged him to wait for reinforcements, Junayd set off from Marw to relieve the city.

The direct route through Bukhārā and along the old 'Royal Road' which ran through the plains north of the mountains was held by the enemy so Junayd decided to go south, through the plains of the Kashka Darya river to Kish (modern Shahr-i Sabz), which he made his base. From there it was only a short distance, some 70 km as the crow flies, to Samarqand but there was a range of mountains between them. He was faced with a choice of routes, either round the western end of the range, which was flat but considerably longer, or over the short but steep 2000 m Tashtakaracha Pass on the direct route.

He was advised that the longer route would be dangerous as the land had not been cultivated for years and the Khāqān would set fire to the tall grass and trees. After some hesitation, Junayd decided on the direct route. The next day they were attacked in the narrow pass by the Turks. Junayd had divided his men into tribal groups on the left and right wings. At first most of the fighting seems to have been done on horseback while Junayd commanded from the centre on foot, at one stage joining the Azd under their banner. No fewer than 18 Azdi standard bearers are said to have been killed one after the other.[71]

When the Khaqan's men pressed the Muslims more vigorously, Junayd's herald (*nādī*) gave orders that they should all dismount and that the commanders should dig *khandaq*s in front of their forces and, though the account is not entirely clear, it seem that this measure saved the surviving Muslims from complete disaster. It was at this point of stalemate that Junayd ordered the reluctant Sawra to come to him from Samarqand, leaving a skeleton garrison in the city: he is said to have admitted openly that the hapless Sawra was being used only as a decoy to divert the attention of the Turks.

Sawra led his men up the northern approaches to the Pass and had almost reached Junayd when the Khaqan's men attacked. After some fierce fighting, Sawra attempted to make a breakthrough to reach Junayd. He took advice from 'Ubāda b. al-Salīl who suggested that they should advance on foot with their spears arrayed, but in the end Sawra decided to go for a cavalry attack. The result was chaos: the Turks set fire to the grass and both sides were caught up in a cloud of smoke and dust. It was the Turks, however, who were victorious and it is said that only 1000 or 2000 of the 12 000 men Sawra had led from Samarqand survived.[72]

Junayd's problems were not yet over. He was tempted to make straight for Samarqand but was persuaded to make a camp. The next day the Turks attacked the uncompleted fortification. Again there was fierce fighting. In the thick of it, Junayd had his herald announce that all slaves who fought would be freed and a number of them did so, using saddle blankets as makeshift armour.[73] Despite fierce attacks, the Turks failed to breach the Muslim ranks and Junayd was eventually able to reach Samarqand.

As with the account of the Battle of 'Ayn al-Warda, the account of the Battle of the Pass shows the importance of infantry warfare, the effectiveness of marching with spears at the ready and the importance of making camp. It also reveals a degree of discussion and argument within the Muslim ranks. Both Junayd and Sawra were faced by senior figures in their own armies who believed that they were taking the wrong course. Junayd's command seems to have inspired little confidence and his men were not afraid to make it clear, like the group of Azd who he joined at one stage of the battle who said openly that they knew he would take credit for success: 'If we win', one of them told him, 'it will be for your benefit; if we perish, you will not weep over us. By my life, if we win and I survive, I will never speak a word to you.'[74] Leaders like al-Muhallab b. Abī Ṣufra or Qutayba b. Muslim who could achieve great things, leaders like Junayd who could not, would find that giving orders was no substitute for gaining respect and that the independent spirit of the Arab tribesmen lived on.

The Syrian army, under 'Abd al-Malik and al-Walīd, 64–96/684–715

Umayyad rule was sustained by the support of the Syrian army. When this army broke up, riven by internal dissension, Umayyad rule collapsed. The description of the Syrian army is central to understanding it. There are constant references to the '*ahl al-Shām*' in the literature, and in reports of contemporary rhetoric. The force is not referred to as the Umayyad army or the army of an individual town or tribal group. This firm location in and identification with the province is very striking, showing that regional – specifically Syrian – loyalties were more important than tribal or even than dynastic ones. When al-Ḥajjāj was exhorting the Syrians to stand firm against the Kharijite Shabīb and his followers in the crucial struggle for Kūfa, it was as *ahl al-Shām* that he addressed them, not by their tribal signifiers, indeed we do not even know what tribes they were drawn from. There are numerous parallel examples. When al-Ḥuṣayn b. Numayr, then commanding the Syrian forces sent to attack Ibn Zubayr, was invited to swear allegiance to Ibn al-Zubayr in 64/684 he agreed, provided that Ibn al-Zubayr moved to Syria. When he refused, al-Ḥuṣayn returned to Syria with his army and gave his allegiance to the Umayyads;[75] he wanted a Syrian Caliphate, the identity of the Caliph was a secondary consideration.

Syria itself was divided into military regions known as *ajnād* (sing., *jund*), a word which also means the soldiers based in a *jund* and hence an army. Islamic tradition ascribes the foundation of these provinces to the Caliph ʻUmar[76] and there seems to be no direct link between them and the late Roman civil provinces in the area. However, it has been convincingly argued that the *jund*s were an adaptation of the commands of the Byzantine *duces*, under whom many Arabs must have served at the time of the Muslim conquests.[77] At first the *jund*s were Damascus, Jordan with its capital at Tiberias, Palestine around Jerusalem and Ascalon and Ḥoms. According to al-Balādhurī,[78] the troops settled in each *jund* were to receive their subsistence (*aṭmā*ʻ) from the tax revenues of the area. Later further divisions were made: Yazīd I (60–4/680–3) separated Qinnasrīn (ancient Chalcis) from the *jund* of Ḥoms and made it a separate province, including Antioch, Manbij and Aleppo, the latter rapidly coming to replace Qinnasrīn as the effective capital. Jazīra had originally been part of Qinnasrīn, but ʻAbd al-Malik separated it at the request of his cousin Muḥammad b. Marwān and the troops in the area then lived off its revenues. According to al-Yaʻqūbī,[79] writing in the third/ninth century, the revenues of the different *jund*s were Damascus, 300 000 *dīnārs*, Palestine 300 000, Ḥoms, 200 000 and Jordan, 100 000 and this probably reflected the relative size of their respective armies.

The *coup d'état* which brought Marwān b. al-Ḥakam to power in 64/684 was led by a group of tribal chiefs from the *jund*s of Jordan and Palestine, and it was they who supported his cause at the great battle at Marj Rāhiṭ in 64/684 which secured his control over Syria. Apart from the Umayyad family and their *mawālī*, Marwān's military support was drawn from the tribes of Kalb, Sakāsik and Sakūn (both branches of Kinda, resident in Syria), Ghassān, Tayyi, Qayn and Tanūkh.[80] The commanders were a member of the Umayyad family, ʻAmr b. Saʻīd b. al-ʻĀṣ, and ʻUbayd Allāh b. Ziyād.[81] According to another report, ʻUbayd Allāh was in command of the cavalry and Mālik b. Hubayra al-Sakūnī of the infantry.[82]

The Umayyads seem to have employed bodies of *mawālī*[83] from the time of Muʻāwiya and, while not very numerous, they may have been of crucial importance in maintaining Umayyad power because of their undoubted loyalty.[84] These were probably clients or freedmen. They may well have been of local

Syrian origin and been either prisoners who had been freed or men who had voluntarily converted to Islam and attached themselves to the Umayyad family and their supporters. According to al-Balādhurī, their *mawālī* were among the first to support Marwān after he arrived in Syria.[85] 'Abbād b. Ziyād b. Abī Sufyān brought 2000 of his *mawālī* and others to join the Marwanid forces at the Battle of Marj Rāhiṭ.[86] They are also recorded as a fighting force with Khālid b. Yazīd b. Mu'āwiya against Zufar b. al-Ḥārith and in the wars against the Jarājima rebels in Lebanon in 'Abd al-Malik's reign where they are described as *jaysh min* (army of) *mawālī* of 'Abd al-Malik and the Banū Umayya.[87] As has been mentioned, the leaders of the *ḥara*s of the Umayyad Caliphs were usually *mawālī* and this probably implies that the soldiers who served in this unit were as well. One of the leaders of the Muslim conquest of Spain is said to have been al-Mughīth al-Rūmī (i.e. the Greek) *mawlā* of the Umayyad Caliph al-Walīd I. Certainly, after the fall of the dynasty, Umayyad *mawālī* played a crucial role in the Umayyad seizure of power in al-Andalus.[88] However, while the Umayyad *mawālī* may have provided a small core following, there can be no doubt that the vast majority of soldiers in the Syrian army were of Arab origin.

The victory of Marwān's supporters at Marj Rāhiṭ was complete but the 6000 troops he is said to have had in his army,[89] drawn from a small number of tribes, were clearly not adequate for the re-establishment of Umayyad control over the entire caliphate. By the time 'Ubayd Allāh b. Ziyād was faced with the Iraqi army of the penitents at 'Ayn al-Warda the next year (Jumada I 65/January 685)[90] he had recruited more widely among the Arab tribes of Syria. His army, described as the *jumū' ahl al-Shām* (host of the Syrians). As well as al-Ḥuṣayn b. Numayr, his commanders included Shuraḥbīl b. Dhī'l-Kilā' al-Ḥimyarī, member of a noble South Arabian family now resident in Ḥoms, who had originally supported al-Ḍaḥḥāk b. Qays, Marwān's opponent at Marj Rāhiṭ.[91] The other three commanders named, Adham b. Muḥriz al-Bāhilī,[92] al-Rabī'a b. al-Mukhāriq al-Ghanawī and Jabala b.'Abd Allāh al-Khath'amī, all came from tribes which were later included in the Qaysī group. Shuraḥbīl's father and Adham himself had served in Mu'āwiya's army. 'Ubayd Allāh b. Ziyād clearly intended to rebuild the Syrian army which had served Mu'āwiya and Yazīd I so well.

The same army met with disaster shortly after in 67/686, when 'Ubayd Allāh b. Ziyād and his Syrian forces, who were said to have numbered 60 000, were decisively defeated by Ibn al-Ashtar on the Khāzir River near Mosul. Besides 'Ubayd Allāh himself, al-Ḥusayn, Shuraḥbīl and al-Rabī'a were all killed.[93]

The Syrian *débâcle* at Khāzir may have been the result of the widening schism among the Syrians between the Qaysī and Yemeni groups. According to one report,[94] 'the whole of Qays was in al-Jazīra and were opponents of Marwān and the family of Marwān. At that time Marwān's army was from Kalb and their commander was Ibn Baḥdal.' Accounts of the battle suggest that this opposition may have undermined the Syrian army because one of the commanders, 'Umayr b. al-Hubāb al-Sulamī was a Qaysī who went over to the enemy in the course of the fighting.[95]

Clearly the report is exaggerated because, as we have seen, 'Ubayd Allāh had recruited commanders from Qaysī tribes, but it does point to a general problem. The origins of the Qays–Yemen dispute have been much discussed and the complexities of the issue lie beyond the scope of this work.[96] It is clear that the division between Qays and Yemen, north and south Arabs, had no roots in the pre-Islamic period. In Syria it emerged in the time of 'Abd al-Malik. Those tribes who came to consider themselves Yamaniya were essentially those tribes who had already been in Syria at the time of the Muslim conquest, or who had arrived in the armies of the conquest, notably Kalb, Sakūn and Sakāsik of Kinda, Ghassān from the Syrian Desert and Lakhm and Judhām from Palestine and Jordan. The Qaysis (Kilāb, Sulaym, 'Uqayl, Bāhila), in contrast, were largely drawn from tribesmen who had migrated north during the reign of Mu'āwiya and settled in the area of the Jazīra, the steppe lands between the Tigris and Euphrates.[97] Here they were in competition with nomad groups already in the area, notably the numerous and well-established tribe of the Banū Taghlib.

The triumph of Marwān and his Kalbī and Kindī supporters at Marj Rāhiṭ was a major defeat for the Qaysī tribes. One of their leaders, Zufar b. al-Ḥārith retreated to Qarqisīya[98] and served as a rallying point for disaffected tribesmen, including the belligerent 'Umayr b. al-Hubāb al-Sulamī. It was he who began the feud with Taghlib which served as the catalyst for the division of the Syrian tribes into two opposed, super-tribal groups. Despite efforts by succeeding Caliphs to keep the peace, the dispute dominated the politics of the Umayyad caliphate.

After the defeat on the Khāzir, 'Abd al-Malik seems to have decided not to undertake a further campaign to conquer Iraq. Instead he set about making contact with disaffected elements among the tribal nobility, the *ashrāf*. When he finally did make a military move in 71/690–1, the work had mostly been done. This time his army was led by members of his own family, perhaps because many of the leading Syrians had expressed misgivings about the campaign, advising the Caliph not to go in person.[99] In the final battle at Maskin, his brother Muḥammad b. Marwān commanded the vanguard and two sons of Yazīd I, 'Abd Allāh and Khālid, commanded the right and left wings, respectively.[100] The triumph of the Syrians was complete.

It remained only to crush the anti-Caliph Ibn al-Zubayr himself, now isolated in Mecca. 'Abd al-Malik sent an army of Syrians, estimated at between 2000 and 5000, with men drawn from all the *jund*s.[101] They were led by Ṭāriq b. 'Amr, a *mawlā* of the Caliph 'Uthmān and al-Ḥajjāj b. Yūsuf al-Thaqafī, later to be 'Abd al-Malik's right-hand man in Iraq.

At first the Syrians did not act as an army of occupation in Iraq but seem to have returned to their own lands. The defence of Iraq against the Khārijīs was, as will be shown below, entrusted to the Iraqis. However, it soon became apparent to 'Abd al-Malik and al-Ḥajjāj, that the Iraqis were either unwilling or unable to defend themselves effectively against the rebels. In 77/696–7, at al-Ḥajjāj's request, the Caliph sent 6000 Syrians under the command of Sufyān b. al-Abrad al-Kalbī and Ḥabīb b. 'Abd al-Raḥmān al-Ḥakamī (from the South Arabian tribe of Madhḥij). It seems to have been their discipline and steadfastness that enabled al-Ḥajjāj to defend Kūfa and drive the rebels back.[102]

It was the Syrian army, too, which enabled al-Ḥajjāj to defeat the major rebellion led by 'Abd al-Raḥman b. Muḥammad b. al-Ash'ath in 81–2/700–1.[103] In the decisive encounter at Dayr al-Jamājim, the Syrian army was commanded by 'Abd al-Raḥmān b. Sulaym al-Kalbī over the right wing, 'Umāra b. Tamīm al-Lakhmī over the left wing, the veteran Sufyān b. al-Abrad al-Kalbī over the cavalry and 'Abd al-Raḥmān b. Ḥabīb al-Ḥakamī over the infantry.[104] All the commanders come from those Yaman tribes who had supported the Marwanid from the beginning and it is likely that most of the army was recruited from the same groups. When the defeated rebel fled east to Sistan, 'Umāra b. Tamīm led 30 000 Syrians in pursuit.[105]

In the aftermath of this major conflict, which really spelled the end of the Iraqi *muqātila* as a military force, al-Ḥajjāj decided to establish a permanent Syrian garrison in Iraq. He founded a new city at the city of Wāsiṭ,[106] roughly half-way between the old garrison centres of Kūfa and Basra. We know disappointingly little about the settlement of the new city but it is clear that it was the base for what was essentially a Syrian army of occupation. In contrast to Basra and Kūfa, where local men held the office, the *ṣāḥib al-shurṭa* in Wāsiṭ was always a Syrian.[107] Furthermore, it seems likely that these Syrians were to be paid from the revenues of Iraq, those revenues which the armies of Iraq had sought to keep for themselves: their *fay'* was being granted away to foreigners. For the first time, the Syrian army was used as a police force beyond its own borders.

Before the end of al-Walīd's reign, Syrian troops are recorded in Ṭabaristān under the command of Sufyān b. al-Abrad in 77/696–7 pursuing the Khārijīs[108] and in Jurjan under the command of Yazīd b. al-Muhallab in 98/716–17 when they were said to have numbered 60 000.[109] Some 6000 Syrians were sent to Sind in about 90/708–9 to help in the conquest under the command of Muḥammad b. al-Qāsim al-Thaqafī.[110] There were 24 000 Syrians settled in Bāb al-Abwāb (Derbent) at the eastern end of the Caucasus in 113/731, where they were provided with salaries and food supplies.[111]

Syrian troops are recorded in Khurāsān. When al-Junayd b. 'Abd Allāh al-Murrī, himself a well-known Syrian leader, was appointed governor of Khurāsān by Ḥishām in 111/730, he came with a number of Syrian troops including men from his own tribe of Murra.[112] His successor, 'Āṣim b.'Abd Allāh al-Hilālī, who was appointed in 116/734, was described as the lord (*sayyid*) of the Syrians, and he may have brought more Syrians with him; certainly we find Syrian contingents of 500 or 1000 in his forces.[113] In 119/737 Asad b.'Abd Allāh had forces from Palestine, Jordan, Ḥoms, Qinnasrīn and Damascus, all the Syrian *junds* in his forces.[114] Compared with the numbers of men of Iraqi origin, the number of Syrians was comparatively small but they were a significant element in the Khurasani military. Gradually, Syrian troops had spread out throughout the Caliphate, supplementing or replacing local forces and becoming the real policemen of the empire.

The troops closest to the Caliph himself were the *shurṭa* (security police) and the *ḥaras* guard but we know little about their composition and their function.[115] The Caliph Ḥishām had a retinue of 800 horsemen, 400 *shurṭa* and 400 *ḥaras*.[116] The commanders of the *shurṭa* (*aṣḥāb al-shurṭa*) were always chosen from a small group of Yamani tribes, Sakāsik, Ghassān and, especially, the 'Ans of Damascus.[117] Not until Marwān II appointed Kawthar b. al-Aswad al-Ghanawī was there a Qaysī commander of the Caliph's *shurṭa*.[118] It is noticeable that commanders of the *shurṭa* might enjoy long periods in office: Ka'b b. Khālid al-'Ansī, for example, served 'Abd al-Malik then, after a break, al-Walīd (86–96/705–15) and Sulaymān (96–9/715–17). 'Umar II (99–101/717–20) chose a new man but Yazīd II (101–5/720–4) reappointed Ka'b who went on to serve Ḥishām for 13 years until he was appointed governor of Armenia.[119] Caliphs might come and go but there was clearly continuity in the military command. The appointment to Armenia is also a sign, if one were needed that Ka'b was regarded as being a figure of substance, not just a glorified domestic servant. The guard, *ḥaras*, by contrast, was usually commanded by *mawālī* (freedmen of non-Arab origin, in this context) and it is likely that the personnel were largely *mawālī* as well. One peculiar feature of the office of commander of the *ḥaras* was that it was sometimes combined with bureaucratic duties and the commander was at the same time clerk of correspondence (*kātib al-rasā'il*) or the holder of the Caliph's seal.[120]

The armies of Iraq

Iraq was certainly the richest province of the Umayyad Caliphate and probably the most populous in both indigenous people and Arab settlers. In the years after the Muslim conquest, very large numbers of Arab tribesmen had settled there and the Azd of Uman continued to arrive in significant numbers during Mu'āwiya's Caliphate. The great garrison cities of Basra and Kūfa both supported huge armies of *muqātila*. It was largely men from these cities who achieved the conquest of Khurāsān, the longest and most hard-fought of all the early Muslim campaigns.

It is therefore paradoxical that by the end of 'Abd al-Malik's reign in 86/705, the Muslim population of Iraq was largely demilitarised and subject to Umayyad governors from outside the province, and the Syrian military stationed in Wāsiṭ and elsewhere. The *fay'* of Iraq, which their ancestors had acquired by force of arms, was lost to them.

This transformation had occurred because of deep divisions among the Muslims of Iraq, the failure of leadership and the ruthlessness of the governor al-Ḥajjāj b. Yūsuf al-Thaqafī. This is not the place to undertake a full investigation of the complex and frequently violent politics of this period[121] but two continuing problems should be noted. The first of these was the problem of the Khārijīs, both the Azāriqa in Khuzistan and Fārs and others, notably Shabīb b. Yazīd al-Shaybānī, in the hinterland of Kūfa and north to the Jazīra. The constant pressure of these anarchic rebels seriously taxed the military resources of the country. Al-Muhallab b. Abī Ṣufra, the most effective of Iraqi military commanders, was largely occupied with fighting the Azāriqa and mobilising the troops of Basra to do so. In the circumstances, he was not prepared to lead the Basrans against an Umayyad take-over, but rather made his peace with the new administration. When the Azāriqa had been finally driven off, he and his able and numerous family moved to Khurāsān. Similarly, the army of Kūfa was hard put to defend the city against Shabīb and indeed they were obliged to rely on Syrian military aid to defend their homes. The Khārijīs were not simply a military threat to the armies of Basra and Kūfa. The sources make it clear that they were in direct competition for resources. The collection of the *kharāj* of Iraq, on which the armies depended for such salaries as they did receive, was forcibly interrupted by the rebels. Khārijī control of areas around Kūfa must have meant that the payment of salaries was difficult if not impossible.

The intra-Muslim conflicts did not end there. Iraqi attempts to resist Syrian control were continuously thwarted by hostility between the tribal nobility, the *ashrāf* and rank-and-file troops, including the non-Arab Muslims, the *mawālī*. While ʿAbd al-Malik was consolidating his power in Syria and Egypt, the Iraqis were spending their military energies on the long war between Muṣʿab b. al-Zubayr, supported by the *ashrāf*, and al-Mukhtār in Kūfa. Even after the defeat of Mukhtār, bitter divisions clearly remained and members of the Iraqi nobility were happy to enter into negotiations with ʿAbd al-Malik imagining, quite wrongly, that Umayyad rule would secure their positions.[122] By the time they realised their mistake, and joined the rebellion of the greatest *sharīf* of them all, ʿAbd al-Raḥmān b. Muḥammad b. al-Ashʿath al-Kindī, it was too late and the Syrian army destroyed them.

There were two groups of specialist archers of Iranian origin serving alongside troops of Arab origin in Iraq, the Bukhāriya (from Bukhārā in Transoxania), who had been recruited by ʿUbayd Allāh b. Ziyād and stationed in Basra by 54/674. They are said to have been 2000 strong and famous archers.[123] They refused to support Ibn Ziyād in Basra after the death of Yazīd b. Muʿāwiya.[124] It seems that they continued in existence as a military unit. Al-Ḥajjāj moved some of them to his new garrison town at Wāsiṭ where their descendants were still to be found in al-Balādhurī's time.[125] They are mentioned in the Umayyad forces opposing the rebellion of Zayd b. ʿAlī in Kūfa in 122/740[126] and supported the Umayyads to the end: 1300 of them supported Ibn Hubayra in his final stand against the ʿAbbasid forces at Wāsiṭ.[127] Later arrivals were the Qīqāniya (from Qīqān),[128] 300 of whom appear in the Umayyad army opposing the rebellion of Zayd b. ʿAlī in 122/740.[129]

It is also likely that converted Persians introduced the idea of *ghilmān* (sing., *ghulām*) into the Muslim military.[130] The word originally means a page. In the Umayyad period they were largely used for menial tasks, supplying water, looking after equipment, rather than as front-line soldiers. However, *ghilmān* were occasionally armed and sent into battle: in 77/696, for example, al-Ḥajjāj armed his *ghilmān* and freedmen to oppose the Kharijite Shabīb's final assault on Kūfa.[131] The governor of Khurāsān, Asad b. ʿAbd Allāh, used a *ghulām* as his standard bearer and others in his vanguard.[132] We also hear of armed *ghilmān* employed by Ṭāriq b. Ziyād, who was in charge of tax-collection in Iraq for the governor Khālid al-Qasrī, presumably employed to enforce tax demands.[133] Similarly we hear of Persians employing slaves (*mamālīk*) in battle; one ʿAbd Allāh b. al-Iṣbahānī had 400 such slaves when fighting for Muṣʿab b. al-Zubayr in Kūfa.[134] These examples are unusual and the numbers involved small, but they are important because they show the origins of a move to military retinues based on ties of slavery and clientage, rather than tribal followings. This was a model which came to dominate military organisation in the ʿAbbasid period.[135]

The army of Kūfa

Kūfa had been settled in the immediate aftermath of the Muslim conquest of al-Madāʾin in 17/638 as an encampment and base for the conquest and occupation of Iraq.[136] Along with Basra, it was one of the two great *miṣrs* where the conquering armies were settled and where the pay was distributed to the troops.

The tribesmen were settled in blocks around a central area which included the great mosque and the governor's palace (*Dār al-imāra*) which adjoined it. Roads radiating from the centre divided the area into districts which were assigned to individual tribes. During the governorate of Ziyād b. Abī Sufyān, the system was rationalised and reduced to just four major groups, the *Ahl al-madīna*, who came from a number of different tribes, mostly from the Hijaz, Tamīm and Hamdān, Madhḥij and Asad, Rabiʿa and Kinda. From the time of their establishment under Ziyād these remained the basic divisions as long as there was a Kūfan army. Despite the tribal origins of the groups, there is little evidence of tribal rivalries in the Kūfa *muqātila*; tensions were more often social, between the *ashrāf* and others, or religious, such as differences in attitude to the house of ʿAlī, and they cut across tribal boundaries.

Leadership of the different Fourths changed according to circumstances, and they seem to have been chosen for particular campaigns, rather than being permanent officials.[137] Choosing them was a matter of some delicacy: they had to be both loyal to the commander and acceptable to the tribal group. There is no record of any leader holding the office for more than one campaign, although sometimes one family, notably the family of Ibn al-Ashʿath in the quarter of Rabīʿa and Kinda, seem to have been regularly chosen. The functions of the leaders seem to have been to recruit from their Fourth, but command in battle was given to commanders who were not leaders of the quarters.

There are also infrequent mentions of the *shurṭa* of Kūfa. At the time of al-Mukhtār's rebellion, the governor had a *shurṭa* of 4000 who seem to have been the main troops immediately available to him to oppose the rebels.[138] Al-Mukhtār himself had both *shurṭa* and *ḥaras*, the latter being commanded, as often, by a *mawlā*.[139] Al-Ḥajjāj had a *shurṭa* in Kūfa commanded by Iraqis, not Syrians,[140] and this policy seems to have been followed by later Umayyad governors. The *ṣāḥib al-shurṭa* in Kūfa, as in Basra and Fusṭāṭ, apparently served, among other functions, as a local liaison officer between the governor, almost always an outsider, and the notables of the city:[141] although appointed by the governor, he had to have some credibility among the citizens in order to be able to do the job. When Yazīd b. al-Muhallab launched his great anti-Umayyad rebellion in Iraq in 101/719, the governor of Kūfa sent the *shuraṭ* out to intercept him but they refused engage him in battle and allowed him to move on.[142] In 119/737 a force of 200 *shuraṭ* of Kūfa were sent against a minor Khārijī revolt, and were too poorly equipped to escape massacre.[143]

The Kūfan army produced few outstanding soldiers. One of the best known was Ibrāhīm b. al-Ashtar al-Nakh'i. His father, Mālik al-Ashtar,[144] had made his reputation as a soldier in the conquests and then as a firm upholder of the rights of the *muqātila* of Iraq to enjoy the *fay'*. His son Ibrāhīm continued to support his father's cause, the rights of the Iraqi *muqātila*. In this cause he was instrumental in Mukhtār's take-over of Kūfa in 66/685 and in the defeat of the counter-coup by the *ashrāf* the next year. In Muḥarram 67/686 he led the Kūfan army to victory against the Syrian forces led by 'Ubayd Allāh b. Ziyād on the river Khāzir near Mawsil.[145] This was almost the only example of an Iraqi army decisively defeating a Syrian one and the sources make it clear that Ibrāhīm's abilities as a commander played a central role in the victory.

Ibrāhīm remained in the Mawsil area while Mukhtār was defeated and killed by Muṣ'ab b. Zubayr, but when Muṣ'ab was confronted by the troops of 'Abd al-Malik in 72/691 in what proved to be the decisive struugle for the control of Iraq, Ibrāhīm was the only Kūfan leader on whom he could rely, the rest having been suborned by the Umayyads. Unfortunately for the Iraqis, Ibrāhīm was killed at the beginning of the battle: as his other troops melted away, Muṣ'ab is said to have lamented 'O Ibrāhīm ! But there is no Ibrāhīm for me now'.

The career of Ibrāhīm b. al-Ashtar is interesting because he represented, as his father had done before him, the interests of the rank-and-file *muqātila* of Iraq and the *mawālī*, not only against the Syrians but against their own *ashrāf* as they struggled to secure the *fay'* to which they believed they were entitled. He consistently supported any leader who could protect them against the Syrians, even if, like Mukhtār and Muṣ'ab, the two were mortal enemies.[146]

Ibrāhīm had no successor among the Kūfan army. After the Umayyad conquest of Iraq, the army of Kūfa came under the command of al-Ḥajjāj and was largely employed against the Khārijīs, who posed a repeated threat to the city and the surrounding countryside. Leaders were chosen from families of the Kūfan *ashrāf* like 'Abd al-Raḥmān b. Mikhnaf al-Azdī (great-uncle of the historian Abū Mikhnaf) and 'Attāb b. Warqā al-Riyāḥī[147] but none of them distinguished themselves and the Khārijīs would probably have taken the city had it not been for the presence of Syrian troops. The failure of the Kūfan military led to them being sidelined. While we have no direct information, we can be reasonably certain that their *'aṭā'* was not being paid, or at least not paid in full, and that the resources of the *fay'* of Iraq were now being diverted to the hated Syrians in their midst. These tensions were to result in a major explosion which came near to toppling Umayyad rule in Iraq.

The accounts of the campaigns against the Khārijīs also show that the numbers of *muqātila* who could actually be raised and put in the field were only a small proportaion of the total numbers said to have been in the *dīwān* of the city at this time.[148] Al-Ḥajjāj's initial response to the outbreak of rebellion was to send out fairly small groups to pursue the Khārijīs, who themselves only numbered a couple of hundred. The first expedition sent against the rebels was composed of 3000 men, 1000 old *muqātila* and 2000 specially recruited for the campaign.[149] After the failure of this first expedition, al-Ḥajjāj ordered the marshals (*'urafā*) to enrol 1000 men from each of the four Fourths. The officials in charge of the *dīwāns* (*aṣḥāb al-dawāwīn*) sat and decided who should be enrolled for the expedition (*ḍarabū al-ba'th*). It was not easy to persuade men to volunteer for this dangerous work and al-Ḥajjāj had to issue dire threats against the unwilling conscripts to force them to go in to action.[150] Later expeditions seem to have been composed of smaller numbers of élite cavalry (*khayl nuqāwa*), 2000 under the command of Suwayd b.'Abd al-Raḥmān al-Sa'dī[151] and 1800 under Zahr b. Qays.[152] It is not clear what the description 'élite cavalry' means in this context and the phrase is not encountered elsewhere, but both the leaders were members of the *ashrāf* of Kūfa and it is likely that their men were chosen from their tribal followings. The last expedition was led by the *sharīf* 'Abd al-Raḥmān b. Muḥammad b. al-Ash'ath with 6000 and another 600 from his own tribesmen (*min qawmihi*) of Kinda and Hadramawt.[153] Finally, when Kūfa itself was under attack from the rebels, a full mobilisation was ordered: 50 000, made up of 40 000 *muqātila* and 10 000 young men (*shabāb*), are said to have been assembled under the command of another *sharīf*, 'Attāb b. Warqā' al-Riyāḥī.[154] None of these armies was successful and it was only with the help of 6000 Syrian troops that the city was saved. These figures suggest that there was no 'standing army' in Kūfa at the time. There were *dīwāns* from which men could be chosen for specific campaigns but these never seem to have numbered more than 6000. In dire emergencies, the whole of the *muqātila*, and at least 1000 *mawālī*,[155] could be gathered, a sort of *arrière ban*, but its military effectiveness was very limited.

Among the leaders of the Kūfan *ashrāf* who were humiliated in the struggles against the Khārijīs was 'Abd al-Raḥmān b. Muḥammad b. al-Ash'ath.[156] Immensely proud of his status, but vacillating and ineffectual in action, he was the direct descendant of the pre-Islamic kings of Kinda and his family had been prominent in Kūfa since its foundation. In the year 80/699–700 al-Ḥajjāj appointed him to lead a large army from Kūfa and Basra to distant Sistan where a Muslim expedition had recently been humiliated by the local ruler, Zunbil.[157] The governor recruited 20 000 Kūfans and 20 000 Basrans and paid them their salaries in full[158] (implying, of course, that this was not normally done). He ordered them to equip themselves with horses and arms.

Al-Ḥajjāj deeply distrusted Ibn al-Ash'ath and it looks very much as if he deliberately set out to break the Iraqi army and its commander. Ibn al-Ash'ath proceeded with great caution in this wild and mountainous region but al-Ḥajjāj replied to his letters with contempt, saying that nothing less than absolute victory would suffice and that the army would have to stay in the field until this was achieved. The harsh conditions and the threat of being away from home for so long led to protests and Ibn al-Ash'ath led his army back to Iraq; al-Muhallab wrote to al-Ḥajjāj, 'the people of Iraq have advanced towards you like a flood'.[159] When he reached Iraq, Basrans and Kūfans alike rushed to support him until their number is said to have reached 100 000.[160] For a moment this army seems to have united the Iraqis as never before: there were members of the *ashrāf* fighting alongside men who had been enthusiastic supporters of Mukhtār against them, Basrans fighting alongside Kūfans and members of all the different tribes. The *qurrā'*, who claimed that the early conquerors of Iraq were the only people entitled to the revenues of the area, were among the most stalwart supporters of the revolt.

The Iraqi army was huge and well supplied, their Syrian opponents fewer in number and short of food. Yet, in the battles of Dayr al-Jamājim and Maskīn, both in the summer of 82/701, the Iraqis were decisively defeated. Their failure was partly a reflection of continuing social divisions and many were suspicious that the *ashrāf* were preparing to desert as they had deserted Muṣ'ab before. The Caliph had offered terms, and Ibn al-Ash'ath himself urged acceptance and was only reluctantly persuaded to fight on.

The defeat of the rebellion, followed by the establishment of the Syrian army in Wāsiṭ meant the effective end of the *muqātila* of Kūfa as a fighting force.[161] Kūfans are found taking to arms again. During the rebellion of Yazīd b. al-Muhallab in 101/719–20, the Kūfan Fourths, one of them commanded by Ibn al-Ash'ath's nephew, are found fighting in the last great Iraqi attempt to overthrow Syrian rule. The Fourths are mentioned again at the time of the revolt of Zayd b. 'Alī in 121/740 with, once again, a nephew of Ibn al-Ash'ath's leading Kinda and Rabī'a,[162] but they do not seem to have played any military role. The fighting in Kūfa was between the supporters of Zayd on one hand and the Syrians on the other.

It is not clear when Kūfans stopped receiving their salaries from the *fay'*. It is likely that payment had been irregular and at a reduced rate since the arrival of the Syrians and that it was stopped almost entirely after the rebellion of Ibn al-Ash'ath. The lack of salaries and the theft of 'their' *fay'* remained a lively source of grievance. When 'Abd al-Malik had wanted to make a compromise with the Iraqis during Ibn al-Ash'ath's rebellion, he offered them salaries like those enjoyed by the Syrians in an attempt to win them over.[163] When Ibn al-Muhallab rebelled, the Caliph Yazīd is said to have offered the Kūfans 'increases' (*ziyādāt*), presumably in their salaries.[164] When Zayd b. 'Alī revolted in the city in 121/740, those who swore allegiance to him did so in order, among other things, 'to pay salaries [*'aṭā'*] to those who had been deprived of it and divide this [the Iraqi] *fay'* among those who were entitled to it'.[165] After the defeat of Zayd's revolt, Yūsuf b. 'Umar is said to have preached a sermon in the mosque denouncing the Kūfans: 'Lament, O people of Kūfa, your disgrace and degradation. You will receive no payment [*'aṭā'*] or rations [*rizq*] from us';[166] he was probably doing no more than confirming the existing position. A final attempt was made at the time of 'Abd Allāh b. 'Umar's governorate when he tried to conciliate the Kūfans by restoring their *'aṭā'* and *rizq* to them. He explained, 'I wanted to *return* your *fay'* to you because I know that you have the best right to it'. The Syrians in the city objected violently, since it was they who now enjoyed these revenues, and the whole project was lost in the general confusion.[167]

By 121/740, the army of Kūfa had ceased to exist, the *muqātila* were no more and the Fourths are never heard of again. At the time of the 'Abbasid revolution, there was no military organisation in Kūfa to join the campaign against the Umayyads or, later, to rival the Khurāsānīs. The once-proud Kūfans had become civilians and subjects, not soldiers and partners. In the end it is hard not to agree with the views forcibly expressed by the 'Alī b. 'Abd Allāh b. al-Ḥasan, writing to Zayd b. 'Alī before his rebellion, 'Cousin! the Kūfans are puffed up with wind on the outside and weak inside. They are loud when circumstances are easy and impatient when you meet them. Their tongues go ahead of them but their hearts do not accompany them. They do not spend their nights preparing for misfortunes nor will they bring about a hoped-for change of government.'[168]

The armies of Basra

The history of the army of Basra is in many ways similar to that of Kūfa, a story of gradual demilitarisation and loss of salaries punctuated by episodes of violent rebellion as elements in Basra attempted to regain their old status.

As the Kūfans were divided into Fourths, so the Basrans were divided into quasi-tribal Fifths (*akhmās*, sing. *khums*). The Fifths were Bakr, 'Abd al-Qays, Tamīm, Azd and Ahl al-'Āliya. Like the Madīna Fourth in Kūfa, the Ahl al-'Āliya comprised a number of tribes from the Hijaz area (Quraysh, Kināna, Azd, Bajīla, Khath'am, Qays 'Aylān and Muzayna)[169] who were represented by only a small number of people. The Fifths of Basra seem to have been units for recruitment and administration, but they were also drawn up in Fifths for battles.[170]

The fullest description we have of the *muqātila* of Basra in action come from the accounts of al-Muhallab's campaigns against the Azāriqa Khārijīs in Fārs and Khuzistan. The Azāriqa threatened to take Basra itself and all the military resources of the city had to be mobilised to prevent this happening. It is said to have been 'Ubayd Allāh b. Ziyād's proud boast that he had increased the number of *muqātila* in the *dīwān* of Basra to 80 000,[171] but in practice it was impossible to mobilise anything like that number. At the height of his struggle against the Azāriqa, al-Muhallab had just 30 000 men registered in the *dīwān* and receiving *'aṭā'*.[172] Al-Ḥajjāj recruited 20 000 Basrans with a similar number of Kūfans to serve under Ibn al-Ash'ath on the ill-fated Sistan expedition of 80/699. Like the governors of Kūfa, the governor of Basra also seem to have had a *shurṭa* to maintain order. In the examples we have, the *shurṭa* was led by local men, even under al-Ḥajjāj, but we have little information about the composition and role of this force.[173]

On his appointment to lead the Basra army against the Azāriqa Khārijīs, al-Muhallab made a remarkable written contract (*kitāb*) with the Fifths. This was in the anarchy of the year 65/684–5 when there was no generally acknowledged governor of the city and tribal rivalries had led to chaos. The Azāriqa were prepared to take advantage of the uncertainty and were on the verge of attacking. Al-Muhallab had been on his way to Khurāsān but was persuaded, or tricked, into taking command of the Basra forces. In exchange for accepting command, he demanded that he should be allowed to keep what he conquered, and that he be paid sufficient revenue from the treasury (*bayt al-māl*) to sustain his men. In addition he demanded, and was given, the right to make his own appointments to commands within the army and it was he who chose the commanders of the Fifths.[174]

The defeat of Ibn al-Ash'ath's rebellion in 82/701 led to the virtual disappearance of the *muqātila* of Basra as a fighting force. As in Kūfa, there was a final attempt to revive their military status at the time of the rebellion of Yazīd b. al-Muhallab. Faced by the rebellion, and aware that the Muhallabīs enjoyed widespread support in the city, the Umayyad governor 'Adī b. Arṭāt al-Fazārī tried to mobilise the Fifths under the leadership of the tribal *ashrāf*, at least some of whom might see the Muhallabīs as rivals. The attempt was not a success and the Basrans almost all moved to join the rebels, not least because Yazīd could afford to pay them more.[175] The Fifths of Basra never seem to have been mobilised again.

The armies of Iran and Khurāsān

The pattern of Muslim conquest meant that Muslim armies and Muslim settlers were very unevenly distributed across Iran. The western and central areas were conquered comparatively quickly, Muslim rule was established but Muslim settlement was slow to follow and, as a result, conversion of the local population was only gradual. Nor was this a frontier area which had to be defended from outside attack. At first troops seem to have been sent on a temporary basis, like the 5000 Kūfans sent in 72/691–2 to Rayy to serve in the garrison (*masālīh*) and collect the *fay'* 'until the time comes for them to return' when they were to be replaced by others.[176] By the year 77/696 small garrisons seem to have been established in a number of cities with a largely law-and-order role, about 2000 in Isfahan, 3000 in Rayy and 4000 in the more disturbed area of Kirman. In Rayy, the government secretaries were able to call up about three-quarters of the available men in an emergency[177] and the fact that a man had his *maktab* there suggests that Rayy, at least, had its own *dīwān*.[178] There was certainly a garrison in Sistan, at the capital Zaranj and the frontier base at Bust, but we have no figures for the number of men involved.[179]

Khurāsān was a frontier province. It covered a huge area with very diverse environments, from the oasis cities like Marw, Bukhārā and Samarqand to the trackless deserts which separated them and the high mountains of the Pamirs. Distances were vast and communications hampered by natural perils like heat, thirst and cold, and man-made ones like bands of marauding Turks and Arabs. The size and diversity of the area meant that there was very little centralised organisation but rather that different areas enjoyed considerable autonomy.

Nor did the frontier with the non-Muslim Turkish and Iranian peoples to the north and east provide a focus or structure. By the later Umayyad period, the Byzantine frontier had became more or less established, not clear lines but a series of connected and garrison outposts in a more or less clear line. In Khurāsān and Transoxania the position was very different. Throughout the Umayyad period, the frontier remained fluid and permeable: major cities like Bukhārā and Samarqand were taken and lost and retaken. Mountain principalities like Khuttal or Ushrūsanā made uncertain and temporary submissions. Military 'organisation' in the province was usually *ad hoc*, responses to particular opportunities or threats, and it is difficult to see any institutional or administrative continuity.

Muslim settlement was on a vastly greater scale in Khurāsān than in the provinces of central and western Iran.[180] In 45/665–6 the governor of Iraq, Ziyād b. Abī Sufyān, sent 50 000 men from Basra and Kūfa, 25 000 from each city, to Khurāsān under the command of al-Rabī' b. Ziyād al-Ḥārithī. This represented the first substantial settlement of Muslims in Khurāsān. Two features were significant about this settlement. The first is that the men came from Kūfa and Basra and remained conscious of their Iraqi origins and loyalties: when Qutayba b. Muslim tried to persuade them to follow him in rebellion in 96/714–15, he started by reminding them of their Iraqi origins and ended by abusing them as, among other things, the 'refuse of Kūfa and Basra'. As late as 102/720–1, more than 60 years after the original immigration, the governor Sa'īd Khudhayna could address them as 'Army of Iraq',[181] though many of them must have been born and bought up in Khurāsān. The Iraqi element was strengthened again in 94/712–13 when Iraqis were sent from Sind to Khurāsān led by the Kūfan *sharīf*, Jahm b. Zaḥr b. Qays al-Ju'fī[182] and in 112/731 when, after the disastrous Muslim losses at the Battle of the Pass, al-Ḥajjāj sent 10 000 more men from Basra and 10 000 from Kūfa. In contrast, Syrian soldiers arrived only later and were probably less numerous.[183]

There is a 'snapshot' of the *muqātila* of Khurāsān in 96/715 when Qutayba b. Muslim made his ill-fated attempt to rouse them in rebellion against the new Caliph Sulaymān b. 'Abd al-Malik. According to this account the vast majority of the troops came from the army of Basra and were divided into their traditional Fifths, each with its own leader. There were 9000 *muqātila* from the Ahl al-'Āliya, 7000 from Bakr, 10 000 from Tamīm, 4000 from 'Abd al-Qays and 10 000 from Azd. There were only 7000 in total from Kūfa and another 7000 *mawālī*, that is non-Arab muslims. This gives a total of 54 000 and Qutayba boasted that he had paid their *'aṭā'* in full and on time and had distributed 'their' *fay'* among them.[184]

In 112/731 al-Junayd b. 'Abd al-Raḥmān gathered his troops for the ill-fated attempt to relieve Samarqand which resulted in the disastrous Muslim defeat at the Battle of the Pass. The Muslim forces in Khurāsān were widely scattered. There were 12 000 or more in Samarqand, 18 000 men had been sent to Tukhāristān and another 10 000 in an unspecified direction. When it came to the battle, al-Junayd had men of the three main tribal groups, Tamīm, Rabī'a and Azd, commanded by leaders chosen from their own *ashrāf*. The vanguard (*muqaddima*) was commanded by 'Uthmān b. 'Abd Allāh b. al-Shikhkhīr al-Ḥarashī, an experienced commander who was not from one of the major groups.[185] There was also a section of the army from Bakr who were ordered, after the initial defeat, to remain in the Kish area and were joined by a number of *mawālī* infantry.[186]

The troops brought with them from Iraq their organisation and their rivalries. It was above all the tribes of Basra who dominated the military of Khurāsān, Tamīm, especially their cavalry, Bakr and Azd were the most important groups. The rivalries which had existed in Basra were intensified and prolonged in Khurāsān. In Basra itself, the force of tribal feud had largely been dissipated by the death of 'Abd al-Malik, though rivalry between the houses of al-Muhallab and Qutayba b. Muslim continued into the 'Abbasid era. In Khurāsān, by contrast, these rivalries gained in ferocity and at times jeopardised Muslim control of the whole area.

There were a number of reasons for this. It was partly because the settlers were spread out rather than being concentrated in one *miṣr*. When Qutayba b. Muslim needed to summon the army in the autumn of 90/708, he could call on 12 000 troops immediately in the Marw area but the rest were scattered in Nishapur, Abiward, Sarakhs and Herat and could not be gathered before the spring.[187] Even within the Marw oasis, different villages 'belonged to' different tribes, who seem to have lived there.[188] When news came of the death of the caliph Yazīd I in 64/684, we are told that, 'The people of Khurāsān rose up against their officials (*'ummāl*) and drove them out. Each tribal group (*qawm*) seized control over a district and civil war (*fitna*) broke out.'[189] Operating many hundreds of kilometres from other Muslim groups, it is not surprising that the tribes, like the Bakris in Herat in 64/683–4 were prepared to resist the claims of members of other tribes, in this case 'Abd Allah b. Khāzim al-Sulamī and his supporters from Tamīm.[190]

In addition to the troops of Basran and Kūfan origin, there were a significant number of non-Arabs who fought along side Muslim forces. These came from two distinct groups. The first were the *mawālī*, non-Arab converts to Islam. As we have seen above, in 96/715 the *mawālī* constituted some 7000 out of a total of 54 000 in the army of Qutayba b. Muslim. They were therefore a significant element in the rank and file of the Muslim armies by that stage. In the reign of 'Umar II a representative of the Khurāsāni *mawālī* said that there were 20 000 of them who joined in the raids on the unbelievers but received neither *'aṭā'* or *rizq*, which suggests that the authorities did not accept them as part of the army.[191] After the Battle of the Pass, al-Junayd was instructed to enlist (*afraḍ farīḍatan*) more troops locally; he recruited 15 000 in addition to the 40 000 being sent from Iraq.[192] There is no indication whether these were converts, *mawālī*, nor whether they were permanent additions to the Muslim forces or simply recruited to deal with a short-term emergency.

Some of the leaders of the Muslim armies were *mawālī*. Among al-Junayd's advisers at the time of the Battle of the Pass in 112/731, there were three Arabs and three *mawālī* who were their equals in 'shrewdness, sound advice and knowledge of warfare', namely, al-Faḍl b. Bassām, *mawlā* of the Banū Layth, 'Abd Allāh b. Abī 'Abd Allāh, *mawlā* of the Banū Sulaym and al-Bakhtarī b. Mujāhid, *mawlā* of the Banū Shaybān.[193] The story of Ḥayyān al-Nabaṭī and his family demonstrates how it was possible for a non-Arab Muslim to rise up the military hierarchy in Umayyad Khurāsān.[194] It is not clear where he came from originally, though it was either Khurāsān or Daylam at the south end of the Caspian Sea (the name al-Nabaṭī, which was usually applied to the non-Arab peasantry of Iraq was, apparently given to him because of his bad Arabic pronunciation and tells us nothing of his origins). He was already a figure of influence and power in 96/715 at the time of Qutayba b. Muslim's deposition, when he was the leader of the 7000 *mawālī* in the army and is described as being in command of the Persians (*a'ājim*). He swung his weight behind the anti-Qutayba faction and secured the appointment of Wakī' b. Ḥassān al-Tamīmī, probably in exchange for a large slice of the *kharāj* of the province. Later on he was able to negotiate a deal between Yazīd b. al-Muhallab and the local ruler of Tabaristan, despite the fact that Yazīd had just inflicted a massive fine on him for being disrespectful to an Arab official. He served subsequent governors as an adviser but was clearly regarded with some suspicion. In the end, it is said, Sa'īd al-Ḥarashī poisoned him by mixing gold dust with his drink, having been told that he was 'the slave [*'abd*, a gratuitously insulting term] most hostile to the Arabs and the tax-collectors' and that he had raised Khurāsān against Qutayba and would do the same again.[195] Despite his ignominious end, his position was inherited by his son Muqātil who served as counsellor for governors of Khurāsān until the fall of the Umayyad regime.[196] Part soldier, part businessman, Ḥayyān's life gives a vivid insight into the opportunities and risks the Muslim conquest offered to some non-Arabs. It shows, too, the deep distrust and contempt that at least some Arabs felt for the *mawālī* they fought alongside.

As well as the *mawālī*, who were of course Muslims, the Arab governors also used non-Muslim levies in their armies. In 94/713 Qutayba levied 20 000 men (*faraḍa 'alā ahl...*) from Bukhārā, Kish, Nasaf and Khwārazm to join his army in the campaign across the Syr Darya to Shāsh and Khujanda.[197] Although the army are referred to as 'the Muslims', it is unlikely that so many men from these Transoxanian districts would have been Muslim at the time and they are not referred to as *mawālī*. All these areas had been conquered or sacked by Qutayba in the previous few years. It is not clear whether this was a compulsory conscription or whether they were volunteers but the Arabic *faraḍa 'alā* may imply that some coercion was involved. In 121/739 the last Umayyad governor, Naṣr b. Sayyār raided Shāsh with 20 000 men from Bukhārā, Samarqand, Kish and Ushrūsanā in his army, as well as the Arab tribal Fifths.[198] Again, it is likely that many of these were not Muslims. In both cases, the levies seem to have been recruited and employed for a single campaign in the north-east limits of the Islamic world.

Military administration seems to have been fairly chaotic. There clearly were *dīwān*s which were kept in the provincial capital; when Asad b. 'Abd Allāh moved the capital from Marw to Balkh in 118/736, he took the *dīwāns* with him[199] and when Naṣr b. Sayyār was threatened by his enemies in Marw, he transferred the *dīwāns* along with the arms stores to the Quhandiz (Old castle) for safe keeping. In 104/722–3, Jumayl b. 'Imrān was sent to Khurāsān, allegedly to 'inspect the *dīwāns*' but in fact to collect intelligence about the governor. As in Iraq, many people whose name appeared in the *dīwāns* were reluctant to come out and fight; in 106/724–5, Naṣr b. Sayyār had to remind the people of Balkh forcefully that, since they had taken their *'aṭā'*, they were obliged to fight and even then many refused point blank.[200]

Overall command of the armies of Khurāsān was taken by the governors. Some of these, most notably Qutayba b. Muslim al-Bāhilī enjoyed long tenures of office and had good military records. Many others were appointed for short periods before political events further west led to their recall. In some cases they were young and inexperienced and few of them had ever visited the province before. They seldom brought large numbers of their own followers with them, nor could many of them count on the wholehearted support of local tribesmen. Some like al-Junayd b. 'Abd al-Raḥmān were, at least at the military level, complete failures. Given the frontier nature of the province at its violent and turbulent population, they were very dependent on the advice and support of local military leaders of long standing who formed a sort of unofficial general staff. Often such men must have had as much influence as the governor on the shaping of strategy.

No one was more reliant on such men that al-Junayd after his defeat at the Battle of the Pass. Al-Madā'inī gives us a list of the leading military strategists in Khurāsān at the time: al-Mujashshir b. Muzāḥim al-Sulamī, 'Abd al-Raḥmān b. Ṣubḥ al-Kharaqī, and 'Ubayd Allāh b. Ḥabīb al-Hajarī. 'Al-Mujashshir would camp the men in their divisions [*rāyātihim*, lit. banners], and post sentries. No one else was as good as him at this. 'Abd al-Raḥmān b. Ṣubḥ was second to none in giving advice if some terrible crisis occurred in warfare, and 'Ubayd Allāh b. Ḥabīb was put in charge of deploying men for battle. There were also men of the *mawālī* who were their equals in wisdom.'[201] All these figures served a number of governors: Ibn Ṣubḥ, for example, had distinguished him self in the army of Sa'īd Khudhayna against the Soghdians in 102/720–1, had been governor of Balkh for Asad b. 'Abd Allāh al-Qasrī in 109/727 and adviser to al-Junayd at the time of the Battle of the Pass.[202] Al-Bakhtarī served al-Junayd, was an adviser to Asad b. 'Abd Allāh in 119/737 and went on to be one of Naṣr b. Sayyār's closest associates before being executed by the 'Abbasids at the time of the Revolution in 130/748.[203] But the most prominent of them was al-Mujashshir. Described by one who knew him as 'intelligent, brave, shrewd but something of a liar',[204] he first appears in 93/712 urging Qutayba to make the surprise attack on Samarqand which led to the capture of the city. Ten years later, he was part of a delegation which successfully urged Ibn Hubayra to dismiss the governor, Sa'īd Khudhayna and replace him with someone more forceful. Successive governors used him as an adviser and employed him to handle tricky situations as al-Ashras did in 110/728–9 when the new Muslims of Samarqand, supported by some pious Arabs, protested about not receiving their tax-exemptions. He was among those who advised al-Junayd to be cautious at the time of the Battle of the Pass and he survived the purge of al-Junayd's officials to serve his successor 'Āṣim b. 'Abd Allāh in 116/734. He advised Asad al-Qasrī in 119/737 and was considered for the top job, governor of Khurāsān in 120/738 but rejected because he was too old.[205]

This group, and there are others like Naṣr b. Sayyār himself who could be added to it, are interesting because they show how continuity of administration and tactics were maintained despite frequent changes at the top and local upheavals. None of them were tribal leaders, they owed their importance to their role on the staff of successive governors and they must take much of the credit for the survival of Umayyad government in the area at this time.

The collapse of the Syrian army

The Syrian army, the *ahl al-Shām*, were the mainstay of Umayyad power as long as the dynasty survived. Until the death of the Caliph Ḥishām in 125/743 we hear remarkably little about their recruitment and organisation. The major expedition against Constantinople in 98–9/716–17 was led by Maslama b. 'Abd al-Malik and the chiefs (*wujūh*) of the Syrians[206] but we know next to nothing more about the composition of the Muslim force. They were regularly in action on the Byzantine frontier and in the Caucasus. When it came to internal security, the Syrians were instrumental in defeating the rebellion of Yazīd b. al-Muhallab. In 122/740 Syrians were responsible for the swift, effective and brutal suppression of the rebellion of Zayd b. 'Alī in Kūfa.[207] We also know that large numbers of Syrians, from all five *junds* were despatched to North Africa to combat a Berber uprising in 123/741. It is said that this force numbered 30 000 when it left Syria: many of them were killed and many others ended up settling in Spain. Very few seem to have returned to Syria, and this must have represented a serious drain on Syrian manpower.[208]

Two points emerge from this very sparse record. The first is that overall leadership of the army was concentrated in the hands of members of the Umayyad family. In Syria and Iraq the most important figures were Maslama b. 'Abd al-Malik and al-Walīd b. al-'Abbās b. 'Abd al-Malik and it was they, rather than the Caliphs, who led the armies on the Byzantine frontier and it was they who defeated Ibn al-Muhallab. From 114/732 we find a new generation taking over, Sulaymān b. Ḥishām on the Byzantine frontier and Marwān b. Muḥammad b. Marwān in the Caucasus. This had the advantage that military leadership was concentrated in the hands of members of the dynasty (except in Khurāsān) so there was little danger of over-mighty generals attempting to usurp power. On the other hand, it did mean that members of the ruling family built up their own military followings, and when it came to succession disputes these could, and were, used against other members of the dynasty.

The second point is that there is little, if any evidence of tensions between tribal groups among the *ahl al-Shām*. In political terms, rivalry between Qays and

Yaman seems to have been increasing in Ḥishām's reign.[209] In Khurāsān, this led to open conflict, in Iraq it was expressed in the dramatic sacking of the Yemeni governor, Khālid al-Qasrī and his replacement by the Qaysī, Yūsuf b. 'Umar al-Thaqafī. These rivalries, however, do not seem to have caused overt division in the army. The Syrians were united and effective faced with Zayd's rebellion in Kūfa and members of all groups joined the disastrous North African adventure.

A characteristic feature of the last decades of Umayyad rule was the emergence of regiments of soldiers called after their commanders, who seem to have raised and led them.[210] The first of these seems to have been the Waḍḍāḥiya, named after al-Waḍḍāḥ, *mawlā* of the Caliph 'Abd al-Malik. They first appear in the historical record in 102/720 when they played a daring role in the defeat of the rebellion of Yazīd b. al-Muhallab. Later they were used for raids deep into Byzantine territory and in 127/744 3000 of them, now commanded by al-Waḍḍāḥ's son, 'Amr, were the first of Marwān II's troops to break into the rebels city of Ḥoms, and shortly afterwards 7000 of them were sent to Egypt to enforce Marwān's authority there.

Equally well known were the Dhakwāniya, said to have been 5000 strong, named after their commander Muslim b. Dahkwān. In the civil war at the time of Marwān's accession, they supported the claims of his rival, Sulaymān b. Ḥishām, and after his defeat some of them followed him in joining the Khārijīs. However, in the final battle on the Zāb when Marwān II was decisively defeated by the 'Abbasids, the Dhakwāniya are found fighting in his army. In his list of Umayyad élite troops, defeated by the *Abnā'*, al-Jāḥiẓ, also mentions the Saḥṣaḥiya, the Dāliqiya and the Rāshidiya,[211] about whom less is known.

In Egypt[212] in 126/744, the governor al-Ḥafṣ b. al-Walīd, was ordered to gather 30 000 recruits (*faraḍa furūḍ*). They were called the Ḥafsiya and were recruited from the non-Arab population. Ḥafṣ was dismissed the next year and the new recruits dropped but they reacted violently to this, expelled the new governor and demanded the reinstatement of Ḥafṣ and the restoration of their position in the *dīwān*. In the confused manoeuvrings which characterised the politics of Egypt in Marwān's reign, they formed a powerful pressure group, while the Caliph's supporters recruited (*faraḍa*) 1000 *mawālī* of the Umayyads and 1000 Qaysī Arabs as a counter-weight.

It has been suggested that these new regiments were in some sense 'private armies' and, in particular, that the Dhākwāniya were the private army of Sulaymān b. Ḥishām.[213] This seems to be an over-simplification. These regiments were distinct from the main body of the Syrians and probably owed some loyalty to their commanders. On the other hand, it is likely that they continued to be paid by public funds. In the case of the Dhākwāniya, whose loyalty to Sulaymān b. Ḥishām is clear, they reverted to being part of Marwān II's forces when Sulaymān disappeared from the scene. Apart from Ḥafṣ b. al-Walīd, none of the men who actually raised and commanded these regiments were members of the Umayyad élite. They were probably *mawālī* entrusted with the recruitment and command of *mawālī* to supplement the manpower of the Arab *ahl al-Shām*.

In 125/743, to all intents and purposes the Syrian army was as united and effective as it had ever been but within seven years it was broken, demoralised, defeated and finally lost its identity completely. The reason for this was the partisan politics which divided the ruling class, which in turn played on and developed then latent divisions in the army.

This is not the place for a detailed narrative of the growing rivalries which at times led elements of the Syrian army to ally with Khārijī or Shi'i rebels rather than accept the leadership of their Syrian rivals. Ordinary soldiers must have been bewildered by constant changes and loss of their cohesion and authority. Many must have shared the sentiments of the Syrians in Iraq when the governor, Yūsuf b. 'Umar, tried to mobilise them against a new Caliph, 'each man would say in reply: "I am a Syrian [*rajul min ahl al-Shām*]. I give the oath of allegiance to the person to whom the Syrians give allegiance and I do as they do."'[214] Among the military in Iraq, Syrian solidarity was more important than tribal rivalries.

After the death of Yazīd III in 126/744, Marwān b. Muḥammad attempted to re-establish the Umayyad regime on a new military base. Marwān had been governor of Armenia and Azerbayjān from 114/732. During this period he had built up an army largely recruited from Qaysī tribesmen from the Jazīra, not from the traditional *junds* of Syria. He established himself in the Jazīran city of Ḥarrān, which became his base, dismissed many of his Syrian troops and recruited extra troops in the Jazīra. According to al-Ṭabarī there were 20 000 of these but Ibn Khayyāt says that there were 26 000 Qays and 7000 from the allied group of Rabī'a. They were joined by the chiefs of Qays from Syria proper, with 4000–5000 men.[215] In doing so, Marwān effectively created a rival to the established Syrian army. He then marched south to take Damascus. There followed a major confrontation at 'Ayn al-Jarr, in the Biqā valley,[216] during which Marwān's men out-manoeuvred Sulaymān's, and attacked his troops from the rear. Sulaymān's men fled back in ignominy to Damascus. Marwān had triumphed over and effectively detroyed the old-established Syrian army.

The reign of Marwān saw major changes in the Umayyad army. Marwān depended for his support on the men of Jazīra and its frontiers in Armenia and Azerbayjān, rather than on the traditional Syrian *junds*, and many of his leading commanders were men like Isḥāq b. Muslim al-'Uqaylī, Qaysī tribesmen who had made their reputations on the northern frontier. True, some Syrian Qaysis, like Yazīd b. 'Umar b. Hubayra played important roles but many, especially the Yemenis, of the old *ahl al-Shām* were reduced to subject status.

Marwān also seems to have organised his army in different ways. His core following are frequently described as *rawābiṭ* (sing., *rābiṭa*). The term had occasionally been used earlier to describe small groups of horsemen, around 500 in strength, established in cities in Iraq and the Jazīra to combat the Khārijīs.[217] Its use to describe much larger groups in Marwān's army may point to a preponderance of mobile cavalry in his forces. When he marched on Damascus, he left his son 'Abd al-Malik at Raqqa with a *rābiṭa* of 40 000 men.[218] In 127/745 he used his *rābiṭa* to capture the rebellious city of Ḥoms and they played a leading role in the defeat of Sulaymān b . Ḥishām.[219] Numbers of the *rawābiṭ* vary; 7000–8000 were sent to Niṣībīn with his son 'Abd Allāh to combat the Khārijīs but 30 000 were despatched to Iraq to support Ibn Dubāra in the pursuit of Sulaymān b. Ḥishām.[220] We are not given much idea where these men came from, although at one stage Marwān was recruiting deserters from the Kharijite cause, who are likely to have been Arab tribesmen, for his *rābiṭa*[221] but the Slav (*saqlabī*) commander from Antioch who fought against Sulaymān b. Ḥishām, may have been a member as well.[222]

Marwān's new army attempted to secure control over Iraq, where the dissensions which had largely been suppressed in the reign of Ḥishām once more came to the fore. The real challenge, however, came from the pro-'Abbasid army of Khurāsān. In military terms, however, it can be seen as the struggle of one frontier army, Marwān's men from the Jazīra and the Caucasus, against another, the pro-'Abbasid troops from Khurāsān. The Syrians and Iraqis, whose rivalries had dominated so much of early Islamic history, were little more than spectators.

The decisive encounter between Marwān's army and the 'Abbasid forces took place on the Zāb river, south east of Mawṣil, at a site called Tell Kushāf.[223] After the fall of Kūfa to the 'Abbasids, a force under 'Abd Allah b. 'Alī was sent north along the Tigris to attack the Jazīra. Marwān came from his capital at Ḥarrān to confront them. There followed a major battle in Jumādā II 132/January 750. As usual, the accounts are confused but the general outlines are fairly clear. Marwān's forces, which are said to have been more than 100 000, significantly outnumbered the 'Abbasid army of 12 000, though the difference is likely to have been exaggerated to glorify the 'Abbasid success. The armies established camps on opposite sides of the river Zāb. The first encounter seems to have been a raiding party sent out by 'Abd Allah b. 'Alī, which forded the river and attacked Marwān's army. The raid was not a success and most of the 'Abbasid force was killed or captured. Marwān then constructed a pontoon bridge across the river. The 'Abbasid commanders, afraid that the defeat of the raiding party would demoralise their army, decided to give battle. Before dawn, the herald (*munādī*), summoned the troops to get their equipment, go to their battle stations and assemble in lines. They were arrayed in the conventional way – centre, right wing and left wing. Marwān grouped his men in around 100 squadrons (*karādīs*), each of 1000–2000 men. Again there was a left wing and right wing while the Caliph himself was in the centre with 30 000 men. He went through his army from one wing to another, inspecting them. The enemy, his herald proclaimed, were not real Khurāsānis, just a rabble from (the nearby town of) Shahrazur.

Battle began when Marwān's left wing attacked the 'Abbasid right and the 'Abbasid troops began to falter. One of 'Abd Allāh's commanders advised him, 'Order them to dismount and you yourself must dismount or panic will spread in the army.' So he did and he and all his troops fought as foot soldiers, kneeling with their spears pointing towards the enemy. They were ordered to keep close together leaving no gaps between them. The archers were placed behind the spearmen and instructed to shoot over them. The armoured horse were stationed behind the archers.

For reasons which are not entirely clear, the Umayyad lines, faced by this disciplined force, broke and fled. Marwān, it was said, could not organise anything that day without disagreement and chaos.[224] It seems as if Marwān had gathered soldiers from every section of the *ahl al-Shām*[225] for this crucial encounter; since many of these had been on opposite sides in the bitter internal conflicts of recent years, it is hardly surprising that they did not trust their commanders or each other. According to one version, the 'Abbasid forces advanced towards the enemy, Marwān, who was bald and not wearing a helmet, received a head wound which incapacitated him and his army broke and fled.[226] In another version,[227] the Umayyad forces attacked but, faced with the Khurāsāni spear wall, began to waver. Then Marwān started to order his men to dismount but the different tribal groups refused: Quḍā'a refused to dismount as the Banū Sulaym had not. And so it went on: every time one tribe was ordered to attack they refused because their rivals had not. Even his *ṣāḥib al-shurṭa* refused to dismount because he would be a sitting target. 'The Syrians attacked us like a mountain of iron' one of the 'Abbasid soldiers remembered afterwards, 'but we knelt down and pointed our spears and they turned away from us like a cloud'.[228] According to another version, Marwān's men started to seize the money he had brought to pay them and make off with it.[229] When the Umayyad army broke, Marwān fled, cutting the pontoon bridge behind him: large numbers of his troops were drowned.

It is difficult to know how far these accounts reflect the true course of the battle and elements in them are probably at best imaginative reconstructions. The picture presented, however, shows the importance of the spear-wall and the discipline necessary to achieve it. Morale and *esprit de corps*, and trust between different units, was crucial to success or failure. It may also be that the battle at Tell Kushāf was the last of its type. The dominance of infantry had been characteristic of early Islamic warfare but never again would the spear-wall be decisive in a major engagement. Ironically, the battle formation which he *ahl al-Shām* seem to have perfected and used to such good effect in Iraq, was now turned against them by the *ahl Khurāsān* and used to destroy their dominance, and even their very identity, for ever.

Notes

1 From the accession to the Caliphate of Marwān b. al-Ḥakam in 64/683 to the final collapse of the Umayyad regime in 132/750, all the Caliphs were descendants of Marwān, as opposed to Mu'āwiya and Yazīd I, who were descendants of Abū Sufyān, and hence known as Sufyanids. For the general history of this period, see J. Wellhausen, *The Arab Kingdom and its Fall*, trans. M. G. Weir (Calcutta, 1927, repr. Beirut, 1963); G. R. Hawting, *The First Dynasty of Islam* (London, 1986); Kennedy, *The Prophet and the Age of the Caliphates: The Islamic Near East from the Sixth to the Eleventh Century* (London, 1986), 82–123.

2 For Egypt in this period, see H. Kennedy, 'Egypt as a Province in the Islamic Caliphate', in C. F. Petry (ed.), *The Cambridge History of Egypt*, i (Cambridge, 1998), 62–85.

3 Bal., *Futūḥ*, 350.

4 Bal., *Ansāb*, iva, 190 (though he notes that some people say this was his son ʻUbayd Allāh).

5 Ṭa, ii, 433–4; Balādhurī (*Ansāb*, ivb, 115–16) gives a version of the same speech in which he claims to have raised the numbers of *muqātila* from 40 000 to 80 000 and the families from 70 000 to 120 000. Other figures recorded in the sources for this time are 60 000 Masʻūdī, *Murūj*, v, 195) and 80 000, but this time including offspring (Jah., 99).

6 Ṭa., i, 2805 though, as always, the number 40 000 should be treated with scepticism.

7 Ṭa., ii, 948.

8 Ṭa., ii, 197.

9 Ṭa., ii, 1290–1.

10 Ṭa., ii, 1533.

11 K. Morimoto, 'The Dīwāns as Registers of the Arabic Stipendaries in Early Islamic Egypt', in R. Curiel and R. Gyselen (eds), *Itinéraires d'Orient: Hommages à Claude Cahen* (Bures-sur-Yvette, 1994), 353–4 , quoting Ibn ʻAbd al-Ḥakam, 102.

12 Ṭa., ii, 1318; Bal. *Futūḥ*, 336 says 120 000 from Syria, Jazīra, the two Miṣrs (Kūfa and Basra) and Khurāsān.

13 Ṭa., ii, 1877.

14 There is no evidence to support this beyond the fact that the Syrian *muqātila* were repeatedly able to defeat their counterparts from Iraq and the large numbers reported in the conflict of 127/744. We have no global totals of Syrian troops.

15 This discussion is based on M. Whitby, 'Recruitment in Roman Armies from Justinian to Heraclius (*ca.* 565–615)', *LAEI*, iii (1995), 61–124 , pp. 73–5.

16 A. H. M. Jones, *The Later Roman Empire 284–602*, 3 vols (Oxford, 1964), ii, 684.

17 Whitby, 'Recruitment', 83.

18 R. MacMullen, 'How Big was the Roman Imperial Army?', *Klio*, 62 (1980), 462–88, pp. 465–6.

19 Whitby, 'Recruitment', 101.

20 See, for example, W. Treadgold, *The Byzantine Revival* (Stanford, 1988), 752–3.

21 M. Whittow, *The Making of Orthodox Byzantium, 600–1025* (London, 1996), 181–93.

22 See the numerous examples given in P. Crone, *Slaves on Horseback* (Cambridge, 1980), 93–123; for a judicious discussion of the position of the *ashrāf*, see Crone, *Slaves*, 31–2.

23 For example, Ṭa., ii, 448 shows how Yazīd b. Muʻāwiya was able to appoint a supporter of his to the crucial position of *ra'īs* of Bakr in Basra. See also K. Athāmina, 'Aʻrāb and Muhājirūn in the Environment of Amṣār', *Studia Islamica*, 66 (1997), 5–25, pp. 19–20.

24 For the emergence of 'generals', as opposed to tribal leaders, to military command, see Crone, *Slaves on Horseback*, 38–40; on the ʻAbbasid *quwwād*, see pp. 99–104.

25 Bal., *Ansāb*, iva, 190 states that he was the first to appoint *ʻurafā* and *manākib* but the sources tend to ascribe all early Islamic administrative innovations to Ziyād.

26 Bal., *Futūḥ*, 187; Lane sv. and Ṭabarī, Gloss, ccclix sv.

27 See the discussion in F. M. Donner, *The Early Islamic Conquests* (Princeton, 1981), 237–9.

28 Ṭa., ii, 242.

29 See Athāmina, 'Aʻrāb and Muhājirūn', 22–4.

30 Ṭa., ii, 866; Bal., *Ansāb*, ix, 271, 275–6.

31 Ṭa., ii, 902.

32 Ṭa., ii, 1244.

33 Among the few exceptions are Abū Maryam ʻAbd Allāh, a Christian convert who was *ʻarīf* of the Banū Zubayd at the time of the Muslim conquest of Egypt (Ṭa., i, 2583), and the unfortunate Shurayk b. ʻAmr al-Yashkūrī, whose execution al-Ḥajjāj ordered when he pleaded that he was unfit to fight (Bal., *Ansāb*, xi, 276).

34 Ṭa., ii, 874; Bal., *Ansāb*, xi, 275; for possible Sasanian precedents and the later development of the function, see C. E. Bosworth, 'Recruitment, Muster and Review in Medieval Islamic Armies', in V. J. Parry and M. E. Yapp (eds), *War, Technology, and Society in the Middle East* (Oxford, 1975), 70–1.

35 Bal., *Ansāb*, xi, 276.

36 Ṭa., ii, 556 . This is a well-known *topos*, designed to show the pious resignation of the commander and his followers: see A. Noth and L. I. Conrad, *The Early Arabic Historical Tradition: A Source Critical Study*, trans. M. Bonner (Princeton, 1994), 120–2.

37 Ṭa., ii, 761; Bal. *Ansāb*, xi, 117, where al-Ḥārith is known by his sobriquet Qabā' (the hedgehog).

38 'Abd al-Ḥamīd, 200–1.

39 al-Harthamī, 34–5.

40 Ṭa., ii, 709–12. The account comes from Abū Mikhnaf.

41 For *katā'ib* (sing., *katība*) see M. Ullmann, *Wörterbuch des klassischen arabischen Sprache* (Wiesbaden, 1957) sv. The *katība* is defined as between 100 and1000 men by the lexicographers: in practice, the numbers are more flexible and the *katība* can be larger or smaller than the *kardūs*.

42 Ṭa., ii, 949–52.

43 Ṭa., ii, 959; see also trans. Rowson n. 427.

44 Ṭa., ii, 1107.

45 Ṭa., ii, 1201–2.

46 Ṭa., ii, 554–5.

47 See Ullmann, *Wörterbuch* sv. where the *kardūs* is defined as between 40 and 50 men, so smaller than the *katība*, but the two terms are not differentiated systematically in the sources.

48 Ṭa., ii, 1944.

49 For the importance of tribal banners, and the designs of many of them, see G. M. Hinds, 'The Banners and Battle Cries of the Arabs at Ṣiffīn (AD 657)', *Al-Abhath*, 24 (1971), 3–42.

50 Ṭa., ii, 479–80.

51 Ṭa., ii, 629.

52 Ṭa., ii, 725, 727.

53 Ṭa., ii, 728.

54 Ṭa., ii, 889.

55 Ṭa., ii, 936–7.

56 Ṭa., ii, 958–61.

57 See pp. 50–1.

58 Ṭa., ii, 1707–10.

59 Ṭa., iii, 123.

60 Ṭa., ii, 585.

61 Ṭa., ii, 903–6.

62 See pp. 100–03.

63 Bal., *Ansāb*, v, 337.

64 Ṭa., ii, 1538–9.

65 'Abd al-Ḥamīd, 204.

66 The main source is Abū Mikhnaf's narrative included in Ṭa., ii , 538–76. There is another account incorporating much of the same material in Ibn A'tham, vi, 58–73, 77–87, but this concentrates more on the religious elements in the story and tells us less about the military campaign. See also Bal., *Ansāb*, v, 208–11.

67 Ṭa., ii, 554–5. The translation is based on Hawting trans., 139–40, with minor modifications.

68 For the climax of the battle, see Ṭa., ii, 560–8.

69 Ṭa., ii, 564.
70 Ṭa., ii, 1532–48. See also the accounts in H. A. R. Gibb, *The Arab Conquests in Central Asia* (London, 1923), 73–6 , W. W. Barthold, *Turkestan Down to the Mongol Invasion* (London, 1968), 189–90 and the comments on the text in L. I. Conrad, 'Notes on al-Ṭabarī's History', *JRAS*, Series 3, 3 (1993), 1–31, pp. 15–16; on the Turks of Transoxania and their military equipment in this period, see E. Esin, 'Ṭabarī's Report on the Warfare with the Türgis and the Testimony of Eighth Century Central Asian Art', *Central Asiatic Journal*, 17 (1973), 130–49.
71 Ṭa., ii, 1536, but this is a well-known *topos*; see pp. 27–9.
72 Ṭa., ii, 1541–2.
73 Ṭa., ii, 1543.
74 Ṭa., ii, 1536.
75 Ṭa., ii, 430–2.
76 Ṭa., i, 2524–5.
77 See J. Haldon, 'The Ajnād and the "Thematic Myth"', *LAEI*, iii (1995), 379–423.
78 Bal., *Futūḥ,* 131–2.
79 Ya'q., *Buldān*, 324–30.
80 For the tribes of Syria at this time and their geographical distribution, see G. Rotter, *Die Umayyaden und der zweite Bürgerkrieg*, (Wiesbaden, 1982), 126–33.
81 Ṭa., ii, 477.
82 Ṭa., ii, 479.
83 The word carries a variety of meanings and it is not always possible to be certain what it means. *Mawālī* could be freedmen, that is ex-slaves or prisoners of war, attached to particular individuals or tribes. It could also be used of blood relatives of a leading figure. On the other hand, the term is used much more generally to describe all non-Arab Muslims. See EI2 *mawlā* (Crone) and I. Hasson 'Les *mawālī* dans l'armée musulmane sous les premiers Umayyades', *JSAI*, 14 (1991), 176–213.
84 Crone, *Slaves on Horseback*, 197–200, argues that there is no clear evidence that these *mawālī* were in fact non-Arab clients of the Umayyads and that the word is used in the older sense to refer to family and supporters but cf. Hasson 'Les *mawālī*', 210.
85 Bal., *Ansāb*, v, 141; also Ṭa., ii, 467–8.
86 Bal., *Ansāb*, v, 136.
87 Bal., *Ansāb*, v, 300.
88 H. Kennedy, *Muslim Spain and Portugal: A Political History of al-Andalus* (London, 1996), 32.
89 Ṭa., ii, 479; Ibn Khayyāṭ, 259, says Marwān had 30 000 and his opponents, 60 000.
90 See pp. 27–9.
91 For his family and career, see Crone, *Slaves on Horseback*, 95.
92 Crone, *Slaves on Horseback*, 168–9.
93 Ṭa., ii, 707–16; Khalifa, 262–3; Ya'q., *Ta'rīkh,* ii, 308–9.
94 Ṭa., ii, 707–8.
95 Ṭa., 707, 713; For 'Umayr's career, see Crone, *Slaves on Horseback*, 107–8.
96 For a comprehensive analysis of the dispute, see P. Crone, 'Were the Qays and Yemen of the Umayyad Period Political parties?', *Der Islam*, 71 (1994), 1–57.
97 See M. Morony, *Iraq after the Muslim conquest* (Princeton, 1984), 229–32.
98 See pp. 27–9.
99 Ṭa., ii, 804–5.
100 Ṭa., ii, 804–14; Bal., *Ansāb*, v, 337–45.
101 Ṭa., ii, 829, 849; Bal., *Ansāb*, v, 355–7.
102 Ṭa., ii, 959–62. There is an alternative account of the conflict, derived from 'Umar b. Shabba, which stresses the role of the Iraqis. See Ṭa. trans., n. 432, where the different accounts are discussed by Rowson; Ya'q., *Ta'rīkh*, ii, 328–9.
103 Ṭa., ii, 1060: Bal., *Ansāb*, ix, 339; see A. A. Dixon, *The Umayyad Caliphate 65–86/*

684–705 (London, 1971), 154 for the uncertainties about the chronology of the rebellion.

104 Ṭa., ii, 1075–6.

105 Ṭa., ii, 1101, 1133–5.

106 For the building of Wāsiṭ, see Ṭa., ii, 1125–6, Bal., *Futūḥ*, 289–92; Ya'q., *Buldān*, 322.

107 Ibn Khayyāṭ, 308, 317, 335, 351.

108 Ṭa., ii, 1018–21.

109 Ṭa., ii, 1318, 1327; Bal., *Futūḥ*, 335–6.

110 Ṭa., ii, 1200, 1256; Bal., *Futūḥ*, 436.

111 Bal., *Futūḥ*, 207–9.

112 Ṭa., ii, 1527, 1533; on al-Junayd see Crone, *Slaves on Horseback*, 98.

113 Ṭa., ii, 1564, 1568–9, 1579–80, 1582.

114 Ṭa., ii, 1609.

115 N. Fries, *Der Heereswesen der Araber zur Zeit der Omaijaden nach Ṭabarī* (Tübingen, 1921), 22–4 discusses the function of these two groups as regular military attendants on Caliphs and governors. For the origins of these units in Mu'āwiya's reign, see pp. 13–14.

116 Bal., *Ansāb*, ivb, 27.

117 Ibn Khayyāṭ, 299, 312, 324, 334–5, 361–2, cf. Crone, *Slaves on Horseback*, 163.

118 Ibn Khayyāṭ, 408.

119 Ibn Khayyāṭ, 299, 312, 319, 334–5, 361–2.

120 Ṭa., ii, 1649; Bal., *Ansāb*, ivb, 4; Ibn Khayyāṭ, 299, 312, 319, 324, 334–5, 361–2.

121 For full accounts of these, see G. Rotter, *Die Umayyaden und der zweite Bürgerkrieg* and Dixon, *The Umayyad Caliphate*.

122 See Ṭa., ii, 804–5; Bal., *Ansāb*, v, 337 and cf. Crone, *Slaves on Horseback*, 111–23.

123 Ṭa., ii, 170., Bal., *Futūḥ*, 376, 410–1, Ya'q., *Ta'rīkh*, ii, 237. See also Narshakhī 37, where Ibn Ziyād is said to have taken 4000 prisoners in the city.

124 Ṭa., ii, 439–40, 443.

125 Bal., *Futūḥ*, 376.

126 Ṭa., ii, 1708.

127 Ṭa., iii, 67.

128 Probably to be identified with Kalat, on the borders of Sind and Baluchistan, about 150 km south of Quetta, G. Le Strange, *Lands of the Eastern Caliphate* (London, 1905, repr. 1966), 332. For early Muslim campaigns there see Bal., *Futūḥ*, 432, 433, 434: Qīqānī horses were presented to Mu'āwiya (Bal., *Futūḥ*, 433).

129 Ṭa., ii, 1702, 1708.

130 For early uses of the term, see D. Sourdel, 'Ghulām', *EI2*.

131 Ṭa., ii, 958.

132 Ṭa., ii, 1582, 1609.

133 Ṭa., ii, 1653.

134 Bal., *Futūḥ*, 366; Morony, *Iraq*, 211. However, it is possible that al-Balādhurī's usage here is anachronistic – i.e. that he was using a term common in his own day but not used by contemporaries.

135 See pp. 118–42.

136 For the geography and history of early Kūfa, see H. Djait, *Al-Kūfa: naissance de la ville islamique* (Paris, 1982).

137 See Ṭa., ii, 643–4, 700–1, 857, 1397.

138 Ṭa., ii, 614, 615–16, 621; Bal., *Ansāb*, v, 224–5.

139 Ṭa., ii, 634; Bal., *Ansāb*, v, 229.

140 Yazīd b. 'Ulāqa al-Saksakī seems to be an exception, Bal., *Ansāb*, xi, 270; Crone, *Slaves on Horseback*, 95–6.

141 Ṭa., ii, 1034; 1855, Ibn Khayyāṭ, 308, 327–8, 335, 351, Crone, *Slaves on Horseback*, 131, 162.

142 Ṭa., ii, 1380.
143 Ṭa., ii, 1634.
144 See p. 11.
145 See pp. 23–4.
146 For an alternative view, see the discussion of Ibrāhīm's motives in Dixon, *Umayyad Caliphate*, 72–4, where he is treated as a lukewarm Shi'ite who disapproved of Mukhtār's extremism.
147 For his family, see Crone, *Slaves on Horseback*, 112–13.
148 Note also the forces of between 4000 and 6000 raised in Kūfa to fight the Khawārīj : Ṭa., ii, 761–2, 825–6, 827.
149 *al-farḍ alladhī faraḍa lahum*, Ṭa., ii, 890.
150 Ṭa., ii, 902–3; see also the account of al-Ḥajjāj's confrontation with the Iraqi *muqātila* at Rustaqābādh, which was partly about whether the Kūfans should be forced to do military service (Bal., *Ansāb*, xi, 266–303); P. Crone, 'Were the Qays and Yemen', 36–7.
151 Ṭa., ii, 911. For Suwayd see W. Caskel, *Gamharat an-Nasab: Das genealogische Wenn das Hisām ibn Muḥammad al-Kalbī*, 2 vols (Leiden, 1996), sn.; Crone, *Slaves on Horseback*, 139.
152 Ṭa., 921. For Zahr, see Caskel, *Gamharat*, sn.
153 Ṭa., ii, 930.
154 Ṭa., ii, 948. For 'Attāb, see Caskel, *Gamharat*, sn.; Crone, *Slaves on Horseback*, 112.
155 Ṭa., ii, 919.
156 For full accounts of Ibn al-Ash'ath's revolt, see R. Sayed, *Die revolte des Ibn al-Asat und die Koranleser* (Freiburg, 1977); Dixon, *Umayyad Caliphate*, 151–68; EI2 sv. Ibn al-Ash'ath (Veccia Vaglieri).
157 See C. E. Bosworth, ''Ubaidallāh b. Abī Bakra and the "Army of Destruction" in Zābulistān (79/698)', *Der Islam*, 50 (1973), 268–83.
158 *kamalan*: Ṭa., ii, 1043–4.
159 Ṭa., ii, 1058–9; Bal., *Ansāb*, xi, 336.
160 Ṭa., ii, 1072.
161 Although 2000 Kūfans are mentioned fighting, unsuccesfully, against the Khawārīj in 100–1/718–20, Ṭa., ii, 1348, 1376.
162 Ṭa., ii, 1702.
163 Ṭa., ii, 1073.
164 Ṭa., ii, 1389.
165 Ṭa., ii, 1687.
166 Ṭa., ii, 1716.
167 Ṭa., ii, 1854–5.
168 Ṭa., ii, 1681; trans. Hillenbrand, 17–18.
169 Ṭa., ii, 1381–2.
170 Ṭa., ii, 586, 1381.
171 See pp. 19–20.
172 Ṭa., ii, 591.
173 Ṭa., ii, 798, 1062; Ibn Khayyāṭ, 308, 335, 351.
174 Ṭa., ii, 584; Bal., *Ansāb*, xi, 102–4.
175 Ṭa., ii, 1380–3.
176 Ṭa., ii, 826.
177 Ṭa., ii, 994, 996–7.
178 Ṭa., ii, 1001.
179 See C. E. Bosworth, *Sistan under the Arabs* (Rome, 1968), 36.
180 See the discussions in M. A. Shaban, *'Abbasid Revolution* (Cambridge, 1970), *passim*; M. Sharon, *Black Banners from the East* (Jerusalem, 1983), 65–71; S. S. Agha, 'The Arab Population in Hurāsān during the Umayyad Period', *Arabica*, 46 (1999),

211–29 accepts the figures given in the Arabic sources for the *muqātila* but argues that the number of dependants has been greatly over-estimated by Wellhausen (*The Arab Kingdom*, 1963, 493) and others who have suggested figures of up to 250 000 for total Arab immigration. See also P. Pourshariati, 'Local Histories of Khurāsān and the Pattern of Arab Settlement', *Studia Iranica*, 27 (1998), 41–81, where it is argued that Arab settlement was much more patchy than assumed in other secondary literature.

181 Ṭa., ii, 1287–9, 1430.

182 Ṭa. ii, 1257; for the family, see Caskel, *Gamharat*, taf. 268 and register sn. Zahr b. Qays and Gahm b. Zahr b. Qays.

183 For Syrian troops in Khurāsān, see p. 34.

184 Ṭa., ii, 1290–1; Bal., *Futūḥ*, 423 has 40 000 Basran *muqātila*, 7000 Kūfans and 7000 *mawālī*.

185 Ṭa., ii, 1534.

186 Ṭa., ii, 1538.

187 Ṭa, ii, 1207.

188 Ṭa., ii, 1026 for villages belonging to Banū Naṣr and Ṭayyi. The whole question of Arab settlement in the Marw oasis has been fruitfully re-examined in E. L. Daniel, 'The "Ahl al-Taqādum" and the Problem of the Constituency of the 'Abbasid Revolution in the Merv Oasis', *Journal of Islamic Studies*, 7 (1996), 150–79.

189 Ṭa., ii, 490.

190 See J. Wellhausen, *The Arab Kingdom and Its Fall*, trans. M. Weir (Calcutta, 1927, repr. Beirut, 1963), 416–18.

191 Ṭa., ii, 1354; many anecdotes concerning 'Umar II need to be treated with caution.

192 Ṭa., ii, 1545; Bal., *Futūḥ*, 429 says that he was given a free hand to recruit as many as he wished (*aṭlaqa yadahu fi farīḍati*).

193 Ṭa., ii, 1544.

194 On Ḥayyān and his family, see P. Crone, 'A Note on Muqātil b. Ḥayyān and Muqātil b. Sulaymān', *Der Islam*, 74 (1997), 238–49.

195 Ṭa., ii, 1290–1, 1294–5, 1329–31, 1430–1; Bal., *Futūḥ*, 423–4.

196 Ṭa., ii, 1504, 1566, 1571, 1614–6, 1998.

197 Ṭa., ii, 1256.

198 Ṭa., ii, 1690.

199 Ṭa., ii, 1591.

200 Ṭa., ii, 1473.

201 See pp. 44–5.

202 Ṭa., ii, 1428, 1497, 1532.

203 Ṭa., ii, 1605, 1661, 1666, 1995.

204 Ṭa., ii, 1662.

205 Ṭa., ii, 1241, 1436, 1438, 1448, 1509, 1529, 1543, 1569, 1608, 1631, 1660.

206 Ṭa., ii, 1315; *'Uyūn*, 24–33 says simply that the *junds* of Syria and Jazīra were summoned and that many *fuqahā* (scholars of religious law) from Syria and Iraq went.

207 Ṭa., ii, 1702–10.

208 The details come largely from later Andalusi sources; see A. D. Taha, *The Muslim Conquest and Settlement of North Africa and Spain* (London, 1989), 202–3.

209 For the best account of these increasing tensions, see Crone, 'Were the Qays and Yemen', 44–57.

210 On these, see K. Athāmina, 'Non-Arab Regiments and Private Militias during the Umayyad Period', *Arabica*, 45 (1998), 347–78, who does not, however, discuss the Egyptian evidence.

211 al-Jāḥiẓ, *Manāqib*, 10; also Ṭa., iii, 40.

212 al-Kindī, *Wulāt*, 82–7.

213 M. A. Shaban, *Islamic History, AD 600–750*, i (Cambridge, 1971), 157.
214 Ṭa., ii, 1838.
215 Ṭa., ii, 1873; Ibn Khayyāṭ, 372; Ya'q., *Ṭa'rīkh*, ii, 403.
216 Ṭa., ii, 1876–8.
217 Athāmina, *Non-Arab Regiments*, 373–4. For *Rawābit* in early 'Abbasid Mosul, see H. Kennedy, 'Central Government and Provincial Elites in the Early 'Abbasid Caliphate' *BSOAS*, 44 (1981a), 26–38.
218 Ṭa., ii, 1876–7.
219 Ṭa., ii, 1893, 1910.
220 Ṭa., ii, 1939, 1945.
221 Ṭa., ii, 1898.
222 Ṭa., ii, 1910.
223 There are two main accounts of the battle. The fullest is al-Azdī, 126–31, the other is Ṭa., iii, 38–42. They share some common features but both incorporate different first-hand accounts. Al-Azdī refers to the encounter as the Battle of Tel Kushāf and I have followed this usage, rather than Battle of the Zāb.
224 Ṭa., iii, 41.
225 Ṭa., iii, 40–1 speaks of traditionally Yemeni groups like Quḍā'a and Sukūn (a branch of Kinda) along with Marwān's Qaysī supporters.
226 al-Azdī, 129.
227 Ṭa., iii, 41–2.
228 Ṭa., iii, 42.
229 Ṭa., iii, 41–2.

CHAPTER THREE

The payment of the military in the early Islamic state

In the centuries after the great conquests, the armies of the Caliphs were mostly paid in cash salaries. In contrast to many post-Roman polities in Europe, grants of land, or of rights to collect taxes directly from the payers, were of only minor importance. The system was not, however, highly centralised and the collection and payment of monies took place at a provincial level rather than through a bureaucratic system centred on Madīna, Damascus or Baghdad. A major consequence of this was that the army directly depended on the state for its subsistence which, in turn, meant that the military had to control the state apparatus, or at least make sure that it operated in their interest. The existing military leadership would have to oppose, either peacefully or violently, any attempt to starve it of salary payments or to replace it with other military groups. Unlike the military aristocracy of western Europe, they had no estates to fall back on if the government failed them or they lost control of it. A further consequence of the system was that membership of the army, or at least a place on the pay-roll, was a desirable position. Many of the political disputes of the first three centuries of Islam were generated by competition between different groups to secure a share of – or, better still, a monopoly of – military status. Conscription, empressment or forcible service was never an important feature of early Islamic warfare (though, of course, there are many examples of people who were happy to collect their salaries, but reluctant to fight).

The key institution for doing this was the *dīwān.* The obscure origins of this word, and its many later ramifications and uses, make it difficult to be certain exactly what is being described. Initially the *dīwān* was simply a list or lists of those entitled to a share of the revenues of the conquered lands. From very early times, however, it was paralleled by a second *dīwān al-kharāj*, or register of taxes due. In time the number of *dīwān*s increased and the word was used for any government department and the list of troops to be paid was more closely defined as the *dīwān al-jund* (department of the army). For the purposes of this discussion, however, the term will be used in its original and evolving sense to describe the military registers.

The origins and early development of the dīwān[1]

Investigation of the origins of the *dīwān* is fraught with the same problems as other areas of early Islamic history. The sources give us detailed, but often contradictory accounts, and they are the result of elaboration and polemic throughout the first century of Islam. The Arabic sources present us with a history of a system inaugurated by the Caliph 'Umar I (13–23/634–44) which provided that the revenues (*fay'*) of the conquered lands would be used to provide salaries (*'aṭā'*) to the conquerors and, perhaps, their descendants. However, it is impossible to know for certain whether such a system was invented in the way described, or indeed whether it ever existed in its 'pure' form at all. The accounts we have may simply represent the claims of disgruntled Iraqis, and others who were excluded from the military *dīwān* in the Marwanid period, about how it ought to have worked.

The traditional Muslim accounts describe the establishment of the *dīwān* by the caliph 'Umar b. al-Khaṭṭab in 20 or 21/640–2.[2] It is likely that mechanisms for the division of revenues had existed in Madīna at the time of the Prophet but the great conquests which followed his death meant that the problem of organising payment was now on a much vaster scale. Because the conquering Muslims were settled in the garrison cities (*amṣār*),[3] they could no longer depend on pastoralism and occasional agriculture for subsistence. Instead they were to live off the tax revenues paid by the local people and collected by local agents.[4] The Muslim troops, the *muqātila*, would be, in effect, a large salariat. This established that payment of the military in the Muslim state was to be based on soldiers paid salaries out of the proceeds of general, public taxation. It was not to be system based on land-tenure or *hospitalitas* or any of the proto- and quasi-feudal relationships which developed in the West after the fall of the Roman Empire. The pattern found in the western half of the Roman empire where, by and large, the public taxation of Roman times fell into abeyance and was replaced by other, more direct ways, in which the military classes derived income from the peasants, simply did not happen in the newly conquered lands. The land tax and poll-tax of the Sasanian and Byzantine regimes, although in new Islamic guises, remained central to the functioning of state and the military.

The establishment of the *dīwān* appears to be the result of a pragmatic response to new circumstances. The origins of the institution are not clear. In the most detailed discussion, Puin argued that attempts to find direct parallels in Sasanian administration are not convincing and there is no reason to suppose that it was a direct borrowing from Sasanian practice.[5] The origins of the system, he claimed, may lie in the provision made for poor *muhājirūn* after they had left their homes in Makka to settle with the Prophet in Madīna.[6]

However, both early Islamic sources and modern scholars have drawn attention to parallels in the pre-Islamic systems of the Byzantine and Persian empires. According to one account reported by al-Balādhurī, 'Umar based his *dīwān* on the system reportedly used by the 'kings of Syria' who used a *dīwān* to organise their army (*jund*).[7] Morony[8] has drawn attention to Sasanian parallels, arguing that the first *dīwān* was developed in Basra at the time of the settlement of the city when al-Mughīra b. Shu'ba, aided by the Persian Payroazh, drew up a list of those entitled to a share of the income in the way the Sasanians had done. 'Umar extended this practice to Kūfa and other areas.[9] Al-Jahshiyārī, a secretary working in the 'Abbasid bureaucracy, certainly considered that the *dīwān* was directly dependent on Sasanian practice.[10] It would probably be reasonable to conclude that while the basic concept of the settlement of the conquerors in *amṣār* and their subsistence on *'aṭā'* was an original idea developed in response to the Muslim conquests, the mechanics and implementation of the system owed much to Byzantine and Sasanian models.

As described in the Arabic sources, 'Umar's setting up of the *dīwān* or *dīwān*s marked a significant development of what had gone before. We have a number of accounts of this, notably in the works of al-Balādhurī and al-Ṭabarī but also of legal scholars like the *qāḍī* Abū Yūsuf and Ibn Sallām.[11] They are in broad agreement on the basic facts. 'Umar set up a *dīwān*, a register of those entitled to *'aṭā'* (a salary). These salaries are reckoned in cash and are given in *dirham*s (silver coins), except in Egypt and Syria where *dīnār*s (gold coins) were used. The relationship between the two currencies fluctuated considerably. At the time of the Prophet it is said to have been 1 *dīnār* = 10 *dirham*s. However there was a persistent silver inflation and by the second/eighth century it was probably 1:12 and by the third/ninth century 1 *dīnār* was worth 20 or 25 *dirham*s.[12] There is general agreement that different groups of people were given different amounts, though there are some variations in the figures and the order of precedence. At the top came the Prophet's surviving wives of whom the favourite, A'isha, is said to have received 12 000 *dirham*s per year. Next come members of the Prophet's family, notably 'Alī b. Abī Ṭālib and al-'Abbās.[13] Below them those who had fought at the Battle of Badr, the Prophet's first encounter with the Meccans in 2/624, each of whom received 5000. Those who joined after Badr but before the treaty of al-Ḥudaybiya in 6/628 received 4000, those who joined after al-Ḥudaybiya but who fought in the *ridda* wars and the earliest campaigns in Iraq, 3000. Those who had fought in the main campaigns in Iraq and Syria were given 2000, or 2500 if they had been especially courageous. The next wave who arrived after the main battle of al-Qādisiya and Yarmūk got 1000 and later groups 500 and 300, all getting the same whether they were strong or weak, Arab or non-Arab. The Persian Ḥamrā and Asāwira troops who came over to the Muslim armies during the conquests were paid *sharaf al-'aṭā'* 2000 *dirham*s, in contrast to Arab tribesmen of 'Akk and Ḥimyar who received only 300 at the same time.[14] Later immigrants received only 200.[15] Different tribes had their own *dīwān*s and the *dīwān*s of Khuzā'a and Ḥimyar are especially noted.[16] We are also told that the Yamanis and Qaysis of Syria and Iraq were all paid on a similar sliding scale.[17]

The setting up of the *dīwān* seems to have been a response to the uncertainties about the division of income in Madīna, Basra and Kūfa, but the system was extended to all the newly conquered provinces. Al-Ya'qūbī says that seven *amṣār* were established in Madīna, Syria (Damascus), the Jazīra (probably Ḥarrān), Kūfa, Basra and two others whose names are lost in a lacuna in the text but were probably Fusṭāṭ in Egypt and possibly Merv in Khurāsān although this did not become a *miṣr* until later. The term *miṣr* (pl. *amṣār*) was used to designate cities where the *dīwān*s were kept and *'aṭā'* was paid out. There was at least an intention that the taxation of each province would be brought to the *miṣr* and paid out there, rather than being despatched to the capital at Madīna or Damascus and paid out from a central treasury. In Syria, the troops were expected to live off the tax-revenues of the districts (*junds*) in which they were settled.[18]

The revenues derived from the taxation of a province claimed to be the *fay'*, the immovable booty which belonged, collectively, to the conquerors and their successors. Those whose names appeared in the *dīwān* were entitled to a share (*farīḍa*) of the proceeds, the proportion depending on their status. The term *farīḍa* is also used in Islamic law as the share of an inheritance to which an heir is entitled[19]: whether there is a direct connection or not, there can be little doubt that the *farīḍa* of the *fay'* was regarded by many Muslims in the same way, as a heritable right. The verbal forms *faraḍa* and *afraḍa* mean to recruit or raise soldiers who would be given a position in the *dīwān*. Each person in the *dīwān* seems to have been assigned a *maktab*[20] or station, where they were expected to serve and where they drew their *'aṭā'*.

While the general outlines are clear, the sources differ on a number of important details. The reports which come down to us are often tendentious and polemical and reflect not just the original form of the *dīwān* but the fierce and sometimes violent controversies to which it gave rise through the next century.

One of the points at issue was whether non-Arabs could be paid salaries. The status of non-Arab Muslims (*mawālī*) was to be a major source of conflict and some of the traditions about the *dīwān* certainly reflect this. It was said that three slaves (*mamlūk*) who fought at Badr were paid the same as all the other participants[21] as were the *mawālī*.[22] A short anecdote shows 'Umar reproving a governor who paid the *'aṭā'* to Arabs but not to the *mawālī*.[23] In response to what must have been a common situation, 'Umar is said to have written to the governors that non-Arab prisoners who converted to Islam and were freed and became *mawālī* should have the same rights and obligations as other Muslims and be paid the same *'aṭā'*.[24]

Individual non-Arabs were also said to have been given high salaries; 'Ammār b. Yāsir was paid 6000 and Salmān the Persian, 4000,[25] proving that non-Arabs could get the highest salaries (*sharaf al-'aṭā'*). Also enjoying high salaries were a number of Persian *dehqan*s from Iraq, including the administrator al-Hurmuzān who was paid 2000.[26] As already noted, other evidence makes it clear that bodies of Persian troops like the Asāwira were paid salaries like the Arabs, from a very early stage.[27]

Another key issue was whether rights to *'aṭā'* were inherited. Here tradition is not at all clear. Some said that the families and offspring of those on the *dīwān* should get allowances and that these were heritable.[28] Sons of the *muhājrūn* were to get 2000 *dirhams*.[29] There is evidence of the payment of child allowances for male children after weaning.[30] Some anecdotes suggest that the *farīḍa* itself, that is the full *'aṭā'*, was heritable but that this was stopped by the Caliph 'Abd al-Malik who allowed this right only to those he wished.[31]

Even more controversial in the Umayyad period was the question of whether the *'aṭā'* was paid as of right or whether the recipient had to do military service in order to earn it. There is no clear and unequivocal link in the sources between the military service and payment of *'aṭā'* in the *dīwān* of 'Umar: payment is the reward for past participation. Nonetheless, the importance of military prowess is stressed at several points, as in the higher payments made to the people who showed outstanding bravery in the conquests. Further light is shed on this by the discussion of whether bedouin should be paid the *'aṭā'* or only Arabs who had settled in the *amṣār*. Ibn Sallām argues that the bedouin, who presumably retained their traditional means of subsistence, should not receive salaries unlike the settled people who 'join with the Muslims in their affairs and support them against their enemies with their bodies and their wealth'.[32] Here he is drawing a clear link between payment and continuing performance but, of course, he is a jurist writing almost two centuries later when the system had long fallen into disuse. Nonetheless, the comments do reflect a real issue and particularly al-Ḥajjāj's determined attempts to link payment to military service. But, as with many aspects of the *dīwān*, the evidence was at best ambiguous and could be argued both ways.

Another issue which gave rise to serious dispute and conflict was the question of the distribution of the surplus (*faḍl*). If the revenue of the *fay'* of a province proved to be more than was required to pay the salaries to those who were entitled to them, what should happen to the extra? Should this pass to the treasury of the Muslims, (*bayt māl al-Muslimīn*), which was under the control of the Caliph, or should it be distributed among the owners of the *fay'* as a sort of bonus? Feelings were to run very high about this, and the controversy is reflected in the accounts of the establishment of the *dīwān*. In one account 'Umar is made to say, 'The *fay'* belongs to the people of the *amṣār* and those who joined them, gave them assistance and stayed with them. It was not allotted to others. Is it not true that the cities and villages were populated by them, that the peace treaties were administered by them, the *jizya* [general taxation in this context] was paid to them, that they made the frontier safe and subdued the enemy?' When someone suggested that a reserve be retained in the treasury, 'Umar dismissed the suggestion as the work of the devil which might lead his successors astray.[33] The polemical nature of the anecdote hardly needs to be stressed. Equally blunt was the advice that 'Alī was said to have given to 'Umar when he was establishing the *dīwān*, 'Divide up each year the money which is collected for you, and do not retain any of it'.[34] The direct linking of both 'Umar and 'Alī to the policy of complete division of the *fay'* is of great importance in the understanding of the polemic which surrounded it and the violent disturbances it occasioned in Iraq and elsewhere in the Umayyad period. It meant that the 'correct' disposal of the *fay'* could be seen as a matter of faith *(dīn)* to be defended against the impious Umayyads, or anyone else who tried to interfere. The issue went to the heart of the contoversy about the distribution of resources. If the surplus went to the Caliph, it was an admission that the revenues were his to dispose of as he saw fit. On the other hand, if the surplus were distributed in the province, it was a clear sign that the revenues belonged as of right to the Muslims of the area and the Caliph and his government could have no say in their distribution.

It is not clear whether the *dīwān* of 'Umar as described in the sources was ever put into effect but after the accession of 'Uthmān contradictions and uncertainties about the distibution of revenues began to manifest themselves. The struggles were essentially a reflection of the competition for resources between different groups in Iraq and Egypt and between the Iraqi and Egyptian Muslims and the Caliph in Madīna. Hinds identifies several elements which gave rise to tensions among the Muslims.[35] The first was the existence of a body of participants in the early conquests who enjoyed a privileged position because of their *sābiqa* and 'Umar's desire to create an Islamic élite. In contrast were the *rawādif*, tribesmen who came to settle after the initial conquest, often on the outskirts of the towns, and who formed a large disadvantaged class with no effective way of improving their position. Another element was the ambiguous position of tribal leaders, like al-Ash'ath b. Qays al-Kindī, who should have had a lowly status in the new Islamic order since he had joined the *ridda* (the anti-Muslim revolts which broke out after the Prophet's death) wars but whose contacts and enduring prestige among their tribesmen meant that they could challenge 'Umar's establishment. These elements competed in a situation where tax-collecting must have been a bit rough and ready and where the virtual cessation of new conquests had put an end to the influx of new resources.

'Uthmān and his advisers made serious attempts to deal with these problems. He appointed governors who would be effective administrators and, in particular, would supervise the distribution of resources. With the appointments of Sa'īd b. al-'Āṣ to Kūfa and 'Abd Allāh b. 'Āmir to Basra in 29/649–50, a new series of expeditions was launched which, it was hoped, would lead to new conquests in the east and north. The Basran expeditions were able to make extensive new conquests in Khurāsān which meant that Ibn 'Āmir was able to rule with a fairly light hand. The Kūfan expeditions to northern Iran and the Caucasus, by contrast, ran into serious difficulties and few, if any, new resources became available. The governor seems to have tried to take control over the payment of *'aṭā'* which led to protests and resistance from those beneficiaries of 'Umar's system, notably the early participants who resented attempts to cut their incomes and who rejected the right of the governor to make decisions about the *fay'* which was theirs by right. Mālik al-Ashtar, the most prominent figure in the opposition, accused Sa'īd of trying to reduce the salaries of the veterans (*ahl al-balā'*) and the allowances of the women and stirred up active opposition, preventing the governor, who had gone to consult the Caliph, from returning to the province.[36] In defence of his policy, the 'Uthmān is said to have claimed that he had returned all the surpluses to the *amṣār* and had taken only the Caliph's fifth;[37] even from this he had taken nothing for himself. The distribution of the revenues had been entrusted to 'the Muslims' (that is, not to government officials).[38]

None of these protestations were enough to deflect the wrath of the discontented elements in Kūfa and Egypt who marched on Madīna and, in mid-35/ early 656, murdered the ageing Caliph, whom they accused of bad faith.[39] While wider religious and political problems certainly contributed to the unrest this, the first and most traumatic outbreak of inter-Muslim violence, was in large measure the result of disputes about the distribution of revenues.

It is not clear whether the armies of the first *fitna* were paid regular salaries or not and there is no mention of *dīwāns*. The short and disturbed reign of 'Alī is unlikely to have produced major military reforms. Hinds notes, 'Although we know little of 'Alī's fiscal measures, we know enough to say that their egalitarian nature, which was a major source of newcomer support for the Shī'ī leaders, was also a major cause of an attitude among other leaders which wavered between indifference and treachery.'[40] At one point he is said to have offered all those who would follow him in an attack on Syria an *'aṭā'* of 500.[41] The young Muḥammad b. Mikhnaf, fighting in 'Alī's army, remarks that he was only seventeen years old at the time and so not yet entitled to the *'aṭā'*.[42] Mālik al-Ashtar exhorted the Iraqis to fight to protect their *dīn* and their *fay'*.[43] Later 'Alī is said to have tried to clarify the relationship between enjoyment of the *fay'* and service,

> Now you have obligations [*ḥaqq*] to me and I have obligations to you. My duties towards you are good counsel to you for as long as I am associated with you, increasing your *fay'*, providing you with knowledge so that you are not ignorant, and educating you so that you acquire knowledge. Your duties to me are the fulfilment of the oath of allegiance [*bay'a*], good advice in private and in public, responding when I call you and obedience when I command you.[44]

Despite the heavily didactic note of this speech the main point is clear; enjoyment of the *fay'* entails military service. Meanwhile, Ibn al-'Abbās, his governor of Basra, was threatening to punish those who deserted their *maktab* and refused to join the army of 'Alī, but he does not seem to have had the authority to do anything about it.[45] Later when 'Alī was trying to form a force to resist an Umayyad takeover in Egypt, he reproached the tribal leaders (*ashrāf*) who had failed to provide him with any troops, saying that they received allowances (*ma'ūna*) and some of them were paid *'aṭā'* but they failed to respond and he contrasted this with the Syrians who would support Mu'āwiya without any payment at all.[46] As has already been noted, he is also said in some accounts of the establishment of the *dīwān* to have called for the distribution of all the surplus among the rightful possessors of the *fay'*.[47] It is impossible to know whether this represents his actual policy, manifesto pledges or simply what later supporters of the 'Alids would have like him to have said.

The evidence of the papyri

Evidence for the day-to-day operation of the system, as opposed to the narrative and polemical accounts in the literary sources, can be pieced together from the evidence provided by papyri found in Egypt and southern Palestine.[48] The earliest important source are the bilingual *entagia* from Nessana, in southern Palestine on the northern fringes of the Negev Desert. They mostly date from 674–7, that is from the reign of Mu'āwiya and before the administrative reforms of 'Abd al-Malik.[49] These are essentially demand notes, written in both Arabic and Greek, to the Christian agriculturists of Nessana requiring them to provide supplies for named bedouin tribes. The supplies are to be paid in wheat and olive oil and in some there is provision for a cash payment instead, perhaps if payment in kind proved impossible to arrange.

Of the seven surviving *entagia*, three (nos. 60–3) order payments to members of the Banū Sa'd b. Mālik, perhaps to be identified with the Banū Sa'd b. Mālik of Judhām, the most powerful tribe in southern Palestine.[50] The beneficiaries of a fourth (no. 64), which was misdirected from another village in the area, might tentatively be identified with the Banū Sa'd b. Zirr of Lakhm, another important group in the area.[51] It is not possible to identify the beneficiaries of the others.

The payments are described as the *rizq* of two or three months in the Muslim year but, because of gaps in the evidence, it is impossible to know if these were regular payments made throughout the year or occasional, one-off handouts. The instructions from the governor to the inhabitants make it clear that the payments were to be made directly to the chiefs of the bedouin groups concerned, who were presumably to be found in the vicinity. There is no mention of any granaries or *dār al-rizq* at the provincial capital at Gaza. Responsibility for distribution must have lain with the clan chiefs rather than with the governor's agents.

Documents from Egypt shed further light on systems of payment in Umayyad times. Morimoto has drawn attention[52] to the papyrus P. Lond. 1447 which dates from the governorate of 'Abd al-'Azīz b. Marwān (65–86/685–705), which is a list of the members of the household and staff of the governor with details of the payments some of them were due. Payments are both in cash and kind and Morimoto notes payments in sheep, oil, sour wine, boiled wine, dates, onions, greens, birds, wine, raisins and wood. This is an important document for the study of administration but it is not, as he remarks, a *dīwān* as such. It does make clear, however, that the bureaucracy in Egypt was overwhelmingly staffed by Greek-using secretaries: there are over 60 Greek-using clerks and only one Arabic-using one.

Another group of documents which throws some light on the question of payments to the military are the letters of Qurra b. Sharīk, governor of Egypt.[53] Two long letters survive from the year 91/710 from the governor to the pagarch (Ar. *ṣaḥab* recte *ṣāḥib*) of Ashqaw (Gr. Aphrodito). In the first,[54] dated to February, he demands cash payments because it is time for him to pay the *'aṭā'* to the *jund* and their families (*'ayāl*) and it is time for the armies to set out (*khurūj al-*

juyūsh). In the second,[55] dated to August (i.e. after the harvest), he orders payments in cereals (*ta'ām*) to be made to the public granary (*al-hurī*) so that he can pay the *arzāq* of the *jund*. The *aṣḥāb* of the granaries will be in charge of receiving it. In this case it looks as if the *rizq* was an annual payment made at harvest time.

Despite similarities of language, the administrative system of Nessana in the 670s and Egypt in 710 were significantly different. In Nessana the villagers were ordered to pay specified amounts of produce directly to the leaders of local bedouin clans. Although the governor had ordered the payments, the produce was not sent to a government granary nor did the governor supervise its distribution. This was a local system which must have put substantial power into the lands of the clan chiefs and deprived the governor of direct authority. In Egypt, on the other hand, the process of collection and distribution was centralised. Both money and grain are forwarded to the governor and it is he who arranges the distribution. He may or may not have done this through clan chiefs, but the ultimate responsibility lay with him.

There are various explanations for these differences. One is that the administrative reforms of 'Abd al-Malik had imposed a more centralised system or it may have been that Egypt always had a more centralised system than southern Palestine. In Palestine, the bedouin recipients of the *rizq* were probably dispersed in their camping grounds whereas in Egypt they were congregated in the capital of Fusṭāṭ. In both cases, however, the papyrus documents give us clear indications of administrative mechanisms which the narrative sources do not.

Puin[56] has drawn attention to a number of Arabic papyrus fragments, mostly of Egyptian origin, which seem to be part of *dīwān*s – or, at least, of lists of Arabic names. The most important[57] gives short lists of names headed by what appear to be sums of money '*wa fī sittīn*' (and in 60) which may imply that the names listed below (Murra b. Abī K . . ., Jund b. al-Athīr, Ḥalbas b. 'Abd . . ., Nawf b. Ṣa' . . ., 'Abd al-Raḥmān) were entitled to 60 *dīnār*s per year. Others appear under different figures. A second papyrus[58] is simply a list of names of heads of households (*manzal*) and others with a note of the numbers in their house. Puin suggests that this is the sort of list which might have been drawn up by the official described by Ibn 'Abd al-Ḥakam, going round the houses in the morning, noting new births and new arrivals so that they could be entered in the *dīwān*.[59]

The evidence of the papyri demonstrates that lists and records were kept but it may also suggest that the *dīwān* took a number of different forms in different places and that practice was more diverse than might appear from the literary sources.

The numismatic evidence[60]

The evidence of the written sources makes it clear that large amounts of coined money were circulated in the collection of taxes and payment of the troops. If we speculate that 80 000 men on the *dīwān* of Basra were paid no more than the minimum of 200 *dirhams* per year, it would require a total of 16 million *dirhams* per year to service the system. If an overall estimate of 300 000 men on the *dīwān* in the whole Caliphate is even approximately correct, we would be talking about at least 60 million *dirhams* or their equivalent being required. Of course, the system is unlikely to have worked as neatly as this and many men may have been paid less than their due, paid in kind or not paid at all. On the other hand some, possibly quite large numbers, received more than the minimum.

Whatever the exact figures, it is clear that early Islamic administration needed vast amounts of coined money to function, and this impression of a cash-rich society is supported by the large numbers of surviving specimens. Furthermore, it could be argued that the payment of the army was the main reason for the minting of very large volumes of coin. This is not the place for a general survey of early Islamic coinage but it is worth examining whether the numismatic evidence can tell us anything about the organisation and payment of the Muslim armies.

The numismatic evidence, however, presents a number of problems. The Sasanian and Byzantine Empires had had very different monetary systems. In the Sasanian empire, the silver drachm, which evolved into the Arabic *dirham*, was the typical coin. These were minted up until the Muslim conquest and the Muslims took over an active tradition of coin-making. In the Byzantine-controlled areas, the principal coins were the gold *nomismata*. However, since these were too valuable for many everyday transactions, they were supplemented by copper *folles*. Whereas in the East, the Muslims took over Sasanian mints, or at least the cities where Sasanian coins had been minted, by the time of the Muslim conquest, Byzantine coin production had been largely concentrated in Constantinople, so no local mints or moneyers came under the conquerors' control.

The early Muslims did not immediately start to mint coins bearing the slogans of the new dispensation or the titles of its rulers. The introduction of a new, specifically Islamic coinage, was slow and happened in some areas much sooner than in others. The first Muslim coins were minted in provinces of the former Sasanian empire. The earliest surviving specimens seem to date from 31/651–2 (that is, from the Caliphate of 'Uthmān). They continued to bear Sasanian royal portraits and are almost indistinguishable from the coins of the Shahs Khusrau II or Yazdgard III except that they have small Arabic inscriptions, typically, *bi'smillāh* (in the name of Allah) or simply the guarantee word *jayyid* (good). From the time of Mu'āwiya on there are Arab–Sasanian coins which bear the date, the name of the Caliph or governor and the place of minting,[61] though sometimes, especially with the name of the mint, secure identification is not always possible.[62] There are also a significant number of coins bearing the name of Ziyād b. Abī Sufyān, giving some credence to the descriptions in the literary sources of his importance in the establishment of administrative system. In Iraq and the East, then, there were established mints before the accession of 'Abd al-Malik. If the system of payment of troops described by al-Balādhurī reflects historical reality, then the minting of coins to service it was essential. If, as he suggests, some people paid taxes in kind because they did not have access to *dirhams*,[63] then there was clearly an unmet demand for more coinage.

These early coins can also be useful for determining the course of political events, notably the succession of governors in various areas; the coins in the name of the Kharijite leader al-Qaṭarī b. al-Fujā'a minted in Fārs and Sistan between 69 and 75 (688–695)[64] provide useful confirmation of the rebellion extensively described in the literary sources.

When we come to look at the coinage of early Umayyad Syria, the position is very different. In fact, there is no evidence that any coins were minted by the Muslim rulers in Syria before 72/692 in the reign of 'Abd al-Malik.[65] However improbable it seems at first sight, the inescapable conclusion of the evidence is that the Muslims of Syria depended on the residue of Byzantine coins from the period before the conquests, imports, mostly coppers, from the Byzantine empire and *dirhams* brought as taxation from Iraq. It is hardly conceivable that the Syrian army would have been paid regular *'aṭā'* without coins being produced to make this possible and, in fact, there is no clear evidence of a *dīwān* system existing in Syria before the time of 'Abd al-Malik. The absence of Muslim coinage adds substance to the impression of a very rudimentary fiscal system in the area. The establishment of mints in Syria for the first time, in the reign of 'Abd al-Malik, may be connected with the introduction of regular payments to the increasingly professional Syrian army.

From 74/693–4, 'Abd al-Malik began a radical currency reform, probably employing moneyers from Iraq, newly conquered by the Umayyad armies. This introduced a standard Islamic coinage. After a brief experiment with representative images, notably the 'standing Caliph' types, in 77/696 a purely epigraphic coinage was introduced. However, the two currency zones, silver in the East and gold and copper in the West, still remained (though some silver *dirhams* were minted in Damascus). Different types of coins are the bearers of different sorts of information. In Syria and Egypt the gold *dīnārs* bear dates but neither the name of the ruler nor the place of minting is given, though it is usually assumed that it must have been Damascus. The post-reform copper coinage usually gives the name of the mint and we find that coppers were struck in some 16 mints in Syria, Palestine and the Jazīra. A few *fulūs* also give the name of the governor or Caliph. *Dirhams* minted in the East after the currency reforms of 'Abd al-Malik are more reticent than ones minted before, but they do still give the date and the name of the mint.[66] Neither *dīnārs* or *dirhams* give the name of the Caliph or governor.

The relationship between the minting of coins and the payment of the army is not simple. Two possible models can be envisaged. In one the tax-payers contribute their produce and valuables to the mint and they are either sold or melted down to make coin to pay the taxes. In the other model, the government sells, melts down or re-coins the taxes in order to pay the troops when required – and, of course, for other government purposes. In the first case, the mints are likely to be where the tax-payers are concentrated, in the second, where the troops are concentrated. In practice, of course, both systems must have operated in different times and in different places.

In addition, coins may have been minted on campaign as an efficient way of distributing booty among the victorious troops. Some indication of how this happened can be seen in the accounts of the conquest of Baykand (Paykent, Uzbekistan, 60 km south west of Bukhārā on the road to the old Oxus crossing at Amul/Charjui). Baykand was a rich commercial city whose merchants travelled to China to do business, and the booty taken from the treasury included 'innumerable vessels of gold and silver and a huge golden idol. Qutayba ordered that this be melted down and 150 000 *dīnār*s were extracted from it'.[67] These were presumably distributed to the troops for they spent vast sums on weapons, clothes and riding animals, and swords and coats of mail were sold for fantastic prices. The account seems to show de-thesaurisation of precious metals, the minting of coins, presumably to make distribution easier, and the consequent emergence of a vibrant market for military equipment. It is not entirely clear that the coins were minted on the spot but if they were, as seems probable, what mint name would they have carried: Marw?

The names of the *dirham* mints of the East give some idea of the centres of government administrative activity. Especially interesting are the mints in the decade 90–100 (708–19), the latter part of al-Ḥajjāj's governorate and that of his immediate successors. At this time, some 20 mints were in regular operation in the East. These can be divided into two main groups; the first in those in southern Iraq and Khuzistan, Wāsiṭ, Junday-Sābūr, Nahr Tīrā, Sūs, al-Ahwāz, Manādhir, Surraq and Dastawā,[68] which were probably chosen because they were revenue-collecting centres in rich agricultural areas. The second group are places in Iran and its borderlands, Rayy, Isfahan, Hamadhan, in Khurāsān, Sarakhs, Marw and Herat, Sistan, Kirman, and in Fārs, Isṭakhr, Darābjird and Bishapur.[69] It is at least plausible that these mint sites also represent the towns were garrisons were established by al-Ḥajjāj in the aftermath of the great revolts which had challenged Umayyad control and that each of these places was the *maktab* for a body of troops. Coins would be minted specifically to pay the *'aṭā'* of the soldiers in the area. It is also possible that the word *fī* (in) which appears before the number of the year in many early post-reform *dirhams*,[70] should actually be read as *fay'*, meaning that this coin was minted as part of the *fay'* for the relevant year. It is noticeable that neither Kūfa nor Basra appear in this list of mints, another sign that their role as centres of government had been taken over by the Syrian garrison town of Wāsiṭ.

Mints need not have been either permanent or static. Bates has convincingly argued[71] that the mints which produced coins ascribed to Armenia, Azerbayjān and other towns in the Jazīra and the Caucasus are simply one mint which moved with the powerful governors of the area; coins were minted when and where they were required and the mint name changed accordingly. Furthermore, the places and dates of minting bear a significant correlation with the known dates of military campaigns and government activity.[72]

After the accession of Ḥishām in 105/724 the policy changed: as al-Maqrīzī, writing much later put it, 'When Ḥishām b. 'Abd al-Malik succeeded, being fond of money, be ordered Khālid b. 'Abd Allāh al-Qasrī [governor of Iraq] . . . to withdraw the dies [*sikak*] from all the towns except Wāsiṭ and he struck *dirhams* only in Wāsiṭ.'[73] Once again the numismatic evidence bears out the written account. Only Wāsiṭ and Damascus in the East[74] are known to have minted coins, at least until the accession of Marwān II in 127/744 when the minting of coins began in Ḥarrān, reflecting his transfer of power to the Jazīra and, no doubt, his need to pay the new troops he was raising. It is quite unclear how the vast sums of money required were distributed from Wāsiṭ to the various places of payment.

The administration of the dīwān in the Umayyad period

The system said to have been established by 'Umar remained the basis for the payment of the armies of the Caliphs throughout the Umayyad and early 'Abbasid period. It is clear, however, that the system was constantly evolving and that the way in which it was put into practice varied at different times and in different places.

The administration of the *dīwāns* seems to have remained in the provincial *amṣār*, though Wāsiṭ replaced Kūfa and Basra after 'Abd al-Malik's take-over of Iraq in 82/701. There is a tradition that the *dīwān* (of Iraq) was burned at the time of the defeat of the rebellion of Ibn al-Ash'ath at Dayr al-Jamājim in that year[75] but the *dīwān* concerned was a record of state lands and the list of those entitled to *'aṭā'* may or may not have perished at the same time.

The narrative sources provide some further information about the operation of the *dīwān* in Iraq.[76] The *dīwāns* in Basra, Kūfa and Syria were probably written in Arabic from the beginning.[77] Ziyād b. Abī Sufyān, later to be governor himself, rose in the service of successive governors because of his position in charge of the *dīwān* and taxation. The lists needed to be updated when the *muqātila* were mobilised. In 37/657–8 'Alī instructed the *ashrāf* of Kūfa to produce up-to-date lists of all those in their tribes and their adult sons and their *mawālī* and slaves.

In al-Balādhurī's *Ansāb al-ashrāf* there is a long account of the administration of Ziyād b. Abī Sufyān in Iraq (45–53/665–673).[78] This is an attempt by a historian of the third/ninth century to reconstruct the earliest phases of Muslim administration. How far it represents what actually happened is, of course, conjectural, but it does at least demonstrate what later Muslims believed had been (or ought to have been) the practice. He quotes report from al-Madā'inī saying that Ziyād collected 60 000 000 *dirhams* from the Basra province.[79] Of these, 36 000 000 were spent on the salaries of the *muqātila*, 16 000 000 on provisions for their children, 2 000 000 on the expenses of government, 2 000 000 were retained in the treasury for contingencies and 4 000 000 were forwarded to Mu'āwiya. 40 000 000 were collected from Kūfa, of which a similar proportion was forwarded to Mu'āwiya. Obviously these are round figures and have been schematised but the point is clear: the overwhelming bulk of the revenues collected were to be distributed among the Muslims of Kūfa and Basra.

The other area in which we are given details about the early operation of a *dīwān* is Egypt.[80] The local historian al-Kindī says that the *dīwān* in Egypt went through a number of editions; 'the first *dīwān* was produced by 'Amr b. al-'Āṣ [in his first term as governor, 38–43/658–63], the second by 'Abd al-'Azīz b. Marwān [65–86/685–705], the third by Qurra b. Sharīk [90–6/709–14] and the fourth by Bishr b. Ṣafwān [101–2/720–1]. After that there is nothing to record except that in the time of the Caliph Ḥishām [109/727–8] the Qays [elements of whom had been settled in the Ḥawf region] were included in the *dīwān*.'[81] In Egypt at least, we have a picture of a register whose membership was fairly stable and was passed down within the same groups until the effective abolition of the Egyptian *dīwān* in the reign of al-Mu'taṣim.[82] The payments in Egypt were to be made in gold *dīnārs* and 'Amr is said to have received special instructions as to who was to get the highest payments of 200 a year, including 'Amr himself 'because of your position as Amir'.[83]

As in Iraq, the establishment of the *dīwān* was linked to the foundation of a new garrison city, at Fusṭāṭ and the organisation of the register, like the settlement of the conquerors, was on modified tribal grounds. It appears from the papyrological evidence at least, that the registers were kept in Greek rather than Arabic.[84] By the reign of Mu'āwiya, we are told that there were 40 000 names in the Egyptian register, of whom 4000 were receiving the highest payment of 200 *dīnārs*.[85]

Evidence about the payment of troops in Syria is almost entirely lacking.[86] 'Alī claimed that the Syrians supported Mu'āwiya without being paid.[87] This may have been no more than a debating point but it may suggest that the system was less developed than in Iraq. The absence of minting in Syria before the time of 'Abd al-Malik may point in the same direction and suggest that the *ahl al-Shām* were dependent for their subsistence on more local and informal arrangements like those shown in the Nessana papyri.

There are varying accounts of the timing of these payments.[88] According to some, the *'aṭā'* was paid every year in Muḥarram (the first month of the Muslim year) and the children were paid their allowances in Ramaḍan. Another account says that the *muqātila* were paid just before Ramadan, 'so that they filled their houses with everything sweet and sour' and the children at the time of the pilgrimage. A later account explains that some of the money was held back and distributed as a *ma'ūna* at the times of the great festivals: each family received 100 *dirhams* at the 'Īd al-Fiṭr (at the end of Ramaḍan) and 50 at the 'Īd al-Aḍḥā (at the time of the Ḥajj).[89]

Muṣ'ab b. al-Zubayr paid his troops fighting the Khārijīs, their *rizq* every month and their *'aṭā'* every year.[90] In Basra, however, he made himself very popular by making a practice of paying the *'aṭā'* twice a year,[91] but this was clearly exceptional. Under al-Ḥajjāj payment seems to have been made before the troops set out on campaign: in 80/699 he mustered the army of 20 000 Kūfans and 20 000 Basrans which he was sending to Sistan under the command of Ibn al-Ash'ath. He paid their *'aṭā'* in full (*kamalan*) and ordered them to equip themselves with horses and full arms. Bonus payments were given to those who were particularly well equipped by 'Abd al-Raḥmān al-Thaqafī, who was reviewing the troops.[92] The papyrus evidence quoted above suggests that troops in Egypt were paid cash in the spring, before they set out on campaign, and received *rizq* after the harvest, but there may have been other payments which we do not know about.

In the reign of Yazīd III (126/744), at the end of the Umayyad period, the people of Ḥoms said that they would give their allegiance to anyone who would pay their *'aṭā'* 'from Muḥarram to Muḥarram' and that they should be given allowances for their male children.[93] In the speech Yazīd made on his accession, he is said to have promised to pay the *'aṭā'* every year and the *rizq* every month[94]. It may be the case that men on active service were paid their wages in advance before they set out. This may be what is meant when the sources speak of *'aṭā'* being paid 'in full' (*kamalan*).[95] While not on active service, those in the *dīwān* would be paid their (probably reduced) salaries once a year.

There is little information about the mechanisms for payment of cash salaries: in the way of things, the sources do not describe normal processes, and from this period we have no description of a pay-day, how it worked, who exactly distributed the money, where it was distributed and how the *dīwān* lists were checked. Morony discusses the evidence from Iraq[96] and notes that Ziyād had a *qubba* (dome), from which he used to review the *jund*[97] and they may have been paid at this time. Ziyād's chamberlain, 'Ajlān said that he had distributed 2 000 000 *dirhams* and 2000 swords in the course of a morning.[98] When 'Ubayd Allāh b. Ziyād was trying to rally support in Basra after the death of Yazīd I, he ordered that all the money in the treasury (*bayt māl*) should be distributed. He announced to the people that this was their *fay'* and that they should take it for their *'aṭā'* and the *arzāq* of their dependants. He ordered the clerks to draw up the lists of names and to be quick about it, ordering someone to supervise them as they worked in the *dīwān* into the night by candlelight. In the end, Ibn Ziyād decided not to distribute the money.[99] Already by this date (64/683–4), the *dīwān* appears to have been a building as well as a register and was staffed by a group of secretaries (*kataba*).

Other forms of payment

Cash payments seem to have formed the major part of the incomes of most of those in the *dīwāns* but they might also be given *rizq* (from the middle Persian *rozik*, meaning daily rations). One of al-Balādhurī's sources describing Ziyād's administration in Iraq claimed, 'we never saw a new moon [which marked the beginning of the month], without going to the *dār al-rizq* and taking supplies for our families, for taxes were collected in kind from those who were short of [*'ajiza 'an*] *dirhams* and the storehouses were full because of that'.[100] Ziyād urged those entitled to collect their rations in person because the servants they sent to do it were pilfering some of them on the way home.[101] Another account says that payments in grain were made at the beginning of Ramaḍan.[102] Ziyād is said to have recruited 500 shaykhs of Basra into his court (*saḥāba*) and given them a *rizq* of between 300 and 500 *dirhams*: whether the *rizq* was a cash payment, or simply the cash value of supplies, is not clear.[103] There was a depôt (*qaryat al-rizq* or *dār al-rizq*) in Basra by 36/656 and the *dār al-rizq* in Kūfa is first attested in 76/695–6.[104]

As we have seen, the evidence of the papyri shows that payments in kind were important in both Palestine and Egypt. In the early ʻAbbasid period, Ibn al-Muqaffaʻ was urging that some of the payments to the army should be made in foodstuffs and fodder to counter the effect of price fluctuations.[105] The use of the term *rizq*, however, does not always imply payment in kind and by the third/ninth century the term had replaced *ʻaṭā'* as the normal word for cash salaries.

We also hear of payments called *maʻūna* (assistance).[106] This was sometimes paid as a gratuity to those not getting *ʻaṭā'* or as a supplement. As has already been noted, Ziyād is supposed to have paid a *maʻūna* to the troops at the great Muslim festivals.[107] When Yazīd b. Muʻāwiya was trying to recruit an army to suppress the rebellion of Ibn al-Zubayr in Madīna in 62/681–2, he offered to pay the *ʻaṭā'* in full (*kamalan*) and give each man a *maʻūna* of 100 *dīnārs*, cash in hand. With such a generous bonus on offer, it is not surprising that 12 000 men are said to have hastened to join up.[108] The *maʻūna* could be paid more regularly. In the long struggles against the Khārijīs in southern Iran, the terrain was harsh, the enemy fierce and there was little prospect of booty: troops had to have generous inducements to serve. In 68/687–8 Muṣʻab b. al-Zubayr, then governor of Iraq, lamented that , in addition to their *rizq* and *ʻaṭā'*, he paid them a *maʻūna* every year, which was equivalent to their stipends and, despite this generosity, they were unable to defeat the rebels.[109] When al-Ḥasan b. Qaḥṭaba was rebuilding Malatya on the Byzantine frontier in the early ʻAbbasid period, he increased the *ʻaṭā'* of the soldiers stationed in this dangerous spot and gave them a *maʻūna*, in this case it would seem, a one off-payment, of 100 *dīnārs*.[110] It seems, then that the *maʻūna* of the Umayyad and early ʻAbbasid period was a bonus payment, not presumably established in the *dīwān*.

The conflict over the surplus (*faḍl*)

As already noted, the question of the distribution of the surplus revenue (*faḍl*) remained controversial.[111] The question of whether any surplus after the payment of salaries and other expenses should be distributed among the people of the province or taken by the government was important in itself, but it also directly related to the question of the ownership and control of the *fay'*.

This conflict of views comes out clearly in the confusion which followed the death of the Caliph Yazīd in 64/683. Various parties attempted to compete for the allegiance of the Iraqis. Ibn al-Zubayr's governor in Kūfa, Ibn Muṭīʻ attempted to win them over with a series of promises. He said that he was instructed to collect the revenue from their *fay'* and distribute it among them. Any surplus (*faḍl*) could be removed from the province only with their consent. In doing so he was following the procedures established by ʻUmar and continued by ʻUthmān.[112]

However, these concessions were not enough for some of the more militant of his audience. Their spokesman demanded that they should follow the conduct (*sīra*) of ʻAlī and that any surplus should be divided among them as of right. They were having nothing to do with the practice of ʻUthmān and even the practice of

'Umar, though better, was not sufficient. This was a clear polemical position, that the Caliph and his representatives have no right to interfere in the distribution of the income at all. We can also see how this point of view is attached to one particular figure, 'Alī: allegiance to 'Alī in early Islamic Iraq was not simply a question of sentiment in favour of the House of the Prophet, it was also a position on a major fiscal issue.

Ibn Muṭī' was driven out by the rebellion of al-Mukhtār b. Abī 'Ubayd in the name of Muḥammad b. al-Ḥanafiya, a son of 'Alī. Al-Mukhtār stood for the retention of the revenues in Iraq and the distribution among those who were entitled. The Umayyad conquest of Iraq and the effective demilitarisation of the Iraqi *muqātila*, probably meant that more revenues were taken to Damascus – though, of course, the Syrian garrison in Wāsiṭ now had to be paid from the Iraqi *fay'*.

How much money was ever actually transferred to the central government is problematic. As we have already seen only about 7 per cent of the revenues of Iraq had been transferred to Mu'āwiya during Ziyād's governorate. Al-Ḥajjāj had won the battle for the *faḍl* in Iraq and while locals might dream of restoring what they held to be the *sīra* of 'Alī, it is likely that any extra revenue was taken to Damascus. As might be expected, al-Ḥajjāj seems to have been efficient at this and when the Caliph Sulaymān appointed Yazīd b. al-Muhallab as governor, he was afraid he would not be able to match the amounts which had been forwarded by his illustrious predecessor. In the end he employed an accountant who arranged to pay the *'atā'* of the local (Syrian) troops but otherwise kept the governor's expenditure under strict control.[113] In 123/741 al-Ḥakam b. al-Ṣalt brought revenues from Iraq to the Caliph Ḥishām[114] and later Yusūf b. 'Umar was under great pressure to forward more money to the Caliph al-Walīd II to pay the Umayyad family and the *'atā'* of the Syrian troops.[115]

The position in Egypt is equally uncertain. In the time of Mu'āwiya, we are told, the governor paid the people of the *dīwān* their salaries, the salaries of their families, their supplies (*arzāq*), their *nawā'ib*, the *nawā'ib* of those who looked after the bridges (?), the rations of the clerks and those who transported the grain to the Hijaz. This left only 600 000 *dīnār*s to be sent to the Caliph. It seems unlikely that 'Abd al-'Azīz b. Marwān sent anything to his brother the Caliph 'Abd al-Malik, during his long period as governor. In the reign of Sulaymān the local financial administrator was claiming that the money he was bringing to the Caliph was ruining the country.[116] It is unlikely that significant quantities of money were forwarded from Khurāsān which, according to the locals, did not produce enough revenue to cover its own costs without booty from continuing conquests.[117]

The disposal of surpluses remained a live issue until the end of the Umayyad Caliphate. When Yazīd III made his famous speech in 126/744 to attract the support of the Syrians, he pledged that if there was a surplus (*faḍl*) he would not transfer it from one town to another until the frontier (*thughr*) had been secured and the needs of its garrison (*masāliḥ*) met; after that, the surplus would be returned to a neighbouring town which was more needy until all the Muslims had an equal share.[118] He was clearly attempting to attract support by returning to the old idea of *fay'* as the property of the Muslims who were entitled to it, but his policies seem to have aroused strong opposition among some groups, notably the people of Ḥoms, who had probably benefited from the privileged position of the Syrians.

From pension to salary

Another important issue was whether membership of the *dīwān* and the receipt of salaries should be a right enjoyed by the conquerors and their descendants or whether it was a payment contingent on military service. Once again, because of the nature of the sources, we know most about the conflicts which occurred in Iraq on this issue. It is clear that many of the Muslims in Iraq claimed the revenues of the province as their *fay'* and held that they, and they alone, were entitled to the revenues it generated.

But this in turn gave rise to a furious debate about who in Iraq was entitled. Al-Mukhtār depended for much of his support on new converts, the *mawālī* and, as we have seen, there was a body of tradition which claimed that 'Umar himself had decided on the rights of the *mawālī* to be inscribed in the *dīwān*. This aroused the fierce opposition of the *ashrāf* of Kūfa who complained that their rightful income was being distributed to their *mawālī* and their slaves were disobeying them. Their orphans and widows would suffer want as a result.[119] There is no mention in this argument of military service as a qualification for a share of the revenues; they were talking about old-established rights. In the end, the conflict between the *ashrāf* and al-Mukhtār brought down his regime and was a major factor in the Umayyad conquest of Iraq shortly afterwards.

After the Umayyad take-over of Iraq, their governors, notably al-Ḥajjāj, were insistent that payment of the *'aṭā'* was dependent on willingness to do military service. It was, in fact, to be a soldier's salary rather than a pension. This took place against the background of the war against the Khārijīs in Khuzistan and Fārs. When in 74/693–4 the men of Kūfa refused to fight and simply returned home, the Umayyad governor, Khālid b. 'Abd Allāh wrote to them saying that they had a duty to join the *jihād* against the rebels. If they did not, then they incurred the wrath of Allāh and they were liable to physical punishment, confiscation of their wealth, cancellation of their *'aṭā'* and exile.[120]

Khālid was not strong enough to make his threats effective but when al-Ḥajjāj b. Yūsuf arrived, he made it clear that he would pursue the same policy with much more vigour. From the beginning he showed that he was going to force the Kūfans and Basrans to join al-Muhallab in the campaign against the rebels. He ordered the *'arīf*s to make sure they complied.[121] Meanwhile, al-Muhallab was given the power and the money to set up a *dīwān* and pay those who actually joined his army and did the fighting.[122]

Al-Ḥajjāj made repeated efforts to enforce military service on the Kūfans, especially in the campaigns against the Khārijīs in central Iraq, ordering those in charge of the *dīwān* and the *'arīf*s to look through the lists and find the men.[123] In 77/696–7, when Kūfa itself was threatened by the rebels, he again threatened them, urging the Kūfans to defend their lands and their *fay'* and promising that if they did not, he would find others to fight their enemies and that these others would 'eat your *fay*".[124] In the end, the Kūfans proved unable to defeat the Khārijīs and it was the Syrians who re-established Umayyad power.[125] The foundation of the city of Wāsiṭ soon after meant that al-Ḥajjāj had implemented his threat: the *fay'* of Iraq was now used to feed the Syrian garrison. Subsequent attempts by the followers of Ibn al-Ash'ath, Yazīd b. al-Muhallab and Zayd b. 'Alī to restore the *fay'* to the Iraqis, or even to resurrect the old concept of *fay'*, were doomed to failure.[126] By the end of 'Abd al-Malik's reign in Iraq, and probably everywhere else in the Caliphate with the possible exception of Egypt and Madīna, the *dīwān* was a register of troops and the *'aṭā'* or *rizq* was paid for military service. The Umayyad state now boasted a professional army.[127]

In 88/707 the Caliph al-Walīd demanded soldiers from Madīna to participate in the campaigns on the Byzantine frontier. He demanded (*ḍaraba 'alayhim al-ba'th*), 2000 men but only 1500 set out while 500 remained and subsidised the others.[128] It seems as if the people of Madīna were seldom required to do military service at all, and it may be that an exception was made in this case because it was a holy war against the Byzantines.

It is not clear how long the stratified system of payments which seems to have characterised the original *dīwān* remained in existence. Ḥujr b. 'Adī, a participant in the early conquests who launched a rebellion against Mu'āwiya's government in 51/671–2, had had an *'aṭā'* of 1500 because of his participation in the early conquests.[129] When 'Abd al-Malik was receiving the oaths of allegiance from the Kūfan tribes after his conquest of Iraq in 71/691 he found one man being paid an *'aṭā'* of 700 *dirham*s and another 300 and ordered the clerks to reverse the payment, though this was a reward for knowledge of poetry rather than military prowess.[130] In Khurāsān in 110/729–30 men were said to be receiving 300 or 600 *dirhams*.[131] It would seem that at this stage, differential salaries were still paid but, as the *'aṭā'* was transformed into a payment for military service rather than a pension, differentials based on the *sābiqa* of the ancestors must have become irrelevant and been phased out. When the Syrians were established as a garrison on Wāsiṭ they were paid more than the Iraqis because they were the government's élite troops, not because of any priority in Islam. Ashtor, quoting al-Mas'ūdī, suggests that the standard rate of pay of Syrian troops in Umayyad times was eight *dīnār*s (or approximately 100 *dirhams*) per month.[132] Al-Walīd II is said to have increased this by ten *dirham*s but this increase was then cancelled by his sucessor Yazīd III, known as 'al-Nāqiṣ' ('the Reducer') as a result.[133] By contrast, the Caliph Ḥishām who presumably enjoyed the highest rate of *'atā'*, had 200 *dīnār*s.[134]

By the end of the Umayyad period, it was generally accepted that the *'aṭā'* was in fact, a salary, a payment for military service. This was a development of the greatest importance. It meant that the Umayyads, and the 'Abbasids after them, had a professional army at their disposal rather than relying on the goodwill of a hereditary caste of *muqātila*. It also confirmed the growing distinction between military and civilian Muslims. Their fiscal status, as much as their equipment and duties, meant that the military were now a separate and definable group in Muslim society. It becomes possible to speak of the Muslim army, rather than the Muslim community in arms.

The payment of troops in the early 'Abbasid period

In early 'Abbasid times, troops serving the government continued to have there names entered in a *dīwān* and to be paid *'aṭā'*. This was now seen as a salary and the concept of *fay'*, as a hereditary resource, which had caused so much dispute in the Umayyad period, was effectively dead. Almost as soon as the 'Abbasid movement became an open rebellion in Khurāsān, Abū Muslim arranged that a new *dīwān* was to be established and a clerk (*kātib*) was sent to the camps to register new recruits. This was done on a new system. Instead of men being registered in tribal groups, the new 'Abbasid *dīwān* listed them according to the villages they had come from.[135] No doubt this was partly because many of the new recruits were local people with no Arab tribal affiliations but it was also a first step to create an *ahl Khurāsān* (people/army of Khurāsān) to rival the *ahl al-Shām* and to put an end to the tribal rivalries which had so divided the Muslims of the province in Umayyad times.

In early 'Abbasid times there seems to have been a gradual move to the monthly payment of salaries, as opposed to the annual distribution of of the Umayyad period. Ibn al-Muqaffa' urged the early 'Abbasids to pay salaries every three or four months on a clearly stated day.[136] However, figures for normal rates of pay are rarely given in the sources. There is a report that Abū Muslim paid the first recruits to the 'Abbasid cause three or four *dirhams* each,[137] but it is not clear what period this was for and it may have simply been a one-off donative. After the victory of the 'Abbasid troops over the Umayyad Caliph Mārwan II in 132/750, the Caliph al-Saffāḥ ordered that members of the victorious army should be given donatives of 500 *dirhams* and that their salaries (*arzāq*) should be raised to 80.[138] This is almost certainly the rate per month,[139] and such evidence as there is suggests that between 60 and 80 per month was a normal rate for regular members of the 'Abbasid forces. This compares with the one or two *dirhams* per day (that is up to 60 *dirhams* per month for skilled men) which labourers employed in the building of Baghdad were paid. The evidence collected by Ashtor[140] suggests that soldiers were paid on about the same level as skilled workers and teachers, although the evidence is very fragmentary and much of it found only in much later sources. At the other end of the spectrum, Ziyād b. 'Ubayd Allāh al-Ḥārithi, a maternal uncle of the Caliph al-Saffāḥ, was offered 2500 *dirhams* per month as governor of Mawṣil[141] and the singer Ibrāhīm al-Mawṣilī collected 4000 *dirhams* in salary (*arzāq*) in his glory days.[142] No doubt other senior members of the élite earned as much, if not more.

It was only exceptional events that caught the notice of the chroniclers. Years after the event, ‘Umar b. Ḥafṣ remembered his father paying troops who had come from Syria in post-haste in groups of ten to help al-Manṣūr against the rebellion of Ibrāhīm the ‘Alid in 145/762–3, ‘I would hold the lamp for him while he paid them by night. I was a young lad at the time.’[143] It is easy to imagine the scene, the Caliph's agent doling out the silver *dirhams* at dead of night by the light of a flickering oil lamp, but this was a crisis situation and clearly not general practice.

We are best informed about the payment of troops in the garrisons on the Byzantine frontier who had a variety of different pay-scales. This was often simply an increase of ten *dīnār*s (120 *dirham*s) on the standard rate, as happened when Faraj b. Sulaym al-Khādim settled Tarsus in 172/788,[144] but there was considerable local variation in practice.

By the reign of al-Ma'mūn a number of small outposts had been established in the Cilician Plain.[145] There was Ḥiṣn ‘Ujayf, named after its founder ‘Ujayf b. ‘Anbaṣa, one of al-Ma'mūn's Iranian supporters, subsequently murdered in the purge which followed al-Mu‘taṣim's seizure of power in 218/833. Ḥiṣn ‘Ujayf ‘and its towers’ (*abrijatahu*), had a garrison (*rasm*) of four horsemen, three guards (*ḥarās*), three foot-soldiers and a preacher (*khaṭīb*). The commander had a salary (*rizq*) of ten *dīnār*s, the horsemen two, the foot-soldiers and guards one and the preacher two. There were other outposts, Burj al-Waṣīfī with eight foot-soldiers, Burj al-Manshā with six, Burj al-Maqṭa‘ with 15 and Burj al-Jazīrī with seven. In all of these the *ra'īs* (chief) was paid a *dīnār* and 1/6 (say, 14 *dirhams*) and the rest a *dīnār*. These figures seem fairly low compared with rates quoted elsewhere but they correspond almost exactly with the rates paid to skilled artisans in Egypt as recorded by the contemporary Aphrodito papyri.[146] It may be that these were local people essentially serving as part-time soldiers.

Further East on the Jazīra frontier there were also permanent garrisons. Al-Manṣūr settled 4000 men from the Jazīra in Malatya after it had been rebuilt following its destruction by the Byzantines. Once again each member of the garrison received 10 *dīnār*s' increase to his *‘aṭā'*. There was also 100 *dīnār*s' *ma‘ūna*.[147] When al-Ḥadath was rebuilt in 169/785–6, 4000 troops were settled there, each being given 40 *dīnār*s as *‘aṭā'* and a cash bonus of 300 *dirham*s each. They were also given places to live (*aqṭa‘ahum al-masākin*). These figures, if correct, suggest that troops who were prepared to serve in the frontier garrisons could command higher rates of pay than those in Baghdad or some more peaceful area.

As often when investigating early Islamic administrative systems from essentially narrative sources, we are much better informed about unusual and difficult periods, After Hārūn's death, there began a long period of civil war, when various parties competed to attract the loyalty of the soldiers. The problem was that after the treasure amassed by Hārūn had been dissipated, it was difficult for the competing parties to raise the necessary sums from the ravaged countryside to pay them.

On his accession in 193/809, al-Amīn ordered that the troops be given a bonus of 24 months' salary.[148] This was not the first time that an accession bonus (the so-called *māl al-bay'a*, money for taking the oath of allegiance) had been paid but this was exceptionally generous, reflecting the new Caliph's need for military support. His brother and rival al-Ma'mūn seems to have offered only 12 months' bonus at this stage.[149] Competition soon developed to win support from the other camp: al-Amīn offered a 12-month bonus to anyone who deserted al-Ma'mūn's cause. When 'Alī b. 'Īsā b. Māhān was recruiting men to join his army to march against al-Ma'mūn, he was allowed to pay 80 *dirhams*[150] and this became the competitive rate: as Ṭāhir's forces began to close in on Baghdad, al-Amīn was able to persuade 5000 of his men to desert by offering to establish them in the *dīwān* at 80 *dirhams*.[151] Shortly afterwards he recruited a whole group of new (and untrained) commanders (*quwwād*) gave them all a one-off gratuity of 500 *dirhams* and a bottle of perfume. This aroused considerable resentment among the regular soldiers, who were not given any *'aṭā'* at this stage and Ṭāhir, who was told of this by his agents in the city, persuaded many of the established military leaders to desert al-Amīn and come over to his side, promising them 80 (*dirhams*) *rizq* with double for the commanders and their sons.[152]

The death of al-Amīn and Ṭāhir's conquest of the city changed the position completely. As one of al-Ma'mūn's agents in Iraq, al-Ḥasan b. Abī Sa'īd, put it, 'Both armies, the army of Ṭāhir and the army of the people of Baghdad, regretted the killing of Muḥammad [al-Amīn] because of the amount of money they had been making'.[153] The victorious Ṭāhir, in fact, seems to have been unable or unwilling to pay his men at all and was faced with a mutiny and he had to borrow 20 000 *dīnār*s from a friend to give them four months' *rizq* and pacify them.

Large numbers of soldiers had been mobilised in the civil war between the brothers and many of these now found themselves unemployed and unpaid. One Abū'l-Sarāyā, an unemployed soldier, began a rebellion in Kūfa in the name of the 'Alids which attracted considerable support, probably mostly from people like himself. He briefly took over Kūfa and much of southern Iraq, even minting his own coins.[154] He was able to pay his cavalry 1000 *dirhams* and his foot-soldiers 500 as one-off payments,[155] but would probably not have been able to keep this up even if his rebellion had not collapsed.

Meanwhile Iraq was divided between the partisans of al-Ḥasan b. Sahl, who had replaced Ṭāhir as al-Ma'mūn's governor in Iraq and his enemies. Fighting dragged on for four years between the death of al-Amīn and the final arrival of al-Ma'mūn in Baghdad in 204/819. For most soldiers, the main concern was to find a commander who could pay them and ensure that their names were in the *dīwān* of whatever regime finally emerged from the chaos, but it was not easy. Constant warfare had destroyed much of the economy and made the collection of taxes very difficult. In 201/817 al-Ḥasan b. Sahl refused to pay the Ḥarbiya[156] troops of Baghdad anything, but was eventually pressured into agreeing to pay six months' arrears, though in the event he paid very little of this.[157] Another of al-Ma'mūn's commanders, 'Alī b. Hishām agreed to give six months' pay when the tax yields came in, with an advance of 50 *dirhams* to see them through Ramaḍan, but again he failed to deliver.[158]

On the other side, in so far as there were clearly defined sides, ʿĪsa b. Muḥammad b. Abī Khālid was able to offer his cavalry only 40 *dirhams* and his foot-soldiers 20, and by the end of the year 201/July 817 most of them were living off protection rackets and robbery.[159] When Ibrāhīm b. al-Mahdī made his ill-starred bid for the Caliphate he could offer prospective supporters only ten *dīnārs*, apparently as a one-off bonus, and even this could not be delivered until the beginning of the next year (Muḥarram, 202/July, 817).[160] When he led the prayers as Caliph for the first time, he promised the soldiers six months' *rizq*, but was unable to pay and, when they rioted, bought them off with 200 *dirhams* each. More ominously, 'he wrote [drafts] for some of them on the Sawad for the value of what they were owed in wheat and barley. They went out to take possession of that and carried off everything they came across as plunder. In this way they took two shares at once, the share of the local people and the share of the authorities (*sulṭān*).'[161]

This seems to have been the nadir of administrative collapse as the *jund* degenerated into banditry. Even when salaries were paid, it was done in very debased coin.[162] The next year, more resources seem to have become available on al-Ma'mūn's side. While the leader of the Baghdad troops, ʿĪsā b. Muḥammad b. Abī Khālid was once again protesting that he could not pay his men until the revenues (*ghullāt*) came in, Ḥumayd b. ʿAbd al-Ḥamīd, acting for al-Ma'mūn, was able to offer 50 *dirhams* in cash, upping it to 60 when the troops said that 50 was unlucky because ʿAlī b. Ḥishām had previously promised them that but had been unable to pay.[163] Not surprisingly, many of the troops were prepared to accept these terms. Ibrāhīm b. al-Mahdī was forced into hiding and the way was open for al-Ma'mūn to make his triumphal entry into Baghdad.

While the sources are not absolutely clear, it seems as if Ḥumayd's offer, and his ability to pay it, no doubt drawing on financial support from the Iranian provinces controlled by al-Ma'mūn, marked the effective end of the long struggles in Baghdad. In the compromise, the army of Baghdad, the once proud *Abnā'*[164] were once again assured their salaries, but at a reduced rate: the 80 *dirhams* they had enjoyed in the early stages of the war now being reduced to 60 in debased coin. It is arguable that when al-Ma'mūn entered Baghdad, he inherited a swollen, ill-disciplined, inefficient and underpaid army.

Qaṭīʿa and *iqṭāʿ*

In addition to salary payments, the military were also rewarded with plots of land (*qaṭīʿa, qaṭā'iʿ*).[165] This term is used in two quite separate senses in the second/eighth century evidence. As well as the housing lots given to soldiers, there were also more extensive land grants also referred to as *qaṭāʿi* and, on occasion, *iqṭāʿ* (which should not be confused with the later *iqṭāʿ* or fief). For the sake of clarity we will call the first sort garrison *qaṭā'iʿ* and the second sort agricultural *qaṭā'iʿ*.

Garrison qaṭā'i'

The historical sources describe the grant of *qaṭā'i'* to soldiers. The *qaṭā'i'* granted to the military in the Umayyad and early 'Abbasid period, had a number of characteristics. They were held in absolute ownership and could be inherited or sold, they were granted on a one-off basis as rewards for past conduct or to encourage men to move to new garrisons, they were urban, always being in cities or fortified towns, they were not given in lieu of salaries or as a source of income and, finally, they were recorded in written deeds (*sijillāt*). Many soldiers were not given them and they did not play any part in the normal system of payment. In many cases, the soldiers were given payments in cash or kind in addition to their *qaṭā'i'*.

Again, accounts of the settlement of troops on the Byzantine frontier provide us with some of the most detailed information. In 84 /703 'Abd al-Malik had established the first permanent garrison in the Cilician plain by settling 300 troops in al-Maṣṣīṣṣa. In early 'Abbasid times al-Saffāḥ raised (*faraḍa*) 400 troops and added them to the garrison (*shiḥna*) and gave them properties (*aqṭa'ahum*). Al-Manṣūr raised another 400. Later it is said that al-Manṣūr raised 1000 men and gave them properties (*qaṭā'i'*) and houses. Al-Mahdī raised another 2000 but gave them no properties because the city was already garrisoned.[166]

The settlement of Tarsus came slightly later. At the beginning of al-Rashīd's reign, he ordered that the ruined site be settled. The project was entrusted to Faraj b. Sulaym al-Khādim, who had a well-known house in Antioch and was later responsible for re-fortifying Adana. He went to Baghdad and recruited 3000 Khurāsānis as a first detachment (*nudba*) of the garrison. He later added 1000 men from Antioch and 1000 from al-Maṣṣīṣṣa. In addition to enhanced salaries, they were also given plots of land. The area to be developed, which lay between two rivers, was surveyed and divided into 4000 plots (*khiṭaṭ*) each one 20 × 20 cubits (say $13m^2$), and these were given to the men. Clearly this was enough to build a (small) house on but not enough to generate any revenue.[167] In Malatya, the Muslim garrison was built houses with two rooms on the upper and two rooms on the lower floor and a stable for each groups of 10–15 men, very much barrack accommodation.[168]

Al-Balādhurī reports the use of *qaṭā'i'* for encouraging settlement in other areas. The coastal cities of Syria and Palestine seem to have been settled by soldiers who were granted *qaṭā'i'* to build houses from the time of the Caliph 'Uthmān onwards, sometimes taking over abandoned properties.[169] 'Abd al-Malik settled troops in Ascalon.[170] In all these cases the *qaṭā'i'* seem to have been residential, rather than revenue-generating estates, though in an ambiguous note al-Balādhurī says that there was a granary (*hurī*,? from Latin horreum) in Ḥoms 'where wheat and oil were brought from/for coastal areas where the people had been given *qaṭā'i'* and documents (*sijillāt*) stating the terms'.[171] The implication of this is not clear but it may mean that they were obliged to pay dues in kind but more probably that the wheat and oil were in fact part of the *qaṭī'a*, i.e. a salary in kind.

We have good documentary information about one *qaṭīʿa* in Mawṣil.[172] This was given to one Wāʾil al-Shaḥḥājī. After the Umayyad Caliph Marwān had been defeated at the battle of the Zāb, Wāʾil had decided to join the ʿAbbasid forces in their pursuit of the fugitive Caliph. He later (146/763–4) served as chief of police in Mawṣil[173] but, apart from this, nothing more is known of his later life. The *qaṭīʿa* was granted to him by the ʿAbbasid Caliph al-Saffāḥ as a reward for this well-timed support. The text of the donation was preserved in the family and shown to the author by one of his descendants. The grant outlines the borders of the property and makes it clear that this was an absolute gift, a reward for past services, and indeed there is no evidence that the beneficiary, Wāʾil, ever formed part of a regular military force.

The most extensive use of the grant of *qaṭāʾiʿ* can be seen in the case of the foundation of Baghdad from 145/762 onwards. One of the great attractions of the site of Baghdad from the point of view of the Caliph al-Manṣūr was that it was a 'greenfield' site, if not necessarily a very verdant one. There were a few existing proprietors, whose rights seem to have been scrupulously protected, but in the main this was 'dead land' which could be brought to life by the development of new canals and of the new city. The capital inevitably became the biggest economic magnet in the Islamic world: it was above all to the capital that tax revenues were brought and that salaries and gifts were dispersed. It contained a large number of élite members of the new regime with very large disposable incomes. Below them was a professional class of secretaries and soldiers who formed a real salariat; they may not have been as wealthy as the élite, but they too needed to buy food and could indulge spending on non-essential items. It was not surprising, therefore, that merchants flocked to the capital and there were numerous and extensive markets, including one which specialised in textiles from Khurāsān, perhaps catering to the wants of homesick soldiers and officials newly settled in the West, and a book *sūq*, which had more than a hundred individual shops.[174]

There is no doubt that al-Manṣūr was well aware of the economic importance of the development of the new city. Among other things, it allowed him to distribute as *qaṭāʾiʿ*, at no cost to himself, plots of land which could prove valuable to their new owners. For the state and its *fonctionnaires*, this was a win–win situation and it undoubtedly contributed to the success of the early ʿAbbasid regime in retaining the loyalty of its supporters. While for many their *qatīʿa* in Baghdad may have amounted to little more than a residential plot in the booming capital city, for the lucky few it was valuable real estate.

Al-Yaʿqūbī's[175] list of the grantees of *qaṭāʾiʿ* shows a whole variety of concessions. It is clear that the members of the ʿAbbasid family and certain administrative officials, notably al-Rabīʿ b. Yūnus, the chamberlain, enjoyed the most extensive properties and al-Rabīʿ was able to develop his commercially and make vast sums. Other lots went to administrative officials like Muhājir b. ʿAmr, director of the Alms Office (*ṣāḥib dīwān al-ṣadaqāt*),[176] or Sulaym, *mawlā* of the Caliph and Director of the Tax Office (*ṣāḥib dīwān al-kharāj*).[177] Muhājir's plot was both residence and government office for the *dīwān* was based in his *qaṭī'a*, just outside the Kūfa Gate of the Round City. At a lower level were officials like Yāsīn, who was in charge of the camel stables,[178] or the secretaries from Anbar who worked in the tax office.[179]

Compared with the members of the royal family and the most privileged elements of the civil bureaucracy, military leaders did not receive over-generous treatment. Al-Musayyab b. Zuhayr al-Ḍabbī, chief of police (*ṣāḥib al-shurṭa*), probably the most important soldier in the capital, had a lot in a prominent position just outside the Kūfa Gate, where he had a house and a mosque 'with a tall minaret'.[180] Al-Ḥasan and Ḥumayd b. Qaḥṭaba, sons of the commander who had led the 'Abbasid armies at the time of the revolution, and both themselves important figures in the military, had a *rabaḍ* which was essentially a family compound with houses for themselves and their households.[181]

Many other soldiers lived in more modest circumstances, especially in the areas which came to be known as the Ḥarbiya, to the north-west of the Round City. Here we find lots for individuals but also whole groups from various districts in Khurāsān and Transoxania who stayed together like 'the people of Balkh, Marw, Khuttal, Bukhārā, and Isfijāb and the subjects of the Ishtākhanj and the Kābul-Shāh, each with their own *qā'id* and *ra'īs*' who lived in the Ḥarbiya quarter.[182] The Khwarazmians had their own *rabaḍ*[183] and there were *qaṭā'i'* for the people of Marwrūdh, led by the important family of Abū Khālid,[184] the Bukharans, who had a mosque with a green minaret,[185] the Kirmanis and Soghdians[186] and even the Afāriqa, from Ifrīqiya (Tunisia).[187]

The establishment of the second part of the city on the East Bank of the Tigris, was meant, at least in part, to provide the heir apparent, al-Mahdī, with the same opportunities for patronage as his father had enjoyed on the other side of the river. More *qaṭā'i'* were distributed, many to individual soldiers, like Khuzayma b. Khāzim al-Ṭamīmī, chief of police to al-Mahdī[188] and bureaucrats but none, apparently to groups as happened on the West Bank. Many soldiers, we are told, lived mingled with the rest of the population and the soldiers' houses (*manāzil al-jund*) lay alongside the houses of ordinary people and merchants.[189]

The *qaṭā'i'* granted in the development of Baghdad seem mostly to have been quite small, indeed al-Mahdī announced that he would not permit the building of large properties on the East Bank. Some people, like al-Rabī' seem to have been able to develop their lands as profitable urban real estate. For most, however, their *qaṭī'a* was simply a house for them and their family.

Agricultural qaṭā'i'

The term *qaṭī'a* is also used to describe much larger areas of agricultural land, especially in the Sawad of Iraq and the Euphrates valley, which were granted to members of the ruling family and other figures in the élite of the Caliphate. These *qaṭā'i'* and other estates were important sources of income for their owners. However, there is no record that such estates were granted as payments to the military, even to such senior figures as the family of Qaḥṭaba b. Shabīb. The evidence seems clear that the military lived off their salaries rather than their landholdings, an impression which is confirmed by their struggles to maintain a place in the *dīwān* during the wars which followed the death of Hārūn al-Rashīd.

In addition to the use of *qata'i* and other sorts of landed property as rewards, a grant known as a *tu'ma* is also mentioned. The word *ṭu'ma* is derived from a root connected with food and eating and it may have implied a means of subsistence. According to Qudāma writing in the early fourth/tenth century, the *tu'ma* was a grant of an estate to a man who took the revenues from it for his lifetime but it returned to the treasury after his death (unlike an *iqṭā'* which was heritable).[190] In the early Islamic period, *tu'ma* is used for extensive grants of the revenues of a whole province or district usually employed by Caliphs to secure the allegiance of powerful leaders. The implication is that they would have complete control of the revenues of the area in exchange for a pledge of obedience. 'Abd al-Malik certainly used the device. He tried to win over the governor of Khurāsān, 'Abd Allah b. Khāzim to his cause by offering him the province as a *tu'ma* for seven or ten years.[191] 'Abd al-Malik's brother 'Abd al-'Azīz is described as having held Egypt as a *tu'ma* during his long governorate (65/685–86/705).[192] His rival Muṣ'ab b. al-Zubayr meanwhile gave Isfahan as a *tu'ma* to Ismā'īl b. Talḥa b. 'Ubayd Allāh, who does not seem to have lived in the city but sent a deputy.[193] Later, when Yazīd II was trying to persuade his brother Ḥishām to renounce his rights to the succession, he offered him the Jazīra province as a *tu'ma*.[194] Not all *tu'ma*s were so big; in 66/685–6 'Abd Allāh b. Khāzim himself offered one of his Arab rivals in Khurāsān 100 000 *dirham*s and the *tu'ma* of the town of Bāsān.[195] The historians tell us nothing about *tu'ma*s after the end of the Umayyad period, but it seems that the device was still in use, at least on a small scale, in Qudāma's day (early fourth/tenth century), when granting them was the responsibility of the *Dīwān al-ḍiyā'*.[196]

Supplies and commissariat

In John Haldon's companion volume, *Warfare, State and Society in the Byzantine World*, there is an extended discussion on the arrangements for the supply of armies on campaign, the provisions which were demanded from the provinces through which the army passed and the means by which these were transported.[197] It is very difficult to write a parallel chapter on the supply of Muslim armies. In most accounts of campaigns, we are given no information whatever about how the army obtained supplies. However, it is not clear how far this is a result of the different nature of the sources and how much it reflects different practice.

As mentioned above, troops during the Umayyad period were given *rizq* or supplies on some occasions: the *dār al-Rizq* is attested in Kūfa from early times and the Egyptian papyri make it clear that oil and grain were requisitioned for the army. These supplies, however, seem to have been distributed at base in the *miṣr*. There is very little evidence of armies being accompanied by a supply train. This was partly due, no doubt, to the almost complete absence of wheeled vehicles[198] which would have made the transport of large quantities of grain problematic. In fact, the only references we have to the use of carts come from campaigns in the northern fringes of the Muslim world, on the Byzantine frontier where they were used to transport wood for making siege engines.[199]

In these remote frontier areas, provision had to be made for garrisons. When Maslama b. ʿAbd al-Malik took Bāb al-Abwāb (Derbent) at the eastern end of the Caucasus in 113/731, he established a garrison of 24 000 Syrians, who were paid *ʿaṭā'*. Al-Balādhurī says[200] that even in his own time (mid-third/ninth century), the people would not accept a governor in their city unless he had money to distribute: the implication must be that the garrison was paid with revenue collected elsewhere in the Caliphate. Maslama fortified the city and provided it with granaries for foodstuffs (*ṭaʿām*), barley and an armoury. When Marwān b. Muḥammad (later the Caliph Marwān II) renewed the assault on the principalities of the Caucasus, he made peace in exchange for numbers of beautiful slaves of both sexes and large quantities of grain, 'to be poured into the granaries of al-Bāb'. However, such careful arrangements for supplying a garrison seem to have remained exceptional.

The clearest evidence of commanders trying to organise supplies for their armies come from the account of al-Afshīn against Bābak in the mountains of Azerbayjān.[201] Al-Afshīn was well aware of the difficulties of supply and organised a convoy system to try to ensure that caravans reached his troops. On occasion he issued rations of biscuit (*kaʿk*) and barley broth (*sawīq*) to his men.[202] Even so, it was not easy: at one stage a vast caravan travelled with more than 1000 steers and other supplies on asses and mules but it was ambushed and all the supplies were stolen.[203] When al-Muʿtaṣim set off on his attack on Amorion in 223/838, he equipped himself 'as no Caliph had ever done before' with supplies for warfare, and he seems to have had a real supply train with equipment for making siege engines and food supplies.[204]

Later in the third/ninth century, when al-Muwaffaq was building up his forces for a sustained campaign against the Zanj rebels in southern Iraq in 267/880–1, he spent a month or so gathering resources,

> Provisions [*miyar*] kept on arriving in a continuous stream, and merchants collected all sorts of merchandise and equipment and brought it to the city of al-Muwaffaqiya [the camp-city he established for the campaign]. Markets were established in the city, and numerous merchants and suppliers of equipment came from every land . . . Abū Aḥmad [al-Muwaffaq] built a Friday mosque and ordered the people to worship there; then he established mints [*dūr al-ḍarab*] that issued *dīnār*s and *dirhams* . . . Money flowed into [the city] and pay [*ʿaṭā'*] was distributed on time.[205]

Here we see clearly how a military campaign leads to a growth in economic and commercial activity.

The armies of al-Afshīn and al-Mu'taṣim seem to have been most unusual in the attention that the commanders paid to supply. When Hārūn invaded the Byzantine empire in 165/782, he took with him vast sums in cash (194 450 *dīnārs* and 21 414 800 *dirhams*) but there is no mention of a supply train.[206] Muslim armies seem to have supplied themselves by buying supplies in markets and from local traders and peasants. The evidence for this is suggestive but not very extensive. When Sulaymān b. Ṣurad was leading the 'Penitents' against the Umayyads in 65/684 a market (*sūq*) was established for them at Qarqīsiya and they brought such provisions as they needed.[207]

Markets were also set up for the Muslims campaigning in the remote areas of southern Afghanistan in 79/698. When the Muslim 'army of destruction' was retreating in disarray and many soldiers were sick and starving, the commander bought up supplies and established markets where grain was sold to the soldiers at what was believed to be an extortionate price.[208] The commander, 'Ubayd Allāh b. Abī Bakra was condemned for his greed and exploitation in a vitriolic poem.[209] We cannot know whether the criticisms were fair or whether the unfortunate commander was doing his best in very difficult conditions. What is clear is that the troops were expected to buy their supplies, with their own money, in markets established for the purpose. When Ibn al-'Ash'ath was sent to revenge the humiliation the next year, markets were again established for the army[210] and markets were set up for Khāzim b. Khuzayma's army when they were pursuing the Khārijīs in Iraq in 138/755–6.[211] The caliph al-Walīd II, when he was being pursued by his enemies in the Palmyra region, offered his troops permission to graze their animals in the standing corn of the local villages. They refused, saying that the green crops would make their animals sick and, anyway, they would accept payment only in cash.[212] Much later, in 267/880–1 al-Muwaffaq, campaigning against the Zanj in Iraq, took possession of large quantities of wheat, barley and rice but rather than distribute it too his men, he ordered that it be sold and the money raised used to pay his men's salaries (*'aṭiyāt*).[213] Once again, we see the army operating in a market economy.

On the campaign against Kamkh in 149/766–7, the Muslim general al-'Abbās b. Muḥammad summoned merchants from the surrounding area and a market was set up. In his account of the expedition, the Zuqnin Chronicler makes an unexpected comment.[213] 'The passage of this army', he says, 'was of great profit to the North [the frontier districts] because they spread many *zouz* [*dirhams*] there, especially new ones: from then on anyone who wanted to make *zouz* could do so without fear. New *zouz* multiplied, especially forgeries. This was the destruction of many men.' It is difficult to know quite what to make of this but it seems as if the army could be a source of profit to the locals. They paid in cash, newly minted cash in many cases, for their provisions. One man's holy war was another man's merchandising opportunity. Besides showing the army as an important economic agent, and potential source of benefit for out-of-the-way areas, it also shows how newly minted coin entered the money supply. The money spent by the army brought an influx of newly coined money into the area, including many forgeries.[214]

There was a clear contrast with Byzantine practice. Ibn Khurdādhbih notes that the Byzantine army was not provided with markets, implying that this was in contrast with Muslim practice.[215] It was therefore something of an innovation when, in 165/782, the Empress Irene agreed to provide markets so that the retreating Muslim troops could purchase supplies.[216]

The evidence is slight, but if the picture is correct it explains why there are so few references to supply trains in the Arabic sources. It may also explain the high degree of mobility and the long distances covered by Muslim armies. Muslim armies were paid in cash and were expected to purchase their supplies (at least when they were in Muslim territory). The evidence of the Zuqnin Chronicler[217] makes it clear that the coming of an army to an out-of-the-way part of the Caliphate could vastly increase the money supply and, no doubt, stimulate the local rural economy and bring it into the wider market economy of the Muslim world.

Conclusion

The armies of the Umayyad and early 'Abbasid period were paid stipends in minted coin. At the beginning of this period, these stipends could be thought of as there hereditary right of those whose names appeared in the *dīwān* registers. During the course of the second/eighth century, the Caliphs and their representatives forced a transformation so that the stipend became a true salary, a payment for work done. Unlike their contemporaries in the West, the soldiers of the Caliphs were never given land grants in lieu of salaries. Sometimes they might be given houses or plots of land on which to build, but not to provide an alternative income. On the rare occasions when larger land grants were given to soldiers it was as a reward for past services, rather than payment for continuing and future ones. Both Umayyads and 'Abbasids normally maintained the separation of the military from tax-collecting: apart from dire emergencies, soldiers were never given the right to collect taxes with which to pay themselves.[218] This was always done by the government *dīwāns*.

Notes

1 For the origins of the *dīwān* based on the Muslim accounts, see G.-R. Puin, *Der Dīwān von 'Umar Ibn al-Haṭṭāb* (Bonn, 1970).
2 The chronology is discussed in Puin, *Dīwān*, 81–2, 94–5.
3 See p. 7.
4 On the rates of taxation and their collection, see D. C. Dennett, *Conversion and Poll-Tax in Early Islam* (Cambridge, Mass., 1950); F. Lokkegaard, *Islamic Taxation in the Classical Period* (Copenhagen, 1953) ; based on the Egyptian evidence but of general interest are K. Morimoto, *The Fiscal Administration of Egypt in the Early Islamic Period* (Dohosa, 1981) and J. K. Simonsen, *Studies in the Genesis and Early Development of the Caliphal Taxation System* (Copenhagen, 1988).
5 Puin, *Dīwān*, 16–18, 27–40.
6 Puin, *Dīwān*, 42–56.
7 Bal., *Futūḥ*, 449. The 'Kings [*mulūk*] of Syria' could refer to the Byzantines or the Ghassanids.

8 M. Morony, *Iraq after the Muslim Conquest* (Princeton, 1984), 56.
9 Morony, *Iraq*, 55–9.
10 al-Jahshiyārī, 17.
11 Bal., *Futūḥ*, 448–61; Ṭa., ii, 2411–18; Abū Yūsuf, 68–73; Ibn Sallām, 271–312, caps. 524–610; al-Jahshiyārī, 16–7, Ya'q., *Ta'rīkh*, ii, 130: a full collection of sources in German translation is given in Puin, *Dīwān*, 126–94.
12 E. Ashtor, *Histoire des prix et salaires dans orient médiéval* (Paris, 1969), 40–1.
13 Since 'Alī was the inspiration of the Shi'a and al-'Abbās the ancestor of the 'Abbasids, it is not surprising that the precedence between these two varies and that one or other are sometimes omitted altogether, depending on the preferences of the author.
14 As an anonymous poet complained in Ṭa., i, 2564.
15 I have followed the list in Ṭa., i, 2412–3; other lists follow the same general lines with variations of detail.
16 Bal., *Futūḥ*, 452; Abū Yūsuf, 72.
17 Bal., *Futūḥ*, 451. According to al-Ya'qūbī (*Ta'rīkh*, ii, 135), salary levels depended on tribal affiliation: Yamanis were given 400, Muḍaris 300 and Rabī'a 200, but this tradition is almost certainly a product of later tribal rivalries rather than reflecting historical reality.
18 Bal., *Futūḥ*, 131–2; see p. 31.
19 EI2 sv, *farā'iḍ*.
20 For example al-Ḥajjāj b. Jāriya had his *maktab* in Rayy (Ṭa., ii, 1001) and Fuḍayl b. Khadīj al-Kindī described himself as one of the 4000 Kūfans and Basrans whose *maktab* was in Kirman (Ṭa., ii, 1060).
21 Bal., *Futūḥ*, 460.
22 Ibn Sallām, 299, cap. 571.
23 Bal., *Futūḥ*, 457.
24 Bal., *Futūḥ*, 458; Ibn Sallām, 300, cap. 572.
25 Bal., *Futūḥ*, 457; Ibn Sallām, 301, caps. 577, 578.
26 Bal., *Futūḥ*, 457–8.
27 See pp. 4–5.
28 Bal., *Futūḥ*, 458.
29 Bal., *Futūḥ*, 451.
30 Bal., *Futūḥ*, 459; Ibn Sallām, 302–7, caps. 580–600.
31 Bal., *Futūḥ*, 458–9; S. S. Agha, 'The Arab Population in Hurāsān during the Umayyad Period', *Arabica*, 46 (1999), 211–29, esp. p. 29.
32 Ibn Sallām, 291 cap. 571; Bal., *Futūḥ*, 458; for further discussion of this issue see K. Athāmina, 'A'rāb and Muhājirūn in the Environment of Amṣār', *Studia Islamica*, 66 (1989), 17–18.
33 Ṭa., i, 2414.
34 Bal., *Futūḥ*, 449.
35 M. Hinds, 'Kūfan Political Alignments and Their Background in the Mid-Seventh Century AD', *IJMES*, 2 (1971a), 346–67, p. 352.
36 Ṭa., i, 2929–30.
37 That is the fifth (*khums*) of the booty which the Prophet had taken for himself and which the Caliphs claimed as his successors.
38 Ṭa., i, 2953.
39 See Hinds, 'The Murder of the Caliph 'Uthmān', *IJMES*, 3 (1972a), 450–69.
40 Hinds, 'Kūfan Political Alignments', 363.
41 Ṭa., i, 3227.
42 Ṭa., i, 3266.
43 Ṭa., i, 3298.
44 Ṭa., i, 3387, trans., 137.
45 Ṭa., i, 3370.

46 Ṭa., i, 3409–10.
47 See pp. 63–4.
48 For an examination of early Muslim government based on documentary sources, see F. M. Donner, 'The Formation of the Islamic State', *JAOS*, 106 (1986), 284–96.
49 C. J. Kraemer, *Excavations at Nessana, vol. 3, Non-Literary Papyri* (Princeton, 1958), 175–97.
50 W. Caskel, *Gamharat al-Nasab: Das genealogische Werk des Hišām ibn Muḥammad al-Kalbī*, 2 vols (Leiden, 1966), taf. 245.
51 Caskel, *Gamharat*, taf. 247: the rareness of the name Zirr and the geographical distribution of Lakhm make this identification just plausible.
52 K. Morimoto, 'The Dīwāns as Registers of the Arabic Stipendiaries in Early Islamic Egypt', in R. Curiel and R. Gyselen (eds), *Itinéraires d'Orient: Hommages à Claude Cahen* (Bures-sur-Yvette, 1994), 362–5.
53 On which see N. Abbott, *The Kurrah Papyri from Aphrodito in the Oriental Institute* (Chicago, 1938).
54 R. Khoury, *Chrestomathie de papyrologie arabe* (Leiden, 1993), no. 90, 153–5.
55 Khoury, *Chrestomathie*, no. 91, 155–60.
56 Puin, *Dīwān*, 120–4.
57 A. Vogliano (ed.), *Papiri della R. Università di Milano* (Milan, 1937), i, 252.
58 D. S. Margoliouth, *Catalogue of Arabic Papyri in the John Rylands Library* (Manchester, 1933), 31.
59 Ibn 'Abd al-Ḥakam, 102; Puin, *Dīwān*, 123–4.
60 The basic introduction to the coinage of the Umayyad period remains J. Walker, *A Catalogue of the Muḥammadan Coins in the British Museum*, i, *The Arab–Sassanian Coins* (1941) and ii, *The Arab–Byzantine and Post-Reform Umaiyad Coins* (1956), but see also the important critique of Walker in M. Bates, 'History, Geography and Numismatics in the First century of Islamic Coinage', *Revue Suisse de Numismatique*, 65 (1986), 231–62. For a more recent update of his views on Syrian coinage with useful annotated bibliography, see M. Bates, 'Byzantine Coinage and its Imitations, Arab Coinage and its Imitations: Arab–Byzantine Coinage', *Aram*, 6 (1994), 381–403. For the transition from Sasanian to Islamic coinage in the East, see Morony, *Iraq*, 38–51. For a recent overview of early Islamic coinage, see S. Heidemann, 'The Merger of Two Currency Zones in Early Islam. The Byzantine and Sasanian Impact on the Circulation in Former Byzantine Syria and Northern Mesopotamia', *Iran*, 36 (1998), 95–112.
61 The earliest example seems to be the coin of 41/661 minted in Darabjird in Fārs in the name of Mu'āwiya, Commander of the Faithful (Morony, *Iraq*, 45–6).
62 See the tables in Walker, *A Catalogue*, i, 36–126, and the discussion of the problems of identification, xcix–ci.
63 Bal., *Ansāb*, iva, 190.
64 Walker, *A Catalogue*, i, 112–13.
65 Following Bates, 'History, Geography and Numismatics', 250–1; Bates has reinforced his argument in a debate with C. Morrisson: see C. Morrisson, 'Le monnayage omayyade et l'histoire administrative et économique de la Syrie', in P. Canivet and J.-P. Rey-Coquais (eds), *La Syrie de Byzance a l'Islam* (Damascus, 1992), 309–17, in which it is argued that coins were minted in Syria from Mu'āwiya's time, and the riposte of M. Bates, 'Commentaire sur l'étude de Cécille Morrisson', in the same volume, 319–21.
66 These are tabulated in Walker, *A Catalogue*, i, lx–lxi. It appears as if changes of governor in Umayyad Iraq were marked by minor variations in coin design, notably the number of small rings around the margins, though governors' names are never given: see A. S. DeShazo and M. Bates, 'The Umayyad Governors of al-'Irāq and the

Changing Annulet Patterns on their Dirhams', *Numismatic Chronicle*, VII Series, 14 (1974), 110–18.

67 Ibn A'tham, vii, 221. The parallel account in al-Ṭabarī, ii, 1188, is less specific about the production of coins. See also Narshakhī, 45, for the vast amounts of booty taken. See also Ṭa., iii, 1989, where it is recorded that al-Muwaffaq, on campaign against the Zanj rebels in southern Iraq in 267/880–1 established mints which issued both *dīnār*s and *dirhams*, presumably to pay his army.

68 Walker, *A Catalogue*, ii, lxxix, identifies this with Dastuva in al-Jibal on which see G. Le Strange, *Lands of the Eastern Caliphate* (London, 1905, repr. 1966), 220, but it must be Dastawā near al-Ahwaz, see al-Ṭabarī, ii, 1062 and Yāqūt, sv.

69 These mints are discussed in Walker, *A Catalogue*, ii, lxx–xcii.

70 Walker, *A Catalogue*, ii, lxiv–lxv.

71 M. Bates, 'The Dirham Mint of the Northern Provinces of the Umayyad Caliphate', *Armenian Numismatic Journal*, Series 1, 15 (1989), 89–111.

72 Bates, 'The Dirham Mint'.

73 Quoted in Walker, *A Catalogue*, ii, lxiii.

74 As opposed to Ifrīqiya (Tunisia) and Spain where coins continued to be produced.

75 Qudāma, ed. Zubaydī, 217; trans. Ben Shemesh, 36.

76 See Morony, *Iraq*, 56–61.

77 al-Jahshiyārī, 38, 'There continued to be two *dīwān*s in Kūfa and Basra, one in Arabic recording the men and their salaries, which had been established by 'Umar, and another recording the sources of revenue in Persian. It was the same in Syria, one in Greek and the other in Arabic.' After the reforms of 'Abd al-Malik, all *dīwāns* were supposed to be in Arabic. But cf. p. 66 for lists of troops in Greek.

78 Bal., *Ansāb*, iva, 170–210.

79 According to 'Ubayd Allāh b. Ziyād's speech to the people of Basra as recorded by al-Mas'ūdī (*Murūj*, 5, 194–5), 60 000 *muqātila* and their families were paid 60 000 000 in *'aṭā'*. On the basis of this evidence, Ashtor (*Histoire des prix et salaires dans orient médiéval*, Paris, 1969, 70), claims that the Umayyads paid 1000 *dirhams* a month. The text, however, proves no such thing: even if the figures are more than rhetoric, they date from a time when payments were made per year, not per month.

80 For a full discussion of the early *dīwān* in Egypt, see Morimoto, 'The Dīwāns', 353–65.

81 al-Kindī, *Wulāt*, 92.

82 al-Kindī, *Wulāt*, 193.

83 Bal., *Futūḥ*, 456.

84 See Morimoto, 'The Dīwāns', 364.

85 Ibn 'Abd al-Ḥakam, 102, 316.

86 The note in Theophanes that Mu'āwiya raised the pay of the Syrians to 200 solidi and lowered that of the Iraqis to 30 should, as noted by the translators, be treated with some scepticism. It looks like a reflection of pay differentials later in the Umayyad period. Theophanes, *Chronographia*, 485–6.

87 Ṭa., i, 3409–10.

88 Ṭa., i, 2486; Bal., *Ansāb*, iva, 190.

89 Bal., *Ansāb*, iva, 206.

90 Ṭa., ii, 755.

91 Bal., *Ansāb*, v, 271.

92 Ṭa., ii, 1043–4: *pace* Morony, the text clearly means that they provided their own horses and equipment as in trans. Rowson, 191–2.

93 Ṭa., ii, 1826. Both these clauses present problems. The first may mean that they should be paid every year at Muḥarram or simply that they should be paid all through the year. The second may imply that the *'aṭā'* should be inherited or simply that they were demanding child allowances; see Hillenbrand trans. 184.

94 Ṭa., ii, 1835. This clause is not given in Ibn Khayyāṭ.
95 Ṭa., ii, 407, 755, 1043–4.
96 Morony, *Iraq*, 59–61.
97 Bal., *Futūḥ*, 358, 364.
98 Bal., *Ansāb*, iva, 189.
99 Ṭa., ii, 439.
100 Bal., *Ansāb*, iva, 190.
101 Bal., *Ansāb*, iva, 181.
102 Bal., *Ansāb*, iva, 206.
103 Ṭa., ii, 78.
104 For a discussion of *rizq* and the Sasanian precedents, see Morony, *Iraq*, 61–4. See also pp. 66–7.
105 Pellat, *Ibn al-Muqaffa'*, 34–7.
106 See Crone, 'Ma'ūna' in EI2.
107 See p. 72.
108 Ṭa., ii, 407; Bal., *Ansāb*, ivb, 33, where the verbal form *yu'āna* (he [the Caliph] helped each man with a hundred *dīnār*s) is used.
109 Ṭa., ii, 755.
110 Bal., *Futūḥ*, 187–8.
111 See pp. 63–4.
112 Ṭa., ii, 603–4; Bal., *Ansāb*, iva, 220–1.
113 Ṭa., ii, 1306–7, al-Jahshiyārī, 49.
114 Ṭa., ii, 1719.
115 Ṭa., ii, 1778–9.
116 Ibn 'Abd al-Hakam, 102; al-Jahshiyārī, 51–2.
117 Ṭa., ii, 1365–6.
118 For the speech, Ṭa., ii, 1834–6, Ibn Khayyāṭ, 365, al-Azdī, 57–8. See also trans. Hillenbrand, 193–5 with further references. I have preferred the wording in Ibn Khayyāṭ, which seems to be clearer, but the differences are not of major significance.
119 Ṭa., ii, 649–50.
120 Ṭa., ii, 858–9.
121 Ṭa., ii, 866, 869–70; Bal., *Ansāb*, xi, 270–1, 274–7.
122 Ṭa., ii, 822, 855–6, 1004.
123 Ṭa., ii, 902–3.
124 Ṭa., ii, 942.
125 See pp. 38–9.
126 However, the rhetoric lingered on: when Dāwud b. 'Alī addressed the Kūfans after the proclamation of the first 'Abbasid Caliph, al-Saffāḥ, he denounced the Umayyads for taking 'your *fay'*, your alms [*ṣadaqa*] and your booty [*maghānim*] and they were promised a 100 *dirham* increase in their *'aṭā'*' (Ṭa., iii, 30–1).
127 The idea of payment of *'aṭā'* for people who were not obliged to do military service remained for some privileged groups, including members of the ruling family and their companions who were paid the *rizq* even though they did not have to go on campaign (Ṭa., ii, 1747–8) and, at least in early 'Abbasid times, the people of Madīna (Ṭa., iii, 483, 701). The Marwanids , we are told, never used to draw the *'aṭā'* unless they went on campaign and the Caliph Hishām gave his stipend to a *mawlā* of his who acted as a substitute: even for the ruling house, there was a clear link between payment and service (Ṭa., ii, 1731–2; M. Bonner, *Aristocratic Violence and Holy War*, New Haven, 1996, 21–4).
128 Ṭa., ii, 1192; see Bonner, *Aristocratic Violence*, 21–2.
129 Bal., *Ansāb*, iva, 232.
130 Ṭa., ii, 814–16.

131 Ṭa., ii, 1518.
132 Ashtor, *Histoire des prix et salaires*, 70.
133 Ṭa., ii, 1825. The phrase used , *'ashratan 'ashratan* may imply that these sums are per month because this formulation is the one usually used in 'Abbasid times for describing monthly salary payments and, besides, ten *dirhams* per year would be too small a sum to be of major importance. However, other discussions at the time imply that salaries were paid annually.
134 Ṭa., ii, 1371–2.
135 Ṭa., ii, 1957, 1969; for the significance of this, see M. Sharon, *The Social and Military Aspects of the 'Abbasid Revolution* (Jerusalem, 1990), 97–107.
136 Pellat, *Ibn al-Muqaffa'*, 34–5.
137 Ṭa., iii, 1969. Ashtor, *Histoire des prix*, 70 is confused in suggesting that this represents a reduction in salaries: if it was 3 or 4 *dirhams per day* (for which there is no textual evidence) it would still amount to more than 80 *dirhams* per month, and hence an increase.
138 Ibn al-Athīr, v, 421.
139 The 'month' was not necessarily a calendar month and 'months' could be extended to make economies: Ashtor, without giving a source, mentions military 'months' of four calendar months (*Histoire des prix*, 71).
140 Ashtor, *Histoire des prix*, 64–72.
141 al-Azdī, 143.
142 *Aghānī*, v, 149.
143 Ṭa., iii, 292.
144 Bal., *Futūḥ*, 169–70.
145 For details, see Ibn al-Adīm, *Bughyat*, i, 209. None of these places can now be identified with any confidence but see pp. 191–2.
146 Ashtor, *Histoire des prix*, 91.
147 Bal., *Futūḥ*, 187.
148 Ṭa., iii, 765.
149 Ṭa., iii, 771–2.
150 Ṭa., iii, 817.
151 Ṭa., iii, 865.
152 Ṭa., iii, 866–7.
153 Ṭa., iii, 924.
154 Ṭa., iii, 978–9.
155 Ṭa., iii, 985.
156 An area to the north east of the Round City of Baghdad, largely settled by soldiers of Khurāsānī origin.
157 Ṭa., iii, 998–9.
158 Ṭa., iii, 999–1001.
159 Ṭa., iii, 1008–11.
160 Ṭa., iii, 1014.
161 Ṭa., iii, 1016.
162 See article '*dirham*' in EI2 (Miles).
163 Ṭa., iii, 1031–3.
164 'Sons', that is, sons of the Khurāsānī troops who had originally come West at the time of the 'Abbasid Revolution.
165 For discussion of this form of landholding, see C. Cahen, 'L'evolution de l'iqta' du IXe au XIII siècle', *Annales: Economies, Sociétés, Civilisations*, 8 (1953), 25–52; A. K. S. Lambton, 'Reflections on the Iqta',' in G. Makdisi (ed.), *Arabic and Islamic Studies in Honor of Hamilton A. R. Gibb* (Cambridge, Mass., 1965), 358–76; A. A. Al-Durī, 'The origins of *iqta'* in Islam', *Al-Abhath*, 22 (1969), 3–22. All three are

concerned primarily to investigate the origins of the *iqṭā'* as it developed from the third/ninth centuries onwards, rather than the position in the second/eighth centuries, and tend to equate *iqṭā'* with *qaṭī'a* . Cahen, however, does make the point, taken up by Lambton, that the later *iqṭā'* evolves from grants of *ighār* and other sorts of immunity rather than from the *qaṭī'a*.

166 Bal., *Futūḥ*, 165–6.

167 Bal., *Futūḥ*, 169–70.

168 Bal., *Futūḥ*, 187.

169 Bal., *Futūḥ*, 128.

170 Bal., *Futūḥ*, 144.

171 Bal., *Futūḥ*, 134.

172 al-Azdī, 158. On this document, see Kennedy, 'Sources of elite incomes' (forthcoming).

173 al-Azdī, 197.

174 Ya'q., *Buldān*, 245.

175 There are two main accounts of the distribution of properties in Baghdad, those of al-Ya'qūbī and al-Khaṭīb al-Baghdādī; see al-Ya'qūbī, *Kitāb al-Buldān*, ed. M. J. de Goeje (Leiden, 1892), 241–54, French trans. G. Wiet (Cairo, 1937), 16–43; al-Khaṭīb al-Baghdādī *Ta'rīkh Baghdād*, 14 vols, (Cairo, 1931), i, 66–127. This can conveniently be consulted in the fully annotated English translation in J. Lassner, *The Topography of Baghdad in the Early Middle Ages* (Detroit, 1970), 29–118. There are considerable differences between the lists and I have based my discussion on al-Ya'qūbī because he gives the fullest information about the earliest distribution of properties, including many details omitted by al-Khaṭīb. Al-Khaṭīb gives more information about the later owners.

176 Ya'q., *Buldān*, 243.

177 Ya'q., *Buldān*, 245.

178 Ya'q., *Buldān*, 243.

179 Ya'q., *Buldān*, 245–6.

180 Ya'q., *Buldān*, 243.

181 Ya'q., *Buldān*, 244, 246.

182 Ya'q., *Buldān*, 248.

183 Ya'q., *Buldān*, 246.

184 Ya'q., *Buldān*, 247.

185 Ya'q., *Buldān*, 246.

186 Ya'q., *Buldān*, 249–50.

187 Ya'q., *Buldān*, 249.

188 Ya'q., *Buldān*, 251.

189 Ya'q., *Buldān*, 253.

190 Qudāma, ed. Zubaydī, 218; trans. Ben Shemesh, 36, though the verb *istaghalla* probably means to derive revenue from, not to cultivate, as he suggests.

191 Ṭa., ii, 831–2.

192 Ya'q., *Ta'rīkh*, ii, 334.

193 Ṭa., ii, 762.

194 Ya'q., *Ta'rīkh*, ii, 376.

195 Ṭa., ii, 697 and trans. (Fishbein) n. 252. The place is probably to be identified with Bāshān near Merv (Le Strange, *Lands*, 399).

196 Qudāma, ed. Zubaydī, 53–4.

197 J. Haldon, *Warfare, State and Society in the Byzantine World, 565–1204* (London, 1999), esp. 287–92.

198 The disappearance of wheeled transport from the Near East has been demonstrated in R. Bulliet, *The Camel and the Wheel* (Cambridge, Mass., 1975).

199 *Chronique de Denys de Tell-Mahré* (The Zuqnin Chronicle), trans. J.-B. Chabot (Paris, 1895), 74.
200 Bal., *Futūḥ*, 206–9; also Ṭa., ii, 1560.
201 For this campaign, see pp. 131–3.
202 Ṭa., iii, 1199.
203 Ṭa., iii, 1178–9.
204 Ṭa., iii, 1236, 1238.
205 Ṭa., iii, 189.
206 Ṭa., iii, 503–4.
207 Ṭa., ii, 552–3.
208 Bal., *Ansāb*, xi, 313–17; Ṭa., ii, 1036–9; On the campaign, see C. E. Bosworth, '‘Ubaidallāh b. Abī Bakra and the "Army of Destruction" in Zābulistān (79/698)', *Der Islam*, 50 (1973), 268–83.
209 Bal., *Ansāb*, xi, 315–7; English trans., and commentary, Bosworth, '‘Ubaidallāh b. Abī Bakra', 280–3.
210 Ṭa., ii, 1045.
211 Ṭa., iii, 123.
212 Ṭa., ii, 1802–3.
213 Ṭa., iii, 1964.
214 *Chronique de Denys*, 80–2.
215 Ibn Khurdādhbih, 112, noted in Haldon, *Warfare, State and Society*, 163.
216 Ṭa., iii, 503–4.
217 *Chronique de Denys*, 80–2.
218 As Ibn al-Muqaffa‘ had advised (Pellat, *Ibn al-Muqaffa‘*, 32–3).

CHAPTER FOUR

Early 'Abbasid warfare, 132–218/750–833

In many ways the coming of the 'Abbasids marked a radical break with the policies and personnel of the Umayyad period. The Umayyad family themselves were removed from office and many of them slaughtered or driven into hiding and exile. The 'Abbasids themselves were determined to show that their regime was something different. They were members of the house of the Prophet, avengers of al-Ḥusayn and all the other martyred 'Alids, and their rule would usher in an era of truly Islamic justice.

In reality, as scholars have begun to point out, there was considerable continuity as well as radical change as a result of the ''Abbasid Revolution'.[1] There was still a large number of professional soldiers whose names were listed in the *dīwān al-jund*[2] and who were paid regular salaries. In the main, they fought as foot-soldiers and many of the senior commanders were members or the ruling family.

At the same time there were major changes. The most important of these were that the *ahl al-Shām* (Syrians) were replaced by the *ahl Khurāsān* (Khurāsānis) as the main military force in the Caliphate. It was now the Khurāsāniya who were the troops on whom the Caliphs relied above all, and it was they who were sent to garrison other parts of the Empire. Many Khurāsānis remained in Khurāsān, many others did not and some moved to and fro as opportunity dictated.[3] Just as some of the *ahl al-Shām* had settled in Wāsiṭ and lived off the revenues of Iraq, so some of the *ahl Khurāsān* settled in Baghdad and lived off the revenues of Iraq. Here their descendants were often known as the *Abnā al-dawla* (the Sons of the Regime). They also provided garrisons in Syria along the Byzantine frontier, and in Ifrīqiya (Tunisia).[4]

In contrast the *ahl al-Shām* were reduced to a greatly inferior status. Ibn al-Muqaffa' advised the Caliph al-Manṣūr that the Syrians should now be deprived of the *'aṭā'*, just as they had previously deprived others.[5] Having lost their position in the *dīwān* they were reduced to the condition of peasants. Some were even offered positions in the Byzantine forces. At one stage the 'Abbasid commander, al-'Abbās b. Muḥammad offered to recruit more Syrians and vast numbers abandoned the harvest and flocked to Ḥarrān. In the end, only 600 were taken on and the rest were disappointed;[6] they would obviously have preferred a position in the military to cultivating the land. Of course, the change was not complete,

Syrians did serve in the 'Abbasid armies,[7] on the Byzantine frontier, for example. Even some of the closest companions of the last Umayyad Caliph, Marwān II, managed to find a place in the élite of the new regime, men like Isḥāq b. Muslim al-'Uqaylī[8] who was a member of the entourages of both Marwān and al-Manṣūr. When the Caliph al-Manṣūr was faced with the rebellion of Ibrāhīm b. 'Abd Allāh the 'Alid in Basra in 145/762 he began to recruit Syrians whom he knew he could rely on against the rebels. There were even occasions when Syrian troops were used to help suppress unrest in Khurāsān.[9] But the *ahl al-Shām* were always marginalised in the 'Abbasid State, it is difficult to know if any of them were permanently inscribed in the *dīwān*[10]: it was now their turn to become tax-paying subjects. Only in Egypt did the descendants of the Umayyad *jund*, now little more than a hereditary oligarchy, continue to enjoy their privileged status. It was not until the reign of al-Mu'taṣim that their names were removed from the *dīwān* and they were replaced by Turkish and other professionals.[11]

Numbers

As with the Umayyads, assessing the total numbers of troops in early 'Abbasid armies is a very approximate science. The 'Abbasid army which was raised in Marw by Abū Muslim was clearly a sizeable military force. The sources consistently suggest that the 'Abbasids had many fewer troops than their Umayyad opponents, but this may simply be a device to glorify them and show that God was on their side. In a major battle fought in central Iran between Qaḥṭaba b. Shabīb leading the 'Abbasid expeditionary force and the Umayyads under 'Āmir b. Ḍubāra we are told that Qaḥṭaba had 20 000 men against 50 000 or more in the so-called 'army or armies' on the other side.[12]

At the Battle of Tell Kushāf (Battle of the Zāb) which finally sealed the fate of the Umayyad Caliphate, the 'Abbasids are again said to have been heavily outnumbered. Marwān is said to have had 120 000 men as opposed to between 12 000 and 20 000 with 'Abd Allāh b. 'Alī, the 'Abbasid commander.[13] These figures should be treated with some caution, but if we estimated the number of Khurāsāni troops coming west at the time of the 'Abbasid revolution at between 20 000 and 30 000, we would probably be fairly near the mark.

We have no overall estimate of the numbers of salaried soldiers in the early 'Abbasid armies but we can get something of a snapshot of the forces available from the accounts of the rebellion of Muḥammad the Pure Soul and his brother Ibrāhīm in 145/762–3. At the time, the Caliph al-Manṣūr is said to have complained that he had no more than 1000 troops with him in Kūfa.[14] The rest of the 'Abbasid forces were scattered, 30 000 in Rayy with his son al-Mahdī, 40 000 in Ifrīqiya and 4000 with 'Isā b. Mūsā fighting the 'Alid pretender, Muḥammad in Madīna.[15] This gives a total of about 75 000 men. In addition, there were local garrisons stationed in various parts of the Caliphate which were probably not counted because they could not easily be moved. There were certainly troops stationed on the Byzantine frontier, probably over 25 000 in various garrisons. We also know that there were smaller forces in various provincial cities, like the 2000 *rābiṭa* maintained in Mawsil to defend the city from the Khārijīs[16] and the 4000 men that the governor of al-Ahwaz had at his disposal, though it is not clear that these were regular, salaried troops.[17] At this time, there is no mention of an 'Abbasid garrison in Basra and the only force available to oppose the rebels was 600 infantry, cavalry and archers hastily gathered by Muḥammad b. Sulaymān, the leading member of the 'Abbasid family in the city.[18] The Caliph was able to send to Syria for reinforcements, possibly from the frontier garrisons, and some 4000 came in small groups.[19] We should also remember the *jund* of Egypt, who received salaries but never seem to have served outside their home province during the early 'Abbasid period. All in all, we can probably estimate some 100 000 salaried troops maintained by the 'Abbasid state in this period. This compares with perhaps 250 000–300 000 whose names were in the *dīwāns* in *c.* 80/700.[20] However, it seems like that the early 'Abbasid army was largely composed of full-time soldiers rather than men who might be called up on campaign but often lived civilian lives. It is possible that the early 'Abbasids maintained a military force approximately the same size as the later Umayyads.

We have more detailed information about the numbers of troops settled on the Byzantine frontier, serving in exchange for salaries and plots for housing in the cities.[21] The Umayyads had settled between 1500 and 2000 troops in al-Maṣṣīṣṣa and in early 'Abbasid times the Caliph al-Saffāḥ sent 400 as a garrison (*shiḥna*) and al-Manṣūr another 400 after that. Al-Mahdī despatched 2000 so there may have been about 4000 troops in the town at the end of his reign. Tarsus, resettled at the beginning of Hārūn al-Rashīd's reign, probably had a garrison of 4000–5000. Further East, early 'Abbasid Caliphs settled 4000 men in Malatya and another 4000 in al-Ḥadath. There must have been similar garrisons in remote outposts like Shimshāṭ and Qālīqāla (Erzerum). The small forts on the Cilician plain discussed earlier[22] had garrisons of no more than a dozen or so. Extrapolating from the figures we do have, it would probably be reasonable to suggest that there were some 25 000 salaried troops settled in the frontier cities by the reign of Hārūn al-Rashīd.

Al-Azdī's history of Mawsil gives more information about the military forces available in a provincial town in this period. In 171/787–8 the newly appointed governor of the city, Rawḥ b. Ṣāliḥ al-Hamdānī was instructed by the Caliph to collect the *ṣadaqa* (alms tax) from the Taghlibi bedouin in the steppes to the west of the city. He collected a force of 4000 but they were ambushed by the tribesmen, their leader was killed and the rest beat an ignominious retreat. In 184/800, after an outbreak of tribal conflict in the city Aḥmad b. Yazīd al-Sulamī was appointed governor and arrived with 4700 horse and 3300 foot.[23]

We also have information about the numbers involved in military expeditions against the Byzantines or other non-Muslims which attracted a significant number of *muṭṭawi'a*, or volunteers. Some such forces were quite small in scale. In 159/775–6 al-Mahdī despatched an expedition to Sind by sea from Basra.[24] It was a mixed force of 2000 men from the *ajnād* of Basra, 1500 *murābiṭāt*,[25] 700 Syrians,

1000 volunteers from Basra and 4000 *Asāwira* and *Sayābija*.[26] The Caliph also sent an agent to make sure that the men were properly equipped. It is curious to find mention of the *junds* of Basra and the *Asāwira* and *Sabābija* at this late date, and the names may simply have been convenient groupings for volunteer troops.

Large armies were assembled for other expeditions. In 162/779 al-Ḥasan b. Qaḥṭaba led 30 000 regular troops (*murtazaq*) as well as volunteers against the Byzantines.[27] In 165/781–22 Hārūn, then heir-apparent, led a force said to have been 100 000 regular troops and on his final expedition in 190/806 he led 135 000 *murtazaq* as well as volunteers.[28] These very large numbers must have included troops who were recruited for that particular campaign rather than being part of a permanent standing army. The next year Harthama b. A'yan led just 30 000 Khurāsānis on the summer campaign[29] and this is likely to have been a more typical number. It is worth remembering that when 'Alī b. 'Īsā b. Māhān led between 40 000 and 50 000 men from Baghdad to attack al-Ma'mūn in Khurāsān, people said it was the largest and best equipped army they had ever seen.[30] The fighting in and around Baghdad from 198/814 to 203/819 seems to have increased the numbers of troops, many of them, no doubt, irregulars hoping to benefit from military salaries, especially at a time when much of the rest of the economy was in ruins. In the final stages of the conflict, immediately before al-Ma'mūn's return to Baghdad, 'Īsā b. Muḥammad b. Abī Khālid, leader of the Baghdadis, commanded an army said to have been 123 000 men. Militarily they were completely useless and their only intention seems to have been to secure payment from the new regime.[31]

The structure of command

The early 'Abbasid period saw the emergence of a class of professional commanders or *quwwād* (sing., *qā'id*). This word, which simply means leader, had been used before, indeed figures like Sufyān b. Abrad al-Kalbī who did so much to secure Iraq for the Umayyads were sort of proto-*quwwād*, but it now came to acquire a quasi-professional meaning and could with caution be translated as 'general'. The *quwwād* of the early 'Abbasid period were in a real sense professional soldiers and depended on their salaries for their income. They were not great land-owners and, in the main they were not recruited from among the *ashrāf*, the old tribal aristocracy.

Their appointment was signalled by the granting of a banner: in his campaign against the Ustādhsīs, Khāzim b. Khuzayma had both a *liwā'* and an *'alam* as a sign of command.[32] They owed their position partly to their military abilities but also to family ties and their role within the 'Abbasid movement. The *qā'id* of the early 'Abbasid period was more than simply a salaried military commander. In many cases he was also a contractor in the sense that he was responsible for recruiting the troops who served under him. They may have been paid by the *dīwān al-jund*, the office which now managed the payment of salaries, but they owed their position to the *qā'id* who led them. This was probably not universal and the position of each *qā'id* must have been different, depending on family ties, relationship to the Caliph, military ability and other variables.

The senior *quwwād* were drawn from a fairly small number of families, most of whom owed their status to the role their founders had played in the 'Abbasid revolution;[33] like the early followers of the Prophet, they had *sābiqa* (precedence) in the movement, in this case the movement which brought the 'Abbasids to power. But *sābiqa* alone was not enough to guarantee success; contacts, ability and good luck were all essential ingredients as well. Status was often passed down within the family until the power bases of most of them were destroyed in the civil war which followed the death of Hārūn al-Rashīd in 193/809. Each case was individual and different and generalisations are difficult but by examining the position of two families of *quwwād* we can begin to see how the system worked.

Khāzim b. Khuzayma al-Tamīmī came from Marwrūdh, which lay on the Murghab river some 200 km south of Marw.[34] He was one of the earliest supporters of the 'Abbasid movement and was an important leader in the armies which marched West in 131/749. He was present at the siege of Wāsiṭ when the last supporters of Umayyad power in Iraq were eliminated. In 134/751–2 he was sent to fight the Khārijīs in Oman and returned to fight the 'Abbasid rebel 'Abd Allāh b. 'Alī and more Khārijīs in the Jazīra. In 141/758–9 he accompanied the Caliph's son, the future al-Mahdī, to Rayy and seems to have spent the next ten years in Khurāsān apart from a hurried expedition from Rayy to Ahwaz in 145/762–3 to wrest the city from the supporters of the 'Alid rebel Ibrāhīm b. 'Abd Allāh. He disappears from the record after 150/765 and it must be presumed that he died in Khurāsān. His family continued to be influential. On the night in 170/787 when the Caliph al-Hādī died, Khāzim's son Khuzayma was able to mobilise 5000 of his own men (*mawālīhi*), armed them, and forced the dead Caliph's son to give up his claim to the throne, so paving the way for the accession of Hārūn al-Rashīd.[35] Khuzayma and his brother 'Abd Allāh were prominent military men in the reign of Hārūn al-Rashīd and Khuzayma built a celebrated palace in Baghdad. Like many of the families of the old Khurāsāniya, the Banū Khuzayma lost most of their power and influence in the civil war which followed Harūn's death in 193/809, but we do hear of one of Khāzim's great-grandsons, Nahshal b. Ṣakhr b. Khuzayma b. Khāzim b. Khuzayma serving the 'Abbasid armies in 251/ 865.[36]

Khāzim came from the Nahshal branch of the famous north-east Arabian tribe of Tamīm . We have no details about how the family came to settle in Marwrūdh, though they must have come in one of the Basran military expeditions to Khurāsān. While they remembered their Arab origins, as their use of the *nisba* Tamīmī shows, they were to some extent Iranianised and we know that Khāzim spoke Persian to his followers and that his sister had married a Khurāsāni called 'Abdawayh.[37] In these circumstances, it is not surprising that tribal contacts were not, in the main, significant in Khāzim's rise into the military élite. There were Arab tribal *ashrāf* in the early 'Abbasid élite, Yazīd b. Mazyad al-Shaybānī, for example, but Khāzim was not one of them. However, if tribal links were comparatively unimportant among the Khurāsāniya, vestiges of tribal solidarity still survived in Basra and when Khāzim was setting out from the city to attack the Khārijīs in Oman, he was joined by a number of Tamīmīs, no other Basrans being mentioned.[38] Even in these changed times, a good *nisba* still counted for something.

Khāzim did have a personal following who were important in his rise to élite status, but their links to him were based on *walā'* and geography rather than tribal loyalties. It was he who had taken Marwrūdh for the 'Abbasids, despite the opposition of other Tamīmīs[39] and he was one of the commanders the people of Marwrūdh during the westward march of the 'Abbasid armies.[40] When he set out for Oman, in addition to 700 soldiers sent by the Caliph, he also chose men he knew he could rely on from his household, his clan (*banū 'amm*), his *mawālī* (which probably means freedmen in this early 'Abbasid context) and the people of Marwrūdh. When he reached Oman he appointed Marwrūdhīs to important positions of command, both his left and right wing being commanded by his fellow townsmen, Muslim al-Arghadī and Ḥumayd al-Wartakānī: it is likely that both of these were first- or second-generation Iranian converts. His scouts (*ṭalā'i'*) were led by Naḍala b. Nu'aym, who came from Nahshal, the same branch of Tamīm as Khāzim himself and may, indeed, have been a cousin.[41] In 138/755–6 Khāzim was sent to fight a Kharijite rebellion in Jazīra. He led 8000 'Marwrūdhīya'. Once again, Naḍala b. Nu'aym was in charge of the scouts, but his other officers, Abū Ḥammād al-Marwazī and Zuhayr b. Muḥammad al-'Āmirī were both men who had served with Khāzim in the armies of the 'Abbasid revolution.

His Marwrūdhī connections proved their worth in 141/758–9 when the governor of Khurāsān, 'Abd al-Jabbār al-Azdī rebelled. Al-Mahdī, who had been sent to Rayy to restore order, appointed Khāzim to lead the expedition against the rebel. When the people of Marwrūdh heard this, they decided not to wait but to fight 'Abd al-Jabbār themselves. He was defeated and captured and their leader, Mujashshir b. Muzāḥim brought the prisoner to Khāzim.[42] Faced with the revolt of Ustādhsīs in 150/757, the Marwrūdhīs again resisted the rebels but this time they were defeated and many of them were slain or fled. When he was put in charge of the campaign, Khāzim rallied those who had fled and incorporated them into his army.[43]

Khāzim valued the right to choose his own forces. He clearly did so in the case of the Omani expedition but the clearest indication of the importance he attached to this was in his response to the rebellion of the Ustādhsīs in Khurāsān. There was a real danger that the whole of the province would be lost to the 'Abbasids so, like al-Muhallab again facing the Khārijīs in Umayyad times, he was in a position to negotiate his own contract. He demanded that al-Mahdī's vizier, Mu'āwiya b. 'Ubayd Allāh, should be forbidden to interfere in the organisation of his campaign. He also demanded to be left in sole charge, to choose his own commanders and to distribute banners as he wished. There is no indication, however, that Khāzim ever enjoyed, or requested, the sort of fiscal independence which al-Muhallab had had. Ibn al-Muqaffa' had advised the Caliph that soldiers were not to be put in charge of tax-collecting[44] and it seems that the early 'Abbasid Caliphs stuck to this.

Khāzim enjoyed considerable moral authority in the 'Abbasid state because of his *sābiqa* in the movement, and the importance of this can be seen in an incident soon after the revolution which almost destroyed his career. For reasons which are not clear a leading figure in the Khurāsāni army, Bassām b. Ibrāhīm, had begun a rebellion in central Iraq in 134/751–2. Khāzim was despatched to deal with him and the rebellion was soon defeated. However, one of the fleeing rebels had passed through a village inhabited by Banū'l-Ḥārith b. Ka'b where he had been sheltered and sent on his way. When Khāzim passed through the village, he was given a cool reception. He turned on the inhabitants, accusing them of aiding the Caliph's enemies, slaughtered most of them and had their houses demolished. None of this would have got him into trouble, indeed quite the opposite, except that the Banū'l-Ḥārith were maternal relations of the reigning Caliph al-Saffāḥ. This was well known to Khāzim, who had reproached them with sheltering their kinsman's enemy. Protests were made and the Caliph resolved to kill Khāzim in revenge. However, several leading figures in the Khurāsāni army protested that this was unjust, in view of his long record of obedience and *sābiqa*. Instead, it was proposed that he be sent to fight the Khārijīs in Oman with at least the possibility that he might never return.[45] The whole incident shows how important the prestige conferred by *sābiqa* could be. It also shows the power of a network, like the network of the Khurāsāniya: membership of such a network was clearly important in maintaining élite status.

Khāzim also enjoyed prestige as a successful military commander, indeed after the death of Qaḥṭaba b. Shabīb, he was probably the most successful commander of the first generation of the Khurāsāniya. Again, the sources give us some indication of the reasons for his success. His strategy was marked by caution. Faced with al-Mulabbad and his Kharijite followers in the Jazīra, he was careful to dig *khandaq*s to protect his troops wherever he went.[46] His defeat of the Ustādhsīs was accomplished by the construction and bold defence of a *khandaq*.[47] In the heat of the battle, he showed the ability to make quick and surprising decisions. In the decisive battle with the Khārijīs, he ordered his men to dismount and fight on foot with their swords, the classic tactic used against the Khārijīs who normally fought on horseback but were now forced to dismount as well. In the confusion and hidden by the dust, he sent his lieutenant, Naḍala b. Nu'aym with mounted archers to the rear of the enemy, who now found themselves attacked from both directions and were rapidly overwhelmed. His victory over the Ustādhsīs was also achieved by a ruse: when two gates of his marching camp were being attacked, he sent a force out of a third to attack the assailants from behind and pretend that they were the expected relieving army. These may not seem particularly subtle devices but they were effective, and the fact that they were reported and passed down into the historical record suggests that they made a significant impact on contemporaries.

Interestingly, Khāzim was associated with technological advances in warfare. In Oman, he was advised by an immigrant from Soghdia who he encountered there, to put rags on the end of his spears and soak them in naphtha (*naft*) and use them to set fire to the flimsy dwellings of the inhabitants.[48] This is presented as an unusual tactic in the warfare of the time. In his battle with Mulabbad, he used a caltrops (*ḥasak*) to impede the Kharijite cavalry, another unusual device.

Khāzim secured his place in the élite by his early commitment to the 'Abbasid cause, by the support he could command among the inhabitants of Marwrūdh, by his control of appointments within his forces and by his track record of military success. By examining his career we can see how the early 'Abbasid army was recruited and led. Though we are better informed about his career than others, he can perhaps be considered as a 'typical' early 'Abbasid *qā'id*.

Ma'n b. Zā'ida al-Shaybānī was a man from a very different background.[49] He came from the bedouin tribe of Shaybān which was powerful in the Jazīra and was, in fact, a distant cousin of Shabīb b. Yazīd al-Shaybānī, the famous Kharijite rebel of the Umayyad period.[50] Far from being an early supporter of the 'Abbasids, he had been one of the fiercest opponents of the armies of the Revolution, joining Ibn Hubayra in the last-ditch attempt to resist them in Wāsiṭ. He was lucky to escape with his life and for some time he remained in hiding until 141/758–9, when he came to the Caliph al-Manṣūr's rescue when his life was threatened by rioters. He was then offered posts in difficult provinces like Yemen and Sistan, where he was killed in 152/722–3 by a band of Khārijīs who disguised themselves as builders to enter his house and catch him unawares. His position was inherited by his nephew, Yazīd b. Mazyad along with a huge retinue (*mawkib ḍakhm*) of his *mawālī* and his tribesmen.[51] Yazīd made himself indispensable to the Caliphs by being almost the only military commander who could take on the Khārijīs who roamed the Jazīra. In 179/795–6, for example, Yazīd managed to regain the favour of Hārūn al-Rashīd, whose accession to the throne he had opposed, by killing the famous rebel al-Walīd b. Ṭarīf. His troops were recruited from his companions (*aṣḥāb*) and his tribe (*'ashīra*).[52] Both Ma'n and his nephew Yazīd were regarded as personifications of traditional Arab virtues and praised extravagantly by poets for their courage and their generosity. While they were both, no doubt, effective soldiers in their own right, it was not just their personal abilities which made them valuable to the 'Abbasids but the fact they could recruit members of their tribe to join the 'Abbasid forces and lead them into battle.

The *quwwād* were pivotal individuals in the early 'Abbasid state, as intermediaries between the troops and their Caliph and as their leaders in the field. There is no evidence, however, that the *quwwād* were responsible for the payment of the troops. It was still expected that they should be paid *'aṭā'* from the proceeds of general taxation. The office which made these payments, the *dīwān al-jund* was staffed not by the *quwwād* or their representatives but by bureaucrats, recruited and appointed by the Caliph and his vizier.

A further development of the idea of the military commander as contractor can be seen in the early attempts to subdue the rebellion of Bābak in Azerbayjān. During the civil war which followed the death of Hārūn al-Rashīd in 193/809, the position of the Muslim settlers in Azerbayjān had deteriorated and when he established himself in power, al-Ma'mūn decided to take action against Bābak and his followers, the non-Muslim Khurramiya. It was not easy; the area was mountainous and inaccessible and the natives determined. Two conventional military expeditions in 204 and 205 (819–20) failed dismally and the Caliph had neither the resources nor the troops to send another.

It was at this stage that Zurayq b. ʻAlī al-Azdī saw his opportunity. Zurayq came from an important Arab family from Mawṣil but he was trying to make his fortune in Azerbayjān by taking lands and exploiting the mineral resources. He now got in touch with a government secretary Aḥmad b. al-Junayd, who in turn informed the Caliph that Zurayq would lead an expedition to conquer the area if he were made governor of Armenia and Azerbayjān. Zurayq recruited an army, said to have numbered 50 000 in Ardabil in 205/autumn 820. Ibn al-Junayd came along, no doubt hoping to profit from what promised to be an exciting opportunity. In the event, the whole expedition was a complete fiasco: the inexperienced secretary was defeated and captured by Bābak's men and Zurayq allowed himself to be bought off and returned to his other political and business interests in the Mawsil area.

Six years later the Caliph decided to launch another expedition. He entrusted the command to Muḥammad b. Ḥumayd al-Ṭūsī, whose father had been one of the his commanders in Iraq during the civil war. This expedition, too, was organised on a contract basis. Muḥammad raised an army out of his own considerable private resources and was able to pay the assembled troops no less than 1 000 000 *dirhams* of his own money before they set out. He first defeated and captured Zurayq, confiscating his estates and then from 212/827 moved into Azerbayjān. Though he was a careful and experienced commander, he too was caught in a narrow defile and slaughtered with his men by Bābak's troops in 213/spring 828. In the cases of the Azerbayjān expeditions, military campaigns had essentially been privatised: the government of al-Ma'mūn lacked both the men and the resources to undertake such a difficult campaign. It was these weaknesses that his successor, al-Mu'taṣim (218–27/833–42), was determined to overcome.

al-Jāḥiẓ on the *Abnā* and *Khurāsāniya*

In his essay on the armies of the Caliphate, the *Manāqib al-Turk*, al-Jāḥiẓ relates a view that the army of the Caliphate in the early third/ninth century was divided into five groups, the Khurāsāniya, the Abnā', the Mawālī, the Arabs and the Turks.[53] Of these, the Turks did not appear in significant numbers until the reign of al-Ma'mūn and they will be treated in Chapter 5. The Arabs are hardly mentioned again and, while their loyalty to the dynasty is stressed, little is said about the fighting skills of the Mawālī. On the other hand, al-Jāḥiẓ devotes considerable space to the weapons and fighting techniques of the Abnā' and Khurāsāniya. It is not always clear how he differentiates between the two groups, and indeed one of the purposes of his essay was to stress their links and similarities, but he seems to use the term Khurāsāniya for the original Khurāsāni supporters of the ʻAbbasids and for those supporters of the regime who remained in the East.[54] They are described as sharing the same land (*ḥayyiz*), as the Turks which places them firmly in Khurāsān and Transoxania. In the extended speech they make extolling their own prowess,[55] they claim that they are the *naqīb*s of the 'Abbasids and the sons of the *naqīb*s (that is, the original leaders of the 'Abbasid movement in its clandestine phase). Only one of their leaders is named and that is the comparatively obscure figure of Hāshim b. al-Ishtākhanj, a Khurāsāni soldier who was arrested and executed by al-Manṣūr in 152/769 apparently for trying to start a revolt in Ifrīqiya, where many of the Khurāsāniya had been posted.[56] It seems most likely that the Khurāsāniya referred to by al-Jāḥiẓ were the Iranian supporters of al-Ma'mūn, like 'Ujayf b. 'Anbaṣa and 'Alī b. Ḥishām whose names were not recorded because they were purged by al-Mu'taṣim. The group may also have included al-Afshīn and Ṭāhir, who we know was an eastern Iranian magnate who claimed than his ancestors had been early supporters of the 'Abbasids.[57]

The Khurāsāniya describe themselves[58] as heavy cavalry, horseman equipped with armour (*tajāfīf*) and other body armour of metal and felt and armed with curved scabbards (that is, curved swords), clubs (*kāfirkūbāt*) and axes (*ṭabarzīnāt*). They boast of their frightening drums and their huge banners (*bunūd*). They train themselves with sports like leaping on horses or polo or attacking birds on spears or the *birjās* (quintain or swinging target on a pole[59]) so that they can perform complex movements like the *karr ba'd al-farr*, that is the wheeling round to attack after a (feigned) flight. Al-Jāḥiẓ's language is chosen for rhetorical effect here, as in other parts of the essay, and it is not always clear what is meant but we can be certain that the Khurāsāniya he speaks of were skilled heavy cavalry.

The spokesman for the Abnā' remarks[60] that his root is in Khurāsān but his branch in Baghdad, confirming that the term is used in the generally accepted way. The Abnā' are said to fight on horses ('we use long spears when foot soldiers and short spears when mounted') but the emphasis is on their role as infantry ('we walk towards the spears') and in hand-to-hand fighting, with knives and daggers if necessary. They boast of their expertise in scaling and breaking into city walls and in amphibious warfare. Above all they are skilled in street fighting, at the gates of the *khandaq*s, in the alleys (*aziqqa*), in the markets and in the villages. Once again al-Jāḥiẓ's language is chosen for literary effect and he seems to want to draw a contrast with the Khurāsāniya. It may be as well that his description of the Abnā' at war owes much to the street fighting in Baghdad during the civil wars which followed the death of Hārūn al-Rashīd. Despite these caveats, however, the discussion does show that infantry warfare was important and that the Abnā' often fought on foot. Neither in the case of the Khurāsāniya, nor of the Abnā', is there any clear discussion of bows and archery.

War on the Byzantine frontier[61]

The Byzantine frontier was the only theatre in which the early 'Abbasid Caliphs attempted to expand the Muslim state by military means. Until the reign of Hārūn al-Rashīd, frontier warfare was limited in scope. There was no attempt to repeat the great Umayyad efforts to take Constantinople itself. Instead policy seems to have been limited to safeguarding the frontier cities, regaining and reoccupying those like Malatya which had been taken by the Byzantines during the chaos of the 'Abbasid revolution and leading raids into Byzantine territory. These raids took place almost every year. The *ṣā'ifa* (summer raid) was as much a part of the symbolic and ritual functions of the Caliph as was organising and providing leadership for the annual *ḥajj* to Makka. It represented a show of authority and Muslim leadership but it did not amount to a campaign of conquest. Little attempt was made to secure bases beyond the Taurus frontier districts. Raids could produce tribute and booty, and could provide an outlet for the enthusiasm of the *muṭṭawi'a*, the volunteers for the *jihād.*

Most of the raids were undertaken by regular soldiers, Khurāsānis and, to a lesser extent Syrians. The campaigns against Byzantium were the only military campaigns in which the Caliphs themselves, and their sons, took part. This seems to have been a deliberate policy, introduced by al-Mahdī from 163/780 to use the *jihād* to bolster the prestige of the dynasty and household and to provide a training ground for his son Hārūn. This resulted in high-profile military operations like that in 165/781 when Hārūn is said to have led 95 793 men as far as the Sea of Marmara. On an even larger scale was the raid of 190/806 when Hārūn, now Caliph is alleged to have led 135 000 men, excluding volunteers and those whose names were not in the *dīwān*. Heracleia was conquered and the inhabitants deported while the Emperor Nicephorus is said to have paid tribute, including an element that was counted as his own personal poll-tax, a sign of humiliation. However, no attempt was made to hold or settle to the conquered city which was simply abandoned. The very large numbers recorded for this expedition are almost certainly exaggerated, to demonstrate the prestige of the Caliph and his role as military leader of the Muslims.

As noted above, none of these campaigns, even the great expedition of 190/806 was recorded in detail by the Arabic chronicles, or at least no such account has come down to us. For a fuller account of the realities of frontier warfare we have to turn to a Syriac Christian source, the Zuqnin Chronicle[62] and the account of the campaign of 149/766–7. The Zuqnin Chronicler was a contemporary, living near the scene of events, the monastery of Zuqnin was near Amida (Diyarbakr), and he himself saw some of the survivors and heard their accounts. Al-Ṭabarī records the campaign in just two and a half lines of text,[63] but he confirms the Zuqnin Chronicler's naming of the leaders.

The army led by al-'Abbās b. Muḥammad, the Caliph al-Manṣūr's brother, and Qaḥṭaba al-Ḥasan b., a veteran Khurāsāni *qā'id*, is said to have been composed of people of many nationalities, including Sindis, Alans, Khazars, Medes, Persians, Kūfis, Arabs and Turks 'like a swarm of caterpillars of every variety'. He alleges that they were of many faiths and some worshipped fire, the sun and the stars. They entered Byzantine territory without encountering any opposition, and began to gorge themselves on the fruits of the land. Like most people in the Zuqnin Chronicle, they soon came to a bad end, many died of dysentery and their animals, especially the camels, perished in vast numbers.

Undaunted, al-'Abbās pressed on to the north. A detachment with some of the workers who had been brought from all over the Jazīra were left at Kharpert to rebuild the fortress there while the main army went north to besiege the castle at Kamkh (Chomacha), the main object of the expedition. The ruins of Kamkh still exist,[64] on a plateau above the waters of the upper Euphrates, about 50 km south-west of Erzincan in eastern Turkey. Al-'Abbās requisitioned carts from the local Armenian population and used them to bring wood to construct siege engines, while the Byzantine garrison constructed engines of their own. Insults were shouted and the siege began. The Muslims, referred to as Persians by the Chronicler, built mobile shelters (presumably the Roman *musculi* which the Arabs called *dabābāt*) and tried to use them to fill up the ditch, but the defenders used their engines to such good effect that they could make no progress. On one side of the castle, there was a gap in the fortifications, and here the defenders laid great logs, weighted with stones. When the Muslims tried a surprise night attack, the logs were rolled down on them and large numbers were killed: 'all their attempts proved futile because God was helping the Romans.'

At this stage the Muslim army divided into two groups. One under al-'Abbās remained to continue the siege while another, said to have been 50 000, set off to pillage. Unfortunately for them, they had no guides and wanted to avoid the main roads for fear that the Byzantines would discover them. They wandered for some time in deserted lands between Byzantine and Armenian territory and many perished of hunger and thirst. Eventually they arrived in a fertile area around Kayseri and began to raid and pillage. Having collected their booty, they them decided to head for Syria. After a while, thinking they had already reached Syria and safety, they camped in a fertile valley with all their loot, only to be surprised by a Byzantine army of 12 000 which had come across them by accident. The Byzantine commander sent to other towns and a large army was assembled. They then launched a night attack, vast numbers of Persians were killed and the survivors were obliged to flee without any of their loot. One of their commanders, called Radad (?) escaped to Malatya while the other, the Taglibi chief Mālik b. Ṭawq, fled to Erzerum with 5000 survivors. It was the dejected remnants of this army who told the Chronicler what had happened.

Meanwhile, back at Kamkh things were not going well for the Muslims. The besiegers were starving and their engines were making no impression. Al-'Abbās sent out messengers and vast numbers of merchants came from the Jazīra, Armenia and elsewhere and established a large market, selling food supplies to the garrison. Unfortunately for them, winter was now coming on and al-'Abbās decided that he had to abandon the siege before the snows set in. The Muslim army proceeded to burn the market so that the goods would not fall into the hands of the garrison after they had gone and there were no pack animals to take it away. Even the workers who were employed at the siege were robbed of their wages and the payments for their donkeys. The emaciated and enfeebled remnants of the army passed Amida on their way south. We probably get much closer to the reality of frontier warfare, with its confusions, hardships and failures, in this account than in the brief and sanitised versions provided by the Arabic historians.

The civil war, 195–204/811–19

After the death of the Caliph Hārūn al-Rashīd in 193/809, the ‘Abbasid Caliphate was torn apart by a long civil war between his two sons, al-Amīn, based in Baghdad, and al-Ma’mūn, based in Merv, the capital of Khurāsān.[65] It developed into a conflict between two different armies. On the one hand there were the Abnā’, now supporting al-Amīn and based in Baghdad. With them were other troops from the western half of the Caliphate, including Arabs. The other army was made up largely of eastern Iranian nobles and their followers. Despite their inferior number, it was the supporters of al-Ma’mūn who proved to be victorious and by 204/819, he had entered Baghdad and, more or less, reunited the Caliphate under his rule.

The civil war was an important turning point in ‘Abbasid history but it remains difficult to explain the triumph of al-Ma’mūn’s numerically inferior armies. The sources we have tend to explain it moral and political terms: al-Ma’mūn was wise and pious while his brother was foolish and feckless. The forces of al-Amīn were over-confident at the beginning and then, when failure began to bite, were paralysed by internal rivalries. But these same sources give only short accounts of the crucial battles which decided the course of the war.

The first, and in many ways decisive, military encounter took place near Rayy in central Iran in Sha‘bān 195/May 811.[66] The two armies were of very different sizes. Al-Amīn’s army, led by the veteran ‘Alī b. ‘Īsā b. Māhān, ex-governor of Khurāsān, is said to have had some 40 000 men while al-Ma’mūn’s commander, Ṭāhir b. al-Ḥusayn, an inexperienced Khurāsāni noble of Arab extraction,[67] had a mere 3800–5000: even allowing for exaggeration of the part of the victors, it was clearly a very uneven encounter.

As so often, the exact course of the battle is uncertain. According to al-Ṭabarī’s first account, ‘Alī’s army approached in overwhelming numbers and Ṭāhir decided to fight ‘like the Khārijīs’, concentrating an attack on the centre of the army. Seven hundred Khwarazmians were despatched, supported by archers from Bukhārā, but the outcome is presented as a single combat between ‘Alī and a warrior from al-Ma’mūn’s army, which left ‘Alī dead and his army in total disarray.[68]

A second, more circumstantial and perhaps more realistic account, gives a more complex picture. At first, Ṭāhir, faced by a much larger army, was advised to fortify himself behind the walls of the ancient city of Rayy and await reinforcement. Ṭāhir rejected this suggestion, arguing that the people of the city, impressed by the size of ‘Alī’s army, would rise against them and hand them over. In the open country, ‘Alī arranged his army in the traditional way, with a left wing, right wing and centre. He divided them into groups of 1000, each with a banner. The men with armour (helmets, *durū‘* and *jawāshin*) were to precede the banner, implying that a large proportion of his men were not so equipped. The groups were to advance in succession and relieve each other. He himself commanded from the centre. Ṭāhir meanwhile arranged his men in *katā’ib* and *karādīs* – that is, mobile cavalry squadrons. When battle was joined, 'Alī's men made gains on the wings but Ṭāhir concentrated his forces in the centre and the battle was effectively brought to a close when 'Alī was killed by an arrow.[69] According to al-Ya'qūbī, 'Alī was out on a reconaissance trip with a few companions when he was spotted by Ṭāhir who was able to cut him off and, while his men dealt with 'Alī's escort, he himself killed their commander. After that, al-Amīn's demoralised army retreated in disorder.

The details are sketchy, but it may be that the battle of Rayy marked a turning point in the military tactics of the period. It looks as if a large, mostly infantry army was defeated by a much smaller cavalry force. This may have marked the end of the large armies of foot-soldiers which were typical of much early Islamic warfare and the superiority of much smaller groups of mounted men, either armoured spearmen or mounted archers.

Al-Amīn's army fled west but this was by no means the end of the conflict. Reinforcements from Baghdad, under the leadership of 'Abd al-Raḥmān b. Jabala were despatched. This time the new commander chose to fortify himself behind the walls and gates of Hamadhan but when the enemy approached they came out to meet them. Twice 'Abd al-Raḥmān's men were driven back to the city and finally Ṭāhir began a blockade while 'Abd al-Raḥman's forces attacked with arrows and stones from the walls. Soon, however, the inhabitants began to resent the occupation and disruption and 'Abd al-Raḥmān was obliged to leave and ask for terms.[70]

Ṭāhir's army and their captives continued to move west to Baghdad but 'Abd al-Raḥmān was not finished yet. In the pass at Asadabad, he launched a surprise attack which caught his captors off their guard. Ṭāhir's men responded as any well-disciplined army of the time would: his foot-soldiers dropped to their knees and defended themselves with swords, shields and arrows while the cavalry gathered their equipment. In the ensuing mêlée, 'Abd al-Raḥmān's men were defeated and their leader, who had dismounted to fight more effectively, was killed.[71]

Ṭāhir's advance them became something of a triumphal progress and we hear little more about the details of battle. In al-Ahwaz, there was a fierce encounter with the forces of the local governor, Muḥammad b. Yazīd al-Muhallabī, who chose to retreat to the protection of the walls at Ahwaz, but the enemy were hard on his heels. Some of Muḥammad's men made a sortie but al-Ma'mūn's men fought them on foot with stones and other missiles. Muḥammad and his companions then dismounted, hamstrung their horses as a sign that they would not flee, and died fighting fiercely.[72] Thereafter, there was little determined opposition to Ṭāhir's advance until he, and al-Ma'mūn's other main commander, Harthama b. A'yan were virtually at the gates of Baghdad.

From Dhu'l-Ḥijja 196/August 812 until Muharram, 198/September 813, the vast city of Baghdad was in the grip of a siege which has no parallel in the warfare of the time. While the Round City of al-Manṣūr was walled, the numerous suburbs where most of the population lived, were not. The siege was not, therefore, attacks on a fortified perimeter, but rather a war of street fighting, house-to-house struggles and temporary improvised fortifications. It was also extremely destructive, above all for the civilian population.

The siege and the contemporary events inside the city are described at length in the accounts collected in al-Ṭabarī's *Ta'rīkh*.[73] These accounts include prose narratives, some ascribed directly to eyewitnesses, and poetry. The emphasis of these accounts is less on the military activities than on the sufferings and privations endured by the non-combatant population. Above all, the accounts lament the damage inflicted by siege engines and by the ill-disciplined soldiers and irregulars who took up arms in one cause or another.

Siege engines were in use from the very beginning of the blockade when Zuhayr b. al-Musayyab al-Ḍabbī set up his camp at Qasr Raqqat Kalwādhā just south of the city. He dug a *khandaq* and set up *manājīq* and *'arrādāt*. At the same time Harthama b. A'yan established a *khandaq* with a wall at Nahr Bīn and placed both types of engine in it.[74] *Manjanīq* is the usual word for a swing beam siege engine. An *'arrāda* is described by the lexicographers as similar to a *manjanīq* but smaller.[75] On some occasions it clearly appears as an anti-personnel weapon.[76] Siege engines were also used by the partisans of al-Amīn to defend the parts of the city they controlled.[77] One supporter of al-Amīn, known simply as al-Samarqandī, even mounted *manājiq* on boats in the Tigris and stones from these caused great destruction in suburbs which had been captured by the besiegers. We also hear of a siege engine called a *khaṭṭāra* from a root describing the motion of an animal's tail when it is lashed up and down. The context is a lament for the destruction of the city by al-Khuraymī and the use may be tropical rather than technical:

> In every gated street and on every side
> There is a siege engine whose moving beam raises its voice.
> With projectiles like men's heads taken from pieces
> Of stone, the evil man loads the sling.
> It is as if over their heads there were flocks
> Of dusky sand grouse taking flight in commotion.[78]

The poem, which is certainly contemporary to the events described, is interesting from the military history angle in that it shows the rough size of the stone missiles used. It also makes it clear that there was a sling (*miqlā'*) attached to the end of the beam and that the projectile was loaded into it to give added acceleration.

A second feature of the narratives of the siege of Baghdad, is the prominence given to the role of the *'ayyārūn* (vagrants or vagabonds) and *'urāt* (naked ones). These terms are used to describe irregulars from non-military backgrounds who came to the aid of al-Amīn in the latter stages of the siege when the regular soldiers had largely deserted him. They were paid no salaries and possessed no armour: their shields were of reeds and their *maghāfir* of palm leaves.[79] In one anecdote[80] a well-equipped Khurāsānī soldier from Ṭāhir's army comes face to face with one of these irregulars, protected only with a reed mat and armed only with a sling. The Khurāsānī, who was mounted, first shoots his arrows but his opponent parries them with his improvised shield and then, to make matters worse, collects the arrows to sell them. When he has no more arrows left, the Khurāsānī tries to close with his sword, but the *'ayyār* hits him in the eye with a stone from his sling and he retreats, defeated and humiliated. Both in poetry and anecdote, a clear contrast is drawn between the regular soldier and the irregular volunteer, not always to the regular's advantage.

Treatises on warfare and the work of al-Harthamī al-Sha'rānī

It seems that the early Islamic world produced little in the way of manuals of warfare or instructional literature about how armies should be led and battles fought. Ibn al-Nadīm (d. 380/990) devotes a short chapter to the subject in his *Fihrist*,[81] a survey of Arabic literature as it existed in his time. He mentions a number of works translated from the Sasanian Persian , a book on 'The Conduct of Wars and the Organisation of the Army' (*Adāb al-ḥurūb wa ṣurat al-'askar*) written for the Caliph al-Manṣūr by one 'Abd al-Jabbār b. 'Adī. There were also works on the administration of armies and siege techniques by authors like al-Shānāq al-Hindī and Ibn Khafīf who are no more than names to us and a book on *Furūsiya* (Chivalry) by al-Ishmīṭī, which must have been an early example of a genre which was to become popular in Mamluke times. No trace of any of these books seems to have survived.

Ibn al-Nadīm also records a book probably called *Al-Ḥiyāl* (The Stratagems)[82] by al-Sha'rānī al-Harthamī composed for the Caliph al-Ma'mūn. This seems to have been an long and elaborate work in two treatises with numerous sub-headings. Nothing is known of this author except that his second *nisba*, al-Harthamī, suggests that he had originally been in the service of Harthama b. A'yan, a famous military commander in the reign of Hārūn. The text of this work seems to have been lost, but there survives in the Koprulu library in Istanbul an MS which claims to be an abridgement of al-Harthamī's work, bearing the title *Siyāsat al-ḥurūb* (the Organisation of Warfare). This seems to be an Arabic adaptation of a classical Greek work on warfare, possibly part of the pseudo-Aristotelian corpus and may well reflect classical Greek warfare more than 'Abbasid practice.[83]

The work was probably undertaken before the tenth century and may indeed be connected with the 'al-Harthamī' to whom it is ascribed. While the text seems to be based on classical military treatises, it is interesting from the point of view of Arabic terminology and shows what views of military organisation were available. How far it was intended as a manual of warfare, and how much as an academic exercise, is difficult to tell.

While we must be grateful for its survival, it is a curiously frustrating work to use. The abbreviator seems to have done his work ruthlessly: all references to sources have been excised and most sections simply begins with *qālū* ('they said'). Equally frustrating is the complete absence of any names of individuals;

even on those rare occasions where specific examples are quoted, the reference is only to 'a certain commander'.[84] This may, of course, have been characteristic of the full original but it seems more likely that all these details, which would have been so interesting to the historian, have been edited out by the abridger. Nor is the surviving text easy to understand, and much of it seems to be composed as a sort of exercise in linguistic virtuosity: the author seldom uses a common word where an obscure one will do.

The author is less interested in practical techniques of fighting than in the organisation of armies and the maintenance of discipline and morale. The section on the defence of fortresses, for example, says nothing about the manning of towers or action to be taken against siege engines, but a good deal about keeping up the spirits of the defenders and preventing dissension and squabbling.[85] And sometimes the text is simply bizarre, like the discussion of how to arrange your line of battle if you only have one soldier.[86]

The work is framed as advice given to the Caliph, either directly from the author or, more commonly, quoting the mysterious 'they' who are the only named source. The imperative is used throughout, 'do this, don't do that, etc.' begins with discussions of the qualities necessary in a commander (*ṣāḥib al-jaysh*, *ra'īs*) and his staff (*aṣḥāb*): they should be God-fearing, brave, patient, and so on. This discussion then[87] moves on to intelligence and the use of scouts and spies, which is one of the author's chief concerns.

Thirty different types of troops are mentioned, including scouts and night-watchmen and horsemen, including the horsemen of the *rābiṭa*, the *shākiriya* and the *shuraṭ*.[88] Later in the text it is explained that one of the functions of the *rābiṭa* and the *shurṭa* is to marshal the army and make sure that they move into camp or fortified positions when ordered to do so.[89] The author also describes different sizes of military formations. The smallest of these number between 300 and 500 men and are called *sarāyā* if they operate at night and *sawārib* if they operate by day. If these formations break up after they have set out, units of fewer than 40 are called *jarā'id*, from 40 to 300 are *manāqib* and from 300 to 500 are *jamarāt*. Anything over 800 men could be called a *jaysh* and a variety of different names are given to different sizes of armies up to a *jaysh jarrār* of 12 000. The section ends with the comment that the best *sarāyā* is 400 men and the best *jaysh* is 4000. Like other sections of the work, these comments seems more concerned with lexicography than the realities of military organisation, but the details may help us to interpret other texts more effectively.

The following sections[90] deal with the organisation of the march and the making of camps. The *ṣāḥib al-ta'bi'a* is the officer responsible for these functions. As always, the importance of intelligence is stressed. The army is to march in an orderly way and the commander is to go in the centre with the *athqāl* (baggage) and *aswāq* (markets, suggesting that the troops were expected to buy their supplies). The camp is to be protected by sentries and *khanādiq* (earthworks) but also by palisades of spears fixed together like a fence (*mutarāṣaf*) and *ḥasak* (here meaning thorny bushes rather than caltrops).[91]

The choosing of a battle field and the arrangement of the army are given considerable attention.[92] The advantages of fighting with your back to the sun and wind are pointed out and using an elevated position so that horsemen can dismount and fight alongside the foot, linked together as one man.[93] If necessary, a squadron of horse (*kardūs*) should be stationed on the flanks of the army to protect the lines.[94] Considerable attention is paid to the drawing up of lines of battle.[95] The lines are described as being arranged in the classical manner with a centre (*qalb* i.e. heart), a right wing (*maymana*) and a left wing (*maysara*). The right wing should lead the attack followed, if all goes well, by the centre, while the function of the left wing is largely defensive.[96]

If the army is large, the line should be arranged in five ranks (*ḥayn*, lit. time), the front row being the main line, the second support, the third with the baggage and civilians, the fourth to support the baggage and the fifth being the rear guard.[97] Drums and horns should be played, religious slogans should be shouted and the author discusses the importance of flags and banners (*band, liwā'*) as rallying places and *'alāmāt* (flags) as a means of signalling.[98] Positions are assigned not only to the military units and but also to officials like the *wazīr* and the *kātib al-rasā'il* (correspondence secretary) and to the doctors and merchants accompanying the army.

The plan of battle is that the right wing will take the offensive and advance on the enemy while the centre remains in position and attack only if the enemy is seen to be retreating. The left wing is to remain on the defensive. If the first attack is not successful and it is necessary to fall back or withdraw, it is essential that this be done in an orderly fashion, without running or panic and that all units return to their positions (*markaz*).[99]

Two sections discuss fortifications and their use in warfare.[100] Much of the discussion revolves around questions of morale and trying to achieve results by guile and the commander is explicitly told not to fight for things that can be achieved by deception and guile.[101] The commander should know the places for the positioning (*naṣab*) of siege engines (*majānīq* and *'arrādāt*), where to find stones for them and their range. He should also know the range of archers, *ḥinshān* (lit., serpents), catapults and slings (*maqāli'*), fire and lassoes. He should also know the use of carts (*'ajal*), *dabbābāt* (mobile shelters), passages, tunnels, holes, ladders, hooks and grappling irons (*salālīm, kalālīb, khaṭāṭīf*).[102] Unfortunately none of these implements is described in any more detail, nor is the commander given further details about how to use them. Similarly in the discussion of the defence of a castle we are given a list of parts of the fortification, gates, corners (*arkān*), towers (*burūj*), battlements (*shuraf*), screens (*sutar*), ramparts (*sudad*), guarding places and watching places, lookouts (*marātib*), trenches (*khanādiq*) and *fārqīnāt* (said by the editor to be a Persian equivalent of *khanādiq*). No further details are given and, as elsewhere in the text, it seems that the list is included more for rhetorical effect than practical utility.

The final sections of the work are concerned with a miscellany of different points,[103] among them that horsemen should not take too much baggage with them on raids or go hunting when on military expeditions. It also includes the only mention of the *'arīf* in the entire text when the author says that he should be the only one of the foot soldiers allowed a horse so that he can supervise his men. There is a list of different types of fighting men (Turks, Daylamites, Greeks, Indians, Kurds, bedouin Arabs and others). The author tells us that all these fight in different ways but fails to give any further details.[104] Finally he concludes with some general observations on the difficulty of making hard and fast rules for the conduct of warfare.

For all its limitations, the work gives us some insight into the problems of military command. The emphasis throughout is on intelligence, of avoiding battle and achieving your objectives by guile and surprise if at all possible. Problems of morale and discipline are very much to the fore, but no mention is made of the payment of the troops.

Conclusion

In organisation and fighting techniques, the early 'Abbasid army had clearly evolved from the Umayyad. Like the later Umayyad armies, soldiers were paid salaries. Like the Umayyad armies, too, they fought largely on foot and armies were sometimes numbered in tens of thousands. It was an army led, and in many cases recruited, by *quwwād* who had replaced the tribal chiefs of the early Islamic period, but this too was a development of later Umayyad practice rather than a radical revolution. What had changed with the Revolution of 132/750 which brought the 'Abbasids to power was the personnel. It is true that some Syrian and Iraqi Arab families, like that of Ma'n b. Zā'ida did play an important role in the army of the new regime, but they were very much a minority. The new army was recruited in Khurāsān from the *ahl Khurāsān* and most of the *ahl al-Shām*, who had defended the Umayyad Caliphate, were demobilised and disempowered. It seems that payment was now made at regular intervals throughout the year, perhaps even monthly, and that this is a further move to the professionalisation of the army which had been characteristic of the later Umayyad period. While the Khurāsāniya and the *Abnā'* had largely replaced the *ahl al-Shām*, military techniques and systems remained largely unchanged and it was not until the civil war which followed Hārūn's death and the coming of al-Mu'taṣim, that major changes were made.

Notes

1 See H. Kennedy, *The Early 'Abbasid Caliphate: A Political History* (London, 1981b), 68, 82–5; P. Crone, *Slaves on Horseback* (Cambridge, 1980), 67; I. Bligh-Abramski, 'Evolution versus Revolution: Umayyad Elements in the 'Abbasid Regime 133/750–320/932', *Der Islam*, 65 (1988), 226–43; A. El'ad, 'Aspects of the Transition from the Umayyad to the 'Abbasid Caliphate', *JSAI*, 19 (1995), 89–132; M. Bonner, *Aristocratic Violence and Holy War* (New Haven, 1996), 45–55 for continuity and discontinuity in the Jazīra.

2 We have very little information about the functioning of the *dīwān al-jund* in the early 'Abbasid period. The names of the heads of the *dīwān*, in so far as they are known, are listed in D. Sourdel, *Le Vizirat 'Abbāside* 2 vols (Damascus, 1959–60), ii, 729–43.
3 See A. Arazi and A. El'ad, 'Epître a l'armée', i, *Studia Islamica*, 66 (1987), 27–70 pp. 54–62 on the spread of the *ahl Khurāsān* and the relationship between those who left and those who stayed behind.
4 See p. 97.
5 C. Pellat, *Ibn al-Muqaffa'*, 46; quoted in M. Sharon, 'The Military Reforms of Abu Muslim', in M. Sharon (ed.), *Studies in Islamic Civilisation in Honour of Professor David Ayalon* (Jerusalem, 1986), 105–44.
6 *Chronique de Denys*, 75, 82, 89–90: the Chronicle repeatedly shows how Arabs and (non-Arab) Syrian peasants and villagers alike were oppressed by the 'Persians' (Khurāsānis) in the early 'Abbasid period; C. Cahen 'Fiscalité, propriété, antagonismes sociaux en haute Mesopotamie au temps des premiers 'abbāsides', *Arabica*, 1 (1954), 136–52, pp. 145–6; Bonner, *Aristocratic Violence*, 55, 68.
7 For more details, see El'ad, 'Aspects of the Transition', 107–111.
8 Crone, *Slaves on Horseback*, 106–7.
9 Ṭa., iii, 356–8 for the role of Bakkār b. Muslim al-'Uqaylī in the suppression of the revolt of the Ustādhsīs in 150/767–8 .
10 El'ad, 'Aspects of the Transition', 107–8.
11 See Kennedy, 'Central Government and Provincial Elites in the Early 'Abbasid Caliphate', *BOAS*, 44 (1981a), 31–8.
12 Ṭa., iii, 4–5. Estimates of the numbers of Ibn Ḍubāra's army range between 50 000 and a wholly fanciful 150 000.
13 Ṭa., iii, 45–7; al-Azdī, 126–7.
14 Or 1500 according to an eye-witness account (Ṭa., iii, 293).
15 Ṭa., iii, 304–5 .
16 al-Azdī, 194–5.
17 Ṭa., iii, 300–1.
18 Ṭa., iii, 300.
19 Ṭa., iii, 292.
20 See pp. 19–21.
21 See pp. 82–3.
22 See p. 79.
23 al-Azdī, 297.
24 Ṭa. iii, 460.
25 Perhaps a local garrison like the *rābiṭa* of Mawsil but it is not clear how, if at all, they were distinguished from the *jund.*
26 For these soldiers, see pp. 4–5.
27 Ṭa., iii, 493; Haldon discusses the numbers involved in Byzantine military expeditions from the seventh to the ninth centuries which go up to 100 000 or more but the author considers that numbers of around 20 000 are 'more reasonable' (J. Haldon, *Warfare, State and Society in the Byzantine World*, 565–1204, London, 1999, 101–3). Except for the major expeditions of Hārūn al-Rashīd, there is no evidence to suggest that the Muslim forces had a large numerical superiority over the Byzantines.
28 Ṭa., iii, 503–5, 709. The figures associated with Hārūn's campaigns may well be exaggerated, to boost his reputation as a commander of the Muslims. It is interesting to compare these figures with the figures for Ottoman armies given in R. Murphey, *Ottoman Warfare, 1500–1700* (London, 1999), 36–49, where he concludes (pp. 41–3) that there was an upper limit of 50 000 for lesser campaigns and a 'generous' 80 000 for Sultan-led campaigns which could rise as high as 100 000. He argues, and I would agree, that numbers significantly over 100 000 should be treated with scepticism.

29 Ṭa., iii, 712.
30 Ṭa., iii, 818.
31 Ṭa., iii, 1007–8.
32 Ṭa., iii, 356: both words mean 'flag' or 'banner' and it is not clear whether there was any distinction in appearance between them. According to Hinds ('The Banners and Battle Cries of the Arabs at Ṣiffīn (AD 657)', *Al-Abhath*, 24 (1971), 104), *liwā'* in the early Islamic period signified a military appointment and *rāyat* (another word for a banner) was the emblem of a kinship group, or in some cases a personal emblem.
33 For the prosopography of the most important of these families, see Crone, *Slaves on Horseback*, 173–89; Kennedy, *The Early 'Abbasid Caliphate*, 78–85.
34 The site, now known as Morghab, lies just south of the Afghanistan–Turkmenistan frontier. It has never been the subject of archaeological investigation, there are no published descriptions and I know of no explorer or researcher who has actually been there.
35 Ṭa., iii, 602–3.
36 For further details of the family, see Crone, *Slaves on Horseback*, 180–1.
37 al-Iṣfahānī, *Maqātil*, 326–9, reading *ṣihr* for *ṣhw* on p. 327.
38 Ṭa., iii, 78.
39 Ṭa., ii, 1959.
40 *Akhbār al-'Abbās*, 335.
41 Ṭa., iii, 78–9, Caskel, *Gamharat al-Nasab: Das genealogische Werk des Hisām ibn Muḥammad al-Kalbī*, 2 vols (Leiden, 1966), taf. 62.
42 Ṭa., iii, 134–5: Mujashshir had been a leading figure in the Umayyad government of Khurāsān but seems to have retired to Marwrūdh after the 'Abbasid Revolution , see pp. 46–7.
43 Ṭa., iii, 354–8.
44 Pellat, *Ibn al-Muqaffa'*, 32–3.
45 Ṭa., iii, 75–8.
46 Ṭa., iii, 122–4.
47 Ṭa., iii, 355–8.
48 Ṭa., iii, 79.
49 For the family, see Crone, *Slaves on Horseback*, 169–70; Kennedy, *The Early 'Abbasid Caliphate*, 84–5.
50 Kennedy, *The Early 'Abbasid Caliphate*, 84–5, Caskel, *Gamharat*, taf. 146.
51 Ya'q., *Ta'rīkh*, ii, 462–3.
52 *Aghānī*, x, 95–6.
53 al-Jāḥiẓ, *Manāqib*, 4.
54 For a full discussion of the differences and links between these two groups, see Arazi and El'ad, 'Epître a l'armée', i, 52–62.
55 al-Jāḥiẓ, *Manāqib*, 8–12.
56 Ṭa., iii, 369.
57 M. Kaabi, 'Les origines ṭāhirides dans la da'wa 'abbāside', *Arabica*, 19 (1972), 145–64.
58 al-Jāḥiẓ, *Manāqib*, 11–12.
59 See p. 53.
60 For the Abnāwī's speech, see al-Jāḥiẓ, *Manāqib*, 15–17.
61 For frontier warfare in this period, see Bonner, *Aristocratic Violence*, 43–106; most of the Arabic sources are translated in E. W. Brooks, 'Byzantium and the Arabs in the Time of the Early 'Abbasids', *English Historical Review*, 15 (1900), 728–47 and 16 (1901), 84–92; also J. F. Haldon and H. Kennedy, 'The Arab–Byzantine Frontier in the Eighth and Ninth Centuries: Military Organization and Society in the Borderlands', *Zbornik Radova Visantoloskog Instituta* (Belgrade), 19 (1980), 79–116.

62 *Chronique de Denys de Tell-Mahré (The Zuqnin Chronicle)*, trans. J. Chabot (Paris, 1895), 72–82; for the economic impact of this campaign, see pp. 87–8.
63 Ṭa., iii, 353.
64 See entry Kemah in T. Sinclair, *Eastern Turkey: An Architectural and Archaeological Survey*, 4 vols (London, 1987–90), ii, 415–22. It is not clear what if any of the existing fortification dates to this period.
65 For a general history of the conflict, Kennedy, *The Early 'Abbasid Caliphate*, 135–63.
66 The main accounts are Ṭa., iii, 797–801, 821– 4; Ya'q., *Ta'rīkh*, ii, 530–1.
67 On Ṭāhir's background, see M. Kaabi, 'Les origines', 145–64.
68 Ṭa., iii, 800–2.
69 Ṭa., iii, 823.
70 Ṭa., iii, 828–9.
71 Ṭa., iii, 831–2.
72 Ṭa., iii, 852–4. The hamstringing of horses is a recurrent *topos*, used to emphasise a refusal to take flight.
73 Ṭa., iii, 868–937; see also Ya'q., *Ta'rīkh*, ii, 532–7.
74 Ṭa., iii, 868–70.
75 Lane sv.
76 Ṭa., iii, 868.
77 Ta., iii, 869.
78 Ṭa., iii, 877. The MS here is not good and some of the readings are problematic. I have adopted the translation suggested by Fishbein trans., pp. 145–6, nn. 552, 553.
79 Ṭa., iii, 877, 886.
80 Ṭa., iii, 885.
81 *Fihrist*, trans. Dodge, 737–8.
82 Various spellings are given in different MSS, but in view of the contents of the book, this seems to most likely: see *Fihrist*, trans. Dodge, 737, n. 31.
83 Ed. 'Abd al-Ra'ūf 'Awn. There are a number of other MSS not used by the editor. On this work and its origins, M. Shatzmiller, 'The Crusades and Islamic Warfare – A Re-evaluation', *Der Islam*, 69 (1992), 247–88, pp. 253–7.
84 Eg. pp. 26 and 53, where *ba'ḍ al-ru'asā* is said to have known the names and characteristics of all 4000 of his *aṣḥāb*.
85 al-Harthamī, 60–4.
86 al-Harthamī, 35.
87 al-Harthamī, 23.
88 al-Harthamī, 26–7.
89 al-Harthamī, 44, 46.
90 al-Harthamī, 29–33.
91 al-Harthamī, 31–2.
92 al-Harthamī, 33–46.
93 al-Harthamī, 34.
94 al-Harthamī, 34, 39.
95 al-Harthamī, 25–8, 48–50.
96 al-Harthamī, 41.
97 al-Harthamī, 36.
98 al-Harthamī, 50.
99 al-Harthamī, 42–3.
100 al-Harthamī, 56–64.
101 al-Harthamī, 61.
102 al-Harthamī, 58–9.
103 al-Harthamī, 65–71.
104 al-Harthamī, 68.

CHAPTER FIVE

The armies of Samarra, 218–56/833–70

The coming of the Turks and the new model army[1]

In the aftermath of the civil wars which followed the death of Hārūn al-Rashīd in 193/809, there was a pressing need to recruit and maintain an effective army whose loyalty would be to the Caliphs alone. The army of the Khurāsāniya and *Abnā'* which had supported the early 'Abbasid Caliphate was broken and demoralised and its loyalty to the new regime was doubtful. The Caliphate had lost control of large areas, notably Syria, Palestine and Egypt and the mountainous districts of northern Iran. These needed to be reconquered if 'Abbasid rule was to be made effective. In order to achieve this, al-Ma'mūn (198–218/813–33) and his successor al-Mu'taṣim (218–27/833–42) looked to new groups[2] who, so to speak, brought no political baggage with them. The best known and most important of these were the Turks, but there were also important contingents from the Iranian principalities of Transoxania, notably Farghāna and Ushrūsanā and Arabs from the Ḥawf districts of Egypt. Al-Ma'mūn's mother had come from Khurāsān and at the beginning of his struggle with his brother al-Amīn, most of his support had come from Khurāsān and Transoxania. It was probably the contacts he developed at this time which led al-Ma'mūn, and later his brother al-Mu'taṣim, to look to these regions when recruiting new soldiers. The army of Baghdad, which had by and large supported his brother, was largely disbanded. However, it is possible that elements of the old *Abnā'* were kept on in the groups known as the *jund* and the *shākiriya*, though the evidence for this is not clear.[3]

Two sources give us a picture of the composition of the army in the reign of al-Mu'taṣim. One is the description of the foundation and settlement of the new capital and garrison city of Samarra from al-Ya'qūbī's geography, *the Kitāb al-Buldān* (Book of Countries), written in 276/889–90 – that is, after the Caliphate had returned to Baghdad. His account naturally focuses on the geography, explaining who was given land where and the places of settlement of the different groups.

The first grants of property in the new city which al-Ya'qūbī mentions were made to prominent the Turkish leaders Ashinās, Khāqān 'Urṭūj and Waṣīf. Ashinās had a number of Turkish commanders (*quwwād*) attached to him and the other came with their followers (*aṣḥāb*) who were presumably also Turks. Nearby were plots for all the Turks (who included Khazars from north of the Caucasus) and the Farāghina. At several points the author notes that the Turks and Farāghina, but not other groups in the military, were settled separately from the rest of the population in specially designated areas. Slave girls were purchased for the Turks and they, and their children, were given allowances from the *dīwān*.[4] The *mawālī* and *ghilmān* had their own *dīwān*,[5] which must have been responsible for the payment of the Turks, and perhaps the Farāghina as well.

As well as the Turks and Farāghina, there were other groups from the north eastern borders of the Islamic world. These included the followers of al-Afshīn, the Ushrūsaniya from his native principality of Ushrūsana and other who were attached to him.[6] At various points, Khurāsāni leaders and their followers are mentioned: the *quwwād* of Khurāsān and their followers (*asbāb*) from the *Shākiriya*.[7] Among the Khurāsāni *quwwād* were al-Ḥasan b. 'Alī al-Ma'mūnī from Badhghīs, and 'Ujayf b. 'Anbasa. Both of these were among al-Ma'mūn's earliest supporters in Khurāsān, but 'Ujayf had been killed in the purge of the supporters of al-Ma'mūn's son al-'Abbāṣ, and al-Ḥasan b. 'Alī does not seem to have held any office under al-Mu'taṣim; it looks as if the leaders of the Khurāsānis were ousted by the Turks. Elsewhere their followers are described as including Arabs, the people of Qumm, Isfahan, Qazvin, al-Jibāl and Azerbayjān,[8] that is from central and western Iran. There were also streets with a mixture of *quwwād* from all the districts of Khurāsān, including the Farāghina, Ushrūsaniya and Ishtākhanjiya.[9] They may have been paid from the *dīwān* of the *jund* and *shākiriya*.[10] Finally there were the Maghāriba, who were granted plots near the river port on the Tigris.[11]

Al-Ya'qūbī's account suggests that the Turks and the Farāghina were the élite of the army, segregated as they were in their own quarters, whereas the other Iranians mingled more freely with the rest of the townspeople. Except for the Maghāriba, all the troops mentioned came from Iran or from beyond the borders of the Muslim world. There was no room in this new army for recruits from Iraq, the Jazīra, Syria, Palestine, the Arabian peninsula or the Arabs of Egypt. It must have seemed to many that the army of the Caliphs was dominated by a sort of Central Asian mafia.

A second important source for the military in the Samarra period is the essay entitled *Manāqib al-Turk* (Qualities of the Turks) by the essayist al-Jāḥiẓ (d. 255/268–9). According to the author's own explanation, this was originally composed during the reign of al-Mu'taṣim but was not finally published until the time of al-Mutawwakil, when it was redrafted to assign a prominent role to al-Fatḥ b. Khāqān, the Caliph's leading confidante. It takes the form of an imaginary dialogue between an unknown critic, who argues that the various groups in the army are separate and, by implication, mutually hostile, and al-Fatḥ. Al-Fatḥ stresses the similarities rather than the differences between the various different groups of troops, thus avoiding friction. Discussion then moves on to the Turks. We are told that at al-Ma'mūn's court, a number of prominent political and military figures had been asked whether they would prefer to face a hundred Khārijīs or a hundred Turks. Most of them say that they regard the Khārijīs as the more formidable opponents, but Ḥumayd b. 'Abd al-Ḥamīd (a prominent Iranian commander) dissents. This gives him an opportunity for a detailed account of the military qualities of the Turks and the ways they excel not only the Khārijīs but other groups in the Caliph's army. The essay is not without its problems, but it is the closest we have from this period to a treatise on the characteristics of the different groups who made up the 'Abbasid armies at this time.

In al-Jāḥiẓ's essay on the army, one of the participants in the debate says that 'today' (i.e. during the reign of al-Mu'taṣim) there were five groups (*aqsām*) in the army, the Khurāsānī, the Turk, the *mawlā*, the Arab and the *Banawī* (i.e. from the *Abnā'*).[12] To an extent this is a rhetorical advice: the speaker wishes to stress the divisions within the army, al-Jāḥiẓ going on to argue that they are all closely related. Of the five, the Khurāsānis and the Turks are described at some length in the essay and can clearly be located in al-Ya'qūbī's account of the settlement of Samarra.[13] The others are more problematic. It is clear that al-Jāḥiẓ uses the term *mawālī* to describe the *mawālī* who participated in the original 'Abbasid revolution, not to describe the Turks (who were also called *mawālī* in third/ninth century sources). The Arabs scarcely emerge as a fighting group. The *Abnā'* describe themselves primarily as foot-soldiers, specialising in street warfare.[14] None of these can be securely located in al-Ya'qūbī's account of Samarra, although it may be that some of them formed part of the *jund* which appears in the sources of the period.[15] On the other hand, their appearance in the essay is probably intended to provide a historical parallel and may not reflect the actual make-up of the army in the Samarra period. Certainly the named heroes of the groups are figures from the bygone era of the early 'Abbasids.

The Turkish military

The Turks, a clearly identifiable group referred to as *atrāk* in the sources, are the most significant of these newcomers. The geographical origins of these Turks is not clear.[16] We know that some of them were Khazars who can be located in the steppes north of the Caucasus, but they were only a minority. It seems likely, however, that most of them were either Ghuzz or Tughuz-ghuz from the lower Syr-Darya or Qarluqs from the Kazakh steppes. Frye and Sayılı have pointed out[17] that many Turks lived in areas of Transoxania where there had long been a Muslim presence. The Turks were probably were distinguished from the Soghdians, Arabs and other settled people in Transoxania because of their language and their nomad lifestyle.[18] Ṭūlūn, almost the only Turk whose geographical origins we know anything about, because his son Aḥmad later became ruler of Egypt, is said to have come from the Tughuz-ghuz who were found in the Syr-Darya basin.[19] It is quite possible that many of the Turks who formed the army in Samarra originally came from areas to the east and north of Samarqand where there had been a Muslim presence for at least a century. We are told that the Samanid family acted as procurers of slaves for the Caliphs.[20] We also know that in around 205/820–1, at just the time the Turks were being sent west to al-Mu‘taṣim, the Samanid Nūḥ b. Asad took Farghana and put an end to the old ruling dynasty, an event which marks the permanent Muslim conquest of the area.[21] Many of the Turks who came to Samarra may have been prisoners of war or taken as tribute at this time. This makes it likely that, while they still lived a nomadic lifestyle, they had come into both Islam and city life before their move to the west.

Individual Turks had been employed in the service of the Caliphs before the third/ninth century but their recruitment by al-Mu‘taṣim marks a new departure. It seems that during the chaos which followed the death of al-Amīn, an ambitious young member of the ‘Abbasid family, Abū Isḥāq (later al-Mu‘taṣim) one of the Caliph al-Rashīd's numerous sons, set about building up a military force of his own responsible directly to him. Initially it seems that he did this by buying Turkish slaves who were already in Baghdad. Around the year 200/815–6, Abū Isḥāq is said to have purchased three slaves Ashinās, Ītākh and Waṣīf from their masters in Baghdad and Bughā the Elder, probably also in Iraq. Apparently Ītākh had been working as a cook, Waṣīf as an armourer (*zarrād*).[22] All these three were later to become leading figures in al-Mu‘taṣim's military household.

After the re-establishment of the ‘Abbasid Caliphate in Baghdad in 204/819, Abū Isḥāq continued to purchase Turkish slaves but he now did so directly from Central Asia. According to one Ja‘far al-Khushakī, who was probably a slave dealer, ‘During al-Ma'mūn's reign al-Mu‘taṣim would send me to Nūḥ b. Asad (the Samanid governor) in Samarqand to purchase Turks. Each year I would bring him a certain number such that, during the reign of al-Ma'mūn, he had accumulated some three thousand young men.'[23]

The geographer al-Iṣṭakhrī, writing in the next century, commented on the preparedness of the frontier men of Shāsh (modern Tashkent) and Farghana[24] for war. ‘This encouraged the Caliphs', he goes on,

> to recruit men from Transoxania and the Turks became their armies because of their because of their superiority of all other races [*ajnās*] in bravery, daring, courage and fearlessness. The nobles [*dahāqīn*] of Transoxania were their [i.e. the Caliphs'] officers [*quwwād*], retinue [*ḥawāshī*] and chosen servants, because of their attentiveness in service, their obedience and their fine appearance in uniform. So they formed the retinue of the Caliphs, their trusted attendants and the heads of their armies, like the Turks and the Farāghina who formed the palace guard [*shiḥna*].

He then goes on to list prominent Khurāsāni officer families.

The legal status of these soldiers is not entirely clear. Modern scholars have seen al-Mu‘taṣim's army as an army of ‘slave-soldiers' and described them as *mamlūks*.[25] In this way, his reforms have been seen as the begining the institution of slave soldiers which became the dominant military and eventually political structure in later medieval Islam. This view has been challenged first by Shaban who argued, without much evidence, that the Turkish leaders were Transoxanian noblemen, and more recently by Amabe.[26] Amabe notes that the evidence for their position as slaves is very limited and neither al-Ṭabarī nor al-Jāḥiẓ make any mention of their supposed servile status. Instead, he argues that they were freemen, many of noble status.

The evidence is not clear either way. Many of the Turks may have been captured or purchased as slaves. Ashinās, Waṣīf and Ītākh certainly were, and Bughā the Elder and his sons were bought by al-Mu'taṣim for 10,000 in 204 (819–20).[27] After their purchase by al-Mu'taṣim, however, they seem to have been freed and the rank-and-file Turks are referred to in the sources as *mawālī*, not as *mamlūks*[28] or *'abīd*, the two words commonly used to describe slaves. The term *ghilmān* (sing., *ghulām*) which means page boy or young man,[29] is also used: in the armies of the Samarra period, this term is applied to Turkish soldiers who were part of the retinue of some commander but does not necessarily imply that they were unfree. *Mawālī* originally meant clients or freedmen and in the reigns of Hārūn and al-Ma'mūn, *mawlā Amīr al-Mu'minīn* is sometimes used as an honorific to describe eastern Iranian aristocrats who took service with the Caliph. In the sources of the Samarra period it is applied also to the Turkish soldiers[30] and among the Turks, particularly to the rank and file. The use of this word implies that they were no longer slaves, even if they had been originally, but were still bound by ties of *walā* to the Caliph. Similarly, the fact that they were paid cash salaries in return for their services, like other troops in the Caliph's armies, also suggests that they had been freed, for slaves, almost by definition, work because they are the property, not the employees, of their masters.

Al-Mu'taṣim developed a new capital to house his new army. In 836/221, three years after his accession, the Caliph fixed on the site of Samarra, on the Tigris some 120 km north of Baghdad.[31] To some extent this was because the new soldiers, particularly those newly arrived Turks and others, often became embroiled in clashes with the population of Baghdad, partly because they did not understand the language and customs of the citizens and partly because many in Baghdad saw them as usurpers, taking over the role of chief military supporters of the 'Abbasid Caliphs. Clashes between the soldiers and local inhabitants in the streets of Baghdad made the Caliph anxious to find a different home for his army. There can also be no doubt that al-Mu'taṣim wanted to move to a new site where he could make land-grants (*qaṭā'i'*) to his followers and reward his chief supporters with valuable property. Baghdad was left under the control of the Tahirid family who maintained their links with the remainder of the old *Abnā'*.

A central question about the arrival of the Turks is whether they brought with them a new style of fighting and new military equipment: was there a military revolution in any sense, or was it simply new faces fighting in the traditional manner? Kaegi[32] has argued that mounted archers had constituted an important element in Roman armies in the wars of Justinian but that they had disappeared during the last decades of the sixth century. As has been noted, there is no evidence that either Muslims or Byzantines employed them on a significant scale during the two centuries which followed the coming of Islam. Byzantine accounts suggest that Turkish mounted archers played an important part in the successes of al-Mu'taṣim's armies in Anatolia.[33] From the Saljuk period onwards, we have extensive written sources which describe the Turco-Mongol horse-archers and, from the fourteenth century, illustrations in manuscripts which give a clear visual representation.

Al-Jāḥiẓ's essay makes it clear that the Turks brought a radically new military technique with them, mounted archery. The firing of arrows from a swiftly moving, and manoeuvring, horse is, obviously, a highly skilled art. It seems that only those brought up to it from a very early age can master it. the key to this was the Turks' relationship to their horses. Their animals were unlike other peoples'[34]: al-Jāḥiẓ refers to the Turkish horse as *bardhūn* (a disparaging word often translated as 'nag', but 'pony' would probably be more appropriate in this generally positive account) as opposed to the Arab *faras*,[35] and says that it had much more endurance. The Turk probably spends more time on horseback than he does on foot.[36] The horse also provides nourishment, from milk or blood. The Turk is also an expert trainer of horses and farrier (*bayṭār*).[37] This combination gives both horse and rider speed, manoeuvrability, endurance and ability to survive without food in all weathers, beyond anything that other troops can rival.

When it comes to battle, it is the mounted archery which distinguishes the Turks. Al-Jāḥīẓ has Ḥumayd comment, 'if a thousand of their horsemen attack they shoot a single volley felling a thousand horsemen' whereas the Khārijīs and the bedouin, the author continues, 'are not known for their shooting from horseback'. Ḥumayd goes on to remark how the Turk can shoot while his mount is moving in any direction at high speed and can fire ten arrows in the time it takes the Khāriji to fire one.[38] Each Turk carries two or three bows and spare strings to go with them. The other characteristic weapon of the Turk is the lasso (*waqh*) and it is hard to believe how skilled they are at catching the rider in one throw.[39]

Their use of tactics, too, is formidable, especially the feigned retreat, which is like poison, for the Turk can fire as effectively backwards and forwards.[40] This skill is a result of upbringing, but also of training. Some of this training takes the form of hunting, for which the Turks have an insatiable appetite and boundless energy.[41] There was also more formal training with the target: the Turks shoot at the target on a spear (*birjās*) or the bird on a pole (*mujaththama*).[42] Further evidence for the importance of the Turks as archers can be found in a comment ascribed to the Arab rebel Naṣr b. Shabath in the reign of al-Ma'mūn to the effect that the power of the Turks was in their arrows and that if they ran out of arrows, they could be led by the hand.[43]

Al-Jāḥiẓ's account, which must date from the early decades of the Turkish presence in the armies of the Caliphate, makes a number of things clear. The Turks were extremely efficient warriors and markedly different from other troops in the Caliphal armies. It is interesting to observe that the characteristics singled out in the *Manāqib* in the early third/ninth centuries are exactly those which commentators would note of the Ghuzz Turks in the time of the Saljuks and of the Mongols in the time of Genghis Khan. This may have been a peaceful recruitment under the watchful eye of the Caliph, rather than a hostile invasion, but the characteristics which made the Turks so effective and so feared were fundamentally the same.

The Turks were formidable fighters but there was a downside as well. According to Ḥumayd, they did not fight for sovereignty over lands and people, religion or even to protect their homes, but only for plunder.[44] They were also fiercely jealous of their privileged status, not wanting to be mixed up with the general run of troops. They felt that they deserved their élite status and would quickly lose patience with a ruler who did not provide it.[45]

The Khurāsānis

The Turks were the most characteristic and probably the most numerous and powerful group in the armies of al-Mu'taṣim and his successors but, as al-Ya'qūbī's account shows, they were by no means the only ones. In his struggle with his brother al-Amīn, al-Ma'mūn had relied heavily on the support of the aristocracy of Khurāsān and Transoxania and after he had established himself as Caliph in Baghdad, he began to recruit Transoxanians on a regular basis. Al-Balādhurī explains what happened:

> Al-Ma'mūn, may God have mercy on him, used to write to his officials in Khurāsān, instructing them to attack those people in Transoxania who had yet to acknowledge ['Abbasid rule] and accept Islam. He would send his envoys to enrol those from among the people of those regions and their princes [*Abnā' mulūkihim*] who wanted to be entered in the *dīwān* and receive stipends. He won them over by extending favours to them. When they responded and came to his gate, he honoured them and presented them with gifts and salaries [*arzāq*]. When al-Mu'taṣim became Caliph he continued the practice such that the élite [*shuhūd*] of his military were recruited from the *jund* of the people of Transoxania, that is from Sughd,[46] Farghāna, Ushrūsanā, Shāsh[47] and elsewhere. Their kings came to him and Islam triumphed over the region.[48]

Two important points emerge from this. The first is that the troops recruited in Transoxania were volunteers, they joined up because of the salaries on offer, and the second is that they were encouraged and led by the local aristocracy. Al-Iṣṭakhrī's account gives the names of some of the local nobles (*dahāqīn*), al-Afshīn (ruler of Ushrūsanā), the family of Abū'l-Sāj (also from Ushrūsanā and probably protégés of al-Afshīn), the Ikhshīd of Samarqand, 'Ujayf b. 'Anbasa of Sughd, the Bukhārā-khudā (local ruler of Bukhārā) and Marzbān b. Türgish.[49] Such men were to play an important role in the military affairs and politics of the Islamic world in the next half century.

The Farāghina, the men of Farghāna, are frequently mentioned in the texts, often, but not always, in partnership with the Turks, with whom they shared a *dīwān*. Some of them at least are described as *'ajam*,[50] which may mean that they were non-Muslims.[51] The principality of Farghāna lay in the Farghāna Valley (Uzbekistan and Tajikistan). Its capital was at Akhsikath on the banks of the Syr-Darya River 25 km south west of the modern town of Namangan. With the Samanid take-over of the area in 205/820–1, it would seem that many Farghanis took service in the armies of the Caliphate. A later biographical dictionary describes one such, Juff b. Yaltakin, who was said to have come from the family of the princes of Farghana. Al-Mu'taṣim heard of his military prowess, and that of his countrymen, and ordered that they be sent to him. When they arrived in Samarra they were welcomed warmly and granted *qaṭā'i'*. Juff had children and died in Baghdad in 247/861.[52] The Farāghina and the Turks were often grouped together and some at least of the Turks may have been obtained from the Farghāna area. However they were clearly distinct, they probably spoke an Iranian language and there is no question of their being slaves.

The Ushrūsaniya came from a very similar background. Like Farghāna, Ushrūsanā[53] was an area whose native princes had long resisted Muslim penetration. It lay to the north and east of Samarqand, west of Farghāna, partly in the plains between the Zarafshan and Syr-Darya (Jaxartes) rivers and partly in the Turkestan mountains to the south. The area had hardly been penetrated by the Muslims before the 'Abbasid period and the ruling dynasty, whose princely title was Afshīn, were able to continue as undisputed rulers. Islam made very little progress and efforts at missionary activity were firmly discouraged by the princes.

In 205/820–1 Ushrūsanā was attacked by the Turks and this may have encouraged the rulers to seek Muslim protection. In 207/822 Ushrūsanā was 'conquered' by Aḥmad b. Abī Khālid and the ruler, Kāwus, and his son al-Faḍl were taken to the Caliphal court. As we have seen, the Ushrūsaniya were given plots of land when Samarra was being laid out. In 215/830–1 another son, Khaydhar, known as al-Afshīn, appears as a leading commander in the army of al-Mu'taṣim in Egypt, where he was responsible for putting down disturbances among the Copts and the bedouin. He went on to become one of the leading figures in al-Mu'taṣim's army until his trial and disgrace in 225/840. The Ushrūsaniya, however, now led by the family of Abū'l-Sāj, continued to play a part in the armies of the Caliphs until the early fourth/tenth century.

The Maghāriba

The Maghāriba ('westerners') were not mentioned by al-Jāḥiẓ but they nonetheless formed an important element in the Samarra army, with a quarter of their own by the river-port. Despite earlier speculation that these troops were Berbers from the Maghrib, Gordon has shown convincingly that they were Arabs[54] from the Hawf districts of lower Egypt, that is the semi-desert lands on each side of the Nile Delta.[55] The Arabs of the Eastern and Western Hawf were not the descendants of the original conquerors, who formed the *jund* of the capital Fusṭāṭ, but were the offspring of later immigrants who had been moved from Syria in Umayyad times.

They had frequently rebelled against the government, refusing to pay taxes, and they may well have wanted places in the Egyptian *dīwān*. In 214/829–30 al-Ma'mūn sent Abū Isḥāq (al-Mu'taṣim) with 4000 Turkish soldiers to Egypt the quell the disturbances. Abū Isḥāq returned from Egypt with a large number of prisoners; the next year there was more unrest and al-Afshīn was sent to suppress it and in 217/832 the Caliph al-Ma'mūn himself travelled to Egypt to sort out the affairs of the province.

It is likely that the Maghāriba were in fact the prisoners taken on these campaigns, and Maghāriba are recorded along with the Turks in al-Mu'taṣim's army attacking Amorion in 223/828 under the command of the Turk Ītākh.[56] Some of them were described as free men (*ḥurr*) but others were slaves (*mamlūk*),[57] which is comprehensible only if they had been captured in warfare. It seems that the Maghāriba were fewer in number than the Turks. A later Persian source says that 4000 were present at a ceremonial parade.[58] The army of Samarra which set out to attack Baghdad in 251/865 contained 2000 Maghāriba in addition to the 5000 Turks and Farāghina.[59] The Maghāriba seem to have fought as foot-soldiers[60] and were considered as lower status than either the Turks or the Khurāsānis. They were certainly paid less[61] and none of their leaders were important political figures.

Jund and *Shākiriya*

In addition to these groups, defined by ethnic and regional origins, there were two others, the *jund* and the *shākiriya*.[62] They are frequently mentioned together and were paid by the same *dīwān*. They are also seen in opposition to the Turks. There is some evidence to suggest that the *jund* incorporated elements of the old *Abnā'* who had been retained in the armies of Samarra. The *shākiriya* may have been free troops of Iranian origin who had come west with al-Ma'mūn at the end of the civil war or in the retinues of Iranian grandees like 'Ujayf b. 'Anbasa or al-Afshīn who had subsequently been purged.

Numbers

At the time of al-Ma'mūn's death in 218/833, the Turkish guard was clearly not a large force, 3000–4000,[63] but it was effective and completely loyal to its master. Al-Mu'taṣim may have continued to purchase Turkish slave soldiers, but numbers were never very large.[64] Töllner, in his study of the Samarra army, estimated that there were between 20 000 and 30 000 troops, of whom about half were Turks.[65] When Abū Aḥmad (later al-Muwaffaq) led the army of Samarra to combat the supporters of al-Musta'īn in Baghdad, he commanded 5000 Turks and Farāghina and 2000 Maghāriba (from the Ḥawf in Egypt).[66] The largest number of Turkish troops recorded in the field seems to be the 19 000 Turks, Maghāriba and their followers (*ḥashūhum*) said by a spy to have been deployed against Baghdad during the siege of 251/865–6.[67] If we assume that about half of these were Maghāriba and others, then the Turks, facing a life and death struggle, numbered less than 10 000 effectives. At other points in the siege, numbers were much smaller: at an important battle at Bāb al-Qaṭī'a, the army sent by al-Mu'tazz consisted of 4000 Turks, of whom half were killed. When Mūsā b. Bughā was appointed as governor of al-Jibāl in 253/867, with a mandate to bring the area back under the control of the Caliph, he led an army of 2443 Turks and others.[68] It is not clear that substantial numbers of Turks were ever stationed outside Iraq on a permanent basis. Faced by a rebellion by the Arab governor of Damascus, al-Mu'tamid was obliged to send Amājūr with 1000 troops, suggesting that there were no reliable troops in the city. In the end Amājūr is said to have defeated the rebel with a force of just 200.[69] There seem to have been few Turkish troops in Egypt and, faced by local disturbances in 252/866, the governor was obliged to ask for assistance from Iraq.[70] These incidents suggest that the Turkish and other élite troops were based in Samarra and sent to other areas only when there was trouble. At other times, local militias like the 400 men at the disposal of the Arab governor of Alexandria, were used to quell disturbances.[71]

We have more figures from the short reign of al-Muhtadī (256/870) when Turkish commanders attempted to mobilise their supporters to challenge the Caliph and each other. Ṣāliḥ b. al-Waṣīf, one of the two or three most important Turkish commanders, managed to raise 5000 supporters at one stage, but they soon drifted away leaving him with a personal following of his own *ghilmān* and *mawālī*.[72] Soon after, the rank and file of the Turks protested to the Caliph about the abuse of power by the senior officers and 1000 cavalry and 3000 infantry gathered to make their point. In response Mūsā b. Bughā, another major player, made a show of strength with 4000 horsemen, with bows, breastplates, spears and battle-axes.[73] In the final push against the unfortunate Caliph the number of Turks 'had swollen to some 10 000 men, united by their common cause'.[74] It should be emphasised that these are the largest recorded figures and often Turkish forces were much smaller, and we would probably be correct in estimating the number of effective Turkish soldiers in Samarra as no more than 15 000 at any given time.

The numbers of Transoxanian troops are very difficult to assess and the Farāghina, who were probably the most numerous, tend to be grouped together with the Turks rather than being numbered separately. At one stage in the campaign against Bābak, the Bukhārā-Khudā is said to have been in command of 1000 horse and 600 infantry, but there is no reason to assume that they all came from his following.[75] In the Amorion campaign, 'Amr al-Farghānī commanded 200 cavalry.[76] When Bughā the Elder was campaigning in Arabia against the bedouin Banū Numayr in 232/846–7, Wājin al-Ushrūsanī, an associate of al-Afshīn's, was sent to support him with just 700 men of the Ushrūsaniya and Ishtāhhanjiya (from the Samarqand area).[77] As noted above, Abū Aḥmad al-Muwaffaq led 5000 Turks and Farāghina against Baghdad in 251/865.[78] In his final struggle with the Turks, al-Muhtadī led a force of 6000, less than 1000 of whom were Turks, the rest being Farāghina cavalry and Maghāriba infantry.[79] None of these figures claims to be a comprehensive number of the Transoxanian troops and they may be unreliable. Taken together, however, they suggest that numbers were quite small, 2000 or 3000 being the largest. Extrapolating, hazardously, from these we could perhaps suggest that the Transoxanian troops employed in the 'Abbasid army might have been as many as 5000, most of them cavalry, but are unlikely to have been significantly more.

It may be interesting to compare the 5000 Turks and Farāghina who set out from Samarra to attack al-Musta'īn in Baghdad and the 40 000–50 000 *Abnā'* 'Alī b. Īsā b. Māhān led from Baghdad to attack al-Ma'mūn in Khuarāsān.[80] The comparison suggests that armies of the Samarra period were significantly smaller than those of the early 'Abbasid age.

Payment

As we have seen, al-Mu'taṣim made major changes in the recruitment and personnel of the armed forces of the Caliphate. So far as we can tell, however, he did not make changes in the methods of payment. His new model army was paid in much the same way as the 'Abbasid army had been paid in the previous century, that is by cash salaries paid by the state out of general taxation. The Turkish and other soldiers were provided with garrison *qaṭā'i'* in the new capital of Samarra, but there is no evidence that, except in the case of a few privileged leaders, either property ownership or direct control of taxation formed a part of the reward system.

This assertion needs to be qualified by drawing attention to the paucity of the evidence. No source gives us a general account of the financial arrangements, and incidental detail is much harder to come by. We are increasingly dependent on one source, al-Ṭabarī's *Ta'rīkh*, and the structure of his history at this point leaves little scope for the introduction of circumstantial detail. In his recent work on the Samarra Caliphate, Gordon has collected such information as there is, and my discussion is largely based on his.

The foundation of the city of Samarra was explicitly intended to provide living quarters for the new Turkish elements in the army at a safe distance from the rest of the population,[81] especially the people of Baghdad, many of who came from groups which had been part of the early 'Abbasid military and certainly resented the privileged position of the newcomers.

The soldiers were settled in the new capital by being given *qaṭā'i'*, just as they had been in Baghdad 80 years before.[82] They tended to be grouped by ethnic and regional origins in certain quarters, Turks together, people of Farghāna together, Maghrabis together, and so on. Sometimes these were under the patronage of a great leader who gathered his followers round him, like the Turks who were settled near Ashinās[83] or the Ushrūsaniya and others who were attached to him (*maḍmūmīn*) around al-Afshīn,[84] but this was by no means always the case and it seems as if most of the settlers were not part of any retinue or following. There is no indication that these *qaṭā'i'* were a source of revenue or income to their owners.

On the other hand, there is evidence that important military leaders were rewarded with property grants and that these were regarded as a source of income.[85] In Samarra itself, leaders like Ashinās were instructed to buy properties from the existing owners and then to develop them by building mosques and markets. Al-Afshīn was also ordered to build a little market for everyday needs, mosques and baths in his *qaṭī'a*.[86] Al-Ya'qūbī says that the lands were purchased for 4000 *dīnārs* (say, 48 000 *dirhams*) and, in a later passage, that the annual revenues of the markets and shops of the city were 10 000 000 *dirhams*.[87] This would represent a massive return on the original investment but the figures should be treated with caution and it is not clear that like is being compared with like. However, we would probably be correct in saying that major figures on the *khāṣṣa* made fortunes out of land ownership in the new city but that these opportunities were not available to rank-and-file troops.

The same was certainly true for agricultural developments which were encouraged on the western bank of the Tigris, opposite the main city itself: al-Ya'qūbī mentions canals called the Isḥāqī, after Isḥāq b. Ibrāhīm the Tahirid, the Ītākhī, after Ītākh, the Turkish military leader, which suggests that they were the result of investments by these leaders. New villages were created and the lands were made into market gardens and orchards and benefited from the proximity of the city markets. Here again, large profits could be made and we are told that the *kharāj* of these areas amounted to 400 000 *dīnārs* per annum.[88]

Military leaders also owned estates (*ḍiyā'*) further afield. Bughā the Elder had a large estate near Basra and probably property in Makka. His son Mūsā had estates in Egypt as did Ītākh. Bughā the Younger had estates in Armenia, where he had conducted military campaigns, Waṣīf in Isfahan and Hamadhan.[89] As part of his reward for his part in the assassination of al-Mutawwakil, Bāghir was given estates in the Sawād of Kūfa, which were administered by a local *dihqān*, and brought in an annual revenue of 2000 *dīnārs*.[90] Ṣāliḥ b. al-Waṣīf's brother-in-law, al-Nūshurī, had estates along the Khurāsān Road in Iraq, where he employed a local Arab as his *wakīl*.[91] In all cases, the owners were, of course absentee landlords, collecting the revenues but remaining based in Samarra.

The disturbed conditions which followed the assassination of al-Mutawwakil in 247/861 meant that military leaders had opportunities to make money in return for protection. The workings of such a deal can be seen in an anecdote in al-Ṭabarī's *Ta'rīkh* which, he says, had been told him by an acquaintance from his native province of Tabaristan.[92] Mūsā b. Bughā had been sent to defend the lands and people of Rayy from the depredations of the supporters of the 'Alid, al-Ḥasan b. Zayd, who controlled the mountains to the north of the city. However, his troops became restless when they heard of the large sums of money their colleagues in Samarra had grabbed after the death of the Caliph al-Mu'tazz in 255/869 and the execution of some of his ministers. They wished to return to share in the spoils and enjoy the *'aṭā'*. The people of Rayy tried to persuade Mūsā to remain and even paid in 500 000 *dirhams* in advanced taxation. They promised that he and his troops would actually be better off remaining in Rayy and living off the taxes they were prepared to pay, than returning to Samarra. Mūsā refused to listen, taking the money they had already paid and leaving them to their fate. The people of Rayy were essentially proposing to employ Mūsā and his men as mercenaries and were encouraging them to set up a semi-independent state in the area. It is likely that the paralysis of government in Samarra after the death of al-Muttawwakil meant that similar deals between the local people and their garrisons were fairly widespread.

For most of the Turkish and other soldiers in Samarra these opportunities did not exist, and a constant theme which runs through the political struggles of this confused period was the need of the troops to secure payment of their salaries. One of the main demands that the *mawālī* made of the Caliph al-Muhtadī in 256/ 870 was that their *'aṭā'* should be paid speedily and that they should get their *arzāq* every two months, though it is not clear what the distinction between these two payments was.[93] The isolation of the Turks, away from the local population and cut off from other economic opportunities, meant that they were wholly dependent on salaries: if they did not receive them, they would starve. The military were engaged in what was, often quite literally, a cutthroat competition for resources.

The rank and file of the Turkish soldiers were segregated from the rest of the population. Though there is little or no direct evidence about their everyday circumstances, they were very recent converts to Islam (if they were Muslims at all), they did not speak the local language[94] and they had limited experience of urban and commercial life. They were, in short, totally dependent on the government for their survival in this alien environment. There is a contrast to be made here with the Khurāsāniya of Baghdad and their descendants, the *Abnā'*, who mingled with the urban population and many of whom must have acquired trades or businesses or access to other resources.

The position was exacerbated by the tensions within the Turkish community. Gordon has argued that we should make a distinction between the 'Baghdad' Turks and the 'Steppe' Turks.[95] The Baghdad group were the leaders like Ashinās, Ītākh, Waṣīf and the Elder and Younger Bughās who were recruited by al-Mu'taṣim within the Muslim world. They seem to have been more acculturated and, as leaders, they were rewarded with landed estates which provided revenues to support themselves and their retinues. Bughā the Elder had 500 of his own *ghilmān* and a similar number of his children, companions and commanders.[96] Ṣāliḥ b. al-Waṣīf had 800 of his own *ghilmān* and *mawālī*.[97] By contrast, the 'Steppe' Turks came straight from their nomad tribal environment and had no such range of economic options. As time went on, they became increasingly resentful, not only of the government which failed to pay them, but also of the resources and lifestyle of the Turkish leadership.

Despite the obvious importance of financial matters, we have few details of the mechanisms involved in payment in Samarra, and almost nothing from other areas, though we know that there were *jund* and *shākiriya* in Baghdad who received salaries.[98] Salary levels are seldom given. When an officer took 100 troops with him to the Byzantine frontier to arrange an exchange of prisoners, he was given 60 000 *dirhams* for their *arzāq*. In Rajab 256/ June 870 we are told that the Caliph al-Muhtadī was offering two *dirhams* a day for Turks and men of similar status and one for the Maghāriba.[99] These rates, 60 and 30 per month, seem low and presumably reflect the financial crisis of the regime, but would also do much to explain the restlessness and dissatisfaction of the rank-and-file troops at this time. In short, the very few figures we have suggest that salary levels for rank-and-file troops were not significantly higher, if at all, than wages in the early 'Abbasid period.

The wars against Bābak

The rebellion of Bābak had begun well before the accession of al-Mu'taṣim, in 201/816–7. It was centred on the city of Badhdh in the remote mountainous area between Ardabīl and Āhar to the south of the Aras (Araxes) river. Bābak's rebellion was associated with a religious movement called the Khurramiya, and it was not so much a rebellion against an established authority as a protest by the indigenous people of the area against Muslim expansion into their homelands.

Until 220/835 the Muslim response to Bābak had been left to local families or freelance adventurers,[100] but in this year the Caliph decided to take over the conflict, probably intending to use it to demonstrate the effectiveness of his army and its commitment to the cause of Islam. The man he chose to lead this great push was Khaydhar b. Kāwus al-Afshīn. Al-Afshīn was hereditary ruler of the small, mountainous principality of Ushrūsanā. Like many magnates in the area, he had supported the cause of al-Ma'mūn and had emerged as one of the leading soldiers in al-Mu'taṣim's army. He led an army largely made up of eastern Iranians like himself, including the Bukhārā-khūdah, the native prince of Bukhārā, but also including some Turks like Bughā the Elder.

The account of the campaign emphasises caution and competence on the part of the military commanders, not heroic actions and wild exploits: the accent is, in fact, on the professionalism with which the campaign was conducted and censure is reserved for those, like Bughā on one occasion and the *muṭawwi'a* (volunteers), who failed to obey orders or maintain discipline. The hero is al-Afshīn himself, but again, the qualities he is lauded for are careful and methodical planning and cautious advance[101] rather than personal courage or brilliance.

Another aspect of this is the specialisation among the troops. In early Islamic armies there were cavalry, foot-soldiers and archers, although it is clear that the roles were often interchangeable. In al-Afshīn's army, however, there were groups divided by function. The most conspicuous of these were the *Kūhbāniya* (mountain-keepers[102]). These may have been local people recruited in the area and their function was to secure the mountain tops and prevent the Muslim armies being attacked from above. On several occasions they used flags (*'alam*, pl. *a'lām*) to signal to the main body of the troops in the valley far below.

As well as the mountain-keepers, there were support troops known as the *kilghariya*. The etymology of this word is not clear[103] but their functions are. They are found bringing water skins and dry biscuit (*ka'k*) to the troops,[104] later the head (*ṣāḥib*) of the *kilgariya* was ordered to take money and weapons to the hard-pressed volunteers who were attacking the walls of Badhdh, and they are described as advancing with axes in their hands.[105] In the final conflict with Bābak's men, they were sent to fill up the pits the enemy had dug with stones so that the Muslim cavalry could advance;[106] al-Afshīn also made extensive use of *fa'ala* (sappers)[107] and there is also mention of a *ṣāḥib al-sharab*, who must have been in charge of the water carriers.[108]

Equally unprecedented was the attention given to medical supplies. In the final assault on Badhdh al-Afshīn had mules loaded with litters for the wounded, supplies of *sawīq* (barley broth) and *ka'k* (biscuit) and sent doctors with them.[109] Later the same day the litters were used to bring back volunteers who had been wounded in the fierce fighting outside the city walls.[110]

The efficiency and organisation extended to the whole field of pay and commissariat. As has already been mentioned, in most early Islamic armies the troops were responsible for providing their own victuals.[111] However, finding supplies in this remote part of Azerbaijān was clearly a problem, especially as al-Afshīn's army remained in the area for two winters. From the beginning he was clearly aware that supplies were going to be a problem. His first actions were to secure a supply route from Ardabil to his first base camp at Barzand, garrisoning forts along the way and introducing a convoy system to prevent Bābak's men for pillaging travellers.[112] The fort at Arshaq, soon to be the scene of bitter fighting, had a garrison of 600 foot and 4000 cavalry.[113] Despite these precautions, there were major problems. Later the same year, a supply caravan (*qāfila*) led by one Abu Ṣāliḥ Āb-kash (the water carrier) was attacked, most of the men with it were killed and the goods were pillaged.[114] This resulted in serious shortages of food and water in the camp at Barzand and al-Afshīn wrote to the governor of Marāgha who despatched a vast caravan (*qāfila ḍakhma*) with supplies, including 1000 head of cattle, and an army escort, but this too was captured by the enemy.[115] Finally supplies were brought from the Jibāl area and Bughā arrived bearing money and reinforcements.[116] Two years later, during the final attack on Badhdh, al-Afshīn was careful to keep his men well supplied with food.[117]

It is clear that there were tensions between the regular army and the volunteers who had come to fight in the Holy War against the unbeliever Bābak. The volunteers (*muṭawwi'a*) seem to have appeared only in the final year of the campaign for the assault on Badhdh itself. The volunteers, supported by one of al-Afshīn's commanders, Ja'far b. Dīnār, felt that they could have taken the city if al-Afshīn had supported them at the crucial moment but Afshīn was concerned that they would be ambushed from behind and firmly rejected what he saw as rash move.[118] Later, the volunteers complained that they were short of supplies and money but they received no help from al-Afshīn who said that his responsibilities lay with the professional troops who would stay with him whatever: 'The road home', he pointed out, 'is wide open'.[119] Later, however, he seems to have relented and sent the volunteers supplies and offered them cash rewards for exceptional bravery. Their wounded were evacuated in the litters he provided.[120]

Nonetheless, there remained important differences between the two elements; the volunteers wanted immediate action and embraced the prospect of martyrdom while al-Afshīn and the regulars wanted victory but not at any price. As their commander recognised, the regulars had more staying power, 'I have with me the Commander of the Faithful's army [*jund*] who are getting their pay [arzāq] by him and they will stay with me in heat and cold. I will not leave here until the snow falls.'[121] When the volunteers realised that the campaign was likely to drag on into the autumn, most of them departed, leaving al-Afshīn and his men to continue the work.

The war also demonstrates modest technological advances. The most obvious of these were developments in communication. Mention has already been made of the use of flags so that the mountain guards could keep in touch with the rest of the army, though it is not clear whether this represented a real semaphore or just a few simple signs. Drums were also used to signal advance. Al-Afshīn is said to have had 21 drums: 'His signals for moving and halting were the beating and silencing of drums because of the great number of troops who were travelling in the mountains and on the narrow paths in their military formations.'[122]

Al-Afshīn continued the tradition of building *khandaq*s (the digging of the trench of his assault camp near Badhdh took the army ten days[123]), to defend his troops, and the more recent practice of using caltrops to defend them.[124] Both cavalry and infantry were deployed, and the Caliph himself had ordered that some squadrons of the cavalry should always be in the saddle to protect the advance.[125] Only foot-archers are mentioned[126] but axes are said to have been used as weapons.[127] Perhaps because of the very difficult terrain, there is no mention of the use of siege engines (*majāniq*) during the assault on Budhdh, though the attackers did make use of two *'arrādas*.[128] They also made use of incendiary warfare and there are references to *naffāṭāṭ*, either as torches or as naptha-hurling weapons.[129]

The Amorion campaign

The Amorion campaign followed immediately after the defeat and execution of Bābak.[130] As in the case of the previous expedition, al-Ṭabarī gives us a full, connected, linear narrative of events[131] with no use of *akhbār* or *isnād*s. The narrative appears to come from someone close to the Turkish commander Ashinās and, as a consequence, somewhat neglects parts of the expedition, like the second prong of the attack led by Al-Afshīn, in which Ashinās did not participate. Although there is an extended account of military events, the author's real interest seems to be in the internal politics of the Caliph's court and army and, in particular, he seems to be trying to justify the brutal purge of al-'Abbās b. al-Ma'mūn and his followers which immediately followed the victory.

The *casus belli* for the campaign was a raid by the Byzantine Emperor Theophilus on the frontier town of Zibaṭra, which resulted in a number of Muslims being taken killed or taken prisoner. Thus, al-Mu'taṣim and his army[132] claimed to be protectors and avengers of the Muslims. The Muslims entered Byzantine territory in Rajab 223/June 838. It was said that al-Mu'taṣim had gathered equipment (*jiḥāz*) like no Caliph had before him, including arms, naphtha and water carriers. He seems to have had a real supply train, with 'baggage, *manājiq*, provisions and the like'[133] which travelled at the rear, but throughout the campaign, food (and even more water), were to cause major problems when the army was on the march through the barren plains of Central Anatolia.

Much of the expedition was taken up with a sort of hide-and-seek with the Byzantine army and in the quest for supplies. Al-Afshīn defeated a Byzantine army and occupied the city of Ankara, which had been deserted by its inhabitants. The Muslim army then reunited for the attack on Amorion itself. The city was defended by a wall which was sturdy enough to resist the Muslim attacks in most places. In one part, however, the wall had been washed away and makeshift repairs made.[134] Alerted by a traitor, the Muslims concentrated on this sector and a small part of the wall was brought down. The Caliph decided on an ambitious use of siege engines. The wall was to be attacked with *manājiq*, 'large in proportion to the height of the wall'. Each *manājiq* was to be worked by four men and they were mounted on wheeled carts (*'ajal*). He also ordered the construction of *dabābāt*, each large enough to hold ten men. *Dabāba* is the modern Arabic word for a tank and it comes from a root meaning to creep along the ground. It is sometimes translated as siege tower[135] but the classical lexicographers make it clear that this was a mobile shelter used to attack the lower part of the wall and was equivalent to the Roman *testudo* or *musculus*.[136]

There still remained the problem of the ditch which surrounded the city. This needed to the filled in if the attackers were to be able to reach the wall and the Caliph is said to have ordered his soldiers to fill sheepskins with stones and throw them into the ditch and so fill it up to make a level approach. In the event, the plan failed because the surface was not firm or level enough and the wheels sank in. The mobile engines proved useless and in the end they were simply burned.

The next day an assault was mounted on the section of the wall which had collapsed but the breach was too small to allow the assailants to gain entry. Al-Mu'taṣim ordered that the large siege engines (*al-manjanīqāt al-kibār*) which had been distributed around the perimeter should be concentrated in this area. The breach was enlarged and the Muslims were able to enter. The commander of the section of the wall surrendered, and though there was sporadic resistance in some of the towers, the city had effectively fallen.[137]

The second siege of Baghdad, Muḥarram–Dhū'l-Ḥijja 251/February–December 865

The history of the second siege of Baghdad, like the first, is covered in detail by al-Ṭabarī. In contrast to the first, however, the narrative is more or less continuous and no sources are mentioned. The narrative concentrates on the defenders. While not openly biased, it contains much more information about the actions of the defenders of the city than of the Turks and Maghribis who were attacking it. As a result, the accounts of warfare may be skewed and, for example, the attackers may have constructed many more siege engines than the one mentioned. That said, however, the account provides a mass of detail about the conduct of the siege.

The second siege of Baghdad was the result of a major division with the army at Samarra. As a result of this, the Caliph al-Musta'īn with a number of his prominent supporters, including Bughā and Waṣīf, left Samarra for the old 'Abbasid capital at Baghdad. Baghdad was effectively ruled at this time as it had been since al-Mu'taṣim had moved the capital to Samarra, by the Tahirid family. The governor, Muḥammad b. 'Abd Allāh b. Ṭāhir, welcomed the Caliph and his entourage to the city and established himself as their protector. Meanwhile in Samarra, the bulk of the Turks and the Maghāriba had elected al-Mu'tazz as their Caliph. He in turn appointed his brother, Abū Aḥmad b. al-Mutawwakil to command a military expedition to Baghdad. Meanwhile Ibn Ṭāhir set about fortifying the city. Previously, only the round city of al-Manṣūr, the centre of government, had had walls, but he now set about enclosing the main inhabited areas on both the east and west banks of the Tigris.

Hostilities began soon after the army arrived from Samarra. The attacking army was comparatively small and Abū Aḥmad left Samarra with only some 5000 Turks and Farāghina and 2000 Maghāriba. After they arrived at Baghdad in Safar 251/March 865 an estimate provided for the defenders of the city by a Baghdad spy put it still lower at 2000 on the east bank and 1000 on the west.[138] At a major battle shortly afterwards at al-Qaṭi'a, 4000 Turkish troops are said to have taken part, of whom 2000 were killed.[139] Subsequently al-Mu'tazz sent 3000 more infantry and cavalry under the command of Mūsā b. Ashinās to help the attackers.[140] Later in the siege, another spy said the attacking army had grown, with 12 000 with Bayākbāk on the west bank and 7000 with Abū Aḥmad on the east[141]: Samarra was almost completely denuded of troops. However, these numbers seem untypically large and nothing like that number is reported in any of the skirmishes which characterised the siege.

We have no gross numbers for the defenders. It seems likely that they were always more numerous than their enemies. Throughout the siege, reinforcements drifted in from different provinces as local military leaders took sides. *Shākiriya* groups came, 300 from the Makka road,[142] 1300 from Raqqa.[143] Bedouin (*a'rāb*) were recruited in significant numbers, and fought as both cavalry and infantry.[144]

Along with these, the authorities in Baghdad began to recruit *'ayyār*s. In contrast to the *'ayyārūn* of the first siege,[145] these were recruited and equipped by Ibn Ṭāhir to supplement rather than rival the regular troops and an officer (*'arīf*) was appointed over them.[146] They were provided with rudimentary arms, including shields made of tar-covered mats and armed with bags of stones, clubs (called *kāfirkūbāt*) and slings.[147] We also hear on one occasion of *'ayyārūn* carrying swords.[148] As in the first siege, we are told of irregulars who put heavily armed troops to flight.[149] Politically this was clearly an attempt to broaden the power base of the Baghdad regime, but militarily the details emphasise the gulf between the professional soldier and the irregular, in both equipment and the style of warfare.

The struggle for Baghdad took the form of assaults by the Samarra troops and counter-attacks by the defenders. It seems that the attackers concentrated on attacking certain sectors, notably the Shammasiya and Anbar Gates, and movement in and out of the city always seems to have been possible. There is no mention of lack of supplies or starvation in the city. The Samarran troops were just too few in number to mount an effective blockade.

Nor did they make use of siege engines. Whereas we have many details of the engines mounted by the defenders, there is only one occasion when the Turks are said to have erected a *manjanīq* by the Khurāsān Gate, but it was damaged by a sortie of the defenders, one of its supports was broken and it was put out of action.[150] Instead, the Turks attacked the defenders with arrows[151] and in two cases these were clearly fired by mounted archers.[152] The attackers also used incendiary weapons to attack gates and siege engines. On one occasion they shot at a *manjanīq* with naphtha and fire but failed to do any damage.[153] Later, however, they succeeded in firing the Anbār Gate and the siege engines which guarded it.[154] On one occasion, one of the Maghribis in the attacking army used a grappling hook (*kullāb*) to scale the walls but he was soon killed and the Baghdadis shot his head from a *manjanīq* into the Turkish ranks.[155] On only one occasion do the attackers seem to have succeeded in entering the fortified perimeter, and then they were driven out after some heavy street fighting and the Anbār Gate, where some of them had entered, was bricked up.[156]

In contrast, the defenders used siege engines to great effect. Both *'arrādāt* and *majāniq* were used essentially as anti-personnel weapons and caused high casualties among the attackers: after one encounter, Ṭabarī's source especially notes that 'most of the killing was done by *majāniq*'.[157] On another occasion a Turkish hero called al-Durghumān was killed when a stone from a *manjanīq* hit him in the chest.[158] Presumably, the burned bricks (*ājar*) which the people of Baghdad were ordered to collect[159] were intended for ammunition for the engines.

The defenders also used siege engines mounted on boats on the river to attack the Turks. We are told of a squadron of ten which arrived from Basra in Safar 251/ March 865. They were called *bawārīj* and each one had a master, three fire-hurlers (*naffāṭīn*), a carpenter, a baker and 35 oarsmen and soldiers. They fired on the Turkish camp by the Shammasiya Gate, forcing them to abandon it and seek a safer site.[160] In an earlier attack on the Shammasiya Gate, the Turks had been driven off by *'arrādāt* mounted on boats.[161] In the last major engagement of the siege (Dhū'l-Qa'ada 251/November–December 865), the Baghdadis attacked the Turks by both land and water, sinking a Turkish boat called, intriguingly, Al-Ḥadīd (the Iron), which had caused the Baghdadis much damage.[162]

The breakdown of the Samarra military

Initially, al-Mu'taṣim's military reorganisation was a success. He managed to create a new army for the 'Abbasid Caliphs which was both obedient and effective. It enabled him to seize the Caliphate on the death of al-Ma'mūn and to cover himself with glory and prestige as champion of the Muslims against the ancient Byzantine foe. His son and successor al-Wāthiq continued the pattern. It was in the reign of al-Mutawwakil that strains and tensions began to become apparent.

At first, relations between the Caliph and the leaders of the Turkish military seemed as close as ever. Al-Mutawwakil was chosen as Caliph by a small group of five leading politicians, two of whom, Ītākh and Waṣīf, were Turkish commanders. However, al-Mutawwakil seems to have been determined to lessen his dependence on the Turkish element in the military and broaden his power base. He took measures to destroy the power of the Turkish leaders. In 235/849 he arranged the arrest and murder of Ītākh, the most prominent of them. It was not easy and the Caliph feared that if he moved against him in Samarra, the Turks would rise in his support, so when Ītākh asked to go on the pilgrimage to Makka, the Caliph saw his opportunity. On his return, Ītākh was invited to Baghdad by the governor, Isḥāq b. Ibrāhīm the Tahirid. There was no love lost between the Turkish commanders in Samarra and the Tahirids of Baghdad and Khurāsān. Furthermore Isḥāq could count on the support of the people of Baghdad and especially of the *shākiriya* military there. Al-Ṭabarī gives a dramatic account of the events which followed,[163] demonstrating a certain *Schadenfreude* which reflects the mixed feelings many Muslims in Iraq had towards the Turks. Ītākh was persuaded to enter Baghdad with sweet words and invited to the riverside house which had belonged to Khuzayma b. Khāzim, a leading member of the *Abnā'*. Here he was skilfully separated from his 300 strong escort of companions and *ghilmān* and the door was locked behind him. Soon his sons and secretaries were brought to join him in prison. Four months later he was dead.

The Caliph had successfully destroyed the most powerful of the Turkish leaders without any open dissent. He had demonstrated that the Caliph was still in charge of the army, but the fact that he had to use subterfuge shows that he was aware of the dangerous power of the military. For their part, other Turkish commanders may have been pleased to benefit from Ītākh's removal but, at the same time, they must have been aware that their own positions were no more secure than his.

On the night of 4 Shawwāl 247/9–10 December 861 as the Caliph and a few intimates were drinking in his palace in Samarra, a group of Turkish soldiers secured the doors and then burst in on him, killing him and his friend and adviser, al-Fatḥ b. Khāqān.

The brutal assassination was the result of tensions which had been building up between the Turkish military and the Caliph, but also within the Turkish military itself. The underlying cause of the problems was financial. The Turks had already used their power to protest against cuts in their pay in 244/858 when the Caliph had temporarily moved to Damascus, and he had been forced to placate them.[164] Now they felt compelled to take action because al-Mutawwakil was recruiting other troops including, according to one source, 12 000 Arabs and *ṣa'ālīk* (bandits or brigands, a term of abuse).[165] Further information about the identity of these soldiers becomes apparent in the events which happened the next day in Samarra. On the morning after the murder, the dead Caliph's minister, 'Ubayd Allāh b.

Yaḥyā b. Khāqān (who may himself be of Turkish origin), was approached by a force estimated at between 5000 and 20 000 *Abnā'*, Persians (*'ajam*), Armenians, *Zawāqīl* (Arab tribesmen from northern Syria and the Jazīra), bedouin (*a'rāb*), *sa'ālīk* and others who urged him to attack the assassins, their newly appointed Caliph al-Muntaṣir and the Turks in general.[166] The *jund* and the *shākiriya* also gathered to express their outrage at the murder.[167] All these military groups threatened the power and position of the Turks. The last straw seems to have been rumours that the Caliph was about to confiscate the estates of Waṣīf, the senior surviving Turkish commander, and give them to his favourite, al-Fatḥ b. Khāqān: they might well feel that their days as the élite force of the Caliph's army were numbered unless they took vigorous action. The accession of al-Muntaṣir in 248/862, the Turks' candidate for the throne, seem to have quelled these anxieties but after the accession of al-Musta'īn, financial problems began to come to the surface. The first indications come from Baghdad in Ṣafar 249/ March 863 when the non-Turkish troops, the *jund* and the *shākiriya* rioted demanding their *arzāq*. The movement developed into an anti-Turkish protest and spread to Samarra, where there was fighting between the Turks and the people.[168] It was not only the non-Turkish soldiers who were feeling the pinch. In response to the riots, Turkish soldiers in Samarra mounted a demonstration against the Caliph's finance officers. Al-Musta'īn had entrusted the treasury to a Turk called Utāmish and he was now blamed for the problems. For the first time we hear of the *mawālī*, the rank-and-file 'steppe' Turks from Dūr and al-Karkh, showing their militancy. Utāmish was dragged from his place of refuge and done to death, after which the troops went on to pillage his palace.[169] The Caliph took measures to keep the loyalty of the Turks and later claimed that he had added 2000 of their children to the *dīwān* and that 4000 of their daughters had been counted among the married (presumably meaning that they were paid).[170] Such generosity must have put a further strain on the treasury. When al-Musta'īn fled to Baghdad in Muḥarram 251/February 865, he left around 500 000 *dīnār*s, which had recently arrived from Syria, in the treasury. The new Caliph in Samarra, al-Mu'tazz ordered that the soldiers be paid an accession bonus of ten months' pay but there was simply not enough money and they had to make do with two.[171]

The civil war and siege of Baghdad which ensued made the situation much worse. Troops in Samarra and Baghdad demanded their pay but it became almost impossible to raise revenue, even from the Sawād of Iraq, never mind more distant provinces. There were occasional windfalls, as when 70 donkeys loaded with money arrived in Baghdad from Fārs and Ahwaz.[172] Probably more typical were the problems in getting money from the lands immediately around Baghdad. The revenues of the lands of Rādhān on the Nahrawān canal, amounting to 12 030 *dīnār*s could be collected only with the help of a Kurdish commander Ibn Jaylawayh, who brought them to Baghdad. He was given 10 000 *dirham*s reward.[173]

In the end, it was lack of financial resources which led to the collapse of al-Musta'īn's regime in Baghdad. In Rajab 251/August 865 the members of the 'Abbasid family in the city staged a demonstration, complaining that they had not been paid their *arzāq*, that the money had gone to other people and threatening that they would open the gates of the city to the besieging Turks if their demands were not met. They were promised one month's pay, which they refused to accept.[174] Soon after, a combination of lack of money to pay the troops and rising dissatisfaction with hardship and high prices among the citizens, prompted Ibn Ṭāhir to open negotiations with the Samarra forces.[175]

The agreement which ended the war was essentially a financial package. The revenues of the state were to be divided, two-thirds going to the Turks and *mawālī* of Samarra, and one-third to Ibn Ṭāhir and the Baghdad army. Al-Musta'īn was to abdicate and to be paid a pension of 30 000 *dīnār*s per year.[176] None of these provisions was honoured: al-Mu'tazz ordered the murder of al-Musta'īn and refused to pay the salaries of the Baghdadis, making it clear that this was the responsibility of the Tahirids.[177] This in turn led to further violence in the city and the final breakdown of Tahirid rule there.

Things were no better in Samarra. A note in al-Ṭabarī's chronicle puts it starkly: the estimated payments required by the Turks, the Maghāriba and the *Shākiriya* for this year (252/866) reportedly reached 200 000 000 *dīnār*s, which was equal to two years' *kharāj* from the entire realm (*mamlaka*).[178] The figure may be exaggerated, but the point is well made: with the loss of almost all revenue from the provinces and the disruption in Iraq itself, the army established by al-Mu'taṣim was completely unaffordable, yet, at the same time, the troops, especially the rank-and-file *mawālī*, would not, and could not, cease their demands for payment.

This was the background to tragic deaths of the Caliphs al-Mu'tazz and al-Muhtadī and the final collapse of the Samarra army. The financial problems led to increased conflict between Turks and Caliphs, Turks and other groups in the military and, above all, between the *mawālī* Turks of Dūr and al-Karkh on one hand and leaders like Ṣāliḥ b. al-Waṣīf and Mūsā b. Bughā, and their retinues, on the other.

In Shawwāl 253/October 867 there was a riot by the Turks and other soldiers demanding their pay. They were confronted by the veteran Waṣīf, the last of the old generation of Turkish commanders who had served under al-Mu'taṣim. 'Take dirt', he told them, 'do you think we have anything to give you?' Honest but tactless, he was immediately lynched by the soldiers.[179] the role of military commander was inherited by Waṣīf's son Ṣāliḥ, who was faced by the same problems as his father. To solve them, he adopted a new and violent tactic. When the Turks complained that they had not been paid, he went to the Caliph and complained that the wealth had been embezzled by three leading administrators, Aḥmad b. Isrā'īl, al-Ḥasan b. Makhlad and Abū Nūḥ 'Īsā b. Ibrāhīm. He caused them to be arrested; they were abused by the Turks and it was decreed that their estates would be confiscated, but no ready cash was produced.[180]

This did not solve the immediate problem of paying the Turks, who now turned to the Caliph, saying that if he could pay them their *arzāq*, they would, in exchange, kill Ṣāliḥ b. al-Waṣīf. The Caliph was clearly tempted by the offer, but had no cash. He approached his mother, the fabulously rich Qabīḥa but she, despite her vast resources, refused to advance him the necessary 50 000 *dīnārs*. The Turks were implacable and without delay, they dragged the unfortunate Caliph from his residence and forced him to abdicate (Rajab 255/July 869). He died in confinement, apparently of thirst, a few days later, aged only 24.

A new Caliph, al-Muhtadī, was chosen but the treasury was still empty and Ṣāliḥ was becoming increasingly desperate to find money for the Turks. However, his luck suddenly changed when he managed to lay his hands on the fortune of the dead Caliph's mother, Qabīḥā. Having so signally failed to help her own son in his hour of need, she was now obliged to sell her possessions. Then 500 000 *dirhams* were brought to Samarra, which solved the pay problem temporarily, and the *jund* and *shākiriya* in Baghdad were also paid something.[181]

Clearly such a windfall would not happen again and Ṣāliḥ cast around for further ways to raise money. He now put the secretaries who had been arrested, to torture, demanding money from them. The new Caliph could only look on in dismay: 'Is there no choice of punishment apart from the whip or death?' he lamented, 'Is imprisonment not enough? We are God's, and to Him we shall return.' Two of the secretaries died under the lash and the third, al-Ḥasan b. Makhlad, was saved by the Caliph only after enduring a terrible beating. Despite the extreme brutality used, the sums raised must have disappointed Ṣāliḥ, 19 000 *dīnārs* from Aḥmad and a jewel worth 30 000 from al-Ḥasan. What was worse, from Ṣāliḥ's point of view, was that a large number of Turks in Samarra, and those who were serving with his rival Mūsā b. Bughā in Rayy, refused to believe that he had extracted so little and firmly believed that he was hiding the rest.[182]

Ṣāliḥ had now run out of options, and simply went into hiding while Mūsā b. Bughā and his men returned from Rayy. A series of discussions now took place between the rank and file of the Turkish soldiery and the Caliph which clearly show the reasons for the tension between the Turkish leaders and the rank-and-file *mawālī*.

On 4 Safar 256/ 11 January 870, there was a public meeting attended by 150 Turkish cavalry and 500 infantry, who drew up a written petition which made a number of demands.[183] Their complaints were not against the Caliph, but against the Turkish commanders. They complained that their salaries (*arzāq*) were always delayed and that the *iqṭā'āt* given to their *quwwād* had used up all the revenues from the estates and the *kharāj*. Furthermore they protested against the special allowances and bonuses (*ma'āwin* and *ziyādāt*) which had been made by their seniors, in breach of previous custom and the payments of salaries to women and other hangers-on who had absorbed all the *kharāj*.

In response, the Caliph sent a letter to be read out in public in which he praised the loyalty of the troops and stressed that he and his family led very frugal lives and that all available money had been paid to them. The *mawālī* then reformulated their requests.[184] In broad terms they asked that the Caliph take direct control for military affairs and that the old customs of the reign of al-Musta'īn be reinstated and they demanded the restoration of a systematic command structure, with an *'arīf* over every nine men, a *khalīfa* over every 50 and a *qā'id* over every 100. Once more the women and extras were to be dropped. On financial matters their main demand was that their *'aṭā'* be paid regularly every two months, that no *mawlā* should enter a *qabāla* contract[185] and that *iqṭā'*s should be abolished.

Shortly afterwards, after further negotiations, the demands were reformulated again.[186] There were five specific points, including the abolition of extras, the abolition of *iqṭā's*, the demotion of gate-keepers (*bawwābīn*) from the *khāssa* (élite) to the *'āmma* (common people),[187] the return to the practice of the reign of al-Musta'īn and what seems to be the abolition of *iljā'* agreements.[188] In addition they demanded that their two main enemies, the *qā'ids* Mūsā b. Bughā and Ṣāliḥ b. al-Waṣīf, should be obliged to account for their wealth and, perhaps most importantly, they demanded that their *'aṭā'* and *arzāq* be paid regularly.

As before, all these demands were designed to limit the power and patronage of the *quwwād* and restore the status of the rank and file as regular, salaried troops dependent directly on the Caliph, or a member of his family, for pay and for promotion. For a moment it seemed as if the two parties would combine against Mūsā and the other Turkish leaders. However, suspicions remained, there was no money to be paid, and Mūsā was able to rally the Turks against the Caliph. On 18 Rajab 256/21 June 870, al-Muhtadī in his turn met a violent death at the hands of his troops.

Conclusion

The Samarra system was now bankrupt, both financially and politically, and only a new beginning could save the power of the Caliphs from complete oblivion. The system established by al-Mu'taṣim was ambitious and efficient as long as all went well. It delivered a small professional army which could suppress rebellion within the Caliphate, as was shown in Egypt and against Bābak, and take on and defeat the Byzantines. The Turkish soldiers, fighting as mounted archers, were the most effective military force of their time. However, the system carried within it a number of dangers. It was highly centralised in Samarra, with a secondary pole in Tahirid-ruled Baghdad: trouble in the capital would mean that the provinces would go their own way very rapidly. Furthermore, it was entirely dependent on large regular payments in coined money. There is no indication that this was a problem under al-Mu'taṣim, al-Wāthiq and al-Mutawwakil. The problems which emerged at first were political rather than financial, the desire of al-Mutawwakil to reduce the power of the Turks and their determination that this should not happen. Political division soon led to financial crisis. The civil war between Samarra and Baghdad bankrupted both cities while the provinces rapidly ceased to send any revenue at all. The government had no method of borrowing in advance of tax-receipts to carry it through bad times; it could resort only to plunder, extortion and the farming out of revenues. Once things had begun to go wrong, it was almost impossible to put them right; the continuous, insistent and violent demand for cash salaries by the military destroyed the governments of al-Musta'īn, al-Mu'tazz and al-Muhtadī and led each Caliph to a grisly end.

Notes

1 There is an extensive literature on the coming of the Turks. For the best general account, see M. Gordon, *The Breaking of a Thousand Swords: A History of the Turkish Community of Samarra, 200–275 AH/815–889 CE* (Albany, 2001); fundamental to the discussion are the papers of D. Ayalon, including 'The Military Reforms of al-Mu'taṣim' in D. Ayalon (ed.), *Islam and the Abode of War* (Aldershot, 1994), 1–39; 'Preliminary Remarks on the *mamlūk* Military Institution in Islam' in V. J. Parry and M. E. Yapp, *War, Technology and Society in the Middle East* (London, 1988), 44–58; 'On the Eunuchs in Islam', *JSAI*, 1 (1979), 67–124 , repr. in D. Ayalon, *Outsiders in Islam: Mamluks, Mongols and Eunuchs* (London, 1988), iii; E. Herzfeld, *Geschichte der Stadt Samarra* (Hamburg, 1948); O. S. A. Ismail, 'Mutaṣim and the Turks', *BSOAS*, 29 (1966), 11–36; H. Töllner, *Die türkischen Garden am Kalifenhof von Samarra, ihre Entstehung und Machtergreifung bis zum Kalifat al-Mu'taḍids* (Bonn, 1971); D. Pipes, *Slave Soldiers and Islam: The Genesis of a Military System* (New Haven, 1981). For an overview of the historical debate, Gordon, *The Breaking of a Thousand Swords*, 6–8.

2 Mas'ūdī, *Murūj*, iv, 350–1 mentions that al-Mu'taṣim gathered the Turks, men from the two Hāwfs of Egypt, the men of Khurāsān, especially Farghāna and Ushrūsanā, and took pleasure in dressing them in fancy uniforms.

3 The origins and identities of these groups has been investigated by Gordon, and my account is based on his analysis.

4 Ya'q., *Buldān*, 257–8, 262.

5 Ya'q., *Buldān*, 267.

6 Ya'q., *Buldān*, 259.

7 Ya'q., *Buldān*, 259.

8 Ya'q., *Buldān*, 261.

9 Ya'q., *Buldān*, 262–3.

10 Ya'q., *Buldān*, 267.

11 Ya'q., *Buldān*, 263.

12 al-Jāḥiẓ., *Manāqib*, 4; for the Khurāsāniya and *Abnā'* see p. 96.

13 See pp. 118–19.

14 For the *Abnā'* in al-Jāḥiẓ.'s essay, see P. Crone, 'The 'Abbāsid Abnā' and Sāsānid Cavalrymen', *JRAS* (1998), 1–19, esp. 5–6, 17–19; Ayalon, 'The Military Reforms', 30–2.

15 The *Abnā'* are mentioned as one of the groups who joined the anti-Turkish movements at the time of al-Muhtadī (255–6/869–7), but their role was minor (Ṭa., iii, 1510; Ya'q., *Ta'rīkḥ*, ii, 618). Descendants of some prominent *Abnā'* families supported the Caliph al-Musta'īn after he had fled to Baghdad (P. Crone, *Slaves on Horseback*, Cambridge, 1980, 181–3).

16 For the geographical and tribal origins of the Turks, Gordon, *The Breaking of a Thousand Swords*, 21–3. Considerable confusion is caused by the use of the term 'Central Asia' to describe the original homeland of these Turks. It is often unclear whether the authors mean Transoxania by this, or the much vaster steppe lands to the east in Sinkiang and Mongolia. There is no evidence that the Turks who formed the army of Samarra came from this larger area.

17 R. N. Frye and A. M. Sayılı, 'Turks in the Middle East before the Saljuqs', *JAOS*, 63 (1943), 194–207.

18 On which, see Al-Jāḥiẓ., *Manāqib*, 39–46.

19 Gordon, *The Breaking of a Thousand Swords*,19–20; F. Amabe, *The Emergence of the 'Abbāsid Autocracy: The 'Abbāsid Army in Khurāsān and Adharbayjān* (Kyoto, 1995), 149–50.
20 Ya'q., *Buldān*, 255–6.
21 See *EI2* 'Farghāna' (Bartold/Spuler).
22 Gordon, *The Breaking of a Thousand Swords*, 19, 23; Amabe, *The Emergence of the 'Abbāsid Autocracy*, 151–3, 156–8, details their careers, but his attempt to claim noble origin for Ashinās and Waṣīf, in defiance of the only evidence we have, is not convincing.
23 Ya'q., *Buldān*, 255–6.
24 Iṣṭakhrī, 290–1. This passage is translated in Gordon, *The Breaking of a Thousand Swords*, 32 and Amabe, *The Emergence of the 'Abbāsid Autocracy*, 150–1 in different ways. The crucial question is whether the Khurāsāni noble families are included among the Turks and Farāghina, as Amabe thinks, or a separate group, as Gordon maintains. The Arabic is ambiguous. My partial translation is based on Gordon, but differs slightly.
25 The debate is dominated by the works of D. Ayalon, notably 'The Military Reforms'; Crone, *Slaves on Horseback*, 74–81; Pipes, *Slave Soldiers and Islam*; Gordon, *The Breaking of a Thousand Swords*, 6–9.
26 M. A. Shaban, *Islamic History: A New Interpretation*, ii (Cambridge, 1976), 66; Amabe, *The Emergence of 'Abbāsid Autocracy*, 140–69; Amabe's argument, though in some ways persuasive, relies heavily on ambiguous texts and speculative interpretations of personal names.
27 al-Ṣūlī, *Awrāq*, 457.
28 The only soldiers who are described as *mamlūk* in the Samarra period are the Maghāriba, some of whom were *mamlūk* and could be sold, while the remainder were free (*ḥurr*) and could not. Ṭa., iii, 1369–70.
29 On the use of the term, see D. Sourdel, 'Ghulām' in EI2.
30 For a full discussion of the uses of the term in this period, see Crone, *Slaves on Horseback*, 74–81; for their manumission, 78.
31 On Samarra, see K. A. C. Creswell, *Early Muslim Architecture*, 2 (Oxford, 1940); J. M. Rogers, 'Samarra, A Study in Medieval Town-Planning' in A. Hourani and S. M. Stern (eds), *The Islamic City* (Oxford, 1970); A. Northedge and R. Falkner, 'The 1986 Survey Season at Samarra' *Iraq*, 49 (1987), 143–73; A. Northedge, *Samarra: Residenz der 'Abbāsidenkalifen* (Tübingen, 1990); Gordon, *The Breaking of a Thousand Swords*, 47–74.
32 See W. Kaegi, 'The Contribution of Archery to the Turkish Conquest of Anatolia', *Speculum*, 39 (1964), 96–108.
33 Kaegi, 'The Contribution of Archery', 99–102.
34 al-Jāḥiẓ., *Manāqib*, 41.
35 al-Jāḥiẓ., *Manāqib*, 27, 29, 39: Lane sv. notes that some authorities say that this is the Turkish, not the Arab, horse.
36 al-Jāḥiẓ., *Manāqib*, 30.
37 al-Jāḥiẓ., *Manāqib*, 29–30.
38 al-Jāḥiẓ., *Manāqib*, 28.
39 al-Jāḥiẓ., *Manāqib*, 29.
40 al-Jāḥiẓ., *Manāqib*, 29.
41 al-Jāḥiẓ., *Manāqib*, 30–1.
42 al-Jāḥiẓ., *Manāqib*, 28. On the *birjās*, see p. 123.
43 Ibn Ṭayfūr, *Kitāb Baghdād*, 143 quoted in Ayalon, 'The Military Reforms', 30.
44 al-Jāḥiẓ., *Manāqib*, 32–3.
45 al-Jāḥiẓ., *Manāqib*, 42–3.
46 The area around Samarqand.

47 The old name for the Tashkent district (Uzbekistan).
48 Bal., *Futūḥ*, 431. The translation is based on Gordon, *The Breaking of a Thousand Swords*, 31, with minor variations.
49 Following the reading suggested by Amabe, *The Emergence of 'Abbāsid Autocracy*, 143.
50 Ya'q., *Buldān*, 258.
51 For the use of *'ajam* in this context, see Crone, 'The 'Abbāsid Abna', 14, n. 119.
52 Ibn Khallikān, *Wafayāt*, biography of Muḥammad b. Tughj al-Ikhshīd, quoted by Gordon, *The Breaking of a Thousand Swords*, 32 .
53 On Ushrūsanā, see E. Esin, 'The Cultural Background of Afsin Haidar of Usrūsanā in the Light of Recent Numismatic and Iconographic Data', in A. Dietrich (ed.), *Akten des VII Kongresses für Arabistik und Islamwissenschaft* (Göttingen, 1976), 126–45.
54 Their only named commander, Naṣr b. Aḥmad al-Zubayrī bears an Arabic name (Ṭa., iii, 1822).
55 Gordon, *The Breaking of a Thousand Swords*, 37–40.
56 Ṭa., iii, 1250.
57 Ṭa., iii, 1369–70.
58 See Ṭa., iii, 1250 trans. (Bosworth), n. 317 quoting Bayhaqi.
59 Ṭa., iii, 1555.
60 Ṭa., iii, 1839.
61 Ṭa., iii, 1369–70, 1820.
62 Gordon, *The Breaking of a Thousand Swords*, 40–2. For a full discussion of the *shākiriya*, see Appendix 1 at the end of this volume.
63 al-Kindī, *Wulāt*, 188 says that al-Mu'taṣim led 4000 Turks to Egypt in 214/829–30, and that number also given in al-Mas'ūdī, *Muruj*, vii, 118.
64 For further discussion of numbers based on archaeological evidence, see Appendix 2 at the end of this volume.
65 Töllner, *Die türkischen Garden*, 45–8.
66 Ṭa., iii, 1555.
67 Ṭa., iii, 1595.
68 Ṭa., iii, 1686.
69 Ṭa., iii, 1840; Ibn al-Athīr, vii, 238.
70 al-Kindī, 207.
71 al-Kindī, 205.
72 Ṭa., iii, 1790.
73 Ṭa., iii, 1800.
74 Ṭa., iii, 1816.
75 Ṭa., iii, 1202–3.
76 Ṭa., iii, 1239.
77 Ṭa., iii, 1362.
78 Ṭa., iii, 1555.
79 Ṭa., iii, 1829.
80 See pp. 108–9.
81 A point stressed in Ya'q., *Buldān*, 258–9.
82 The settlement is described in Ya'q., *Buldān*, 255–68.
83 Ya'q., *Buldān*, 258.
84 Ya'q., *Buldān*, 259.
85 The income of the military leaders and financial opportunities available to them are discussed in M. Gordon, 'The Turkish Officers of Samarra: Revenue and the Exercise of Authority', *JESHO*, 42 (1999), 466–93 and in *The Breaking of a Thousand Swords*, 118–24.
86 Ya'q., *Buldān*, 258–9.
87 Ya'q., *Buldān*, 258, 263.

88 Ya'q., *Buldān*, 264.
89 Gordon, *The Breaking of a Thousand Swords*, 120–1.
90 Ṭa., iii, 1535.
91 Ṭa., iii, 1735.
92 Ṭa., iii, 1736–9; see the discussion in Gordon, 'The Turkish Officers', 471–2.
93 Ṭa., iii, 1801.
94 See Ṭa., iii, 1535, where the Turks need an interpreter and express their disapproval by saying 'yok, yok' and iii, 1789 where they 'jabber away in Turkish', interrupting al-Muhtadī's audience.
95 Gordon, *The Breaking of a Thousand Swords*, 143–4.
96 Ṭa., iii, 1695.
97 Ṭa., iii, 1790.
98 Ṭa., iii, 1717.
99 Ṭa., iii, 1820.
100 See pp. 103–4.
101 E.g. Ṭa., iii, 1207.
102 Ṭa., iii, 1188 and trans. Bosworth, n. 138.
103 Ṭa., iii, 1199 and Gloss. sv., but see trans. Bosworth, n. 165 who suggests it comes from Persian *gil-kar*, one who works with clay (e.g. clay bricks in building).
104 Ṭa., iii, 1199.
105 Ṭa., iii, 1212.
106 Ṭa., iii, 1216–7.
107 E.g. Ṭa., iii, 1199, 1200.
108 Ṭa., iii, 1212.
109 Ṭa., iii, 1210–1.
110 Ṭa., iii, 1214.
111 See pp. 85–8.
112 Ṭa., iii, 1172–4.
113 Ṭa., iii, 1177.
114 Ṭa., iii, 1188.
115 Ṭa., iii, 1189.
116 Ṭa., iii, 1189. The supplies may have come from Sīrawan in Luristan but, as the Ṭabarī editor (de Goeje) notes, '*lectio suspecta est*', and it seems more likely that the source was closer at hand.
117 Ṭa., iii, 1199, 1209–12.
118 Ṭa., iii, 1207.
119 Ṭa., iii, 1209.
120 Ṭa., iii, 1211–12.
121 Ṭa., iii, 1209.
122 Ṭa., iii, 1203.
123 Ṭa., iii, 1200–1.
124 Ṭa., iii, 1197.
125 Ṭa., iii, 1197–8.
126 Ṭa., iii, 1214.
127 Ṭa., iii, 1212.
128 Smaller engines, Ṭa., iii, 1213.
129 Ṭa., iii, 1202, 1215 and trans. Bosworth, 56, n.169.
130 On this campaign, see A. A. Vasiliev, *Byzance et les Arabes*, 1 (Brussels, 1958–60), 144–77; Kaegi, 'The Contribution of Archery', 99–102; Treadgold, *The Byzantine Revival* (Stanford, 1988), 297–305.
131 Ṭa., iii, 1234–56.
132 Unfortunately, we have no figures for the total size of the army. However, they all seem to have been regulars and there is no mention of volunteers.

133 Ṭa., iii, 1237–8.
134 Ṭa., iii, 1245.
135 Ṭa., iii, 1248 trans. (Bosworth), n. 313. Bosworth bases this on the definition in Dozy sv. However, Dozy's authorities are thirteenth-century and later histories of the Mongols: siege towers are well attested from the Crusader period and after.
136 See Lane sv.
137 Ṭa., iii, 1248–53.
138 Ṭa., iii, 1555, 1557–8.
139 Ṭa., iii, 1564: it must be remembered that these figures are provided by the (optimistic) defenders.
140 Ṭa., iii, 1588.
141 Ta., iii, 1595.
142 Ṭa., iii, 1559.
143 Ṭa., iii, 1595 and other small groups.
144 Ṭa., iii, 1560, 1580, 1599–1600.
145 See pp. 110–11.
146 Ṭa., iii, 1552.
147 Ṭa., iii, 1552, 1586–7, 1592–3. There is perhaps a direct contrast here with the picture of Bughā and Waṣīf riding out in their coat of mail and Ibn Ṭāhir proudly sporting his grand-father's breastplate (*ṣudra*), and iron arm-piece (Ṭa., iii, 1558).
148 Ṭa., iii, 1589.
149 Ṭa., iii, 1592–3.
150 Ṭa., iii, 1561.
151 Ṭa., iii, 1559, 1578, 1592–3.
152 Ṭa., iii, 1559, 1592–3.
153 Ṭa., iii, 1578.
154 Ṭa., iii, 1621.
155 Ṭa., iii, 1587.
156 Ṭa., iii, 1621–2.
157 Ṭa., iii, 1560, also 1559, 1583.
158 Ṭa., iii, 1579.
159 Ṭa., iii, 1561.
160 Ṭa., iii, 1582–3.
161 Ṭa., iii, 1578.
162 Ṭa., iii, 1626–7.
163 Ṭa., iii, 1384–7.
164 Ṭa., iii, 1436; for an interesting discussion of this move and its motives, see P. Cobb, 'Al-Mutawwakil's Damascus: A New 'Abbāsid Capital?', *JNES*, 58 (1999), 241–57.
165 al-Mas'ūdī, *Tanbīh*, 329; see the discussion of Mutawwakil's assassination in Gordon, *The Breaking of a Thousand Swords*, 83–90.
166 Ṭa., iii, 1463.
167 Ṭa., iii, 1478–9.
168 Ṭa., iii, 1510–2.
169 Ṭa., iii, 1512–5.
170 Ṭa., iii, 1544.
171 Ṭa., iii, 1545.
172 Ṭa., iii, 1576–7.
173 Ṭa., iii, 1554.
174 Ṭa., iii, 1616.
175 Ṭa., iii, 1628–30.
176 Ṭa., iii, 1640.
177 Ṭa., iii, 1661–2.
178 Ṭa., iii, 1685.

179 Ṭa., iii, 1687–8.
180 Ta., iii, 1707–9.
181 Ṭa., iii, 1715–20.
182 Ṭa., iii, 1720–5, 1738.
183 On these negotiations, see Gordon, *The Breaking of a Thousand Swords*, 124–9.
184 Ṭa., iii, 1798–9.
185 See trans. Waines, 1801, n. 273. The text is doubtful but it would appear that this was an attempt to prevent *quwwād* from guaranteeing certain sums to the treasury but collecting more in taxes, and so making a profit at the expense of the treasury and, by extension, at the expense of soldiers who were dependent on salaries.
186 Ṭa., iii, 1800–1.
187 This obscure demand was presumably intended to restrict the power of the *quwwād* to make promotions .
188 The text is not clear and may well be corrupt.

CHAPTER SIX

The last armies of the Caliphs, 256–324/870–936

The period between the end of the anarchy in Samarra and the final collapse of the power of the Caliphs in 324/936 saw the power and effectiveness of the army, like the territorial extent of the Caliphate, in steady decline.[1] The Caliphs retained only a small proportion of the area they had ruled at the time of the assassination of al-Mutawwakil in 247/861. Khurāsān and all of eastern and central Iran were effectively lost, as were Syria and Egypt (though nominal authority over these area was briefly regained between 292/905 and 323/935). The Arabian peninsula, too, had largely slipped from the authority of Baghdad. The Caliphs might claim to be the successors of al-Manṣūr and al-Rashīd but in reality ruled only southern and central Iraq and a few areas of western Iran, and even in these areas their authority was challenged by insurgents like the Zanj[2] and the Qarāmiṭa.[3] The army of the Caliphs had become no more than one Islamic army among many: the Samanids in Khurāsān and the Tulunids in Egypt, for example, maintained powerful military forces. However, these last armies of the Caliphate are interesting: we are comparatively well informed about both organisation and personnel, and they represent the culmination of that trend towards professionalisation of the military and its separation from the rest of Muslim society which had begun with the *ahl al-Shām* in Umayyad times.

Al-Muwaffaq and his son al-Mu'taḍid succeeded in working out a *modus vivendi* with the Turkish leaders. They were able to build up an army strong enough to defeat the Zanj rebels of southern Iraq but after the end of the Zanj war in 270/883, the effectiveness of the army seems to have declined. Now composed almost entirely of *ghilmān*, it seems to have lacked popular legitimacy and military skill.

On 16 Rajab 256/19 June 870, Aḥmad son of al-Mutawwakil was chosen as Caliph.[4] We have no information as to who made the choice or why they chose Aḥmad, who seems to have lived in comparative obscurity up to this point and, even as Caliph, kept a very low profile. In contrast to his short-lived predecessors, his reign was 22 years and he died peacefully of natural causes. His accession brought to an end the period of violent military unrest and, except for a few minor incidents late in the reign, there is no record of mutiny or riots over pay. Instead, a moderately effective army was built up and some political credibility was restored to the Caliphate.

The responsibility for this changed state of affairs lay not with the Caliph but with his brother Abū Aḥmad, known as al-Muwaffaq. Abū Aḥmad was already very experienced in politics and warfare. He is first heard of on the night of the murder of his father, al-Mutawwakil, when he played a decidedly ambiguous role. According to two accounts in al-Ṭabarī, he was in the palace at the time and had been drinking with his father. At one point he left the room to go to the lavatory and came across the assassins already armed. Later, it is said, he tried to defend his father but retired to his chamber when he saw it was useless.[5] There are reasons for thinking that his role may not have been entirely innocent. Among the assassins, according to some accounts, was Mūsā b. Bughā who was to be his ally in the turbulent years which followed the assassination and his right-hand man in the rebuilding of the army after 256/870.[6] It is possible, therefore, that Abū Aḥmad had already had close links with the young Turks before the murder, or that they were forged on that night.

Whether he played a murky role in his father's death or not, Abū Aḥmad's connection with the Turkish interest became open in the civil war between al-Mu'tazz and al-Musta'īn. In Muḥarram 251/February 865, immediately after al-Musta'īn and his allies had fled to Baghdad, al-Mu'tazz appointed his brother Abū Aḥmad to lead the expeditionary force of 5000 Turks and Farāghina against them. Significantly, at the same time, Mūsā b. Bughā, who was cultivated by both sides, decided to join al-Mu'tazz's side, confirming his close links with Abū Aḥmad.[7] Throughout the siege of Baghdad which ensued, it was he who led the Turks and on at least one occasion[8] prevented a rout by his personal intervention. It was he who conducted the clandestine negotiations with Muḥammad b. 'Abd Allāh the Tahirid which brought the civil war to an end.[9]

After his victory, Abū Aḥmad returned to Samarra, where he was invested with robes and honours by his brother[10] and he was able to secure the reinstatement of Bughā the Younger, one of the leading Turks who had gone to Baghdad (and was also, it should be noted, one of the assassins of al-Mutawwakil). However, the tables were soon turned when al-Mu'tazz imprisoned his two brothers, al-Mu'ayyad and Abū Aḥmad. Al-Mu'ayyad was soon murdered in prison but it is clear that Abū Aḥmad was protected by his powerful Turkish friends: as Mūsā b. Bughā explained to the Caliph, 'They [the Turks] wanted to free Abū Aḥmad b. al-Mutawwakil on account of their closeness to him during the recent conflict.'[11] He was later released and sent to Basra but allowed to return to Baghdad and there was popular demand in the city for him to succeed his brother al-Mu'tazz when al-Muhtadī was chosen in Samarra.[12]

He was in Makka when his brother was chosen as Caliph to succeed the unfortunate al-Muhtadī in 256/870 and came straight to Samarra.[13] Soon after, he was appointed to an extensive governorate which included Baghdad and southern Iraq, Fārs, the Hijaz and Yemen,[14] so making him the most powerful man in the Caliphate. It also meant that he was responsible for making war on the Zanj rebels of southern Iraq, by far the most serious challenge facing the Caliphate.

Abū Aḥmad, who took the quasi-Caliphal title of al-Muwaffaq, came to an amicable working relationship with an important section of the Turkish military. In a sense this is not surprising, and the close personal contacts he had had with some of the leaders, notably Mūsā b. Bughā, and the rank and file over many years must have helped enormously. So did his status as the Caliph's brother. During the reign of al-Muhtadī, the Turkish rank and file, the *mawālī*, had made a series of demands. Among these was the request that 'the Commander of the Faithful should turn over the command to one of his brothers or someone else who could act as an intermediary between him [the Caliph] and them in their affairs'.[15] Their main purpose was that they should no longer be dependent for salaries, promotions and other matters on leaders like Ṣāliḥ b. al-Waṣīf and Mūsā b. Bughā, whom they distrusted. It may have been in direct response to this demand that al-Mu'tamid appointed his brother in this role.

Though we have no direct evidence, there was probably another aspect to this settlement. It is likely that al-Muwaffaq guaranteed to the Turks that they, and they alone, would form the military élite of the new army. There would be no other groups, no *shākiriya*, Ushrūsaniya, Farāghina or Maghāriba to compete with them for a share of government revenues. These other groups largely disappear from the record: though individual members of the Farāghina, and leaders who had been connected with the *shākiriya* are still found, the regiments themselves lost their identities. If this is the case, then it goes some way to explaining how the revenues which had proved so inadequate for the military in the reigns of al-Mu'tazz and and al-Muhtadī, seem to have been sufficient under al-Muwaffaq. This is all the more strking in that the resource base of the Caliphate was further dimished by the Zanj revolt and the temporary loss of Fārs to the Saffarids.

Al-Muwaffaq depended on a small number of Turkish leaders whom he had known for some time.[16] Many, but by no means all, of these were second-generation Turks – that is, their fathers had been involved in the military and, typically, they bore Muslim not Turkish names. When al-Muwaffaq set out to fight the Zanj in 265/879, his army commanders were Mūsā b. Utāmish, Isḥāq b. Kundājīq, Yanghajūr b. Urkhūz and al-Faḍl b. Mūsā b. Bughā[17]. With the exception of Yanghajūr, these were all sons or grandsons of prominent members of the Samarra Turkish élite.

Chief among them, until his death in 263/877[18] was Mūsā b. Bughā. Not only was he the most powerful military commander in his own right, but almost all the Turks who held important positions under the new regime were in some sense his protégés or were connected with him. After his death his sons, Aḥmad, Muḥammad and al-Faḍl continued to be important figures in al-Muwaffaq's long struggle against the Zanj, so marking the third generation of the Turkish military. Al-Faḍl was still a military leader in the reign of of al-Muktafī when he is found defending Kūfa against the Qarāmiṭa rebels in 293/906.[19] Mūsā also had his own *quwwād,* among them Kayghalagh and Isḥāq b. Kundājīq,[20] who became powerful and influential governors in the Jazīra and Jibāl, respectively. Also closely associated with Mūsā b. Bughā and al-Muwaffaq was Mufliḥ (killed in 258/872 fighting the Zanj[21]), who had been in al-Muwaffaq's army in the siege of Baghdad and second in command to Mūsā in Rayy[22] and an important supporter of his during the intrigues in the reign of al-Muhtadī.

There are also many new names in the military élite. In many cases these are, so to speak, onomastic happaxes – that is, they are simply single names which tell us little about the origins or connections of their bearers. Many of these, Tashtimur, Takīn, for example, are clearly Turkish, others, like Ju'lān and Abbā, are specifically qualified as 'al-Turkī' and we must presume that they were first-generation arrivals from Central Asia. The most important of these new men promoted by al-Muwaffaq seems to have been Masrūr al-Balkhī.[23] He has an Arabic first name and presumably came originally from Balkh (northern Afghanistan); at one point he is described as a *mawlā* of al-Muwaffaq.[24] Second-generation Turks usually have specifically Muslim names (Aḥmad, Mūsā, etc.) but Masrūr has no such connotations and he may have come from an Iranian or Turkish Muslim background.

During the long war against the Zanj, a new generation of military leaders emerged.[25] These were connected with the rise to prominence of al-Muwaffaq's son Abū'l-'Abbās who subsequently became Caliph with the title of al-Mu'taḍid. In Rabi ii 266/ November–December 879 al-Mu'taḍid was appointed by his father to lead a new campaign against the Zanj who had just entered and sacked the city of Wāsiṭ. An army of 10 000 cavalry and infantry was gathered and equipped. The boats so necessary for fighting in the marshes of southern Iraq were under the command of one Nuṣayr Abū Ḥamza until his death in action in 269/883.[26] Nuṣayr is said to have been a Daylamī by origin and was a *mawlā* of a court official, Sa'īd b. Ṣāliḥ al-Ḥājib. Nuṣayr was a key figure in the 'Abbasid war effort, but nothing is known of his origins.

Figures like Masrūr al-Balkhī, al-Shāh b. Mīkāl and the sons of Mūsā b. Bughā, all connected with the old Samarra regime, continued to be important in al-Mu'taḍid's forces, but we can also observe the rise to power of a new group, the *ghilmān* of al-Mu'taḍid. The group can be seen together for the first time in an account of a riverboat expedition organised by al-Mu'taḍid in 267/880–1. After the prince himself, the second in command was Zīrak al-Turkī. Zīrak was something of a veteran by this time, having first come to prominence in the reign of al-Mutawwakil in 234/848–9, when he was sent with 200 000 (!) Turkish horsemen against the rebel Ibn al-Ba'īth in Azerbayjān and he was campaigning in the Caucasus in 238/852–3 with Bughā the Elder.[27] Nothing is heard of him during the period of the anarchy in Samarra, but it is likely that he passed from the forces of Bughā to those of his son Mūsā b. Bughā and that he, like many others in the army at this time, owed his position to Mūsā's patronage.

The rest of the force was composed of a group of al-Mu'taḍid's *ghilmān*,[28] the leading figures being named as Badr, Mu'nīs, Rashīq al-Ḥajjājī, Yumn, Khafīf, Yusr, Nadhīr and Waṣīf. None of these are recorded before and they may have been recruited and trained by Zīrak. In the long struggle against the Zanj which followed, the *ghilmān* were the élite force which bore the brunt of the fighting . It should be noted that they are described as *ghilmān* and not as *mawālī*, as the previous generation of Turks had been. This may mean that, unlike the *mawālī*, they remained as slaves in law, but the evidence is not conclusive.[29] It was these commanders and their children who provided the leaders of the 'Abbasid army down its final disintegration.

An obvious difference between these *ghilmān* and the Turkish *mawālī* comes in the naming patterns. As already mentioned, the first-generation Turks have recognisably Turkish names, Bektimur, Takīn, and the like, and their sons have clearly Muslim ones, Aḥmad, Mūsā, and so on. The *ghilmān* of al-Mu'taḍid, on the other hand, have what can only be described as pet-names. Thus of the group named above, Badr means 'full moon', Mu'nis means 'cheerful, friendly', Rashīq means 'slender, graceful', Yumn means 'good fortune', Khafīf means 'nimble, lively', Yusr means 'ease, prosperity'; Nadhīr is more serious, meaning 'pledged to God, a herald or warner' while Waṣīf simply means 'servant, page'. They are all Arabic, either nouns or adjectives, and refer either to their real or imagined physical characteristics or are names of good omen. When they refer to characteristics, they describe youth and beauty, not strength, bravery or heroism, yet men like Badr and Rashīq became senior military commanders and political figures of considerable importance. This is all rather peculiar and it is difficult to know what to make of it. It may be that it shows that the Turkish *mawālī* were purchased or recruited when they were already fairly mature and they brought with them their Turkish names, whereas the *ghilmān* were acquired as infants, or at least very young, and had Arabic given to them by their new masters. They were also, of course, names that give no indication of race or origin.

It is probable that most of the *ghilmān* were of Turkish origin though we hear of 30 Daylamite *ghilmān* (from Daylam, at the south-west corner of the Caspian sea).[30] Some of them, like Naṣr al-Qushūrī, from Qushūra in Daghestan, were from the Caucasus area. They were paid salaries (*'aṭā'*, *rizq*) along with the other troops.[31]

The *ghilmān* of al-Mu'taḍid had an important political role. Like al-Mu'taṣim before him, al-Mu'taḍid was able to use the military support he had cultivated to secure the Caliphate for himself. In the years after the final defeat of the Zanj, relations between the young prince and his father, al-Muwaffaq, had deteriorated. Why this happened is not clear and the sources are very sketchy. It may be that al-Muwaffaq was refusing to pay his son's *ghilmān* now the military emergency was over. In 270/884 al-Mu'taḍid's troops in Baghdad began a violent protest against al-Muwaffaq's vizier, Ṣā'id b. Makhlad, who had refused to pay them, and the disturbance was brought to an end only when the vizier acceded to their demands.[32] In 275/889 al-Muwaffaq had his son arrested and put in prison. This resulted in violent protest in Baghdad and al-Mu'taḍid's *ghilmān* prepared their arms and their horses. Al-Muwaffaq came from Samarra and was able to reassure them about his son's safety and the affair died down but it must have showed to those concerned that al-Mu'taḍid was the real power in the city.

In Muḥarram 278/May 891 al-Muwaffaq entered Baghdad, a dying man. It seems that al-Mu'taḍid was still under house arrest at this time and power in the city was in the hands of a commander called Abū'l-Ṣaqr (Father of the Falcon) and his Berber followers. He had apparently been embezzling money and making unjust tax demands in order to win the support of unnamed military commanders. He now tried to ensure that al-Mu'taḍid remained in confinement while he sent for the Caliph al-Mu'tamid and his son and heir al-Mufawwaḍ, hoping to use them to secure his own position when al-Muwaffaq died. His plans were thwarted by the *ghilmān* of al-Mu'taḍid and his father, who released him from confinement. When al-Muwaffaq finally passed away in Safar 278/June 891, Abū'l-Ṣaqr and his supporters were arrested while al-Mu'taḍid replaced his cousin al-Mufawwaḍ as heir-apparent, the oath of allegiance having been taken to him by the commanders and the *ghilmān*.[33] When he finally succeeded to the throne on his uncle's death in Rajab 279/October 892, his first action was to appoint Badr as Chief of Security and his right-hand man.[34]

The accounts we have of the accession of al-Mu'taḍid are patchy and much remains obscure. It is clear, however, that it was his military support among the *ghilmān* which enabled him to defeat his rivals and became the most powerful and effective Caliph since al-Mutawwakil.

The war against the Zanj, Ramaḍan 255–Safar 270/August 870–August 883[35]

The war against the Zanj rebels of southern Iraq is the most fully and extensively described campaign in the whole of early Islamic historical writing apart from the campaigns of the Prophet and the early conquests.[36] The most important source for the history of the war is the 'Account of the Chief of the Zanj and his Battles' of Muḥammad b. al-Ḥasan b. Sahl, known as Shaylama,[37] large sections of which are preserved almost in their entirety in al-Ṭabarī's *Ta'rīkh*. Shaylama had originally been a partisan of the leader of the Zanj, 'Alī b. Muḥammad but, like many of the rebels, his accepted the offer of an amnesty and joined the 'Abbasids. He thus had access to information from both sides and knew almost all the main participants personally. He may well have written the book to ingratiate himself with the 'Abbasids and make amends for his previous support of the rebels. Certainly the account is not a neutral and disinterested historical record. It is obviously hostile to the Zanj and particularly to their leader, who is always referred to by insulting epithets rather than his true name. It is also clearly written to glorify the role of the 'Abbasid Abū Aḥmad al-Muwaffaq, who was effectively regent for his brother, the Caliph al-Mu'tamid, at the time, and al-Muwaffaq's son Abu'l-'Abbās, who later reigned as the Caliph al-Mu'taḍid. This means that, despite the fact that we have a first-hand account of much of the conflict, we have to treat it with some caution, especially when the skill and wisdom of the leadership is being discussed.

The campaign against the Zanj went through two distinct phases. In the first, the Zanj were on the offensive and the local representatives of the 'Abbāsids were unable to prevent their advance; the great city of Basra fell to them and many of the inhabitants were slaughtered, Ahwaz and Wāsiṭ were both taken. Al-Muwaffaq's military intervention was little more than a holding operation to prevent the rebels from expanding their domains. This began to change, at least according to Shaylama, with the appointment of Abū'l-'Abbās (al-Mu'taḍid) as commander in Rabī' ii 266/November–December 879 and the arrival, a year later, of his father al-Muwaffaq. From this point there was a slow but steady 'Abbasid advance which culminated in the isolation of the Zanj around their capital at Mukhtāra in the southern marshes.

The war against the Zanj was unique in the annals of early Islamic warfare in that it was an entirely amphibious struggle. The strongholds of the Zanj lay in the southern marshes of Iraq, a flat area of land divided and parcelled up by natural rivers and numerous man-made canals. It was impossible to move very far in this area without water transport and there had to be boats for men, equipment and supplies. We have the names of numerous different sorts of boats, but without illustrations or detailed descriptions it is difficult to have a clear idea what is being described. It is not clear, either, that the names are applied consistently in the accounts that have come down to us. It would seem that they were shallow draft vessels, propelled by oars. They varied in size from large vessels with 40 oarsmen to tiny craft which can have been little bigger than canoes for use in the narrowest channels. There were specialist boats for carrying horses[38] and siege engines were mounted in boats,[39] as they had been on the Tigris in both sieges of Baghdad. Faced by a bombardment by 'stones, arrows, slings, *manājiq*, *'arrādāt* and molten lead', al-Muwaffaq ordered that his boats should be armoured with fireproof wooden screens, covered with hide and an anti-inflammatory mixture.[40]

We have many references to the numbers of troops in the 'Abbasid armies. Until the members of the 'Abbasid family took control of the campaign, the number of government troops seems to have been very small, though assessment is made difficult by the fact that almost all the information in this section of Shaylama's account comes from Zanj sources – that is to say, they are reporting their impressions of the size of government forces, and may be ill-informed or exaggerating. A Turk called Abū Hilāl is said to have had 4000 troops under his command, who were probably local levies.[41] Shortly afterwards a composite force set out from Basra to attack the Zanj. According to the Zanj spy it consisted of 1200 fighting slaves (*khawal muqātil*), 1000 troops from the *aṣḥāb* of the governor al-Zaynabī, 2000 from the Basran factions of the Bilāliya and Sa'diya and 200 cavalry. This motley force quarrelled with the inhabitants of Ubulla, who they were supposed to protect, and when they were attacked by the Zanj, only the slaves seem to have done any real fighting.[42] The same force of Zanj was later held off by a force of 1000 Maghāriba, fighting with spears.[43] When Basra was taken by the Zanj, it was defended by just 50 government cavalry[44] but the governor of Ahwaz, the Turk Aṣghajūn, had a force of 370 mounted archers who successfully drove the Zanj back.[45] Four hundred government cavalry under Ibn Laythaway drove the Zanj back from Tustar.[46] The first phase of the war, therefore, the government forces were small units gathered together on an *ad hoc* basis by local governors and tax collectors.

On his appointment in 266/879, Abū'l-'Abbās was accompanied by an army of 10 000 cavalry and infantry, well equipped and supported by boats. At least some of these troops were *ghilmān* who were to provide the leadership and the backbone of the 'Abbasid army in the war to come. In 269/883 the army was reinforced by an enormous (*kathīf*) army of 10 000, led by Ṣā'id b. Makhlad, al-Muwaffaq's secretary, who brought them from Samarra.[47] Shortly afterwards, Lu'lu', Ibn Ṭūlūn's governor of Raqqa, came over to the 'Abbasids to join the Holy War and brought with him 'an enormous [*'adhīm*] army of men from Farghāna, Turks, men from Rūm, Berbers, Sūdān and others of Ibn Ṭūlūn's best troops.'[48] There could not be a clearer example of the use of the device of Holy War to attract support to the 'Abbasid cause. The government army was also swelled by deserting Zanj, many of whom were given payments (*arzāq*) as inducements to defect[49] and by volunteers. At one stage there are said to have been 50 000 government troops against 300 000 Zanj,[50] but these numbers are probably exaggerated on both sides. Despite the very large numbers, the brunt of the battle was always born by much smaller numbers of *ghilmān*. This army was very well-equipped with weapons, boats and support staff like sappers (*fa'ala*).

The campaign was characterised by naval attacks, often led by Abū'l-'Abbās in person. There were continuous struggles to keep waterways open or closed, to capture or burn wooden bridges and to safeguard supplies to the government troops and deny them to the Zanj. Perhaps because much of the fighting was done from boats, archery was supremely important. Archers in boats were used to attack enemy forces on land[51] and water,[52] to give cover to sappers (*fa'ala*) as they tried to demolish the walls of Zanj strongholds[53] and prisoners were shot to death with arrows.[54] Abū'l-'Abbās himself often fought as an archer;[55] on one occasion he fired so many arrows that his fingers bled[56] and on another he aroused universal admiration by shooting a crane in full flight.[57] He was also at the receiving end and is portrayed after a hard fight between his boats and those of the Zanj with 25 arrows sticking out of the felt coat (*kīz*) he was wearing over his armour. Yet more arrows were extracted from the felt caps (*labābīd*, sing. *lubāda*) of the other sailors in his boat. Both spears (*rimāḥ*), and to a lesser extent swords, were used in close combat, but it seems clear that bows and arrows were the decisive weapons.

Catapults were used, especially in the final siege of Mukhtāra but, as has already been noted in the second siege of Baghdad, these were almost exclusively employed as anti-personnel weapons by the defenders. The Zanj regularly mounted both *manājiq* and *'arrādāt* on the tops of the walls.[58] The government forces also used catapults mounted on ships, but apparently only as anti-personnel weapons[59] or to fire the severed heads of captives into a city to discourage the defenders.[60]

We also hear of *nāvakiya* bows being used by the defenders along with the catapults. The word is probably a diminutive of the Persian *nāv*, meaning a trough or pipe.[61] The *nāvakiya* bows were clearly static, since they were burned along with the catapults on one occasion, but they fired arrows not stones.[62] We should probably think of them as large bows, which may have shot arrows through tubes or down grooves to improve aiming. There is also mention in the same passage of the defenders using cross-bows (*qissī al-rijl*).[63]

The government forces attacked fortifications by firing arrows at the defenders and by the use of specially prepared ladders.[64] On one occasion grappling hooks (*kalālīb*) were used to pull down the Zanj banners. Once the wall head had been secured, the catapults could be burned and sappers (*fa'la*) brought in to demolish the wall and allow access to the rest of the army.[65] Because many of the buildings and other strategic structures, like bridges, were made of wood, incendiary devices were used and a team of skilled *naffāṭīn* were employed in an effort to burn wooden fortifications.[66]

The army of al-Mu'taḍid and al-Muktafī, 279–295/892–908

Al-Mu'taḍid came to the throne with many years of military experience behind him and strong personal following among his *ghilmān*. He was a keen horseman and took care to inspect both his troops and their mounts in person. However, it is clear that he was hampered from the beginning of his reign by lack of money. The élite *ghilmān* seem to have been employed largely as palace guards and escorts while inferior troops were sent to provincial centres like Wāsiṭ and Kūfa. Despite the Caliph's personal enthusiasm, the military record of his forces was not impressive and they were unable to defend the settled populations against the attacks of the Qarmaṭ (Carmathian) insurgents. Even more humiliating was the government's failure to protect pilgrims on the Ḥajj, large numbers of whom were slaughtered on their way from Iraq to the Holy Cities in the Hijaz. Many of these unfortunates came from Khurāsān and other eastern areas outside the Caliph's control, and these disasters must have further undermined the prestige of the Baghdad government in those lands.

There survives a unique snapshot of the Caliph's army at the time of al-Mu'taḍid's accession in a document which is essentially an outline budget of the government.[67] Income is mentioned as a global total. It was paid to the treasury under the terms of a guarantee (*ḍamān*) by the tax-farmer Aḥmad b. Muḥammad al-Ṭā'ī and it seems that he was responsible for supervising and paying the tax-collectors. Expenditure, on the other hand, is catalogued in some detail. The overwhelming bulk of the expenditure is directly connected with the military. Of the total expenditure of 7915 *dīnār*s per day, some 5121 are entirely military, 1943 in areas (like riding animals and stables) which served both military and non-military and only 851 in areas like the bureaucracy and the harim which can be described as truly civilian (though even in this case, the bureaucrats' main purpose seems to have been to arrange the payment of the army). It seems reasonable to conclude that something over 80 per cent of recorded government expenditure was devoted to maintaining the army.[68]

The organisation of different groups of soldiers is described in some detail, but the categories and distinctions are by no means clear and it is not always possible to make sense of them.

The first group described[69] were foot-soldiers who were employed as guards around the palace. and were known as the *Aṣḥāb al-Maṣāff* or *Maṣāffiya* because they stood in lines *(ṣaff*, pl. *ṣufūf*) on ceremonial occasions. These were in two groups. There were the whites, comprising the Jannābīs and the Basrans and those who served at the gates of (*'alā'l-abwāb*) the commanders of the Mufliḥiya, Daylamites, Ṭabariya and Maghāriba. Of these, Tabaris and the Daylamites came from the mountains of northern Iran, as probably did the Mufliḥiya, who may have been recruited when Mufliḥ was serving with Mūsā b. Bughā in the Rayy area. The Maghāriba originally came from Egypt.[70] The Basrans may have been ex-supporters of the Zanj, as many of the black soldiers were. Jannāba (modern Bandar-i Jannāve, on the Iranian shore of the Gulf about 100 km from its head) was famous as the birthplace of the Qarmaṭ leader Abū Ṭāhir al-Jannābī, and it is likely that the Jannābiya were ex-supporters of the Qarmatis.

The black foot-soldiers were slaves, originally from Nubia and the Zaghāwa and purchased in Makka and Egypt. There were also non-Arab supporters of the Zanj. These were clearly of low status and paid very little, and their pay was supplemented by a bread ration. They guarded the Bāb al-Khāṣṣa, or Inner Gate.

The daily pay of the two groups was 300 for the blacks and 700 for the whites – that is, some 30 000 per month. From this, Amabe estimates that the total numbers were 3000 in each group.[71]

The next group were the *ghilmān* who had been freed by al-Muwaffaq and their names added to the list of the freemen (*aḥrār*) and they were mixed with the free *quwwād* and *mawālī*.[72] They had a 40-day pay interval but this was increased to 50 because of bad behaviour and eventually al-Mu'taḍid transferred them to the body of the freemen and gave them a 60-day interval (i.e. their salaries were progressively reduced). They were commanded by a *ḥājib* and 25 deputies. On campaign, they were provided with riding animals from the stables.

In addition al-Mu'taḍid acquired *mamlūks* who were stationed in the palace and its rooms (*ḥujar*) and were consquently known as the *Ḥujariya*. They were put under the control of eunuch tutors (*al-khudum al-ustādhīn*) and were not allowed to go out or ride without them. They were to form the main cavalry force in the last 'Abbasid armies. They first appear as a group on campaign in 287/900.[73]

The freedmen of al-Muwaffaq and the *mamlūks* of al-Mu'taḍid formed the 'cavalry, freemen and the select', whose total salary bill was 1500 *dinar*s per day and were reviewed by the Caliph in person.[74] The procedure is described in some detail in the budget. The review took place in the square in front of one of the palaces, the Caliph and his vizier, 'Ubayd Allāh b. Sulaymān, watched from an elevated position. Below them, and hidden from the soldiers, were the clerks of the pay-office (*kuttāb al-'aṭā'*). 'Each officer [*qā'id*] came forward with a list in which were written the names of his men and their salaries. A servant took this and brought it to al-Mu'taḍid. Then 'Ubayd Allāh b. Sulaymān summoned them one after the other. Each one entered the *maydān* and was tested on the *birjās* [quintain]. If he shot well, was in control of himself, was firmly seated in his saddle and his shot hit the target, or came near, his name was marked with a J, meaning *jayyid* [good]. One who was less good was given a Ṭ meaning *muṭawwasiṭ* [middling]. One who lagged behind and could not ride well or hit his target was given a D, meaning *dūn* [inferior].'[75] The most competent were called the Special Forces (*'askar al-khāṣṣa*) with a pay interval[76] of 90 days, the next were called Service Forces (*'askar al-khidma*), who were entrusted with security duties in the neighbourhood of the capital under the command of Badr and had a pay interval of 120 days. The third category were appointed to help tax-collecting and for police duties in Baghdad, Kūfa and Wāsiṭ. It seems that this last group were paid from contributions from the districts rather than by the treasury.

They were divided into units (*qiyādāt*, i.e. a unit commmanded by a *qā'id*), whose names are listed as the Nāṣirī mamlūks (i.e. slaves of al-Muwaffaq), the Bughā'iya, the Masrūriya, the Bakjūriya, the Yānisiya, the Azkūtakīniya, the Kayghalaghiya and the Kundājiya. These names are very interesting. Each *qiyāda* was led, and possibly recruited, by one of the Turkish (or other) leaders who had been part of the group who had put al-Muwaffaq in power and kept him there. Most of these Turkish leaders had originally been connected to Mūsā b. Bughā. The evidence also suggests that these groups fought as cavalry, and probably as mounted archers.

There was also a budget for the *shurṭa* of Baghdad and their deputies, those in charge of the prisons and the patrols (*ṭawf*), and the cavalry and the foot-soldiers who were stationed at the gates. The policing cost a mere 50 *dīnār*s per day, compared with the *Maṣāffī* infantry and the *ghilmān* who cost 1000 *dinar*s. The document goes on to detail numerous classes of servants and retainers, with their various wages.

The budget gives us a picture of the different groups who made up the army. It also provides a unique insight into the responsibilities of government in this period. It comes as no surprise to see that the government paid the wages of the *qāḍī* of Baghdad and the expenses of the Friday mosques, but the expenditure on the hospital and the feeding of prisoners is unexpected. It is also striking how small the sums involved are compared with the pay and expenses of the army.

The army seems to have been largely recruited from slaves, captives (like the ex-supporters of the Zanj, and marginal groups like the Nubians). Whether they were a 'slave army' is, however, questionable. Certain groups, like the Ḥujariya were acquired as *mamlūks* and had restrictions placed on their movements, which suggests that they were unfree while the *ghilmān* seem to have served as freemen.

It is clear that some of the soldiers were eunuchs and that eunuch status was no barrier to advancement.[77] Eunuchs began to appear in the military, as well as at court, in the early 'Abbasid period, often serving on the Byzantine frontier, like Faraj al-Khādim al-Turkī who rebuilt Tarsus in 170/787. The tradition was revived in the post-Samarra period when we find Yāzmān al-Khādim leading raids on Byzantine territory from Tarsus in 270–8/883–91. Eunuchs continued to lead expeditions from Tarsus as late as Thumal al-Khādim in 330/941–2. Some eunuchs, like Yāzmān had their own *ghilmān*. The best known of all the military eunuchs was undoubtedly Mu'nis al-Khādim, al-Muqtadir's main military commander. However, eunuchs never seem to have formed more than a small proportion of the military. In Muslim Spain, the *saqāliba* (Slav eunuchs) came to be an important part of the military élite in the fourth/ninth century and a major political force. In the 'Abbasid armies, however, they remained individuals, who might become very important but they were never a party or pressure group.

It is noticeable how closely the army was connected with the court and court functions. The Caliph does not seem to have maintained or paid sigificant numbers of troops outside the Baghdad metropolitan area. Such 'Abbasid forces as there were in Basra, Kūfa or other provincial areas must have been paid from local resources.

The armies of al-Muqtadir's reign, 295–320/908–932

As contemporaries recognised, the reign of al-Muqtadir was disastrous for the 'Abbasid Caliphate. The achievements of his two predecessors in rebuilding the power of the Caliphs was lost in a confusion of intrigue, cruelty and financial mismanagement. We are very well informed about this melancholy tale.[78] The great history of al-Ṭabarī gives only a bare outline of the events of the early part of al-Muqtadir's reign and finally ends with the year 302/915. However, it was continued by the Andalusi historian, 'Arīb b. Sa'd of Cordova, who provides a narrative up to 320/932, surprisingly well-informed considering that he was living so far away. Fortunately this is supplemented by the work of Abū 'Alī Miskawayh, whose *Tajārib al-umam* continues the story in much greater detail. Unlike al-Ṭabarī, Miskawayh was a bureaucrat and his main interests lie in administrative history. Though he himself lived a century after the events of al-Muqtadir's reign, he uses earlier bureaucratic sources some of whom, like Thābit b. Sinān, were eye-witnesses. Miskawayh and his sources have a keen interested in the interplay of personalities, and above all in the fiscal administration of the Caliphate during these troubled years. They are much less interested in the detail of military activity and often seem to regard the army, with some justification, as little more than a dangerous nuisance.

The chronicle has its heroes and its villains and a clear philosophy of government. The main hero is 'Alī b.'Īsā, 'the good vizier', the classic image of the competent, honest, pious and forthright administrator. Along with him is his chief ally, the military leader Mu'nis al-Khādim (the Eunuch), who is again portrayed as competent, honest and loyal to the Caliph.[79] On the other side, there is a whole rogues' gallery of foolish, dishonest, incompetent and vicious players who end up by ruining not just themselves but the 'Abbasid state itself. The Caliph is shown as both weak and cruel, dominated by his mother and the harim and wholly selfish. Finally there is the prince of darkness himself, the vizier 'Alī b. Muḥammad b. al-Furāt, lordly, cultured and generous, a brilliant adminstrator but fatally flawed by his ambition, his greed and his inability to curb the excesses of his son al-Muḥassin.

The action is played out against a background of disintegration and bankruptcy.

The revenues fail while the enemies of the state, the Daylamites in Iran and above all the savage Qarāmiṭa (Carmathians) of the Arabian and Syrian deserts rampage through provinces and, in the case of the Qarāmiṭa, almost take Baghdad itself. Miskawayh's work is as much a treatise on good and bad government as it is a historical record.

The army of al-Muqtadir's reign was commonly divided into *ghilmān* who were cavalry, and the *rijjāla* or footmen. The Ḥujariya established by al-Mu'taḍid were a section of the *ghilmān* and it seems that sometimes the term Ḥujariya was used to describe them all. Similarly, the Maṣāffiya were included in the foot-soldiers.

By the time of al-Muqtadir's accession, the Ḥujariya were well established and highly paid. Al-Muktafī had increased their salaries, apparently to win them over from their loyalty to his father's right-hand man Badr, whom he wished to have executed. The senior ones men were paid 16 *dīnār*s and the younger 12. Their status increased further after 296/908 when they probably formed the core of the force of *ghilmān* which Mu'nis al-Khādim used to restore al-Muqtadir after an unsuccessful coup in favour of a rival 'Abbasid, Ibn al-Mu'tazz.[80] They maintained their reputation for militancy over pay: in 303/915–6, 700 of them rioted and burned the stables of the vizier 'Alī b. 'Īsā.[81] The next year a group of them were appointed as a permanent escort for the vizier Ibn al-Furāt, newly restored to office[82] but by 312/924 they were demanding his dismissal[83] and shortly afterwards were influential in securing his execution.[84] They were mobilised to defend the capital from the Qarāmiṭa during the crisis of 315/927–8 but do not seem to have played an important part in the action.[85] By this time, the cavalry are said to have numbered 12 000 and they were able to destroy their long-time rivals, the Maṣāffi infantry.[86] They were also extremely aggressive in defence of their status *vis-à-vis* the rival Sājī *ghilmān*.[87] In the chaotic years which followed the death of al-Muqtadir, they played an important role in the deposition of the Caliph al-Qāhir (322/934) and were supporters of Yāqūt and his sons. Their involvement in politics was their undoing. In 325/936 Ibn Rā'iq, by this time the most powerful man in Iraq, ordered them to accompany the Caliph al-Rāḍī to his base in Wāsiṭ. Despite their misgivings, most of them left the capital. When they arrived, he began by inspecting them and rejecting 'the interlopers, the substitutes, the women the traders and the refugees'. The Ḥujarīs reacted to this challenge with their customary violence but this time they had met their match: in Muḥarram 325/December 936 there was a sharp battle and the Ḥujarīs were soundly defeated. Many of them were killed and the rest fled to Baghdad where they were attacked by the chief of police and dispersed. The remnants went into hiding and their dwellings were pillaged and burned.[88] Although a few of them survived, and even appear as supporters of Ibn Rā'iq, they were destroyed as a unit and with them disappeared the last elements of the army which al-Muwaffaq and al-Mu'taḍid had constructed.

The Ḥujarī *ghilmān* fought as mounted archers and there are numerous references to the hail of arrows they unleashed on their enemies.[89] During the attack on the partisans of Ibn al-Mu'tazz, the *ghilmān* are described as wearing cuirasses (*jawāshin*) and helmets (*khuwadh*).[90] The *Ḥujarī ghilmān* were the the power base of the most prominent generals, like Rā'iq and above all Mu'nis al-Khādim. Like most of the 'Abbasid army, however, they remained firmly Baghdad-based: they seldom went on military expeditions[91] and never provided garrisons for other towns.

The Maṣāffis are less often singled out for mention by name, but there are numerous references to the foot-soldiers of Baghdad, the *rijjāla*. They were more numerous than the Ḥujarī *ghilmān*.[92] Like the Ḥujarīs, the Maṣāffis were mobilised to defend Baghdad from the Qarāmiṭa in the winter of 315/927–8[93] but are otherwise mostly encountered in accounts of palace intrigues and pay mutinies. They were also influential in the deposition of al-Qāhir and the restoration of al-Muqtadir in 317/929.[94] Shortly after this they were destroyed.[95] The reasons for this were basically financial: after al-Muqtadir's restoration, there were widespread army mutinies and the authorities blamed their inability to pay the cavalry on the demands of the Maṣāffi infantry. This led to open warfare between the two groups and the cavalry, including the Ḥujarīs, drove them out of the Palace. Muḥammad b. Yāqūt proclaimed that they must not remain in Baghdad, their properties were confiscated and their houses and those of the *'urāfā* destroyed. Finally the remnants fled to Wāsiṭ where they tried to regroup but were defeated and massacred by Mu'nis. 'After this', says the chronicler, 'they raised no banner again.'[96] In the budget the cost of the infantry is estimated at 30 000 *dīnār*s per month. When 'Alī b. 'Īsā became vizier for the second time in 314–5/927, he found that their pay was 80 000[97] (presumably per month), while at the time of their destruction it is said to have been '130 000 dīnārs for every month of the lunar year' (i.e. calendar months, not fiscal months). The payment of their salaries was a major burden on the state finances and their numbers seem to have increased substantially since the time of al-Mu'taḍid. In 306–6/917–8 there were said to have been 10 000 Maṣāffī infantry[98] and in 317/929, just before their destruction, they were 20 000 strong.[99]

The third named corps of *ghilmān* were the Sājiya, named after the family of Abū'l-Sāj. Abū'l-Sāj himself came originally from Ushrūsanā, and had served in the armies of the Caliphate as a military contractor during the Samarra period. His position had been inherited by his sons Muḥammad and Yūsuf. By the reign of al-Muqtadir, Yūsuf had effectively established himself in Armenia and Azerbayjān as a semi-independent ruler. In the budget there is reference to cavalry known as the *jabaliyūn* or mountain men, who were paid by the lord of Azerbayjān. The reference is not entirely clear, but it may imply that the Sājids were obliged to provide and pay for some horsemen for the Caliph's army. These may have been the nucleus of the later Sājiya *ghilmān*.

These first appear by name in the historical record in 311/924. At this time Ibn al-Furāt was trying to remove his rival Mu'nis from the capital and send him with an army to Raqqa. Among the troops to be attached to him were the Ḥujarīya and the Sājiya *ghilmān*.[100] In 314/926 Ibn Abū'l-Sāj was invited to Iraq to lead the defence against the Qarāmiṭa. In return all the revenues of the eastern provinces were assigned to him for the support of his *quwwād, jund* and *ghilmān*. The vizier 'Alī b. 'Īsā is said to have remarked to the Caliph that it would have been much more effective to employ 5000 Asadī bedouin to guard the *Ḥajj* and 5,000 Shaybānīs to resist the Qarāmiṭa and, furthermore, they would do it for a quarter of the price, but his advice was disregarded.[101] The campaign ended in a complete débâcle the next year when Ibn Abū'l-Sāj was defeated, captured and subsequently executed by the Qarāmiṭa.[102] It is probable that his surviving *ghilmān* were then incorporated into the 'Abbasid army under the leadership of Mu'nis. He promised them equal pay with the élite Ḥujarīs, but apparently failed to deliver: the Ḥujaris had a pay-month of 50 days but the Sājīs had one of 60 'at the same rate as slaves [*mamālīk*]'. They then joined forces with the Caliph al-Qāhir against Mu'nis in the conspiracy which led to the old general's execution.[103] Along with the Ḥujarīs, they subsequently joined the forces of Yāqūt[104] and they are mentioned as guarding the palace in 323/935 when Ibn Muqla was moving to undermine the position of Yāqūt and his sons. Like the Ḥujarīs, their nemesis came at the hands of Ibn Rā'iq, who disbanded the corps and seized their possessions in 324/936.[105]

We have few details about the composition of the Sājiya. Like the other corps, they were usually led by commanders like Mu'nis who were not of their number. The only member of the corps who is named seems to have been Mākird the Daylamite,[106] though he might simply have been attached to them by the Caliph. This would suggest, as seems probable, that the Sājiya were recruited among the mountains peoples of Azerbayjān and Daylam. The account of the disastrous battle against the Qarāmiṭa make it clear that they fought primarily as archers.[107] Numbers are difficult to estimate, but we are told that in the campaign against the Qarāmiṭa in 315/927–8 Mu'nis sent his *ḥājib* Yalbaq with 6000 commanders and *ghilmān* of Ibn Abū'l-Sāj to try to rescue their master from captivity.[108]

All these groups were essentially Baghdad-based, and their main military function was 'guarding' the Caliph and his officers and palaces. Despite the pressing threats from the Qarāmiṭa rebels and others, provincial towns in the Caliph's control seem to have had to take responsibility for their own defence, at least until forces could be sent from the capital. Typical of such an encounter was the successful defence of Kūfa against the Qarāmiṭa in 293/906, shortly before al-Muktafī's death. The Qarāmiṭa, mostly brigands from the surrounding countryside, mustered some 800 horsemen with coats of mail and cuirasses and numerous foot-soldiers. The governor of the city, Isḥāq b. 'Imrān, assembled the *jund* and arrayed them for battle. After a short conflict, the rebels fled and the Kūfans set about restoring their moat and walls. Meanwhile the governor wrote to the authorities (*al-Sulṭān*) who sent a substantial force to help him and ordered another commander to pursue the fleeing Qarāmiṭa.[109] Later, in 301/913–4 we hear of the army of Mawṣil (*jund ahl al-Mawṣil*) who defended their city against the Kurds.[110]

Other towns defended themselves as best they could against marauders from the desert. The people of Hīt on the Euphrates, forewarned by a previous attack, set up siege engines (*'arrādāt* and *manjanīqāt*) on their town walls and drove off the attackers, killing several of them.[111] The people of Raqqa were much less well prepared but resisted fiercely 'hurling water (? in jars), dust, bricks and poisoned arrows from the roofs of their houses',[112] a simple but in the end effective form of defence as the attackers fled. In none of these cases is there any sign of government troops.

The attack on Basra by the Qarāmiṭā in 311/923 had a very different outcome.[113] One thousand seven hundred rebel foot-soldiers used ladders to climb the walls. They then jammed the gates open so that they could not be trapped in the city and proceeded to create mayhem, burning the mosque and slaughtering large numbers of the inhabitants. The governor, Sabuk al-Mufliḥī, thought that they were just bedouin and incautiously rushed to meet them and was defeated and killed. The people of Basra resisted bravely but 'they had no one from the government with them'.[114] Only after the rebels had departed did government troops finally arrive. The vizier, 'Alī b. 'Īsā was accused of delaying the payment (*arzāq*) of the sentries so that they had deserted their posts on the fateful night.[115] In this case, the policy of concentrating forces in the capital proved disastrous for the city, and the general prosperity of the Caliphate.

Responsibility for local defence was also assumed by tax-farmers like 'Alī b. Aḥmad al-Rāsibī at Junday Sabur, Sūs and Mādharāyā (in the Sawad between 150 and 300 km south-east of Baghdad). In addition to sending 1 400 000 *dīnār*s to the capital, he also agreed to take responsibility for the defence (*ḥarb*) of his district and for the garrison (*shiḥna*) 'without the assistance of any officials of the Sultān'.[116]

Total numbers of troops available to the government at this time are hard to assess. The highest figures recorded are the 40 000 cavalry, infantry and others commanded by Mu'nis[117] and the 42 000 found by Mu'nis and Naṣr al-Qushūrī in the lists (*jarā'id*) of those who joined the Baghdad forces against the Qarāmiṭa in the winter of 315/927–8. This did not include the bedouin or Mu'nis' and Naṣr's own *ghilmān*.[118] However, this was a major crisis when it seemed as if Baghdad itself was about to be sacked by the rebels and the large numbers were no doubt the result of mass mobilisation. Despite their overwhelming superiority in numbers, the Baghdad forces proved woefully inadequate against a enemy force which numbered no more than 1700.[119]

In normal circumstances, numbers were much smaller. There were 9000 horse and foot in the *shurṭa* of Baghdad at the time of the fall of Ibn al-Furāt's first ministry in 299/911–2 but they were unable to prevent pillaging and general mayhem in the city.[120] Six thousand men, including 1000 Arab tribesmen from Shaybān, were found to escort the Ḥajj in 313/925 but they were defeated by the Qarāmiṭa and were unable to prevent the rebels entering Kūfa.[121] In the tense series of stand-offs which preceded the death of al-Muqtadir in 320/932, Mu'nis commanded 800 men and Muḥammad b. Yāqūt, defending the Caliph, had 2000 horse including (?) the Ḥujariya.[122] If we count only effective regular troops, it seems that 2000 was a large army and it is doubtful whether as many as 10 000 could ever be mustered efficiently.

The end came in 324/936 when the Caliph al-Rāḍī, faced by complete bankruptcy and the consequent disintegration of the remnants of the army, agreed to allow Ibn Rā'iq to assume both military and civil power as Amir of Amirs. It was a hollow triumph and proved to be just a prelude to the take-over by the Daylamite Buyids in 334/946. At the time, the change may have seemed to more than another desperate expedient but in retrospect it can be seen as a turning point. For the first time (apart from a few irregular exceptions), the military had taken control of their own payment. With the loss of financial power, the Caliph no longer had an army under his control. The struggle that Caliphs from 'Umar b. al-Khaṭṭāb onwards had waged to establish a military under the command of the successors of the Prophet was finally and irrevocably lost. The 'Abbasid dynasty survived, but only as powerless figureheads.

Notes

1 The best, indeed almost the only account of the 'Abbasid army in this period is F. Amabe, *The Emergence of the 'Abbāsid Autocracy: The 'Abbāsid Army in Khurāsān and Asharbayjān* (Kyoto, 1995), 219–43. His prosopography is meticulous, but sometimes, as in the case of numbers and rates of pay, his conclusions are more definite that the sources will sustain.

2 See pp. 153–6.

3 The Qarāmiṭa were a branch of the Fatimid Shi'a who were widely supported among the bedouin tribes of Eastern Arabia and the Syrian desert and began raiding settled lands from 284/907, see H. Halm, *The Empire of the Mahdī* (Leiden, 1996), 51–7, 180–92.

4 On his accession, see M. Gordon, *The Breaking of a Thousand Swords: A History of the Turkish Community of Samarra, 200–275 AH/815–889 CE* (Albany, 2001), 141–3, who lays less emphasis on his previous relations with Turkish military leaders.

5 Ṭa., iii, 1459–60, 1461.

6 Mūsā was also the son of al-Mutawwakil's maternal aunt, so he and Aḥmad were cousins (Ṭa., iii, 1459).

7 Ṭa., iii, 1554–5.

8 Ṭa., iii, 1627.

9 Ṭa., iii, 1640–1.

10 Ṭa., iii, 1657.

11 Ṭa., iii, 1669.

12 Ṭa., iii, 1714–5.

13 Ṭa., iii, 1840.

14 Ṭa., iii, 1841–2.

15 Ṭa., iii, 1801.

16 Amabe, *The Emergence of the 'Abbāsid Autocracy*, 219–21 also notes that dissident commanders from the Samarra military found service with Ibn Ṭūlūn in Egypt.

17 Ṭa., iii, 1930.

18 Ṭa., iii, 1916.

19 Ṭa., iii, 1927, 1930, 1939, 1956, 1989, 2048–9, 2256.

20 Ṭa., iii, 2048–9.

21 Ṭa., iii, 1862–5.

22 Ṭa., iii, 1614, 1686–7, 1736–8.
23 See for example, Ṭa., iii, 1898–9, 1908, 1927, 1974.
24 Ṭa., iii, 2003.
25 See Amabe, *The Emergence of the 'Abbāsid Autocracy*, 221–7.
26 Ṭa., iii, 2046–7; al-Mas'udī, Murūj, vii, 44.
27 Ṭa., iii, 1381–2, 1414–6. It remains possible that there were two different Zīraks and that this one is not connected with al-Mutaḍid's commander, but the name is very rare and it is most probable that they were one and the same.
28 For the *ghilmān* in this period, see D. Sourdel, 'Ghulām', EI2.
29 This view is challenged by Amabe, *The Emergence of the 'Abbāsid Autocracy*, 224–5, who argues that many of them were free. Working from the information that their pay was 1000 *dīnār*s per day, and 'If we suppose their per capita daily salary was 0.5 *dīnār*, we get 2000 men in all.' While the estimate seems realistic, there is no hard evidence for it since we do not know the daily *per capita* salary, which could have been have been twice as much or half as much, or more or less. Amabe then argues that, 'This comparatively large number means that not all of them were really purchased slaves' but, again, this is supposition, not fact.
30 Ṭa., iii, 2012.
31 Ṭa., iii, 1964, 1976,.
32 Ṭa., iii, 2104.
33 Ṭa., iii, 2118–24.
34 Ṭa., iii, 2133.
35 The date given in Ṭa., iii, 2098.
36 The bulk of Ṭa., iii, 1742–2102 is devoted to it. For modern accounts of the revolt see A. Popovic, *La révolte des esclaves en Iraq au IIIe/IXe siecle* (Paris, 1976) and Amabe, *The Emergence of the 'Abbāsid Autocracy*, 173–95.
37 For his life, see *Fihrist* trans. Dodge, 279. For further discussion on this source, see H. Kennedy, 'Caliphs and their Chroniclers in the 'Abbasid Period (Third/Ninth Century)', in C. Robinson (ed.), *Essays in Honour of D. S. Richards* (forthcoming).
38 *raqqiyat*, Ṭa., iii, 2074.
39 Ṭa., iii, 1995–6, 2052: *manjanīq* and '*arrāda* are both mentioned..
40 *al-adwiya allatī tamna'u al-nār min al-iḥrāq*, Ṭa., iii, 2042–3.
41 Ṭa., iii, 1765; see Popovic, *La révolte*, 88, n.3.
42 Ṭa., iii, 1769–72; the use of *khawal* for slaves here is unusual but it makes it clear that they were not élite slave soldiers who would have been called *ghilmān.*
43 Ṭa., iii, 1771.
44 Ṭa., iii, 1851.
45 Ṭa., iii, 1866.
46 Ṭa., iii, 1911.
47 Ṭa., iii, 2079–80.
48 Ṭa., iii, 2080.
49 e.g. Ṭa., iii, 1980–1, 2023.
50 Ṭa., iii, 1986–7; Ṭa., iii, 2076 also says 50 000 'Abbasid troops.
51 Ṭa., iii, 1966, 1983, 2023–4.
52 Ṭa., iii, 1998.
53 Ṭa., iii, 2011, 2054.
54 Ṭa., iii, 1992.
55 Ṭa., iii, 1955, 1969.
56 Ṭa., iii, 1954.
57 Ṭa., iii, 1957.
58 Ṭa., iii, 1982–3, 2052.
59 Ṭa., iii, 2052.
60 Ṭa., iii, 1995.

61 See Steingass sv.
62 Ṭa., iii, 2004.
63 See EI2, 'Kaws' (Boudot-Lamotte).
64 Ṭa., iii, 1946, 2004, 2035, 2057–8.
65 Ṭa., iii, 2005, 2035.
66 Ṭa., iii, 2042–3.
67 For the text, see al-Hilāl b. al-Muḥassin al-Ṣābī, *al-Wuzarā*, ed. A. A. Farraj (Cairo, 1958), 15–27. For a full discussion with commentary, see H. Busse, 'Das Hofbudget des Chalifen al-Mu'taḍid billāh (278/892–289/902)', *Der Islam*, 43 (1967), 11–36; for a more general discussion of payment in the later 'Abbasid army, W. Hoenerbach, 'Zur Heereswerwaltung der 'Abbāsiden', *Der Islam*, 29 (1950), 257–90; also, C. E. Bosworth 'Recruitment, Muster and Review in Medieval Islamic Armies', in V. J. Parry and M. E. Yapp (eds), *War, Technology and Society in the Middle East* (Oxford, 1975), 58–77 pp. 72–4, Amabe, *The Emergence of the 'Abbāsid Autocracy*.
68 See p. 71 for comparable figures from early Umayyad Iraq.
69 al-Hilāl, 15–6.
70 See pp. 125–6 for the Maghāriba in the Samarra period. It is not clear, however, whether there was a direct connection between them and the Maghāriba mentioned her and there is no indication where al-Mu'taḍid's Maghāriba were recruited.
71 Amabe, *The Emergence of the 'Abbāsid Autocracy*, 222, though, since we do not know how much each man was paid, this is little more than guess work; see p. 161 for their subsequent history and final destruction.
72 al-Hilāl, 16–17.
73 Ṭa., iii, 2198.
74 al-Hilāl, 17–19.
75 al-Hilāl, 17. Busse (19) understands them to be throwing spears (*Lanze*). But no spears are mentioned: the verb used, *ramā*, is the normal one for the shooting of arrows and suggests that mounted archery, rather than javelin throwing, was being tested.
76 The word used is *shahr*, meaning 'month'.
77 For military eunuchs, see D. Ayalon, 'On the Eunuchs in Islam', *JSAI*, 1 (1979), 67–124; Amabe, *The Emergence of the 'Abbāsid Autocracy*, 228–31. As often, the Arabic vocabulary is ambiguous. The word *khādim* originally meant 'servant' but in the 'Abbasid period it often, but not, as Ayalon insists, always, means 'eunuch'. As Amabe notes, even the word *khasī* (castrated) can be used figuratively and does not necessarily denote a eunuch.
78 For this period see the classic account, H. Bowen, *The Life and Times of Ali b. Isa, the Good Vizier* (Cambridge, 1928); also Amabe, *The Emergence of the 'Abbāsid Autocracy*, 234–41.
79 For the biography and achievements of Mu'nis, see Amabe, *The Emergence of the 'Abbāsid Autocracy*, 230–1.
80 Ṭa., iii, 2282; Misk., i, i, 6; 'Arīb, 27–8. The name Ḥujarīya as such is not mentioned, cf. Amabe, *The Emergence of the 'Abbāsid Autocracy*, 228 refers to them as the *ghilmān*.
81 Misk., i, 38: the text speaks of '*al-rijjāla al-ḥujariya*' (the *Ḥujari* foot-soldiers) but the text should be emended to *al-rijjāla wa'l-ḥujariya* (foot-soldiers and Ḥujarīya); 'Arīb, 58, where they are simply called *ghilmān*.
82 'Arīb, 62.
83 Misk., i, 124–5.
84 Misk., i, 137–8.
85 Misk., i, 176–7.
86 'Arīb, 141, 142, 148.
87 Misk., i, 261, 286. They were paid every 50 days, the Sājīs every 60.

88 Misk., i, 357–8.
89 E.g. 'Arīb, 28, 148; Misk., i, 126, 197.
90 Misk., i, 6.
91 An exception were the Ḥujarīs sent to help the defence of Kūfa from the Qarāmīta in 293/ 906 ('Arīb, 12).
92 'Arīb, 58, 142.
93 Misk., i, 176, 183.
94 Misk., i, 195–6.
95 The violent destruction of the infantry is described in Misk., i, 202–4 and 'Arīb, 148–9.
96 Misk., i, 202–3.
97 Misk., i, 157.
98 Hilāl, 56.
99 'Arīb, 142, 148.
100 Misk., i, 117.
101 'Arīb, 139.
102 This campaign also provides us with the clearest account of the use of pigeon post in early Islamic warfare: with the fighting so close to Baghdad, the vizier 'Alī b.'Īsā needed to be kept informed so he organised 100 pigeons, each with a handler, who would bring him news of developments every hour. Curiously, the messages are said to have been written directly on the birds' wings (Misk., i, 179).
103 Misk., i, 261–4.
104 Misk., i, 297.
105 Misk., i, 351.
106 Misk., i, 351.
107 Misk., i, 174.
108 Misk., i, 178.
109 'Arīb, 12–13.
110 'Arīb, 42.
111 Misk., i, 183.
112 'Arīb, 134.
113 Misk., i, 104–5; 'Arīb, 110–11.
114 *wa lā sulṭān ma'hum*, 'Arīb, 111.
115 Misk., i, 109. This was, however, part of a politically motivated interrogation and does not necessarily mean that the government was responsible for paying their salaries.
116 'Arīb, 44.
117 Misk., i, 176.
118 Misk., i, 180.
119 Misk., i, 179.
120 Misk., i, 20.
121 Misk., i, 145–6.
122 Misk., i, 233–4. This was not the total number of al-Muqtadir's supporters since another force was despatched at the same time.

CHAPTER SEVEN

Weapons and equipment in early Muslim armies

Reconstructing the military equipment of early Muslim armies is problematic. Compared with Roman armies – or, indeed, later mediaeval Muslim armies – the range of visual representation is very small, often imprecise and difficult to date. Physically very little material evidence has survived and again, much of it is difficult to date.[1] Literary sources and lexicographical works often mention items of military equipment but rarely describe them unless they are in some way out of the ordinary.[2] High quality military equipment, both body armour and weapons, were greatly esteemed and described and apostrophised in prose and poetry.[3] Taking all these sources together, we can build up a fairly full picture of the sorts of military equipment which were available to soldiers during the first two centuries of Islam. However, it should always be remembered that many men fought without the benefit of full military kit and that body armour, in particular, was probably quite rare.

The standard form of protective body armour was the coat of mail *(dir'*, pl. *durū')*.[4] In addition *sard* or *zard* are used for mail in general or a coat of mail with the verbal forms *sarada* and *zarada* being used for the making of mail.[5] In the classical Roman period, body armour seems to have been mostly lamellar, that is using small plates of metal sewn on to a cloth or leather garment to provide protection. Mail was certainly known in the Roman army from the third century[6] and by the time of the Muslim conquests it was probably the main form of body armour for both Byzantine and Sasanian soldiers. In the Qur'ān, the making of coats of mail is one of the blessings conferred by God on David.[7] The early Islamic sources treat the coat of mail as a standard piece of military equipment. It could be worn under a cloak *(qabā')* to disguise it, as Ibn al-Ashtar and his followers did in Kūfa when they were taking over the city in the name of al-Mukhtār in 66/685.[8] In 145/762 the 'Alid rebel, Ibrāhīm b. 'Abd Allāh was killed when he loosened his mail coat (*qabā' zarad*) because of the heat and was caught by a stray arrow.[9] There are also references to the practice of wearing two coats of mail (*dir'ayn*), the under one being shorter or even made of fabric or leather.[10]

Mail required a considerable investment and it is likely that only a small proportion of the soldiers in any army could afford it. When Qutayba b. Muslim was appointed governor of Khurāsān in 85/704 it was said that there were only

350 coats of mail (*dir'an*) in the entire province, which is not very many for a military force of some 50 000 men.[11] And they were expensive: after the fall of Paykand to the Muslims in 87/706, coats of mail were sold for 700 *dirhams*, while spears and shields fetched between 50 and 70.[12] Mail was passed on from one generation to another as a prized possession: one of Marwān II's followers at the Battle of Tell Kushāf in 132/750 recalled that when he went into battle he took his sword and his mail which he had inherited from his father, his grandfather and his grandfather's grandfather and which had been in the family since the time of the Jāhiliya before the coming of Islam,[13] which is to say that it was well over 100 years old.

The Khārijīs who fought al-Muhallab are described at one point as being heavily armoured with *maghāfir* which came down to their chests, coats of mail (*durū'*) which trailed on the ground and leggings made of mail (*sūq min al-zard*) which they attached to their belts with hooks.[14] The word *ḥalqa* (ring) for coat of mail is attested in the lexicography[15] but only rarely in the Chronicle evidence.[16] The Turkish leader Kūrṣūl is described as wearing 'brocade leggings (*rānā*) with rings (*ḥalaq*) in them'.[17] The use of mail leggings, at least in Iran, is confirmed by representations in wall-painting and on silver dishes. The most important wall-paintings come from the site at Shahristan in Tajikistan, the ancient capital of the principality of Ushrūsanā.[18] This is particularly interesting, as Ushrūsanā was place of origin of important contingents in the armies of the Caliphs in the third/ninth century. Unfortunately the paintings are poorly preserved and poorly published but they clearly show figures with long mail coats with sleeves and leggings.[19] The mounted warriors on a silver dish from the Hermitage, a 'battle plate', dating from the eighth to the tenth century, are shown wearing either mailed or lamellar leggings reaching to their ankles.[20] These eastern Iranian examples may well be more heavily and effectively armoured than the early Muslim ones further west.

As well as *dir'*, the word *jawshan* is also found for a coat of mail and, on one occasion, *al-ḥuṭamiya*.[21] *Jawshan* has been translated as 'breastplate' but it may be simply a Persian synonym for a coat of mail, or possibly lamellar body armour.[22] Al-Ḥārith b. Surayj was offered the choice between armour (*jawshan*) and 100 000 *dirhams* and had chosen the armour, though this was presumably, a luxury product.[23] In an account of the 'Alid rebellion of 145/762–3 we hear of a *tannūr*, which is clearly, from the context, a piece of armour.[24] It was gilded and was said to have belonged to Muṣ'ab b. al-Zubayr; since Muṣ'ab had been killed in 71/690, this is another example of armour being passed down from one generation to another. It broke the neck of the wearer when he fell off his horse, so it was probably a rigid cuirass. At the time of the Zanj rebellion, a man is said to have thrown first his helmet, then his shield and finally his iron *tannūr* at his pursuer.[25] Body armour is also referred to as *la'ma*[26] and at one point a warrior is described as *mustala'ma fī'l-ḥadīd* so that only his eyes were visible.[27]

The wearing of protective armour was by no means universal and sometimes men chose to fight without it. At the battle of Karbalā, al-Ḥusayn is said to have been wearing a silk shirt (*qamīṣ*, *jubba*) trousers (*sarāwīl*) and a turban but no armour.[28] One of his followers took off his *mighfar* and coat of mail before his final attack on the enemy.[29] When Ibn al-Zubayr went to say farewell to his mother before the encounter in which he was killed, he took off his coat of mail and went to his death in a silk shirt.[30] In these cases, the lack or armour is to be understood as a sign of preparing for martyrdom, almost a suicidal gesture.

We also find references to horses and men being *mujaffaf*. The word seems originally to describe horse armour, but is sometimes applied to the rider as well to mean heavy cavalry.[31] When al-Ḥusayn b. 'Alī reached Karbalā in 60/680, the Umayyad governor 'Ubayd Allāh b. Ziyād sent squadron of *mujaffafa* (probably from the *shurṭa*) and 500 archers to oppose him. In 83/702 'Abd al-Malik b. al-Muhallab is described as *mujaffaf*, whereas most of the Syrians' horses were unprotected.[32] In an account of the Battle of the Pass, a distinction seems to be made between the *mujaffafat al-khayl*, or heavy cavalry, and the *mujarrida*, or unarmoured horse.[33] What the horse armour was made of is not clear and there is no indication that horses wore mail or any other sort of iron protection.[34]

Along with the body armour, the helmet was the most important piece of protective equipment. The most common word for helmet is *bayḍa*, which also means an egg.[35] The Syrian forces at Ṣiffīn were lined up with spears (*rimāḥ*) and shields (*daraq*) and helmets (*bayḍ*) on their heads.[36] The *bayḍa* is described by Abū 'Ubayda[37] as 'a helmet of iron which is composed of plates like the bones of the skull, the edges whereof are joined together with nails; and sometimes of one piece'.[38] This description is strikingly confirmed by some of the surviving Byzantine and Sasanian examples.[39] In 85/704 a Turkish army is described as having tapering helmets *(bayḍa dhāt qawnas)*,[40] which were clearly thought of as being characteristically Turkish. Again, the description should be compared with the examples shown by Nicolle.[41] Sometimes helmets had nose-pieces, described as *anf al-bayḍa*[42] and a story recounts that the Turkish Khāqān was saved from injury to his nose because he had a Tibetan helmet, which presumably had an integral nose- or face-guard.[43] Khālid al-Barbarī, fighting the 'Alid rebels in Madīna in 169/786, is described as having a nose-piece on his helmet *(anf al-bayḍa)*, a sword and a mace attached to his belt. Nose-guards can be seen on two of the figures from the royal palace at Shahristan.[44] In general, though, both written accounts and the archaeological survivals suggest that nose-guards were unusual.

Another commonly used piece of protective headgear was the *mighfar*. The word *mighfar* is sometimes used as a term for an aventail, that is a piece of mail, or sometimes fabric, attached to the rim of the helmet and hanging down behind to protect the neck. More commonly, at least in the early period, it meant a mail coif or hood covering the top as well as the sides and back of the head.[45] According to al-Naḍr b. Shumayl (d. 203–4/818–20) the *mighfar* is 'a piece of mail [*ḥalaq* = ring, therefore real chain-mail] which a man puts beneath the helmet hanging down upon the neck . . . a man throws it upon his head, and it reaches to the coat of mail, then the helmet is put over it and the *mighfar* hangs down upon the shoulders. Sometimes, also, the *mighfar* is made of brocade or silk beneath the helmet.'[46] It is occasionally mentioned along with the *bayda*; when the Muslim envoys to Kashgar in 96/714–15 wanted to impress their hosts with their warlike qualities, they dressed in their helmets and *maghāfir* and carried their spears, swords and bows.[47] On other occasions the term *mighfar* may have included the helmet as well: both al-Ḥajjāj and Ibn al-Zubayr are described as wearing a coat of mail and a *mighfar* into battle, with no mention of a helmet.[48] In one account of the rebellion of Zayd b.'Alī in Kūfa in 122/740 there is a description of a Syrian horseman 'veiled in iron' (*muqanna' bi'l-ḥadīd*) riding down one of Zayd's supporters and ordering that his *mighfar* be taken off so that he could be beaten to death with iron bars.[49] It may be that the term *mighfar* was generally used to refer to a flexible mail head-covering rather than a rigid *bayḍa*.

Representations of *maghāfir* are rare but two clear examples have appeared in an archaeological context, probably dating from the early second/eighth century. These are two ivory plaques unearthed in the remains of the large dwelling, probably the *manzil* (residence) of the 'Abbasid family, at Humayma in southern Jordan. Two standing military figures holding spears have their heads and shoulders covered with a mail hood. A small rounded peak at the tope of the head suggests that they may be wearing these over a pointed helmet.[50]

Shields were carried by both mounted warriors and foot-soldiers, though many figures are shown without them and they are little celebrated in the poetry.[51] Such illustrations as survive show the early Islamic shield as a small disk, certainly less than a metre in diameter.[52] Interestingly, the general word for a shield, *turs*, was also used figuratively for the sun. Shields seem to have been made of wood or of leather and the word *daraqa* may have been used specifically to describe a leather shield.[53]

Stirrups must be included among the military equipment used. The early history of the stirrup is both obscure and controversial. It is clear that stirrups were unknown in classical antiquity and that there is no reliable dated evidence of the use of the metal stirrup in either the Middle East or Europe until the seventh century.[54] There is no reason to suppose that they were known to the Arabs of the Jāhiliya or to either the Muslims or their opponents at the time of the early Islamic conquests. The Arabic word *rikāb* attracted very little attention from the lexicographers, which suggests that there were no references in the earliest Arabic literature. The Persian word for stirrup derives from the Arabic, so there are no linguistic grounds for seeing the idea as an established Persian technology adopted by the Muslims. As White recognised, the scattered and incidental early mentions of stirrups are not reliable evidence and should probably be dismissed as anachronistic or tropical.[55]

Two literary sources give clear accounts of the adoption of the stirrup by Muslim soldiers. Al-Jāḥiẓ, writing in the third/ninth century, makes the Persians boast of the primitive nature of early Arab warfare, 'You were accustomed to ride your horses in battle bare-back and, whenever a horse did have a saddle on its back, it was made of leather and had no stirrups. But stirrups are among the best trappings of war for both the lancer who wields his spear and the swordsman who brandishes his sword, since they may stand in them or use them as support.' To which the author, retorting on the part of the Arabs says, 'As to stirrups it is agreed that they are very old, but iron stirrups were not used by the Arabs before the days of the Azāriqa [a groups of Khārijīs, active in Fārs and Khuzistan from about 680].'[56] The other reference is in the *Kāmil* of al-Mubarrad, who tells us that 'stirrups were first made of wood and therefore broke very easily, with the result that whenever the warrior wished to brandish his sword, or a lancer strike with his spear, he had no support. Consequently al-Muhallab ordered that they be made of iron. He thus became the first to have stirrups made of iron.'[57] Al-Muhallab made his reputation fighting against the Azāriqa, first for the anti-Caliph Ibn al-Zubayr and then for the Umayyad 'Abd al-Malik. The accounts may or may not be entirely accurate, but we can be certain that in the third/ninth century it was widely believed that iron stirrups, in contrast to swords, spears and other military equipment, were a new invention and that they had appeared during the struggles between al-Muhallab and the Khārijīs in south-western Iran at the end of the seventh century.

From the beginning of the late first/seventh century we get more incidental mentions in literature, especially in descriptions of fighting in Khurāsān. One of the earliest convincing references comes from the year 65/684–5 in a description of a horseback duel between 'Abd Allāh b. Khāzim and one of his rivals for control of Khurāsān, al-Ḥarīsh b. Hilāl al-Sa'dī. In the course of the encounter al-Ḥarīsh's stirrup snapped (*inqaṭa'a rikāb* which could mean either the stirrup or the stirrup-leather).[58] Indeed, we mostly hear of them when the equipment fails, as when the straps (*suyūr*) of Naṣr b. Sayyār's stirrups broke at the Battle of the Pass, though he continued to use the broken pieces of leather as weapons.[59]

The archaeological and visual evidence for the use of stirrups in the Islamic world is compatible with the chronology suggested by the literary evidence. Two Coptic ivories, which can probably be dated to the seventh to ninth centuries, show mounted warriors with Roman-type armour using stirrups, one apparently showing loop stirrups which may have been made of leather.[60] That stirrups were in use in Transoxania at the time of the Muslim invasions is shown by the ring stirrups used by princes depicted in the Soghdian wall paintings from old Samarqand, which must predate the Muslim invasions and destruction of the city in the early eighth century.[61] Almost certainly post-dating the Muslim conquest, and probably made for a Muslim patron, is the magnificent repoussé silver gilt dish, now in the Hermitage in St Petersburg, which shows a mounted hunter, drawing a bow to fire backwards.[62] Clear evidence for the use of stirrups among the Muslim élite comes from a fresco painting recovered in the excavations of the Umayyad palace at Qasr al-Hayr al-Gharbī in Syria, which shows a mounted hunter, with a bow but no helmet or body armour and clearly using iron stirrups.[63]

Few examples of early stirrups have survived, but one magnificent pair of silver stirrups, said to have come from Cheragh Ali Tepe in northern Iran, and now in the Romisch–Germanisches Zentralmuseum in Mainz, are thought to date from the late Sasanian period (end of the sixth or beginning of the seventh century).[64] Though a seventh-century date must be more likely than a sixth in view of the other sources on the early diffusion of stirrups, they are a striking example of the new technology.

Lynn White suggested that the introduction of stirrups in Western Europe led to the development of the heavily armoured horseman and ultimately to the social structures designed to support such specialised warriors. Few would now support this argument in its simple form, but it may be that the stirrup was one of the factors which encouraged the development of the Western knight. It is not clear that it had any similar effect in the Islamic world. Mounted archers, for example, are well attested from the classical and Sasanian material and they seem to have been very effective without the use of stirrups.[65] It must have been the case, however, that their introduction gave the mounted warrior greater stability and encouraged the widespread use of the mounted archer and the replacement of infantry by cavalry as the dominant force on the battlefield by the early third/ninth century.[66]

Weapons

The main offensive weapon was the *sayf*, the straight, hilted sword.[67] There seems to be no evidence for the use of the curved sword or scimitar from the Marwanid period, though Khurāsāni soldiers in the early third/ninth century are said to have had curved scabbards.[68] These were thrusting as well as slashing weapons. Swords were carried on baldrics or straps around the shoulder or the waist in the early Roman fashion, not hung on belts.

Schwarzlose has collected references to swords in early Arabic literature.[69] The best swords came from India (*hindī* swords) followed by those made in the Indian fashion (*muhannad*) in Yemen which, along with Syria, was the most famous centre of manufacture. Swords were named after their place of production, or at least supposed place of production. There were *qala'ī* from a site in central Arabia or Iraq or Malaysia,[70] Diyāfī swords from Iraq, Baylamānī from Baylamān which was either in Yemen or India[71] and Mushrafī, from a site which was also either in Yemen or Syria.[72] It is a curious characteristic of these names that the locations of the places are so uncertain, which suggests that even by the earliest Islamic times the names referred to types rather than places of production. There were also *ḥanafī* swords, said to have been named after the early Islamic hero al-Aḥnaf b. Qays; Ma'n b. Zā'ida, the great Arab warrior of the early 'Abbasid period, is described as having a long *ḥanafī* sword which dragged along the ground, as part of his attempt to attract the attention of the Caliph al-Manṣūr.[73] The names of a few famous sword makers are recorded, Surayj of central Arabia and Khabbāb of Makka, though the fact that these have no tribal identifications suggest that they came from low-status groups, perhaps similar to the Ṣulubba who acted as smiths in Arabia until the twentieth century. Famous swords had names like the Ṣamṣāma of Ma'dikarib and, of course, the Dhū'l-Fiqār of the Prophet himself.

They were tempered (or, as the Arabs put it, 'the sword drank the water'), and were polished by the swordsmith (*sayqal*), using a wooden *midwas* which held the stone. Their virtues were apostrophised by the poets.

In al-Jāḥiẓ's essay on the Turks, there is a detailed description of the stages involved in the making of a sword. The purpose of the description is to draw a contrast between the specialised tradesmen employed by the most soldiers and the Turks who, the author claims, make their own weapons from scratch.

> The person who melts the sword's iron and liquefies it, who purifies and refines it is different from the person who hammers and forges it. The person who hammers and forges it is different from the one who fashions it, the one who gives it a straight edge and puts on the finish is different from the one who tempers and whets it. The one who whets it is different from the one who puts on the pommel [*qubay'a*] and secures the *sīlān* [the tang or tongue at the end of the blade which is inserted in to the hilt]. The person who attaches the nails of the *sīlān*, the two knobs [*shāribay*] of the pommel and the blade is different from the one who carves the wood of the scabbard. The person who carves the wood of the scabbard is different from the one who tans its leather and the person who tans its leather is different from the one who decorates it. The person who decorates it and puts on the metal tip is different from the one who sews its belt. And so it is with the saddle, the arrow, the quiver [*ja'ba*], the spear and all arms which wound or protect.

In the third/ninth century, Ya'qūb b. Isḥāq al-Kindī (d. *c.* 256/870), otherwise known as the 'Philosopher of the Arabs', composed a treatise on swords. This purports to be a response to a request by the Caliph to describe the different types of swords and is called, appropriately, *al-Suyūf wa ajnāsiha* (Swords and their Types).[74] It is a curiously austere work, there are no traditions of the Prophet, no improving anecdotes and no effusive dedications. The author immediately settles to his task of describing the different sorts of swords. His main interest is in evaluating different swords for their strength and sharpness. He is especially concerned with the patterning in the steel of the blade, the *jawhar* (lit., jewel) or *firind* which reveals its true qualities. The best steel seems to have come from Sarandīb (Sri Lanka), though that may have simply been the entrepôt for metal from further east, and the best swords were made in Yemen or Khurāsān. Other, inferior, swords were made in Kūfa, Basra and Egypt. There were also Frankish (*Franjiya*) swords, but it is not clear whether this refers simply to imports from Europe or simply a type of sword.[75] He also gives the name of famous sword makers of early Islamic times, Zayd al-Ṣāni' from Kūfa and Sulaymān of Basra (fl. 95–109/713–27),[76] but no further information about them. The most expensive swords seem to have been the Yemeni, which would sell from between 50 and 100 *dīnārs* while a Qala'ī sword of the same dimensions would fetch only between 5 and 10: forgery was common.[77] Swords from Basra might cost 2½ *dīnārs*, those from Damascus 15–20 *dirhams* and, at the bottom end of the market, Egyptian swords could be had for just 10 *dirhams*.[78] Thus the most expensive Yemeni swords could cost more than a hundred times as much as the cheapest Egyptian.[79] The difference lay not in rich ornament or jewel-encrusted hilts but in the quality of the blades. A soldier of the early 'Abbasid period, on 60 *dirhams* a month could easily afford the Egyptian model but would have to save at least 10 months' salary to buy a Yemeni one.

Al-Kindī also provides the dimensions of some of the blades. The best were around 96 cm in length and 6–9 cm in width and might weigh up to 1½ kg.[80] Their fighting qualities were more dubious and the most expensive ones were probably display weapons rather than designed for use in warfare.[81]

There are two significant differences between the descriptions of swords collected by Schwarzlose from the ancient Arab poets and al-Kindī's treatment. Not surprisingly, Persian vocabulary is much more apparent in al-Kindī in the descriptions of swords and Khurāsān has joined Yemen as a major centre of production. Al-Kindī also describes the market for swords and their prices. But in other ways, the swords discussed by the third/ninth-century philosopher were remarkably similar to those the ancient poets gloried in, and there is little evidence of major change in design or manufacture.

Surviving examples of early Islamic swords, as well as pictorial representations, are few in number and difficult to date.[82] A number of swords discovered in northern Iran, some of them with scabbards and finely decorated can be dated to late Sasanian times. Around 100 cm in length, they have straight blades but, apparently, no hand guards.[83] We also have the fine sabre from Nishapur dated to the ninty–tenth centuries which may be typical of the arms carried by Turkish soldiers in the employ of the 'Abbasid dynasty.[84]

A particular problem is posed by the collection of weapons said to have been of early Islamic provenance now in the Topkapı Museum and Armoury in Istanbul. These include swords ascribed the Prophet Muḥammad himself and other early Caliphs and heroes. Their dating is not clear and the hilts and mountings have certainly been replaced, but some of the broad, straight blades may indeed be of early Islamic origin, even if not the actual weapons of the individuals to whom they are said to have belonged. If so, they are the most important witness to the sword making of the early Muslim period.[85]

Along with the sword went the spear or *rumḥ* (pl., *rimāḥ*). This was an thrusting weapon with an iron point[86] often used with devastating effect against cavalry charges. We are told of spears which were 13 and 14 cubits long (perhaps 6 or 7 m) but these were clearly unusually long ones, chosen to hold banners aloft.[87] Spears were used in infantry encounters, before the fighting closed to sword length.[88] Early Muslim spearheads had long edged blades and were used for slashing from side to side as well as thrusting straight ahead. This is suggested by the two-handed grip used by the hunter depicted in the Umayyad period wall paintings at Qusayr Amra. Such a side-to-side movement of the spear may be the 'thrusting of [spears] from left to right' described in an account of a battle against the Khārijīs in 68/687–8.[89] Spears were obviously considered an essential part of military equipment: after al-Junayd b. 'Abd al-Raḥmān was worsted by the Turks in the Battle of the Pass, the Caliph Ḥishām sent 30 000 spears and 30 000 shields to re-equip the Muslim armies.[90] Despite some illustrations of mounted figure holding spears,[91] the spear almost always appears as an infantry weapon in the literary sources; cavalry duels were typically fought with swords.

There are also references to another sort of spear, the *ḥarba* (pl., *ḥirāb*). This may have been a short throwing spear with a long blade. There is no record of *ḥirāb* being used in battle, though the Caliph 'Abd al-Malik is said to have used one when he murdered his cousin and rival 'Amr b. Sa'īd al-Ashdaq in the palace at Damascus. The main use of the *ḥarba* was as a symbol of authority to be carried before a Caliph or governor, usually by the *ṣāḥib al-shurṭā*.[92]

Iron maces or bars were often used. The most common term is *'amūd* (pl., *'umud* or *'amad*), a word which also means a tent-pole: some of the references may be to wooden staves rather than iron maces. Indeed tent-poles were sometimes used as weapons, as when the pages at the Muslim camp defended the camp against the Turks, using poles as weapons and horse blankets (*barādhi'*) as armour.[93] Ibn al-Ashtar's men fought the Syrians with spears and maces when the armies closed at close quarters.[94] Other terms are also used: Shabīb b. Ṣāliḥ, the Kharijite leader, had an iron stick (*'aṣā ḥadīd*) weighing 12 ratls (about 4 kg) which he carried into battle.[95] Ṣāliḥ b. 'Abd al-Raḥmān carried a small, yellow *dabūsiya* (club) when he led the Syrian troops to meet Yazīd b. al-Muhallab.[96]

Another weapon which seems to be recorded for the first time is the *ḥasak* or caltrops, used by Khāzim b. Khuzayma to impede the advance of Kharijite cavalry.[97]

Muslim armies also used incendiary material. The word used to describe this is *nafṭ*.[98] This is sometimes used to describe the mixtures known as 'Greek fire', which were said to have been developed by one Kallinikos and used to defend Constantinople against Muslim attack in the seventh century, and used by Muslim forces to counter-attack. However, the *nafṭ* used in early Islamic land warfare may have been no more than crude oil. *Nafṭ* is described as coming out of the ground at Khāniqīn in Iraq[99] and at Baku on the Caspian (both, of course, in modern oil producing areas). The oil at Baku is described by the geographer Yāqūt in the early thirteenth century, 'There [Baku] there is a huge spring (*'ain*) of oil, the revenues from which amount to 1000 *dirhams* a day. Next to it is another one which flows with white *nafṭ* like liquid mercury which runs night and day without stopping and produces revenues like the first one. A merchant whom I trust told me that he saw there land which always burned with fire. I reckon that the fire was dropped into it by some person and is never extinguished because of mineral composition.'[100] The *nafṭ* here is clearly crude oil and it burns without any chemical additives; it did not need to be mixed with anything else to make an inflammable liquid. The oil of Baku was known to the Muslims at least since early 'Abbasid times, when al-Manṣūr ordered that it should be taxed.[101] When Khāzim b. Khuzayma was attacking the Khārijīs in Oman in 134/751–2 he was advised by a Soghdian living there to order his men to put rags soaked in *nafṭ* on the ends of their spears, ignite them and walk forward to set fire to the flimsy dwellings of the Omanis, which they duly did.[102] From this account it appears that this was a new and unusual tactic and it is not clear where the *naft* came from. It was used during the first siege of Baghdad when al-Amīn ordered that the Ḥarbiya quarter be shot at with *naft* and fire and there was *naft* and fire in the streets of Baghdad.[103] Al-Afshīn used it during his attack on Bābak's stronghold.[104] Waṣīf ordered the *naft* throwers to burn down shops and houses in Samarra during civil disturbances in 249/863 and the historian al-Ṭabarī himself saw the burned out ruins.[105] Others were more scrupulous: in the second siege of Baghdad, Sulaymān b. 'Abd Allāh b. Ṭāhir refused to sanction the use of *naft* by his men, presumably because of the damage he feared it would cause in the city.[106] *Naft* could also be launched from boats.[107]

Naft is usually described as being shot or hurled, but it is not clear whether special equipment was used for this or whether it was simply used on ordinary arrows as Khāzim b. Khuzayma had done. Its usefulness was clearly limited and we find it being employed only in urban warfare for the destruction of wooden buildings. *Naffāṭīn* were clearly specialists, like the sappers, but do not seem to have been counted among the military élite.

Finally there were the bows.[108] Archers formed an important part of early Muslim armies. In contrast to many western mediaeval societies, where archery was often regarded as socially inferior to fighting with sword or lance, archery was highly esteemed among the Muslims and a considerable literature was developed about it, though none now survives from before the twelfth century. We know little of the bows (*qaws*, pl., *aqwās*) themselves or the arrows and there are no surviving examples from this period. There seems to have been a division between the Arab bow, which was light, and the more effective and heavier Persian bow,[109] though it is not clear that there was any difference in design or construction. The lexicographers describe the arrow (*sahm*) as being of two sorts, the *nabl* or Arab arrow and the *nushshāb*[110] or Persian arrow. Ibn Shumayl describes the *nabl* as having an iron head (*naṣl*)[111] and feathers (*rīsh*). The surviving representations show both horse and foot archers using composite bows with the double S shape which had been used by the Sasanians and remained characteristic of Muslim bows for centuries to come.[112] The quiver (*ja'ba* or *kināna*) was made of leather or wood. According to Ibn Shumayl, the *ja'ba* is a quiver with a broad open top which tapers towards the bottom, so that when the arrows are put in point downwards, their feathers are not damaged.[113] The range of a bow shot is discussed by the lexicographers, the majority of whom put it between 300 and 400 cubits.[114] Taking a cubit as about 0.600 m, this suggests a range between 180 and 240 m. It is clear that archers mostly fought on foot[115] during the Umayyad period and probably into the early 'Abbasid era as well. From the third/ninth century, however, the mounted archer largely replaced the footman and became the backbone of the military forces of the Caliphate[116]. It is not clear whether this change was accompanied by the introduction of a new sort of bow, but it is probable that the soldiers from Transoxania who brought the new techniques also brought with them a shorter composite bow of the sort we are familiar with from Seljuk and Mongol times.

Conclusion

The Arabs of the pre-Islamic period and the years of the conquests had comparatively simple military equipment but they did have, or at least some of them did have, swords, bows, helmets, shields and body armour. Apart from the stirrup, whose importance should not be exaggerated, there seems to have been no major technical advances in military equipment during the first three Islamic centuries. However, it is likely that there was a gradual assimilation of Persian, and possibly Byzantine, military equipment. This was not radically different but more powerful (like the bows) and more developed (like body armour). By the third/ninth state of the art military equipment was probably too expensive for anyone but professional soldiers and senior cadres of the Caliphate to afford. The possession of such equipment was another factor which distinguished the soldier from the civilian.

Notes

1 The visual evidence has been collected and discussed in D. Nicolle, 'Arms of the Umayyad Era', in Y. Lev (ed.), *War and Society in the Eastern Mediterranean* (Leiden, 1997), 9–100; for late Roman and Sasanian precedents see the important article by A. D. H. Bivar, 'Cavalry Equipment and Tactics on the Euphrates Frontier', *Dumbarton Oaks Papers*, 26 (1972), 271–91; for Byzantine military equipment, see J. Haldon, *Warfare, State and Society in the Byzantine World, 565–1204* (London, 1999), 128–34 and T. Kolias, *Byzantinische Waffen* (Vienna, 1988); interested readers should also consult D. Nicolle, *The Armies of Islam 7th–11th Centuries* (London, 1982) and *Armies of the Muslim Conquest* (London, 1993), both with imaginative and largely convincing reconstructions of arms and armour drawn by A. McBride.

2 Evidence from ancient Arabic poetry has been collected in F. W. Schwarzlose, *Die Waffen der alten Araber aus ihren Dichtern dargestellt* (Leipzig, 1886, repr. New York, 1982). See also N. Fries, *Das Heereswesen der Araber zur Zeit der Omaijaden nach Ṭabarī* (Tübingen, 1921), 48–54.

3 See, for example, the description of ideal military equipment in 'Abd al-Ḥamīd, 196–7.

4 For the extensive lexicography of a body armour, see Schwarzlose, *Die Waffen*, 322–48; for the technical terms for military equipment in Greek, Arabic and Persian see the glossary in Bivar 'Cavalry Equipment', 291.

5 See Lane svv. According to Schwarzlose, *Die Waffen* (322), *zarad* is simply the Persian for *dir'* though it had clearly become Arabised and been given an Arabic verbal form.

6 See P. Southern and K. R. Dixon, *The Late Roman Army* (London, 1996), 96–9; Bivar, 'Cavalry Equipment'.

7 Qur'ān xxi, 80; xxxiv, 10–11. The word *dir'* is not used: the coats of mail are called *labūs* and *sābighāt* and *sarada* for the making of them.

8 Ṭa., ii, 615.

9 Ṭa., iii, 316.

10 Ṭa., ii, 1443; Schwarzlose, *Die Waffen*, 330–1; see also A. Musil, *The Manners and Customs of the Rwala Bedouin* (New York, 1928b), 387 for an account of mail being worn under or between other garments.

11 Ṭa., ii, 1180, though it must be said that this story was circulated by Qutayba's supporters to emphasise his achievements.
12 Ṭa., ii, 1188–9, ; Ibn A'tham, vii, 221; Narshakhī, 46. The story is recounted to show how rich the Muslims were after the conquest, and the prices are quoted to show how high they were.
13 al-Azdī, 129–30.
14 Ṭa., ii, 587.
15 Lane sv.; Schwarzlose, *Die Waffen*, 339–41.
16 For example, Bal., *Futūḥ*, 23, 61 where the term seems to be used for arms in general. The term seems to have been used only in material dating from the time of the Prophet and may well have been largely obsolete by the Marwanid period.
17 Ṭa., ii, 1690.
18 The excavations are published in N. N. Negmatov, *Srednevekovyi Shakhristan* (Dushanbe, 1966). Unfortunately the quality of the illustrations is extremely poor; see also, N. N. Negmatov, 'O Zhipovisi Dvortsa Afshinov Ustrushani (De la Peinture du Palais Royal d'Oustrouchana; Communication Preliminaire)', *Sovetskaya Arkeologiya,* 1973, 183–202.
19 Nicolle, 'Arms of the Umayyad Era', nos. 67A–D with comments.
20 Nicolle, 'Arms of the Umayyad Era', nos. 76A–G with discussion.
21 Ṭa., ii, 1202. For a discussion of this obscure word see Ṭa., Gloss, cxcvi sv. ḥṭm: it may be derived from the place of manufacture or the name of the maker. See also the use of *zaghaf* as a coat of mail in Ṭa., ii, 1432, though there seems to be no lexicographical support for this.
22 J. W. Allan, *Persian Metal Technology 700–1300 AD* (London, 1979), 97, 98; A. S. Melikian-Chirvani, 'Notes sur la terminologie de la métallurgie et des armes dans l'Iran musulman', *JESHO*, 24 (1981), 310–16, p. 312. There seems to be no archaeological evidence for the use of plate armour in the early Islamic period. *Jawshan* is not found in the early Arabic sources used by Schwarzlose, *Die Waffen*, nor in 'Abd al-Ḥamīd al-Kātib's description of armour.
23 Or the anecdote is meant to show al-Ḥarith's austerity and commitment to warfare, Ṭa., ii, 1889.
24 Ṭa., iii, 233.
25 Ṭa., iii, 1777. The translator, Waines, a scholar well known for his interest in culinary history, has the man 'heaving a metal oven' at his pursuer (trans., 60).
26 Ṭa., iii, 315.
27 Ṭa., iii, 239.
28 Ṭa., ii, 364–5.
29 Ṭa., ii, 354.
30 Ṭa., ii, 847–8.
31 See for example Ṭa., ii, 1153 where Ibn Khāzim deploys 300 *mujjafaf* against the Turks and the term is helpfully translated as 'cataphracts' by Hinds. See also Melikian-Chirvani, 'Notes', 314 for the continuing use of horse armour in Iran after the Muslim conquest, cf. Allan, *Persian Metal Technology*, 96, who argues that it fell into disuse.
32 Ṭa., ii, 1100.
33 Ṭa., ii, 1535–6.
34 Nicolle suggests that this was 'soft' horse armour, consisting of felt or quilted material (personal communication).
35 Schwarzlose, *Die Waffen*, 349–51 for the vocabulary of helmets.
36 Ṭa., i, 3268.
37 Ma'mar b. al-Muthannā al-Taymī , d. c. 210/825–6. For his works, see *Fihrist,* trans. Dodge, 115–18.
38 Lane, sv.
39 See Nicolle, 'Arms of the Umayyad Era', 98, nos. 172–9; B. J. Overlaet (ed.),

Hofkunst van de Sassanieden (Brussels, 1993), nos. 30, 31, 32, 33, 34; see also B. J. Overlaet, 'Contribution to Sasanian Armament in Connection with a Decorated Helmet', *Iranica Antiqua*, 17 (1982), 189–206.

40 Ṭa., ii, 1153 with Hinds trans. n. 365.

41 Nicolle, 'Arms of the Umayyad Era', 98, nos. 181, 182, 184.

42 Ṭa., ii, 1383–4.

43 Ṭa., ii, 1521–2.

44 Nicolle, 'Arms of the Umayyad Era', no. 67B.

45 Nicolle, personal communication.

46 See the discussion in Lane 2274–5 sv. For the life and work of Ibn Shumayl, see *Fihrist*, trans. Dodge , 112–13.

47 Ṭa., ii, 1278.

48 Ṭa., ii, 831, 847.

49 Ṭa., ii, 1704. The Khāqān's soldiers are described as *muqanna'* in a poem (Ṭa., ii, 1554).

50 R. Foote, 'Frescoes and Carved Ivory from the 'Abbasid Family Homestead at al-Humeima', *Journal of Roman Archaeology*, 12 (1999), 423–30.

51 Schwarzlose, *Die Waffen*, 351–6.

52 Nicolle, 'Arms of the Umayyad Era', 15, nos. 76B, 84, but note also the large oval shield with a prominent central boss in a statue from Khirbet al-Mafjar which, as Nicolle notes (no. 16E) may be anachronistic, reflecting a Roman–Byzantine protype.

53 Lane sv.

54 For the origin and diffusion of the stirrup, see L. White, *Medieval Technology and Social Change* (Oxford, 1962), 14–28.

55 As, for example, Ṭa., ii, 120 when Ḥujr b. 'Adī has stirrups on his mule in 51/671.

56 al-Jāḥiẓ, *Al-Bayān wa'l-tabyīn* (Cairo, 1926–7), iii, 8, 12; quoted in White, *Medieval Technology*, 18.

57 al-Mubarrad, *Kāmil*, ed. W. Wright (Leipzig, 1886), 675; quoted in White, *Medieval Technology*, 18, 142.

58 Ṭa., ii, 596–7; see also Ṭa., ii, 785 where the same term is used.

59 Ṭa., ii, 1546.

60 Nicolle, 'Arms of the Umayyad Era', nos. 84, 85. The dating of these ivories is unclear and much of the argument is circular, that these must be eighth century or later since they show stirrups. Nonetheless there is a clear contrast with other, probably earlier, ivories which clearly show riders without stirrups.

61 C. Silvi Antonini, 'The Painting in the Palace of Afrosiyab (Samarkand)', *Rivista degli Studi Orientali*, 63 (1989), 109–44, esp. figs. 7, 8; for evidence of stirrups in the late Sasanian period, see also M. Michalak, 'The Origins and Development of Sassanian Heavy Cavalry', *Folia Orientalia* 24 (1987), 73–86, 83.

62 Nicolle, 'Arms of the Umayyad Era', no. 75.

63 D. Schlumberger, *Qasr El-Heir El Gharbi* (Paris, 1986), pl. 34. Dated by the excavator to c. 109/728–9.

64 Overlaet, *Hofkunst* 187, no. 48.

65 See Bivar, 'Cavalry Equipment', esp. 286–7.

66 See Cahen, 'Les changements technique militaires dans le Proche Orient mediéval et leur importance historique', in V. J. Parry and M. E. Yapp (eds), *War, Technology, and Society in the Middle East* (Oxford, 1975), 116.

67 On Sasanian swords, see K. Masia, 'The Evolution of Swords and Daggers in the Sasanian Empire', *Iranica Antiqua*, 35 (2000), 185–289; for discussion of early Islamic swords and their manufacture, see al-Kindī, *Al-Suyūf wa Ajnāsiha*, ed. Abd al-Rahman Zaki, *Bulletin of the Faculty of Arts, Cairo*, 14 (1952) , Arabic section, 1–36. Schwarzlose, *Die Waffen*, 124–209; Allan, *Persian Metal Technology*; Melikian-Chirvani, 'Notes'; Y. Raghib, 'La fabrication des lames damassées en Orient',

JESHO, 40 (1997), 30–70. For illustrations and surviving examples, see A. R. Zaky, 'Medieval Arab Arms', in. R. Elgood (ed.), *Islamic Arms and Armour* (London, 1979), 202–12; Nicolle, 'Arms of the Umayyad Era', nos. 101–30.

68 al-Jāḥiẓ, *Manāqib*, 11.

69 Schwarzlose, *Die Waffen*, 124–209.

70 Schwarzlose, *Die Waffen*, 130 and Zaki al-Kindī, 8, no. 15, both look for a site in the Middle East, Raghib 'La fabrication des lames damassées', 60, n. 337, argues for an Arabised form of Kalang in Malaysia, an ancient port near Kuala Lumpur.

71 See Yāqūt sn.

72 See Lane sv, but possibly named after a pre-Islamic armourer called Mushārif, Raghib, 'La fabrication des lames damassées' 54, n. 288.

73 Ṭa., ii, 1223; iii, 394.

74 For an assessment of this work, stressing that it is concerned with metallurgy rather than military affairs, see M. Shatzmiller, 'The Crusades and Islamic Warfare – A Re-evaluation' *Der Islam*, 69 (1992), 247–88, 251–2.

75 Shatzmiller, 'The Crusades and Islamic Warfare', 32–3.

76 Shatzmiller, 'The Crusades and Islamic Warfare', 10, 31, 35.

77 Shatzmiller, 'The Crusades and Islamic Warfare', 22; Qala'ī swords are probably named after a toponym Qal'at (castle), whose location cannot be identified with certainty: see Shatzmiller, 'The Crusades and Islamic Warfare', 8 n. 15 for a full discussion of the possibilities.

78 Shatzmiller, 'The Crusades and Islamic Warfare', 34–5.

79 On a conservative ratio of 12 *dirhams* to the *dīnār.*

80 Raghib, 'La fabrication des lames damassées', 61.

81 Raghib, 'La fabrication des lames damassées', 62–4.

82 Examples with parallels from outside the Islamic world are given in Nicolle, 'Arms of the Umayyad Era', nos. 101–31.

83 Nicolle, 'Arms of the Umayyad Era', 124; Overlaet, *Hofkunst*, 178–9, nos. 37–41.

84 Now in the Metropolitan Museum, New York; Nicolle, 'Arms of the Umayyad Era', no. 130.

85 Nicolle, 'Arms of the Umayyad Era', 101–11 and the discussion on 50; some of them a fully illustrated in A. Zaky, 'Medieval Arab Arms', 204–5.

86 Lane sv.; Fries, *Das Heereswesen*, 50–1; see also A. Musil, *The Manners and Customs of the Rwala Bedouin*, 132–3 for the use of both *rumḥ* and *ḥarba* in the early twentieth century.

87 Ṭa., ii, 1954; see the spears with banners used to corral the hunted beasts in the Qusayr Amra paintings, Nicolle, 'Arms of the Umayyad Era', no. 4B.

88 Ṭa., ii, 761.

89 Ṭa., ii, 761 *'al-ṭa'n shazaran'*; for the Qusayr Amra spearsman, see Nicolle, 'Arms of the Umayyad Era', no. 5C; for further discussion of the broad-headed spear, with illustrations, see Nicolle, 'Arms and Warfare in Classical Islam', in R. Elgood (ed.), *Islamic Arms and Armour* (London, 1979), 162–86, 180–1, 184–5, figs. 51–61.

90 Ṭa., ii, 1545.

91 E.g. Nicolle, 'Arms of the Umayyad Era', no. 85 and, of course, the reliefs of Sasanian Kings as mounted lancers from Naqsh-i Rustam and elsewhere.

92 See Ṭa. ii, 790–1, 862 and Gloss. clxxxvii sv.; Fries, *Das Heereswesen*, 50.

93 Ṭa., ii, 1597–9.

94 Ṭa., ii, 712.

95 Ṭa., ii, 927.

96 Ṭa., ii, 1307.

97 Ṭa., iii, 123.

98 See V. Christides, *Naft*, in EI2, which is largely concerned with Greek fire and its use in naval warfare; see also Haldon, *Warfare, State and Society*, 138.

99 Le Strange, *Lands of the Eastern Caliphate* (London, 1905, repr. 1966), 63.
100 Yāqūt, sn. Bākūya.
101 Bal., *Futūḥ,* 210, referring to the *naffāṭa arḍ Shirwān.*
102 Ṭa., iii, 79.
103 Ṭa., iii, 869, 887.
104 Ṭa., iii, 1215 mentions *naffāṭīn* (*nafṭ*-throwing men) and *naffāṭāt* (presumably *nafṭ*-throwing equipment).
105 Ṭa., iii, 1511–2: the *naffāṭīn . . . qadhafū . . . b'il-nār* the shops and houses.
106 Ṭa., iii, 1731.
107 Ṭa., iii, 1636.
108 For a good introduction to archery in mediaeval Islam with full bibliography, see the article 'Kaws' (A. Boudot-Lamothe), EI2.
109 Fries, *Das Heereswesen*, 52; Schwarzlose, *Die Waffen*, 250–1 gives the word *'atal* for the heavier, thicker Persian bow, but it does not seem to be used in the historical sources. Nicolle suggests that the Arab bow was longer and more suited to infantry warfare (personal communication).
110 *nabl* and *nushshāb* are both collective words for arrows, *sahm* is used for a single arrow. For the effectiveness of arrows in causing injury and penetrating skull, see Fries, *Das Heereswesen*, 53 but the reference to poisoned arrows is based on a misreading of Ṭa., ii, 350: in fact, as the translator (Howard) correctly says, al-Jamalī was putting his name on his arrows before firing, presumably so that he could tell how many men he personally had killed.
111 Lane sv. *sahm.*
112 Nicolle, 'Arms of the Umayyad Era', nos. 6B, 12, 15, 75.
113 Lane sv. *ja'ba.*
114 Lane sv. *ghalwa.* Other variants include 200 cubits and 1/25th of a *farsang*.
115 For example, the painted figure from Khirbet Mafjar, a foot-archer firing while using his round shield to defend himself, Nicolle, 'Arms of the Umayyad Era', no. 15.
116 See pp. 123–4.

CHAPTER EIGHT

Fortification and siege warfare

Siege warfare played a comparatively small part in early Islamic military activity. In general it seems that Muslim armies did not like to find themselves confined within walls but would rather have had the freedom of manoeuvre in the open countryside. Many must have agreed with Zufar b. al-Ḥārith's attitude: when the army of 'Abd al-Malik set up their siege engines to bombard the walls of Qarqīsiyā, saying that they were going to make a breach to attack him, he retorted, 'We will not fight you from behind walls and gates, but will come out against you.'[1] In 64/684 the Bakrī tribesmen of Herat rebelled against the governor, 'Abd Allāh b. Khāzim. The governor sent a military expeditions against them and they debated how best to resist. Their leader, Aws b. Tha'laba urged them to 'stick to the town, for it is well fortified (*ḥaṣīna*)' and 'Abd Allāh would be obliged to offer them terms, presumably because he would be unable to mount an effective siege. The Bakrīs, however, rejected this option and preferred instead to leave the town and encamp behind a *khandaq*.[2] A century and a half later, in 195/811 when Ṭāhir b. al-Ḥusayn was leading the troops of al-Ma'mūn against al-Amīn's armies, his companions urged him to take refuge behind the city walls of Rayy. Ṭāhir, like the Bakrīs, decided that he would rather fight in open country, keeping the city behind him so that the could take refuge there if things went wrong.[3] There was clearly a body of military opinion which held that its was either dishonourable or too restricting to shelter behind walls.

When people did use fortifications, the result was more likely to be a period of negotiation rather than an assault. When Ibn Muṭī' was besieged by al-Mukhtār in the governor's palace (*qaṣr*) in Kūfa, no attempt was made to organise an assault. Apart from firing arrows at the defenders when they appeared to shout insults, no offensive action took place: after three days, Ibn Muṭī' agreed to terms.[4] When the tables were turned, al-Mukhtār himself was besieged in his *qaṣr* for four months. Again, no attempt was made to attack the building, except by firing arrows against any defenders incautious enough to put their heads above the parapets. Food and water was denied to the defenders, but even this simple blockade took some time to organise. The siege ended only when al-Mukhtār and his men made a desperate sally outside the *qaṣr*.[5]

When al-Walīd II's enemies set out to hunt him down in 126/744, he considered taking refuge in the fortified town of Tadmur (Palmyra), but was afraid that the people would prove hostile. After considering other options, he went to the *qaṣr* at Bakhrā, about 25 km to the south. This was a rectangular fort, probably of Roman origin (one of al-Walīd's advisers described it as well-fortified (ḥaṣīn) built by the *'ajam*,[6] with boldly projecting hollow towers.[7] Here he fortified himself and waited. His enemies brought with them no siege engines but entered the *qaṣr* simply by climbing over the walls.[8]

There were occasions when serious sieges were undertaken, mostly during warfare on the frontiers against non-Muslims. There were also two major sieges of Baghdad in 196–8/812–3 and 251/865–6,[9] but both these were concentrated on a blockade and street fighting rather than on attempts to destroy fortifications.

Siege engines[10]

The main Muslim siege weapon was the *manjanīq* (pl., *manājiq*). This was a swing-beam engine, similar to the trebuchet used in Western mediaeval siege warfare. The swing-beam engine seems to have originated in China and have been brought to the West by the Avars and is first heard of at the siege of Thessalonica, probably in 597. This machine proved more efficient than anything previously known and rapidly displaced the torsion artillery (that is, artillery powered by twisted ropes or sinews) used in classical times. There is no evidence for the use of torsion artillery in the Islamic world. The early medieval engines were all traction trebuchets, that is to say, they were operated by men pulling ropes to bring the short end of the beam down, rather than using counter-weights, as was common from the thirteenth century onwards. The *'arrāda* was simply a smaller-scale version of the swing-beam engine, usually mounted on a single pole.

Manājiq are mentioned in accounts of the early Muslim conquests, for example at al-Madā'in when the defending Persians used them against the Arabs. A certain Sa'd Shirzād, presumably a Persian renegade, then constructed 20 with which the Muslims could counter them.[11] Al-Ḥajjāj famously used a *manjanīq* to bombard the Ka'ba, then held by Ibn al-Zubayr, in 73/692.[12] They are sometimes mentioned as breaching fortifications, as at Samarqand in 93/712, where they made a breach (*thalamū thalmatan*) which the defenders blocked up with sacks of grain.[13]

After the Battle of Marj Rāhiṭ which assured Umayyad control over Syria, the leader of the defeated Qasī party, Zufar b. al-Ḥārith, fled to Qarqīsiyā. The Caliph 'Abd al-Malik came to besiege him and set up *manājiq* around the walls and began to bombard them. The siege is said to have lasted for a (formulaic) 40 days and considerable damage was done, including the destruction of four towers. However, the besieged fought back and made several sorties and the confrontation was brought to an end by negotiation, not by the storming of the fortifications.[14]

Manājiq were employed in both the sieges of Baghdad. In the siege of 196–8/812–14 the siege engines were said to have been used for the indiscriminate bombardment of the civilian population and to have inflicted terrible casualties.[15] At the siege of Amorion in 223/838, al-Mu'taṣim used 'big *manājiq*' to fill up the ditches with sheepskins full of earth. Chevedden has argued that this sees the introduction of a new sort of 'hybrid trebuchet', using both traction and counter-weight propulsion.[16] *Manājiq* were also effective in opening a breach in the walls, at a place where improvised repairs had been made after flood-damage.[17]

It must be emphasised that accounts of *manājiq* being used with effect against walls are exceptional. Both *manājiq* and *'arrādāt* were used more commonly as anti-personnel weapons.[18] Defenders made as much use of them as attackers and there are examples of them being used to good effect in open battle where neither side were using fortifications.[19] Compared with the Romans before or the Mamluks after, early Muslim use of artillery against fortified enclosures was sporadic and largely ineffective. They caused terror and considerable loss of life among people but there is little evidence of effective assaults on major fortified sites. Furthermore, such engines were used at least as much by defenders as by attackers. Until the third/ninth centuries, there are few mentions of sappers or specialists in artillery in Muslim armies (though that does not mean that they did not exist). It is only with the military reforms of al-Mu'taṣim, that such specialists appear in the sources.

Fortification

The history of early Islamic fortification has hardly been investigated. Creswell's classic essay, 'Fortification in Islam before 1250'[20] established a simple framework, but is now seriously out of date. Since then there have been studies of individual sites but little attempt at an overview.[21]

The Arabic sources use a variety of words for castles or fortress. *Ḥiṣn* is commonly used of a structure which is purely military in character. The word *qal'a*, later the normal word for a castle, is less common in the first centuries of Islam. Q*aṣr*, which seems to be derived from the Latin *castrum*, is used of a high-status dwelling usually, but not always, fortified. The residential/military castle, so typical of Western Europe from the eleventh century and, to a lesser extent, of the Middle East from the period of the Seljuks and their successors, was virtually unknown in the early Islamic world, apart from some survivals from Sasanian times in Fārs and elsewhere.

Most of the existing cities the Muslims took over after the great conquests had been surrounded by walls. Northedge has drawn attention to two different traditions of city fortification in the Middle East.[22] One is the classical style with vertical stone, or occasionally fired brick, walls, usually strengthened with interval towers, either square or round. These towers could be either solid or hollow. Hollow towers often contained chambers which were provided with arrow slits or small windows from which projectiles could be fired along the side of the walls.

The second tradition was a Mesopotamian or Iranian one which consisted of piling up huge banks of mud-brick and pisé, a technique which can be seen at its most impressive in the pre-Islamic city of Marw and the massive ramparts of old Samarqand and Balkh.

In Syria the ancient city walls seem to have continued in use. In Damascus, the ancient enceinte seems to have survived virtually unchanged into the twentieth century. In Ḥoms the Roman walls were formidable enough in late Umayyad times to cause serious problems to the forces of Marwān II. When he finally took the city, he destroyed a considerable length of wall to present the city being held against him again.[23]

Walls clearly had their uses, but the great garrison cities of early Islam seem to have been left without them. The great Iraqi miṣrs of Kūfa and Basra had no walls until the 'Abbasid period, when al-Manṣūr is said to have ordered the building of walls around the two cities at the expense of the inhabitants in 155/772. In Kūfa each of the inhabitants was obliged to pay 40 *dirhams* for the wall (*sūr*) and the digging of the moat (*khandaq*).[24] Basra certainly had walls at the time of the invasion of the Qarāmiṭa. The walls of Mawṣil were built by Muḥammad b. Marwān, brother of the Caliph 'Abd al-Malik in about 106/724–5,[25] probably to protect the city against the Kharijites of the Jazīra steppes. Fusṭāṭ in Egypt remained unwalled until its virtual destruction in the late twelfth century. The Round City of Baghdad certainly had impressive fortifications but the rest of the sprawling metropolis seems to have been open at the time of the siege of 196–8/812–13. In the second siege of 251/865 it had walls with elaborate gates. In Samarra, individual palaces and complexes had walls, but there was no wall surrounding the whole built-up area. In the early ninth century Aleppo was unfortified, with the result that the citizens could not defend themselves against the bedouin.[26] The position in Marw is particularly interesting in this respect.[27] As far as can be determined from the archaeological and written record, the old walled city was gradually abandoned in favour of new, unwalled suburbs along the Majan canal to the west. It was not until Seljuk times in the late eleventh century that this area was surrounded by a wall. Aerial photographs show an extensive network of walls around Rayy where a virtually new city was constructed during the residence of al-Mahdī, but these have never been investigated on the ground and are now largely destroyed.[28]

Caliphs were often concerned that city walls would encourage the citizens to defy the government. Marwān II is said to have destroyed the walls of all the cities of Syria except Antioch which he intended to use as a refuge.[29] Al-Rashīd had the walls of Mawṣil demolished in 181/797 after the citizens had protested against government taxation. According to one account, he guaranteed an amnesty to all the citizens provided they demolished the sections of wall nearest them with their own hands.[30] During the disturbance at the beginning of al-Ma'mūn's reign, the people of Edessa were obliged to reconstruct the walls, which had been demolished in al-Manṣūr's time, at their own expense.[31] When the authority of the government was restored, the Caliph ordered the destruction of the walls of Cyrrhus, Qinnasrīn and 'all the fortifications of Jazīra and Syria'.[32] There was no place for city walls in a properly ordered state where security was assured by the authorities.

There are no surviving walls of a major city dating from the Umayyad period.

However, we do have we have the examples of fortifications of semi-urban structures which seem to have contained a mixture of official and residential buildings. The most important examples of these are Amman, Anjar, Aqaba and Qaṣr al-Ḥayr al-Sharqī.

The fortifications on the citadel of Amman[33] followed the lines of the Roman and pre-Roman circuit, but they were substantially rebuilt in Umayyad times. The walls are all in stone, often constructed of reused ashlar blocks. Sometimes these are arranged in an ordered fabric of headers and stretchers, sometimes as a more rubble masonry. They are strengthened by shallow. pilaster buttresses and irregularly spaced towers, positioned at the gates or where the line of the wall changed. The towers contain small chambers but do not project very far from the wall. One of the Umayyad towers seems to have been 11–12 m in height and to have had three stories[34] and this may have been typical, but none of the towers survives above the ground floor and it is not clear whether they had arrow slits or not. The walls enclose an extensive area (90 000 m^2) on the citadel hill, but it should be remembered that much of the city, including the Umayyad mosque, sadly demolished in the 1920s, lay in the valley below and seems to have been unfortified.[35]

Anjar is a more problematic site, partly because the publication has been very partial.[36] This almost square urban site (310 m x 370 m) consists of a single line of wall with between eight and ten small, rounded towers on each side: these tower are all solid. At each corner there are projecting round towers with chambers inside. There are four gates in the middle of the four sides. At no point does the wall remain higher than a few courses, and there is no indication what wall-head defences there might have been.

The third example, Aqaba, is again problematic. It is much smaller than Anjar (165 m x 140 m). Once again it is a rectangular enclosure with four gates. The walls are defended with boldly projecting, D-shaped interval towers. These are all hollow. The towers are very similar to those in legionary fortresses like Lajjun of the fourth century and, while there certainly was extensive Umayyad occupation on the site, it is possible that the fortifications are Roman in origin and tell us little about early Islamic military architecture.

The other type of Umayyad fortifications which survive are the *quṣūr* (sing., *qaṣr*). The word combines the idea of palace and castle. The ruins of a considerable number of these structures survive. Their dating is often problematic and their functions are not always clear. Almost all of them are square or rectangular in plan and almost all have a perimeter wall strengthened by solid round towers of fairly modest dimensions. It is not usually clear how far these were intended to be serious military defences and how much they were added to create an imposing effect.

In many cases these structures have been ruined, and only their ground plans, or the lower parts of the fortifications, have been preserved. In two of them, however, the structures have been preserved to wall-head level. Kharana, east of Amman, is usually interpreted as a caravanserai.[37] There are many puzzling things about this building, particularly the use of Sasanian-style rubble masonry covered with plaster rather than the ashlar more typically associated with Syrian building. The building presents a formidable face to the outside world. There are no windows, only slits, and one small door. There are towers on each of the sides, all of which are solid. There are no signs, however, of more specifically military features: there are no surviving battlements, no chambers in the towers and no machicolations and, from their position high above the floor levels, it is more likely that the slits are for ventilation than for archery.

Qaṣr al-Ḥayr al-Sharqī,[38] to the north-east of Palmyra, is a complex site which includes two fortified enclosures, a small one variously interpreted as a caravanserai or a *qaṣr* and a larger, semi-urban one, about 163 m^2. On both of these, the fortifications consist of round, solid interval towers. There are no hollow towers at the corners, as at Anjar. In the smaller enclosure, the walls, largely constructed in a friable local limestone, mostly stand to their full height, some 10.5 m. The walls are about 210 cm in width and are entirely solid with no openings except at one point where a slit lights a spiral staircase in a tower. The wall-head had an external parapet which survives in places between the towers of the entrance gate and seems to have had an internal parapet as well. This may have created a wall-head passage such as existed at al-Ukhaydir .[39] However, there are no indications of arrow slits or crenellations. The interval towers reach only to wall-head height but the corner towers, and the two which flanked the main gate, were provided with small round chambers roofed by brick domes. Once again, there are no openings in the outside walls of these chambers. The gate, like all the gates at Qaṣr al-Ḥayr al-Sharqī, seems to have been a simple entrance with wooden doors. There is no evidence of multiple gates or of a portcullis, nor of a covered passage or *dihlīz* of the sort described as existing in Baghdad and found in the gates of al-Ukhaydir. There is a three corbel box-machicolation over the main gate at the height of the wall-head.[40]

The fortifications of the large enclosure are much less well preserved but show some interesting features. Some of the towers, notably the tower to the south of the west gate, preserve arrow slits in the brick parapet, as do towers 24 and 27. In the case of tower 27, the arrow slit seems to be positioned to enable a defender to fire along the sides of the walls.[41] All the gates were provided with box-machicolations above the entrance.

The defences at Qaṣr al-Ḥayr al-Sharqī are massive enough, but technically quite simple. It is surprising to see that there is no ditch or other obstacle to keep siege engines away, and that provision for wall-head defence and flanking fire was very limited. Only the machicolations over the gates seem to show an awareness of the possibilities of active defence. We must conclude that the walls and towers were designed for show and for protection against bedouin raids and perhaps the Khārijīs, who were often active in this part of the desert, but not against an army equipped with siege engines.

There are some signs that the early ʿAbbasid period showed an increased interest in fortification. When al-Manṣūr founded his new city of Baghdad in 145/762, he ordered the construction of elaborate fortifications for the Round City which was the administrative hub of the city.[42] From the outside these consisted of a ditch and then two lines of walls separated by an open space (*faṣīl*). The inner wall was lined with round interval towers which are estimated to have been about 20 m high, that is almost exactly the height of the towers at al-Ukhaydir. At the wall-head there were rounded battlements (*sharafāt*). There were four gates, each of which consisted of a gate in the outer wall, followed by a passage and then a more elaborate gate in the inner wall, surmounted by a dome chamber at the upper level. No trace of these fortifications now survives.

The whole city of Baghdad was fortified at the time of the second siege in 251/865. The walls had a *khandaq* outside them and shelters *(miẓallāt)* on the inside for horses to shelter from the sun and the rain. Special attention was given to the gates, each one of which had a *dihlīz* or covered hallway attached to it where 100 infantry and 100 cavalry could be stationed.[43]

The entrance of the Shammāsiya Gate was defended by five *shadākhāt*[44] which stretched across the road. These are described in the text as made of cross-beams and boards with protruding spikes. Outside the gate there was a second gate equal to it in thickness and armoured with iron sheets, suspended with ropes in such a way that if an enemy were to enter , the hanging gate would be dropped on him and he would be killed.[45] It is clear that there were spiked wooden barriers in front of the gate itself and then a hanging gate or portcullis.[46] On the outer gate an *'arrāda* was set up and on the inner gate there were five big *manājiq,* one of them called the Angry One, and six more *'arrādāt.*[47] Other gates were similarly defended: the Baradān gate had four *shadākhāt* and eight *'arrādāt*, four on each side. Each *manjanīq* and *'arrāda* had men assigned to pull on the ropes and one man to fire (presumably to load and let go of the sling).[48] This description makes it clear that the siege engines were traction, not counter-weight, driven, that is to say that the short arm was brought down by men pulling on it. The whole programme of fortification must have been completed very rapidly and is said to have cost 330 000 *dīnār*s.[49]

Something of the appearance of the fortifications at Baghdad can be seen from the surviving remains of the walls at Raqqa.[50] Here the walls enclosed an area approximately D-shaped, with the straight line flanking the Euphrates. There was an outer and an inner wall, as at Baghdad. The inner wall was defended by large, round towers, faced with fired brick, resting on a stone foundation. The towers appear to have been solid and, since they are ruined to a fairly low level, there are no surviving traces of wall-head defences.

The only early 'Abbasid fortification of which substantial remains still exist is the castle palace of al-Ukhaydir, some 50 km into the desert to the west of Karbalā in southern Iraq.[51] This vast *qaṣr* was almost certainly built by the 'Abbasid prince 'Īsā b. Mūsā after his retreat into internal exile in around 159/776. The palace is a large fortified enclosure approximately 170 m square. The outside wall is almost intact up to the wall-head level at 17 m. There are round towers at each corner, ten half-round towers at regular intervals on each side and quarter-round towers flanking each of the three gates. The surface of the walls is not flat but articulated by two, tall, pointed blind arches between each of the towers. All the towers are solid and there are no arrow slits or other openings in the walls.

At the wall-head, there was a covered walkway. On the exterior, this opened into a chamber at the top of each tower. Every one of these rooms is now ruined but it is likely that they had arrow slits facing outwards and sideways. Along the wall-head, there are also arrow slits accessible from the passage.

The gates are more complex than anything surviving from Umayyad military architecture. They are vaulted halls about 10 m in length. Above them there are two stories of vaulted chambers, in the same position as those described above the original gates of the Round City of Baghdad, only vaulted, not domed. Near the outer end, there is clear evidence of a groove for a portcullis or rising door. With the hall (*dihlīz*) and the groove for the portcullis outside the main door, the gates at al-Ukhaydir look very much like a simplified version of the gate described in the account of the second siege of Baghdad.

The evidence from al-Ukhaydir suggests that the military architecture here was much more developed than anything seen in the Umayyad *quṣūr*. This can be seen in the arrow slits at the wall-head and in the towers and the provision of a portcullis. The palace was clearly designed so that attack could be resisted by archers. This may be because the early 'Abbasid builders or their patron put more emphasis on defence but it may be in part a result of the accidents of survival: as has been noted, Qaṣr al-Ḥayr al-Sharqī is the only one of the Umayyad buildings in which any of the wall head defences have survived, and these are very fragmentary. Nevertheless, the fact that the chambers on top of the towers at Qaṣr al-Ḥayr al-Sharqī have no arrow slits and the gates are simple entrances, does suggest that the military aspects of the architecture were genuinely less developed. The probable builder of the palace, 'Īsā b. Mūsā had good reason to fear for his life, and it may be that this is reflected in the architecture of his palace. No other early 'Abbasid military building is sufficiently well preserved to show whether this was unique or commonplace.

We know from accounts in the literary sources that the 'Abbasids devoted considerable resources to building of fortifications on the Byzantine frontier. Al-Balādhurī's account of the frontiers tells of the rebuilding of cities (*mudūn*, sing., *madīna*) and fortresses (*ḥuṣūn*, sing., *ḥiṣn*) from Tarsus in the west to Malatya in the east during the early 'Abbasid period.[52] The great men of the state and occasionally even Caliphs themselves played an active part in this. Unfortunately the sources tell us little about the military architecture. Various materials were used: Malatya was rebuilt in stone while nearby al-Ḥadath was built in mud-brick (*labin*) which disintegrated in the winter rains.[53] The building of the fortifications was probably done largely by the soldiers themselves, but we do hear of professional workmen (*fa'ala*) being recruited. At the rebuilding of Malatya in 140/757 al-Ḥasan b. Qaḥṭaba ordered special rewards for those who reached the battlements (*sharaf*) of their part of the wall first and the work, including the construction of the mosque, was completed in six months.[54]

The archaeological record of this activity is meagre. Some sites like Tarsus and

Adana in the Cilician plain have been completely built over, others like Malatya and al-Ḥadath have simply not been investigated. However, the magnificent survey work of Robert Edwards in Cilicia has produced one or two sites which may be ascribed to ʿAbbasid work in this period.[55]

The ʿAbbasids built a series of small forts which seem to have been designed to control the passes which led through the Amanus mountains from the Cilician plain in the west to Marʿash and Dābiq further east. The fort at Haruniye was built on the orders of the Caliph Hārūn al-Rashīd in around 183/799 and, remarkably, the village still bears his name today. The Arab geographers describe it as a 'small fort' (*ḥiṣn ṣaghīr*), which perfectly describes the small, oblong enclosure castle, about 75 m × 30 m, surveyed by Edwards.[56] He notes that 'the design is much too compact to be Armenian' and that there are three stages of building on the same plan, the earliest being in squared limestone and basalt masonry. The entrance is a simple gate between two square towers while at the other end there is a postern flanked by a large D-shaped tower. The north curtain is penetrated by a row of arched embrasures with arrow slits with a rounded stirrup arch at the bottom. Edwards claims that the embrasures are 'the only certain examples of Arab embrasures in Cilicia'. If this were true, it would show that the wall was penetrated by arrow slits in a way found in no other early Islamic fortifications where, we have seen, the arrow slits were to be found only at the wall-head level. Unfortunately the dating is obscure, and it seems more likely that the construction dates from a later period; it may be only the design of the ground plan which dates back to the original foundation.

Some 20 km south-west of Haruniye lies the site of Karafrenk.[57] There are reasons for believing that this the site known to the Arabs as Kanīsat al-Sawdā (the Black Church),[58] which is said to have been fortified and garrisoned during the reign of Hārūn al-Rashīd. Unlike Haruniye, the surviving structure at Karafrenk, now incorporated into several houses, clearly resembles other early Islamic fortifications. It is a small, square enclosure, some 15 m across. At each corner there are solid round towers which now stand to a height of about 5 m. There is no evidence of the provision of arrow slits in the curtain wall. The style of military architecture is unlike either Armenian, Crusader or Mamlūk work and an early Islamic origin is plausible. If this is true. it offers an important insight into the establishment of the frontier, showing a small but carefully planned military establishment.

There are a number of other sites for which I believe it is possible to suggest an early Islamic origin. In his geographical survey of Cilicia, Ibn al-ʿAdīm mentions a number of small fortresses in the Tarsus area including Ḥiṣn ʿUjayf, Ḥiṣn Shākir, Ḥiṣn al-Jawzāt and a number of towers.[59] None of these have been securely identified. Edwards has identified a number of small military sites in the Tarsus area whose origins and ancient names are quite unknown. These include Yaka,[60] Tece[61] and perhaps Tumil[62] on the route west from the city and Kutluku[63] to the north-east. All these are small, rectangular enclosure castles, Tece,[64] Tumil and Kutluku all have round corner towers, solid in the case of Tece, hollow at Tumil and Kutluku. Yaka has fragments of rectangular and rounded hollow towers. There are no surviving arrow slits in either the towers or the curtain walls, but all the sites are fairly ruined. Edwards suggests that these are Crusader sites, but on stylistic grounds these could equally well be early Islamic.[65]

A fragmentary inscription in the name of the Caliph al-Mutawwakil recovered at 'Ain Zarba led Hellenkemper to assign one of the defensive walls to the 'Abbasid period, but this is not at all certain.[66] At Amida (Diyarbakr) inscriptions record the rebuilding of the Harput and Mardin gates in 909 on the orders of the Caliph al-Muqtadir.[67]

Conclusion

Siege warfare played a comparatively small part in the military activities of the armies of the Caliphs. In the first two centuries of Islam, there seems to have been a dislike for static and restricted forms of warfare and no evidence for organised siegecraft. Only in armies of the Samarra period and after is there evidence of specialist forces. Cities, citadels and individual buildings were certainly fortified, though often as much for display as for defence.

Notes

1 Bal., *Ansāb*, v, 301.
2 Ṭa., iii, 491–2; for the *khandaq* and its uses, see pp. 26–7.
3 Ṭa., iii, 821–2.
4 Ṭa., iii, 630–3; Bal., *Ansāb*, v, 227–8.
5 Ṭa., iii, 734–8, 749; Bal., *Ansāb*, v, 260–1.
6 Ṭa., iii, 1796: *'ajam* are often Persians but the term can be used for any Arabs and, given the geographical location close to Palmyra, Roman is probably more likely.
7 For the plan and a brief description, see A. Musil, *Palmyrena* (New York, 1928a), 141–3.
8 Ṭa., iii, 1796–1807.
9 See pp. 109–11, 134–6 for accounts of these sieges.
10 The best accounts discussions of Muslim siege engines see P. E. Chevedden, 'The Artillery of King James the Conqueror' in P. E. Chevedden *et al.* (eds), *Iberia and the Mediterranean World of the Middle Ages* (Leiden, 1996), 47–94 and P. E. Chevedden, 'The Hybrid Trebuchet' in D. Kagay and T. Vann (eds), *On the Social Origins of Mediaeval Institutions* (Leiden, 1998), 179–200; see also C. E. Bosworth, *'Ḥiṣār'*, in EI2. I have followed Chevedden's conclusions in this account. For siege weapons in the contemporary Byzantine armies, see J. Haldon, *Warfare, State and Society in the Byzantine World, 565–1204* (London, 1999), 134–8.
11 Ṭa., i, 2427.
12 Ṭa., ii, 844–5; *Ansāb*, v, 362–3.
13 Ṭa., ii, 1244–5.
14 The siege is described in Bal., *Ansāb*, v, 301–4: the author was clearly more interested in the poetry generated by the conflict than the mechanics of siege warfare.
15 See pp. 109–11 for further details.
16 Chevedden, 'The Hybrid Trebuchet', 188–9.
17 Ṭa., iii, 1245.
18 See p. 155.
19 Ṭa., ii, 1692; Michael the Syrian, iii, 95.

20 M. Gough, ‘Anavarza’, *Anatolian Studies*, 2 (1952), 85–120.
21 See articles ‘Burdj’ and ‘Sūr’, EI2.
22 ‘Sūr’, EI2.
23 Ṭa., ii, 1893–4.
24 Ṭa., iii, 373–4.
25 al-Azdī, 25.
26 Michael the Syrian, iii, 31.
27 On Merv, see H. Kennedy ‘Medieval Merv: An Historical Overview’, in G. Herrmann, *Monuments of Merv: Traditional Buildings of the Karakum* (London, 1999), 27–44.
28 For Rayy and other ancient city sites in Iran, see the superb aerial photographs in E. F. Schmidt, *Flights over the Ancient Cities of Iran* (Chicago, 1940).
29 Theophanes, 588.
30 al-Azdī, 285–6.
31 Michael the Syrian, iii, 22, 27.
32 Michael the Syrian, iii, 75.
33 For a full description and discussion, see J. Wood, ‘The Fortifications’, in A. Northedge, *Studies on Roman and Islamic ‘Amman* (Oxford, 1992), 105–27.
34 Wood, ‘The Fortifications’, 107, 124.
35 Wood, ‘The Fortifications’, 162.
36 On Anjar, see R. Hillenbrand, ‘Anjar and Early Islamic Urbanism’ in G. P. Brogiolo and B. Ward-Perkins (eds), *The Idea and Ideal of the Town Between Late Antiquity and the Early Middle Ages* (Leiden, 1999), 59–98 (with full bibliography).
37 On Kharana, see S. K. Urice, *Qasr Kharana in the Transjordan* (Durham, 1987).
38 On Qaṣr al-Ḥayr al-Sharqī, see O. Grabar, *City in the Desert*, 2 vols (Cambridge, Mass., 1978). Still useful for the discussion of the walls is the account in K. A. C. Creswell, *Early Muslim Architecture*, 2 vols (Oxford, 1932–40), i, 330–49; see also K. A. C. Creswell, *A Short Account of Early Muslim Architecture*, rev. and supplemented by J. W. Allan (hereafter, ‘Cresswell, rev. Allan’), 149–64.
39 See pp. 189–90.
40 For the Byzantine origin of this type of box-machicolation, see Creswell, *Early Muslim Architecture*, i, 345–7 and Creswell, rev. Allan, 163.
41 Creswell, *Early Muslim Architecture*, i, 336, fig. 410.
42 Creswell, ‘Fortification in Islam before 1250’, *Proceedings of the British Academy* (1952), 91–108.
43 Ṭa., iii, 1551–2. The covered area is later referred to as a *sarab*, Ṭa., iii, 1559.
44 The word, which is not attested elsewhere, comes from a root meaning ‘to crush’. The Ṭabarī glossator, with uncharacteristic vagueness, simply describes it as ‘machina bellica defensioni portae destinata’ and Dozy and the translator (Saliba) have followed this.
45 Ṭa., iii, 1551.
46 See pp. 190 for the description of the gate at al-Ukhaydir which has both a large *dihlīz* and provision for a portcullis.
47 Ṭa., iii, 1551. There are a number of problems with this passage; the text is doubtful in at least one place and it really makes sense only if we understand ‘inner’ by ‘outer’ and vice versa (since it is logical to suppose that the heavier artillery was mounted on the inner gate, the single *‘arrāda* on the outer), but it is important as the clearest description we have of fortified gates.
48 Ṭa., iii, 1552.
49 Ṭa., iii, 1551.
50 M. Meinecke, *Patterns of Stylistic Changes in Islamic Architecture* (New York, 1996), 5–30; M. Meinecke article, ‘Rakka’, EI2; Creswell, *Early Muslim Architecture*, ii, 39–42; Creswell rev. Allan, 243–4; M. al-Khalaf, ‘Die ‘abbāsidische Stadtmauer von ar-Raqqa/ar-Rāfiqa’, *Damaszener Mitteilungen*, 2 (1985), 123–31.

51 The best account remains is still Creswell's in *Early Muslim Architecture*, ii, 50–100, where a strong case is made for ascribing the building to 'Īsā b. Mūsā: attempts to find alternative patrons are unconvincing, see Creswell, ed. Allan, 248–64.
52 Bal., *Futūḥ*, 163–71, 183–92.
53 Bal., *Futūḥ*, 187, 191.
54 Bal., *Futūh*, 187.
55 R. W. Edwards, *The Fortifications of Cilician Armenia* (Dumbarton Oaks, 1987).
56 Edwards, *The Fortifications*, 143–7, pls. 96–100.
57 Edwards, *The Fortifications*, 154–7, pls. 111–14.
58 The evidence of the literary sources is discussed in Edwards, *The Fortifications*, 156, n. 3.
59 Ibn al-'Adīm, *Bughya*, 209–13.
60 Edwards, *The Fortifications*, 265–7, pls. 270–1.
61 Edwards, *The Fortifications*, 241–4, pls. 232–4.
62 Edwards, *The Fortifications*, 254–5, pls. 249–50.
63 Edwards, *The Fortifications*, 169–71, pls. 132–3.
64 The tower in the centre of the enclosure at Tece is clearly not early Islamic and may well be Crusader but may have been built later than the enceinte, to which it is not physically connected.
65 Edwards suggests that they are Crusader basically because they are not Armenian, which is clearly the case, and because of the masonry. However, there is little evidence of Crusader settlement in this area and the simple rectangular castrum plan is not found in Crusader work of the late twelfth and thirteenth centuries. On the other hand, there is evidence of early Islamic fortification in the area and the surviving remains are not incompatible with such a dating. The use of Edwards' style IX masonry (a squared ashlar) could again be early Islamic, as illustrated by the earliest phase of construction at Haruniye where style IX is employed.
66 Gough, 'Anavarza', 85–120, 98; H. Hellenkemper, *Bürgen der Kreuzritterzeit in der Grafschaft Edessa und im Königreich Kleinarmenien* (Bonn, 1976), 196.
67 Sinclair, *Eastern Turkey: An Architectural and Archaeological Survey*, 4 vols (London, 1990), iii, 170–6.

CHAPTER NINE

Postscript

The granting of the title of Amīr al-umarā (Amir of Amirs) to Ibn Rā'iq in 324/936 marked the end of the armies of the Caliphs. It was a story which had begun when the Caliph 'Umar (13-23/634-44), or whoever was responsible, established the *dīwān* and settled the Muslims in the *amṣār*. When this happened, certain rules were established which were to guide the military and political development of the early Muslim State. Above all, there was the idea that there should be an army paid cash salaries out of the proceeds of general taxation. It was inevitable that Caliphs who wished to make their authority real and effective would wish to take control of this process. As the numbers of Muslims increased, it was inevitable, too, that only some of them would be paid soldiers: the Muslim community would become divided between soldiers and civilians. Given the importance of the military in the fiscal and hence political structure of the state, this came also to be a distinction between rulers and subjects.

If 'Umar had not settled the conquering Muslims in the *amṣār* and established the *dīwān*, a landed military aristocracy might have emerged as it did in Western Europe, an aristocracy not directly dependent on the State for its subsistence, but living on the proceeds of its estates. This in turn might have meant less military control of the State and, almost paradoxically, more freedom of manoeuvre for the ruler.

Throughout the early Caliphate, the principle was maintained that the military should be paid out of the receipts of taxation. But they were not to collect these dues themselves: they were dependant on the *dīwān* and its bureaucrats, and ultimately on the Caliph, to pay them.

The system had a profound effect on the economic life of the Islamic world. One of the most obvious contrasts between the Muslim world of the early Middle Ages and contemporary Byzantine and Western European polities was the extent to which the Muslim world operated a monetary economy. Taxes were paid in cash, goods services and soldiers were paid for in cash. As we have seen, most of the monies collected by the State were paid to the soldiery. And because the soldiers were increasingly specialised and professional, they paid for both everyday supplies and luxury goods in cash. Whether in cities or on campaign, the military provided a market which attracted merchants from far and wide, to sell them goods or to buy their booty. If the early Caliphs had permitted or encouraged the Muslims to settle the land they had conquered and live off its produce, such a thriving monetary economy might never have developed. Coins would have become as rare, and as useless for everyday life, as they were in the Christian world.

The creation of a new army by al-Muʿtaṣim (218-227/833-42) has often been seen as a turning point. Historians have frequently drawn attention to the idea of military slavery or slave soldiers as characteristic of Islamic society and have seen the origins of the 'Mamlūk Institution' in the military reforms of al-Muʿtaṣim. Looked at from this perspective, the adoption of slave soldiers can be seen as the failure of the early Muslim polity to generate a functioning civil society. But the issue of the legal status of soldiers in the Caliphate remains something of an irrelevance. Perhaps the most striking feature of the discussion is that we simply do not know whether the majority of the *mawālī* and *ghilmān* in the armies of the Caliphs in the third/ninth and early fourth/tenth centuries served as free or unfree men, and how this affected their role in practical terms. The troops who formed the last armies of the Caliphs were paid salaries – or, at least, they were supposed to be paid salaries – they had families and children (apart, that is, from the small proportion who were eunuchs) and they came and went as they pleased. It was only the need to earn a living which kept them in service.

The characteristic feature of the armies of the Caliphs in the Samarra and post-Samarra years was not their legal status but the fact that they were recruited from groups and areas which were marginal to the main Muslim community, both geographically (coming mostly from Transoxania, or the Caucasus) or ethnically (being in many cases Turks, as opposed to Arabs or Iranians). This position, was, however, a logical consequence of developments which had occurred much earlier. In the days of the early Caliphate, most of the Muslims, both Arabs and converts, had formed the military and been paid pensions. It was under 'Abd al-Malik (65-86/685-705) and his right-hand man al-Ḥajjāj, that this began to change. They realised that if the rule of the Caliphs was to be effective, they needed a military force which depended on the state for its salaries (rather than the hereditary right to a share of the *fay'*) and which accepted these salaries as payment for military service. The Syrians, the *ahl al-Shām*, became the first professional army in Islam and, as far as many Muslims in other areas were concerned, they were an alien military élite. The 'Abbasid revolution of 132/750 meant the replacement of the *ahl al-Shām* by the *ahl Khurāsān* and their *Abnā'* in Baghdad. When al-Muʿtaṣim sought to reconstruct the 'Abbasid army after the divisions and traumas of civil war, he turned to Transoxanians, both Turkish and Iranian and, to a lesser extent, men from the Caucasus and North Africa.

The choice of men from these marginal areas to form the élite of the armed forces was not because others refused to join up or because most Muslims disdained to serve a Caliphate which they felt had abandoned the ways of true Islam. The grandees of Hārūn al-Rashīd's court may have regarded rank-and-file soldiers with contempt, the *'ulamā* may have regarded them with fear and loathing (though we have no real evidence for this). But, because of the system of salary payments being in the military was regarded as a desirable career. Many of the major political confrontations in the Caliphate were caused by conflicts between different groups competing to be part of the army. In Umayyad times, the Iraqis resented the role of the Syrians as the military élite, in early 'Abbasid times, Syrians were desperate to be taken on as soldiers. The civil war in Baghdad was prolonged after the death of al-Amīn in 198/813 by different groups who wanted to form part of the military.

Given this enthusiasm, why did Caliphs of the third/ninth century look to marginal peoples? The dependence of the military on the state, and hence their need to control it, meant that Caliphs were reluctant to entrust military powers to subjects who were already well established on the political stage, even to close relatives. How much more efficient it would be, or so it seemed, to have a military drawn from outsiders, non-Arabs, non-Muslims even non-men (eunuchs). It was partly because they came with no political baggage: being, at least in the beginning, deracinated, they might be thought to be loyal to the Caliph alone, whereas recruits from nearer home would have their own political agenda. They might also bring skills, especially in horsemanship and mounted archery, which the peoples of the Islamic heartlands could not offer. But the effect of relying on these marginal groups was to alienate and disenfranchise most ordinary Muslims. Now reduced to the status of tax-paying subjects, they would feel little incentive to support the political power of the Caliphate.

The restriction of the army to certain groups was not just a result of Caliphal policy. It was also because of pressure from the military themselves. It all came back to the old question: who was entitled to the *fay'*, or, in third/ninth-century terms, who was to be paid salaries. Groups who were part of the military violently resented the attempts of outsiders to claim a share of the resources which taxation provided. The *ahl al-Shām* complained bitterly when, in the last days of the Umayyad Caliphate, there was talk of sharing the *fay'* of Iraq with the Iraqis. Attempts to forge an alliance between the *Abna'* of Baghdad and the Syrians against al-Ma'mūn's forces foundered on the refusal of the Baghdad forces to share their status with the Syrians. The assassination of the Caliph al-Mutawwakil in 247/861, which began the anarchy in Samarra, seems to have been, at least in part, because the Turkish military were afraid that the Caliph was favouring rival groups to challenge their monopoly of the military élite. The débâcle of al-Muqtadir's rule was precipitated by the desire of military groups like the Maṣāffiya and Ḥujariya to exclude their rivals from the enjoyment of ever more limited resources. When the vizier, 'Alī b. 'Īsā suggested that the government would be better off employing the bedouin than the existing military, he may have had a point, but it could never have happened: the existing army would never have tolerated rivals.

This lay at the heart of the problem. The new military was wholly dependent on the state for its very survival. Isolated and feared by most of the population, their main, and increasingly their only, concern was to dominate the State apparatus. If a Caliph was unwilling, or unable to satisfy their demands, then the Caliph would have to be replaced. The middle 'Abbasid Caliphate had, in a real sense, become a military dictatorship in which government functioned only as a vehicle for maintaining an army whose only function was to maintain itself. As the resource base remorselessly declined, the competition became more bitter until finally the military, with its desperation and short-termism, destroyed the political power of the Caliphate entirely.

APPENDIX 1

The origins of the shākiriya

In accounts of the army of Samarra, there are numerous references to a regiment called the *shākiriya*. The nature and identity of this group is never discussed in the sources and we can only speculate on where they were recruited, how they were paid, and the significance of the name itself. The term *shākiriya* has been the subject of some discussion in the academic literature[1] but this has not entirely succeeded in clarifying its meaning and importance. The word seems to be an Arabization of the Persian *chākir*, meaning either a household servant or the personal guard of a ruler or other important figure. In the history of the Umayyad period, there are a number of mentions of the *shākiriya* of important military and political figures. However, with one exception,[2] the term is used only in a Transoxanian context.

In 77/696 the brothers Ḥurayth and Thābit b. Quṭba appear among the commanders of the Umayyad forces in Transoxania. They are described as *mawālī* of the Arab tribe of Khuzāʿa, but from the context they were clearly important figures in local society who had converted to Islam and thrown in their lot with the Arabs. In 82/701 they are recorded as having an escort of 300 *shākiriya* and Arabs who were attached to them (*munqaṭaʿūn lahumā*).[3] Later we hear of Thābit being guarded by his *shākiriya* at night while on campaign.[4]

The Banū Quṭba brothers were not the only Transoxanian aristocrats to have their *shākiriya*. Ṭarkhūn, the Ikhṣhīd of Soghdia and leader of the local princes, had a *shākiriya* who lit camp fires for him and were supposed to guard him from surprise attack.[5] We also find them hunting with their masters[6] and providing a 'Tibetan horn' as an improvised drinking vessel.[7] In addition to these quasi-domestic roles, *shākiriya* are recorded as taking part in military campaigns, along with other soldiers, either on the Muslim side[8] or on the side of their enemies.[9]

The question of the social status of these soldiers is problematic. Narshakhī gives a description of the queen of Bukhārā being attended by a *shākiriya* drawn from the sons of members of the local nobility and arrayed in great splendour, from which Barthold concluded that the *shākiriya* was a sort of military household, or *comitatus*, of young nobles similar to those found in mediaeval Europe from Carolingian times.[10] In fact it seems more likely that the description of the Queen's retinue is given to make the point that she was exceptional, rather than that this aristocratic *shākiriya* was the norm.

Further evidence for the comparatively humble status of the *shākiris* can be found in two anecdotes from the Umayyad period in Transoxania. In one of them, Sulaymān b. Ṣūl, who may in fact have been of princely origin, was sent as an ambassador to the ruler of Farghāna. On being asked by the ruler who he was, he answered that he was 'a *shākirī* of the deputy secretary of the Amir'.[11] The implication seems to be that he was man of no great consequence who was simply obeying orders. More telling is a story about Ghūrak, the local prince of Samarqand. In the aftermath of the disastrous Arab defeat by the Khāqān of the Turks at the Battle of the Pass in 112/730, a group of fugitives were hunted down by Ghūrak, the local ruler of Samarqand, who had been fighting on the same side as the Turks. He offered them a safe-conduct (*aman*) which they accepted but when they came to the Khāqān, he refused to accept the safe conduct and the Muslims knew they would be slaughtered. When they reproached Ghūrak, he excused himself with the words, 'I am a slave of the Khāqān from his *shākiriya*.'[12] At one level this suggests that the *shākiriya* of a great ruler like the Khāqān could indeed be made up of aristocrats, but in context it may mean something different. Ghūrak was trying to say that he could not be held responsible because as a member of the *shākiriya* he was equivalent to an *'abd* (slave) and had no power to make independent decisions. Whether he was a formal member of the *shākiriya*, or whether he was simply using this as a excuse for his failure to protect the lives of those who had surrendered, is impossible to know.

The evidence from the Umayyad period suggests that in the first phase of the development of the *shākiriya* the term refers to the military retinues of Iranian princes and others in Transoxania. There is no clear record of an Arab being served by a *shākiriya* and the Arab followers of the Banū Quṭba are clearly distinguished from their (non-Arab) *shākiriya*. Their social status is not clear: the men who lit Ṭarkhūn's camp fires and fled so ignominiously when his tent was attacked are unlikely to have been aristocratic. There is no indication that they were slaves, but some that they were bound to accept the decisions of their masters.

The *shākiriya* of the 'Abbasids

Curiously, the 'Abbasid Revolution, which brought so many Iranian ideas and personnel to the central Islamic lands, saw the almost complete disappearance of the term *shākiriya* from the historical record. We hear of *shākiriya* in a letter written by Ṭāhir to al-Ma'mūn explaining the circumstances of the killing of his brother al-Ma'mūn. In it he explains how he posted a group of his most trusted men (*khāṣṣa thiqātī*) and his *shākiriya* both horsemen and foot) to prevent al-Amīn's escape.[13] In this case, the term is clearly being used by a Khurāsāni noble (Ṭāhir) in the sense of a military retinue. The term reappears in the reign of al-Mu'taṣim with an enigmatic notice, dated 225/839–40, to the effect that the Caliph arrested Ja'far b. Dīnār al-Khayyāṭ 'on account of his attack on the *shākiriya* who were with him'.[14] By the reign of al-Wāthiq, if not before, a group called the *shākiriya* had become part of the regular forces of the Caliphal armies –

a regiment, in effect, with its own identity. In 230/844–5, 200 *shākiriya* horsemen were sent to the Hijaz to try to control the depredations of the Banū Sulaym bedouin.[15] By the time of al-Mutawwakil's accession in 232/847 they had become an important political force. In conjunction with the soldiers simply known as the *jund*, they became a counter-weight to the power of the Turks and the new Caliph seems to have shown his favour to them by paying them an accession bonus which was twice that offered to the Turks and the Maghāriba.[16] Later in al-Mutawwakil's reign, the heir-apparent, al-Muntaṣir, was made to swear that he would not deprive his brothers of the services of any of their commanders, *jund, shākiriya, mawālī* or *ghilmān*.[17]

As far as we can tell from the sources, the *shākiriya* always served as cavalry, and seem to have had their own stables.[18] As with other military groups at this time, numbers were fairly small; we hear of the 40 *shākiriya* who came to Baghdad from Samarra,[19] of 500 *shākiriya* cavalry being sent out from Baghdad.[20] The 1300 from Raqqa were the largest, and many forces were much smaller.

The *shākiriya* of the Samarra period were part of the regular army of the Caliph. They probably numbered several thousand and were paid, normally, salaries on a regular basis like other elements in the army. There was a separate *dīwān* in Samarra for the *jund* and the *shākiriya*.[21]

In contrast to the Turks, who were stationed almost entirely in Samarra, with a small force in Egypt, the *shākiriya* were more widely dispersed. Some of them were stationed on *qaṭā'i'* in Samarra[22] but their main strength seems to have lain in Baghdad, Raqqa and along the Makka (pilgrimage) Road and perhaps in Azerbayjān, where 900 of them were despatched by al-Mutawwakil to fight the rebel Ibn al-Ba'īth.[23] There were also *shākiriya* permanently stationed in Egypt[24] and Fārs.[25]

Their ethnic origins are not clear but there is some evidence that they were of Khurasani origin: al-Ya'qūbī describes how there was *qaṭā'i'* in Samarra for 'the commanders from Khurāsān and their followers [*aṣḥāb*] in the *jund* and the *shākiriya*',[26] and al-Ṭabarī describes the *shākiriya* and the Farāghina being led by Khurāsānī commanders.[27] One of the few *shākirī* commanders to be named was 'Abd Allāh b. Maḥmūd, whose *nisba* al-Sarakhsī clearly shows that he was of Khurasani origin.[28]

Politically they seem to have identified with the interests of the Tahirids of Baghdad. When in 235/849 Isḥāq b. Ibrāhīm, the Tahirid governor of Baghdad, was entrusted with the delicate task of luring Ītākh, the Turkish leader, to the place where he was to be killed in Baghdad, he was supported by a group of *shākiriya*.[29] The formal investiture of al-Musta'īn in Samarra in 248/862 was disrupted by the appearance of 50 *shākiriya* horsemen from the *aṣḥāb* of Muḥammad b. 'Abd Allāh the Tahirid,[30] somewhat ironically in view of Muḥammad's subsequent role as al-Musta'īn's chief supporter.

The links between the *shākiriya* and the Tahirid family, especially Muḥammad b. 'Abd Allāh, are most apparent in the war between the supporters of al-Mu'tazz in Samarra and the supporters of al-Musta'īn in Baghdad in 251/865–6. Muḥammad

b. 'Abd Allāh was the governor of the city and the main organiser of the defence and the *shākiriya* formed an important element in the Baghdad forces. *Shākiriya* from other areas of the Caliphate came to Baghdad to join the defenders, including 300 from the Makka Road[31] and 1300 from Raqqa.[32] Al-Ḥusayn b. Ismā'īl, a member of a junior branch of the Tahirid family, was one of the main commanders of the *shākiriya* in the later stages of the civil war.

The political settlement which ended the siege of Baghdad seems to have led to a breach between the *shākiriya* and Ibn Ṭāhir, who they felt had sold out to al-Mu'tazz and the Samarra faction, and there were riots when their pay was not forthcoming.[33] As a result of this protest, they seem to have to have maintained their position in the city and were still being paid their salaries (*murtazaqa*) in 255/869.[34]

The death of Muḥammad b. 'Abd Allāh in Dhū'l-Qa'da 253/November 867 further widened the breach between the Tahirids and the *shākiriya.* He was replaced in 255/869 by his brother Sulaymān b. 'Abd Allāh, who arrived from Khurāsān with a considerable number of new troops and *sa'ālīk* from Rayy. These newcomers were led by a brutal and rapacious military man called Muḥammad b. Aws al-Balkhī, who had already acquired an unsavoury reputation for his activities in Ṭabaristān. There then began a virtual civil war in Baghdad between Ibn Aws and the newcomers on one hand and the *shākiriya* and other Baghdadis on the other. The latter were led by 'their' Tahirid, al-Ḥusayn b. Ismā'īl and al-Shāh b. Mīkāl, described elsewhere as the *mawlā* of Tahir.[35] The issue, as so often, was money. Ibn Aws demanded that his men should be paid from the revenues of the Tahirid estates in Iraq. This would have meant that there was no money to pay the *shākiriya.* After a short conflict, during which Sulaymān looked on helplessly, Ibn Aws and his followers were driven from the city and retreated to the Nahrawān area, where they lived off pillage of the unfortunate local people. [36]

The *shākiriya* also played a political role in Samarra in the tumultuous events of al-Muhtadī's short reign. Again, they can be seen as opponents of the Turks in the city, escorting the Caliph out of danger[37] and involved in open conflict with the Turks, when one of their long-time commanders 'Attāb b. 'Attāb was killed.[38]

The *shākiriya* virtually disappear from the historical record after the settlement between the Caliph al-Mu'tamid, his brother al-Muwaffaq and the Turks in 256/870. Although we have no evidence, it is possible that the Turks made the disbanding of their long-standing rivals a condition of their acceptance of 'Abbasid authority. Other regiments, like the Farāghina and the Maghāriba also lost their identity at this time. Elements from the *shākiriya* may have continued to serve in Baghdad and some commanders closely associated with them still had important roles. As late as 271/884–5, al-Ḥusayn b. Ismā'īl was acting as *ṣāḥib al-shurṭa* in Baghdad on behalf of Muḥammad b.Ṭāhir[39] and it is possible that he employed some of his old *shākiriya* comrades in the police. Al-Shāh b. Mīkāl appears as one of the cavalry commanders in the war against the Zanj in 267/880–1[40] and his son Muḥammad was appointed to command the guard (*ḥaras*) by the Caliph al-Mu'taḍid on his accession in 279/892.[41] Again, it is possible that members of the old *shākiriya* served with him but there is no specific mention of them in the sources.

The information is scattered and often confusing but we can arrive at some tentative conclusions about the middle 'Abbasid *shākiriya*. They were regular, salaried members of the 'Abbasid armed force and they usually fought as cavalry. Elements of them were stationed in a number of provinces of the Caliphate but their main strength lay in Samarra and Baghdad. It is difficult to estimate numbers but, given the references we do have, the total number of effectives can hardly have been more than 5000. Such indications as we have suggest that they came from Khurāsān and were Iranian (and possibly Arab) by origin, not Turkish. Politically, they were closely associated with the interests of the Tahirid family in Baghdad.

The question remains as what connection, if any, these *shākiriya* had with their namesakes in the Umayyad period, especially as there is almost a century between the mentions of the *shākiriya* of the Khurasani leaders in Umayyad times and the appearance of the 'Abbasid *shākiriya*. On the other hand, the choice of the name for an élite group in the 'Abbasid army must have been intended to signify some connection. In this context, it should be remembered that the Tahirids were by origin Khurāsāni aristocrats, that is that they came from the same social group as those who had had *shākirī* retinues in Umayyad times. As we have seen, Ṭāhir himself had a *shākiriya* of his own during the siege of Baghdad. I would tentatively suggest that the *shākiriya* were recruited by the Tahirids in Khurāsān for service in Baghdad and the west, and that the use of the term was a sort of honorific, referring back to a heroic and chivalrous past. The Turkish soldiers are often referred to as the *mawālī* in this period and it may well be the *shākiriya* was chosen as a Persian equivalent of the Arabic word: it signified élite but dependent troops while at the same time, asserting their Iranian heritage.

Notes

1 See Fries, *Das Heereswesen der Araber zur Zeit der Omaijaden nach Ṭabarī* (Tübingen, 1921), 24–5; Ṭa., iii, 132–3 trans. (Bosworth), n. 506; Athāmina, 'Non-Arab Regiments and Private Militias during the Umayyad Period', *Arabica*, 40 (1998), 347–75, 363–4; C. I. Beckwith, 'Aspects of the Early History of the Central Asian Guard Corps in Islam', *Archivum Eurasiae Medii Aevi*, 4 (1984), 29–43, argues that *chakars* were the warrior retinue bound to the service of a Turkish chief: the evidence is interesting but not conclusive; Gordon, *The Breaking of a Thousand Swords: A History of the Turkish Community of Samarra, 200–275 AH/815–889 CE* (Albany, 2001), 40–2; I am grateful to Michael Bates for allowing me to see his unpublished paper on the *shākiriya* which provided some valuable information.

2 In 77/696–7 one Khālid b. 'Attāb is described (Ṭa., ii, 965) as leading his *shākiriya* against the Kharijites in Iraq. There are, however, a number of reasons for not taking this as evidence of a *shākiriya* at this stage. It is earlier than any other mention and is set in Iraq, whereas all the other Umayyad references are to Khurāsān, a country with which the Arab Khālid b. 'Attāb had no known connection. It is possible that some confusion has crept in with between Khālid b. 'Attāb and the Khurāsāni commander

'Attāb b. 'Attāb, who was one of the leaders of the *shākiriya* of Samarra in 265/870 (Ṭa., iii, 1826).

3 Ṭa., ii, 1082.
4 Ṭa., ii, 1155.
5 Ṭa,. ii, 1159–60.
6 Ṭa., ii, 1330–1.
7 Ṭa., ii, 1631.
8 Ṭa., ii, 1528.
9 Ṭa., ii, 1604 where the Khāqān is supported by the princes of Khurāsān and 'their *shākiriya*'.
10 Narshakhī, 9–10: Barthold, *Turkestan Down to the Mongol Invasion* (London, 1968), 180, 183; see also Beckwith, 'Aspects of the Early History of the Central Asian Guard Corps' for this view.
11 Ṭa., ii, 1695.
12 Ṭa., ii, 1542.
13 Ṭa., iii, 928. The letter, quoted in full on the authority of al-Madā'inī, shows every sign of being genuine. The translation (Bosworth) of *shākiriya* as 'hired men' can hardly be correct in this context.
14 Ṭa., iii, 1302–3.
15 Ṭa., iii, 1336–7.
16 Ṭa., iii, 1369–70.
17 Meaning their troops from all the main groups in the military. Ṭa., iii, 1398
18 Ṭa., iii, 1494 where it seems to be said that the deposed brothers of al-Muntaṣir would no longer have access to their mounts.
19 Ṭa., iii, 1560.
20 Ṭa., iii, 1605.
21 Ya'q., *Buldān*, 267.
22 Ya'q., *Buldān*, 259–60.
23 Ṭa., iii, 1380, 1381.
24 Ṭa., iii, 1430–1.
25 Ṭa., iii, 1534.
26 Ya'q., *Buldān*, 259.
27 Ṭa., iii, 1826.
28 Ṭa., iii, 1517, Sarakhs being near Merv.
29 Ṭa., iii, 1385.
30 Ṭa., iii, 1503–4.
31 Ṭa., iii, 1559.
32 Ṭa., iii, 1595.
33 Ṭa., iii, 1661–2.
34 Ṭa., iii, 1717.
35 Ṭa., iii, 1574.
36 Ṭa., iii, 1725–32.
37 Ṭa., iii, 1788.
38 Ṭa., iii, 1822.
39 Ṭa., iii, 2107.
40 Ṭa., iii, 1950, 1956.
41 Ṭa., iii, 2133.

APPENDIX 2

Numbers of the ʻAbbasid army in Samarra

Assessing the numbers of soldiers in early Islamic armies is always difficult. The figures we are given are usually, at best, approximations, at worst, wildly inaccurate. We cannot rely on the literary sources as anything more than a rough and sometimes mistaken guide. Any methodology which enables us to find more concrete data is therefore to be welcomed and treated very seriously.

Derek Kennet has recently developed an argument about the numbers of the ʻAbbasid army in Samarra based on the accommodation units in the cantonments.[1] Building on Herzfeld's original work, Northedge and Kennet have succeeded, convincingly, in identifying most of the areas of the city described in the sources, notably in al-Yāqūbī's, *Kitāb al-Buldān*. Kennet has then examined the areas which are known to have been settled by the commanders of the Turkish troops. Many, though not all, of these are well enough preserved to allow the number of units to be counted with some accuracy. In the area thought to have been al-Karkh, for example, there are 'a series of roughly square houses measuring between 10 m and 35 m on each side'.[2] Kennet then takes the *'irāfa* of ten men as the basic division of the army and suggests that one *'irāfa* was housed in each of the houses.[3] By multiplying the number of houses which can be traced on the ground by ten, he believes it is possible to estimate the overall numbers of troops.

The results Kennet comes up with are surprisingly large: he suggests that at the time of the first foundation of the city in the time of al-Mu'taṣim there were 94 353 soldiers living in cantonments[4] (of whom between 70 961 and 87 115 were Turks)[5] and that early in the reign of al-Mutawwakil (but before the development of his new city of al-Mutawwakiliya) this had risen to 156 678. This is much larger than the estimate produced by Töllner, who suggested between 20 000 and 30 000, of whom half were Turks.[6]

It is also much larger than the numbers mentioned in al-Ṭabarī's detailed narratives of the Samarra era. For instance, when Abū Aḥmad al-Muwaffaq led the armies of Samarra to attack Baghdad in the civil war with al-Musta'īn, he commanded 5000 Turks and Farāghina and 2000 Maghāriba.[7] When Mūsā b. Bughā led a campaign to bring al-Jibāl back under the Caliph's control in 253/867 he led an army of 2443 Turks and others. In the disturbed reign of al-Muhtadī, when the Turks were fighting for their survival as a military force in Samarra,

Ṣāliḥ b. al-Waṣīf managed to raise 5000 men,[8] most of whom soon drifted away; his opponent Mūsā b. Bughā made a show of strength with 4000 horsemen.[9] In the final push against the unfortunate Caliph the number of Turks 'had swollen to 10 000 men, united by their common cause'.[10] It should be emphasised that the struggle against the Baghdadis and the assertion of control over the Caliphate in the time of al-Muhtadī were causes that were likely to produce the maximum response from the Turks. In both cases they were fighting for the cause that they held most dear: their salaries. So if there were about 150 000 soldiers in Samarra, of whom up to 100 000 were Turks, this is not a very impressive turn-out; what were they all doing? Clearly something is wrong somewhere with our figures.

One of the problems may lie in the picture of the cantonment houses, each one of which held an *'irāfa*. It should be noted first that there is no direct evidence for this. The only parallel we have is the account in al-Balādhurī of the garrison in Malatya on the Byzantine frontier a century before, where an *'irāfa* of ten to fifteen men were settled in a house with four rooms and a stable.[11] This could provide the model for the cantonment house. But this assumes that all the Turks lived as single men in barracks. Now this was clearly not the case: al-Ya'qūbī says[12] that al-Mu'taṣim purchased slave girls for them who were married to them. The names of the girls and their offspring were recorded in the *dīwān*. This puts a different slant on the physical evidence. It might be possible, if a bit intimate, for ten men to live in each cantonment house, but hardly for ten families, particularly when it is remembered that these were comparatively affluent people by the standards of their day. In this context, we should also bear in mind al-Ya'qūbī's observation that the houses in Samarra were more extensive than those in Baghdad.[13] If we assumed that at least some of the cantonment houses were dwellings for individual families, it would clearly have a dramatic effect on the overall numbers, reducing them by anything up to 90 per cent.

But the problems with the archaeological evidence go further. The idea of the cantonment, essentially a grouping of barrack buildings in a confined area, may not be a helpful one. At first glance it is clearly logical to see these rows of near uniform structures as having been constructed by commanders to house their men, most of them Turks with no local contacts and, probably, no tradition of urban living. But there is no evidence for this in the written sources. There is no Arabic word for cantonment at all. Al-Ya'qūbī says that the Caliph and his military commanders built many buildings on their *qaṭā'i'*. These included mosques, baths and markets but there are no mention whatever of commanders constructing dwellings. Now it could be argued that this was because it was too obvious to be worth mentioning, but nonetheless, it should give rise to thought.

At the heart of Kennet's methodology, there is a simple assumption. He takes it as obvious that the soldiers lived in planned cantonments and civilians lived in area where the urban planning was less formal.[14] This is not, however, supported (or contradicted) by the sources since, as has already been noted, there is no mention at all of the building of dwellings for the troops, still less that they were laid out in this strictly orthogonal pattern. We do, however, have evidence that other buildings were laid out in straight line. When the first phase of the city was being laid out we are told that al-Mu'taṣim, 'laid out the lines (*ṣufūf*) of the sūqs', giving each trade and group a separate space as it was in Baghdad.[15] When al-Mutawwakil was developing the area around his new mosque, he laid out wide streets and rows of shops, each row of shops (*ṣaff al-ḥawānīt*) having its own trade. 'And from each row of shops to the one next door there were lanes [*durūb*] and alleys [*sikak*] in which were the lots [*qaṭā'i'*] of the common people.'[16] This is clearly describing a planned orthogonal layout of streets and plots, yet it is specifically said that these belong to the *'āmma*, the common people, and this was clearly not a military district but a commercial quarter.

How, then, should we understand the development of these quarters? Samarra grew extremely quickly. Not just soldiers but many workmen were brought to the city by the Caliphs and great numbers of merchants and craftsmen were attracted by the economic opportunities. Clearly large numbers of dwellings required to be built quickly. Are some of the regularly planned cantonments simply speculative building projects to house immigrants of all sorts to the city? Large sums of money were to be made (the rents of the city and its markets are said to have amounted to 10 million *dirham*s per year[17]) . In the rapidly developing industrial cities of nineteenth-century Britain, large numbers of dwellings were constructed in regular rows creating an essentially orthogonal townscape, but these were not barracks; they were built that way because it was the cheapest and quickest way to house large numbers of people in a rapidly developing city. This is not to deny that some of the planned housing may have been for soldiers and their families, indeed al-Ya'qūbī makes it clear that the Turks and Farāghina (though not apparently other soldiers) originally had separated quarters, but we have no real means of knowing how much of the planned development was occupied by the military or, conversely, how much unplanned development they occupied.

The archaeological evidence presented by Kennet shows clearly that the building in Samarra was divided in to formally planned areas and areas with a looser pattern of housing and streets . He has managed to identify many of these areas by name. What he does not demonstrate is that all the planned areas were for military occupation, still less that the military occupation was on the density he claims (since he has overlooked the possibility that many of these houses were family dwellings). From the point of view of urban design, élite dwellings and the political history, all this is very interesting: as a way of estimating the numbers of troops in Samarra it is, I would suggest, useless.

In privileging the numbers given in the written sources, I am not unaware that they may be unreliable in various ways but I am inclined to take them seriously. The events are close to al-Ṭabarī's own lifetime and his narratives are sober and matter of fact. There seems no good reason why he should have drastically reduced the numbers of troops involved; indeed, except in accounts of heroism against great odds, literary sources tend to inflate rather than depress numbers. Furthermore the numbers given, though not very often quoted, are generally consistent with each other in the general order of magnitude. None of this is proof positive and the discussion will no doubt continue but, until new evidence emerges, Töllner's estimate is the most convincing we have.

Notes

1 D. Kennet, 'Military Cantonments at Samarra', in C. F. Robinson (ed.), *Multi-disciplinary Approaches to Samarra: A Ninth-Century Islamic City* (Oxford, 2000). I am most grateful to Derek Kennet for allowing me to see this paper before publication: despite our disagreements on interpretation, I think this is a very valuable piece of work which marks a clear advance in our understanding and use of the archaeological sources.
2 Kennet, 'Military Cantonments', 2.
3 Kennet, 'Military Cantonments', 10.
4 Kennet, 'Military Cantonments', 14.
5 Kennet, 'Military Cantonments', 15.
6 Töllner, *Die türkischen Garden am Kalifenhof von Samarra, ihre Entstelhung und Machtergreifung bis zum Kalifat al Mu'taḍids* (Bonn, 1971), 45–48, noted by Kennet, 'Military Cantonments', 15; note also the numbers of slaves owned by al-Mu'taṣim, quoted by Pipes, *Slave Soldiers and Islam: The Genesis of a Military System* (New Haven, 1981).
7 Ta., iii, 1555.
8 Ṭa., iii, 1790.
9 Ṭa., iii, 1800.
10 Ṭa., iii, 1816. This very low turn-out would be all the more striking if, as Kennet, 'Military Cantonments', 16 suggests, 'the massive growth in numbers of troops at Samarra which he proposes was due to the power struggle between different parties at Samarra as commanders continued to recruit in order to boost their own standing'.
11 Kennet, 'Military Cantonments', 10.
12 Ya'q., *Buldān*, 258–9.
13 Ya'q., *Buldān*, 263, ll, 11–12.
14 Kennet, 'Military Cantonments', 'we can define areas occupied by ordinary civilians (which obviously result from numerous individual building projects rather than an overall scheme)'.
15 Ya'q., *Buldān*, 258, ll, 9–10.
16 Ya'q., *Buldān*, 265, ll, 14–19.
17 Ya'q., *Buldān*, 263, ll, 15–16.

Glossary

'abd	slave (cf. *mamlūk*)
Abnā' al-dawla	descendants of Khurāsānī supporters of the 'Abbasids, settled in Iraq
ahl	family or people, hence army, as in '*ahl al-Shām*', army of Syria
amīr	commander or governor
amīr al-mu'minīn	commander of the faithful, official title of the Caliph
'arīf	officer in charge of payment and discipline of small group (ten–fifteen) of soldiers
ashrāf	plural of *sharīf*
'aṭā'	pension paid to Muslims after the conquests, later salary paid to troops
dirham	silver coin
dīnār	gold coin (worth between 12 and 20 *dirhams*)
dīwān	list of troops registered for pay
fay'	total revenue yields from a province
fitna	civil war within the Muslim community (cf. *jihād*)
ghilmān	plural of *ghulām*
ghulām	originally boy or page; from third/ninth century soldier, usually mounted and of Turkish origin, sometimes of slave status
ḥajj	Muslim pilgrimage to Makka
ḥaras	guards of Caliph or governor
jāhilīya	time of 'ignorance' before the coming of Islam
jihād	holy war against non-Muslims
jund	army; in Syria, district or sub-province
khādim	servant, eunuch
kharāj	taxation, later specifically land-tax
khandaq	lit. ditch, hence camp fortified with earth or rubble ramparts
mamlūk	slave, owned person
mawālī	plural of mawlā
mawlā	(i) freedman, ex-slave; (ii) any non-Arab convert to Islam; (iii) rank-and-file Turkish soldier in the army of Samarra

miṣr	city founded for Muslims to settle in; provincial capital
muqātila	Muslim fighters entitled to *'aṭā'*
qāḍī	Muslim judge
qā'id	military officer
qaṣr	fortress or palace
qaṭā'i'	plural of *qaṭī'a*
qaṭī'a	plot of land given as private property
quwwād	plural of *qā'id*
rizq	originally supplies, payment in kind to troops, later military salary in any form
ṣāḥib al-shurṭa	commander of the *shurṭa*
ṣā'ifa	summer raid aganist the Byzantines
sharīf	member of Arab tribal aristocracy
shurṭa	military police
'urāfā'	plural of *'arīf*
wazīr	vizier, chief minister

Bibliography

Primary Sources

Primary sources are referred to in the notes under the abbreviated name of the author. Only when there are two works by the same author, like al-Balādhurī is a short title also given.

'Abd al-Ḥamīd b. Yaḥyā al-Kātib, *Risāla*, in, ed. Muḥammad Kurd 'Alī, *Rasā'il al-Bulaghā'* (Cairo, 1946), 173–210.

'Arīb: 'Arīb b. Sa'd al-Qurṭubī, *Ṣillat Ta'rīkh al-Ṭabarī*, ed. M. J. de Goeje (Leiden, 1897).

al-Azdī: al-Azdī, Abū Zakarīyā Yazīd b. Muḥammad, *Ta'rīkh al-Mawṣil*, ed. 'Alī Ḥabība (Cairo, 1967).

Bal., Ansāb: al-Balādhurī, Aḥmad b. Yaḥyā, *Ansāb al-Ashrāf*; there are two major, but partial editions of this text. The following are the editions I have referred to: *Anonyme Arabische Chronik Band XI*, ed. W. Ahlwardt (Leipzig, 1883); vol. III, ed. A. A. Ad-Duri (Wiesbaden, 1978); vol. IVA, ed. M. Schloessinger (Jerusalem, 1971); vol. IVB, ed. M. Schloessinger (Jerusalem, 1938); vol. V, ed. S. D. F. Goitein (Jerusalem, 1936); vol. VIB, ed. K. Athāmina (Jerusalem, 1993).

——Futūḥ: al-Balādhurī, Aḥmad b. Yaḥyā, *Futūh al-Buldān*, ed. M. J. de Goeje (Leiden, 1866, repr. Leiden, 1968).

al-Dīnawarī, Abū Ḥanīfa Aḥmad b. Dāwūd, *Al-Akhbār al-Ṭiwāl* eds V. Guirgass and I. I. Krachkovskii (Leiden, 1912).

Fihrist: *see* al-Nadīm.

al-Harthamī, *Mukhtaṣar Siyāsat al-Ḥurub*, ed. 'Abd al-Ra'ūf 'Awn (Cairo, 1964).

al-Hilāl b. al-Muḥassin al-Ṣābī, *al-Wuzarā'*, ed. 'Abd al-Sattār Aḥmad Farrāj (Cairo, 1958).

Ibn 'Abd al-Ḥakam, Abū'l-Qāsim 'Abd al-Raḥmān b. 'Abd Allāh, *Futūḥ Miṣr*, ed. C. C. Torrey (New Haven, 1921).

Ibn al-'Adīm, Kamāl al-Dīn, *Bughyat al-Ṭalab fī Ta'rīkh Ḥalab*, ed. Suhayl Zakkār, 12 vols (Damascus, 1988).

Ibn al-Athīr, 'Izz al-Dīn, *Al-Kāmil fī'l-Ta'rīkh*, ed. C. J. Tornberg, 13 vols (Leiden, 1867, repr. Beirut, 1982).

Ibn A'tham, al-Kūfī, Abū Muḥammad, Kitāb al-Futūh, ed. M. A. Khan *et al.*, 8 vols (Hyderabad, 1968–75).

Ibn Ḥawqal, Abū'l-Qāsim, *Kitāb Ṣūrat al-Arḍ*, ed. J. H. Kramers (Leiden, 1939).

Ibn Khayyāṭ, Khalīfa, *Ta'rīkh* , ed. Akram Ḍiyā' al-'Umarī (Beirut, 1977).

Ibn Khurdādhbih, 'Ubayd Allāh b. 'Abd Allāh, *Kitāb al-Masālik wa'l-Mamālik*, ed. M. J. de Goeje (Leiden, 1889).

Ibn Miskawayh, Abū 'Alī Aḥmad b. Muḥammad, *Tajārib al-Umam*, ed. H. F. Amedroz with English trans. by D. S. Margoliouth, *The Experiences of the Nations*, 7 vols (London, 1920–1).

Ibn al-Muqaffa', *Risāla fī 'l-Ṣaḥāba*, ed. C. Pellat (1976).

Ibn Sallām, Abū 'Ubayd al-Qāsim, *Kitāb al-Amwāl*, ed. Muḥammd Khalīl Harās (Beirut, 1988), references are to section nos.

Ibn Ṭayfūr, Aḥmad b. Abī Ṭahir, *Kitāb Baghdād*, ed. H. Keller (Leipzig, 1908) .

al-Iṣfahānī, Abū'l-Faraj, 'Alī b. al-Ḥusayn, *Maqātil al-Ṭālibiyīn*, ed. Aḥmad Ṣaqr (Cairo, 1949).

——*Kitāb al-Aghānī,* ed. Muḥammad Hatim (Cairo, 1963).

al-Iṣtakhrī, Abū Ishāq Ibrāhīm b. Muḥammad, *Kitāb Masālik wa'l-Mamālik*, ed. M. J. de Goeje (Leiden, 1927).

al-Jāḥiẓ, 'Amr b. Baḥr, *Manāqib al-Turk*, in G. van Vloten (ed.), *Tria Opusula Auctore Abu Othman Amr ibn Bahr al-Djahiz Basrensi* (Leiden, 1903, repr. Leiden, 1968), 1–56.

——*Al-Bayān wa'l-Tabyīn* (Cairo, 1926–7).

al-Jahshiyārī, Muḥammad b. 'Abdūs, *Kitāb al-Wuzarā*, eds M. al-Saqqā *et al.* (Cairo, 1938).

al-Kalbī, Hishām b. Muḥammad, *Jamharat al-Nasab*: *see* W. Caskel in secondary sources, p. 214.

al-Khaṭib al-Baghdādī, *Ta'rikh Baghdad*, 14 vols (Cairo, 1931).

al-Kindī, Muḥammad b. Yusūf, *Kitāb al-Wulāt*, ed. R. Guest (London, 1912).

al-Kindī, Ya'qūb b. Ishāq, *Al-Suyūf wa Ajnāsiha* , ed. Abd al-Rahman Zaki, *Bulletin of the Faculty of Arts, Cairo*, vol 14 (1952), Arabic section, 1–36.

al-Mas'ūdī, 'Alī b. al-Ḥusayn, *Murūj al-Dhahab*, ed. C. Pellat, 7 vols (Beirut, 1966–79).

——*al-Tanbīh wa'l-Ishrāf* (Beirut, 1981).

Michael the Syrian, *Chronicle*, ed. with French trans., J.-B. Chabot, 4 vols (Paris, 1899–1924).

al-Minqarī, Naṣr b. Muzāḥim, *Waq'at Ṣiffīn*, ed. 'Abd al-Sallām Muḥammad Hārūn (Beirut, 1990).

al-Mubarrad, *Kāmil*, ed. W. Wright (Leipzig, 1886).

al-Nadīm, Muḥammad b. Isḥāq, *Fihrist*, ed. G. Flügel (Leipzig, 1871–2), references are to trans. B. Dodge, *The Fihrist of al-Nadīm*, 2 vols (New York, 1970).

Narshakhī, Muḥammad b. Ja'far, *History of Bukhara* trans. R. Frye (Cambridge, Mass., 1954).

Palmer, A., *The Seventh Century in West-Syrian Chronicles* (Liverpool, 1993).

Qudāma b. Ja'far, *al-Kharāj wa Ṣinā'at al-Kitāba*, ed. Muḥammad Ḥusayn al-Zubaydī (Baghdad, 1981).

——*Kitāb al-Kharāj*, partial trans. with commentary, A. Ben Shemesh (Leiden and London, 1965).

Sebeos, *The Armenian History Attributed to Sebeos*, trans. R. W. Thomson with historical commentary by J. Howard-Johnston with T. Greenwood, 2 vols (Liverpool, 1999).

al-Ṣūlī, Abū Bakr Muḥammad b. Yaḥyā, *Kitāb al-Awrāq*, ed. A. Khalidov (St Petersburg, 1998).

Ṭa.: al-Ṭabarī, Muḥammad b. Jarīr, *Ta'rīkh al-Rusul wa'l-Mulūk*, eds M. J. de Goeje *et al.*, 3 vols (Leiden, 1879–1901); English trans., ed. E. Yarshater, 38 vols (Albany, 1985–2000). References are always to the pagination of the Leiden edition which can be found in the margins of the translation.

Theophanes Confessor, *Chronicle*, trans. and commentary, C. Mango and R. Scott (Oxford, 1997).

Yaḥyā b. Ādam, *Kitāb al-Kharāj*, trans. and commentary, A. Ben Shemesh (Leiden, 1967).

Ya'q., *Buldān*: al-Ya'qūbī, Aḥmad b. Abī Ya'qūb, *Kitāb al-Buldān*, ed. M. J. de Goeje (Leiden, 1892).

Ya'q., *Ta'rīkh*: al-Ya'qūbī, Aḥmad b. Abī Ya'qūb, *Ta'rīkh*, ed. M. Houtsma, 2 vols (Leiden, 1883).

Yāqūt, Ya'qūb b. 'Abd Allāh, *Mu'jam al-Buldān*, ed. F. Wüstenfeld (Leipzig, 1886), references are given to name of place sn. (sub nomine).

Abū Yūsuf Ya'qūb b. Ibrāhīm al-Anṣārī, *Kitab al-Kharāj*, trans. A. Ben Shemesh (Leiden and London, 1969) .

Zuqnin Chronicle: *Chronique de Denys de Tell-Mahré*, French trans. J-B. Chabot (Paris, 1895).

Secondary sources

Abbott, N., *The Kurrah Papyri from Aphrodito in the Oriental Institute* (Chicago, 1938).

Agha S. S., 'The Arab Population in Hurāsān during the Umayyad Period', *Arabica*, 46 (1999), 211–29.

Allan, J. W., *Persian Metal Technology 700–1300 AD* (London, 1979).

Amabe, F., *The Emergence of the 'Abbāsid Autocracy: The 'Abbāsid Army in Khurāsān and Adharbayjān* (Kyoto, 1995).

Arazi, A. and El'ad, A., 'Epître a l'armée', i, *Studia Islamica*, 66 (1987), 27–70 and ii, *Studia Islamica*, 67 (1988), 29–73.

Ashtor, E., *Histoire des prix et salaires dans orient médiéval* (Paris, 1969).

Athāmina, K., 'A'rāb and Muhājirūn in the Environment of Amṣār', *Studia Islamica*, 66 (1987), 5–25.

—— 'Non-Arab Regiments and Private Militias during the Umayyad Period', *Arabica*, 45 (1998), 347–75.

Ayalon, D., 'Preliminary Remarks on the Mamlūk Institution in Islam', in V. J. Parry and M. E. Yapp (eds), *War, Technology, and Society in the Middle East* (Oxford, 1975), 44–58.

—— 'On the Eunuchs in Islam', *JSAI*, 1 (1979), 67–124 , repr. in D. Ayalon, *Outsiders in Islam: Mamluks, Mongols and Eunuchs* (London, 1988), iii.

—— 'The Military Reforms of al-Mu'taṣim', in D. Ayalon (ed.), *Islam and the Abode of War* (Aldershot, 1994), 1–39.

Barthold, W. W., *Turkestan Down to the Mongol Invasion* (London, 1968).

Bates, M., 'History, Geography and Numismatics in the First Century of Islamic Coinage', *Revue Suisse de Numismatique*, 65 (1986), 231–62.

—— 'The Dirham Mint of the Northern Provinces of the Umayyad Caliphate', *Armenian Numismatic Journal*, Series 1, 15 (1989), 89–111.

—— 'Commentaire sur l'étude de Cécille Morrison', in P. Canivet and J.-P. Rey-Coquais (eds), *La Syrie de Byzance a l'Islam* (Damascus, 1992), 3191–21.

—— 'Byzantine Coinage and its Imitations, Arab Coinage and its Imitations: Arab–Byzantine Coinage', *Aram*, 6 (1994), 381–403.

Beckwith, C. I., 'Aspects of the Early History of the Central Asian Guard Corps in Islam', *Archivum Eurasiae Medii Aevi*, 4 (1984), 29–43.

Bivar, A. H. D., 'Cavalry Equipment and Tactics on the Euphrates Frontier', *Dumbarton Oaks Papers*, 26 (1972), 271–91.

Bligh-Abramski, I., 'Evolution versus Revolution: Umayyad Elements in the 'Abbasid Regime 133/750–320/932', *Der Islam*, 65 (1988), 226–43.

Bonner, M., 'Some Observations Concerning the Early Development of jihād on the Arab–Byzantine Frontier', *Studia Islamica*, 75 (1992), 5–31.

—— 'The Naming of the Frontier: 'Awāṣim, Thughūr and the Arab Geographers', *BSOAS*, 57 (1994), 17–24.

——*Aristocratic Violence and Holy War* (New Haven, 1996).

Bosworth, C. E., *Sistan under the Arabs* (Rome, 1968).

—— 'Ubaidallāh b. Abī Bakra and the "Army of Destruction"' in Zābulistān (79/698)', *Der Islam*, 50 (1973), 268–83.

—— 'Recruitment, Muster and Review in Medieval Islamic Armies', in V. J. Parry and M. E. Yapp (eds), *War, Technology, and Society in the Middle East* (Oxford, 1975).

—— 'The City of Tarsus and the Arab–Byzantine Frontier in Early and Middle 'Abbasid Times' *Oriens*, 33 (1992), 268–86.

Bowen, H., *The Life and Times of Ali b. Isa, the Good Vizier* (Cambridge, 1928).

Brooks, E. W., 'Byzantium and the Arabs in the Time of the Early 'Abbasids', *English Historical Review*, 15 (1900), 728–47 and 16 (1901), 84–92.

Bulliet, R., *The Camel and the Wheel* (Cambridge, Mass., 1975).

Busse, H., 'Das Hofbudget des Chalifen al-Mu'taḍid billāh (278/892–289/902)', *Der Islam*, 43 (1967), 11–36.

Butler, A. J., *The Arab Conquest of Egypt*, 2nd edn, ed. P. M. Fraser (Oxford, 1978).

Cahen, C., 'L'évolution de l'iqta' du IXe au XIII siècle', *Annales: Economies, Sociétés, Civilisations'*, 8 (1953), 25–52.

—— 'Les changements technique militaires dans le Proche Orient mediéval et leur importance historique', in V. J. Parry and M. E. Yapp (eds), *War, Technology, and Society in the Middle East* (Oxford, 1975), 113–24.

—— 'Fiscalité, propriété, antagonismes sociaux en haute Mesopotamie au temps des premiers 'Abbāsides', *Arabica*, 1 (1954), 136–52.

Caskel, W., *Gamharat an-Nasab: Das genealogische Werk des Hisām ibn Muḥammad al-Kalbī*, 2 vols (Leiden, 1966): references are either to the tables, taf (*Tafeln*) in vol. 1 or the Register, sn (sub nomine) in vol. 2.

Chevedden, P. E., 'The Artillery of King James the Conqueror', in P. E. Chevedden *et al.* (eds), *Iberia and the Mediterranean World of the Middle Ages* (Leiden, 1996), 47–94.

—— 'The Hybrid Trebuchet', in D. Kagay and T. Vann, (eds), *On the Social Origins of Mediaeval Institutions* (Leiden, 1998), 179–200.

Cobb, P., 'Al-Mutawwakil's Damascus: A New 'Abbāsid Capital?', *JNES*, 58 (1999), 241–57.

Cole, D. P., *Nomads of the Nomads: the Āl Murrah Bedouin of the Empty Quarter* (Chicago, 1975).

Conrad, L. I., 'Seven and the *tasbī'*: On the Implications of a Numerical Symbolism for the Study of Medieval Islamic History', *JESHO*, 31 (1988), 42–73.

—— 'The Conquest of Arwād: A Source Critical Study in the Historiography of the Medieval Near East', *LAEI*, i (1992), 317–401.

—— 'Notes on al-Ṭabarī's History', *JRAS*, Series 3, 3 (1993), 1–31 .

Creswell, K. A. C., *Early Muslim Architecture*, 2 vols (Oxford, 1932–40).

——'Fortification in Islam before 1250', *Proceedings of the British Academy* (1952), 89–125.
——*A Short Account of Early Muslim Architecture* (revised and supplemented by J. W. Allan) (London, 1989).
Crone, P., *Slaves on Horseback* (Cambridge, 1980).
——*Meccan Trade and the Rise of Islam* (Princeton, 1987).
——'Were the Qays and Yemen of the Umayyad Period Political Parties?', *Der Islam*, 71 (1994), 1–57.
——'A Note on Muqātil b. Ḥayyān and Muqātil b. Sulaymān', *Der Islam*, 74 (1997), 238–49.
——'The 'Abbāsid Abnā' and Sāsānid Cavalrymen', *JRAS* (1998), 1–19.
Crone, P. and Cook, M., *Hagarism: The Making of the Islamic World* (Cambridge, 1977).
Daniel, E. L., *The Political and Social History of Khurasan under 'Abbasid Rule, 747–82* (Minneapolis and Chicago, 1979).
——'The 'Ahl al-Taqādum' and the Problem of the Constituency of the 'Abbasid Revolution in the Merv Oasis', *Journal of Islamic Studies*, 7 (1996), 150–79.
——'Persians and the Advent of the 'Abbasids Reconsidered', *JAOS*, 117 (1997), 542–8.
Dennett, D. C., *Conversion and Poll-Tax in Early Islam* (Cambridge, Mass., 1950).
DeShazo, A. S. and Bates, M., 'The Umayyad Governors of al-'Irāq and the Changing Annulet Patterns on their Dirhams', *Numismatic Chronicle*, VII Series, 14 (1974), 110–18.
Dixon, A. A., *The Umayyad Caliphate 65–86/684–705* (London, 1971).
Djait, H., *Al-Kūfa: naissance de la ville islamique* (Paris, 1982).
Donner, F. M., *The Early Islamic Conquests* (Princeton, 1981).
——'The Formation of the Islamic State', *JAOS*, 106 (1986), 284–96.
——'The Growth of Military Institutions in the Early Caliphate and their Relation to Civilian Authority', *Al-Qantara*, xiv (1991), 311–26.
——'Centralized Authority and Military Autonomy in the Early Muslim Conquests', *LAEI*, iii (1995), 337–60.
——*Narratives of Islamic Origins: The Beginnings of Islamic Historical Writing* (Princeton, 1998).
Dozy, R., *Supplément aux Dictionnaires Arabes*, 2 vols (Leiden and Paris, 1967).
Durī, A. A., ' The Origins of *iqta'* in Islam', *Al-Abhath*, 22 (1969), 3–22.
——*The Rise of Historical Writing Among the Arabs*, trans., L. I. Conrad (Princeton, 1983).
Edwards, R. W., *The Fortifications of Cilician Armenia* (Dumbarton Oaks, 1987).
El'ad, A., 'Aspects of the Transition from the Umayyad to the 'Abbāsid Caliphate', *JSAI*, 19 (1995), 89–132.
Elgood, R. (ed.) , *Islamic Arms and Armour* (London, 1979).
Esin, E., 'Ṭabarī's Report on the Warfare with the Türgis and the Testimony of Eighth Century Central Asian Art', *Central Asiatic Journal*, 17 (1973), 130–49.
——'The Cultural Background of Afsin Haidar of Usrusana in the Light of Recent Numismatic and Iconographic Data', in A. Dietrich (ed.), *Akten des VII Kongresses für Arabistik und Islamwissenschaft* (Göttingen, 1976), 126–45.
Foote, R., 'Frescoes and Carved Ivory from the 'Abbasid Family Homestead at al-Humeima', *Journal of Roman Archaeology*, 12 (1999), 423–30.
Fries, N., *Das Heereswesen der Araber zur Zeit der Omaijaden nach Ṭabarī* (Tübingen, 1921).

Frye R. N. and Sayili, A. M., 'Turks in the Middle East before the Saljuqs', *JAOS*, 63 (1943), 194–207.

Gibb, H. A. R., *The Arab Conquests in Central Asia* (London, 1923).

Gordon, M., 'The Turkish Officers of Samarra: Revenue and the Exercise of Authority', *JESHO*, 42 (1999), 466–93.

——*The Breaking of a Thousand Swords: A History of the Turkish Community of Samarra, 200–275 AH/815–889 CE* (Albany, 2001).

Gough, M., 'Anavarza', *Anatolian Studies*, 2 (1952), 85–120.

Grabar, O., *City in the Desert*, 2 vols (Cambridge, Mass., 1978).

Haldon, J. F., *Byzantium in the Seventh Century* (Cambridge, 1990), 63–4.

——'The Ajnād and the "Thematic Myth"', *LAEI*, iii (1995), 379–423.

——*Warfare, State and Society in the Byzantine World, 565–1204* (London, 1999).

Haldon, J. and Kennedy, H., 'The Arab–Byzantine Frontier in the Eighth and Ninth Centuries: Military Organization and Society in the Borderlands', *Zbornik Radova Visantoloskog Instituta* (Belgrade), 19 (1980), 79–116.

Halm, H., *The Empire of the Mahdī* (Leiden, 1996).

Hasson, I., 'Les *mawālī* dans l'armée musulmane sous les premiers Umayyādes', *JSAI*, 14 (1991), 176–213.

Hawting, G. R., *The First Dynasty of Islam* (London, 1986).

Heidemann, S., 'The Merger of Two Currency Zones in Early Islam. The Byzantine and Sasanian Impact on the Circulation in Former Byzantine Syria and Northern Mesopotamia', *Iran*, 36 (1998), 95–112.

Hellenkemper, H., *Bürgen der Kreuzritterzeit in der Grafschaft Edessa und im Königreich Kleinarmenien* (Bonn, 1976).

Herrmann, G., *Monuments of Merv: Traditional Buildings of the Karakum* (London, 1999).

Herzfeld, E., *Geschichte der Stadt Samarra* (Hamburg, 1948).

Hill, D. R., 'The Role of the Camel and the Horse in the Early Arab Conquests' in V. J. Parry and M. E. Yapp (eds), *War, Technology, and Society in the Middle East* (Oxford, 1975), 32–43.

Hillenbrand, R., *Islamic Architecture* (Edinburgh, 1994).

——''Anjar and Early Islamic Urbanism' in G. P. Brogiolo and B. Ward-Perkins (eds), *The Idea and Ideal of the Town between Late Antiquity and the Early Middle Ages* (Leiden, 1999), 59–98.

Hinds, G. M., 'Kūfan Political Alignments and their Background in the Mid-Seventh Century AD', *IJMES*, 2 (1971a), 346–67, repr. in Hinds, *Studies in Early Islamic History*, ed. G. R. Hawting (Princeton, 1996) (hereafter, '*Studies*'), 1–28.

——'The Banners and Battle Cries of the Arabs at Ṣiffīn (AD 657)', *Al-Abhath*, 24 (1971b), 3–42, repr. in Hinds, *Studies*, 97–142.

——'The Murder of the Caliph 'Uthmān', *IJMES*, 3 (1972a), 450–69, repr. in Hinds, *Studies*, 29–55.

——'The Ṣiffīn Arbitration Agreement', *JSS*, 17 (1972b), 93–129, repr. in Hinds, *Studies*, 56–96.

——'The First Arab Conquests in Fārs', *Iran*, 22 (1984), 39–53, repr. in Hinds, *Studies*, 199–231.

——*Studies in Early Islamic History*, ed. G. R. Hawting (Princeton, 1996).

Hoenerbach, W., 'Zur Heereswerwaltung der 'Abbāsiden', *Der Islam*, 29 (1950), 257–90.

Hoyland, R., *Seeing Islam as Others Saw It: A Survey and Evaluation of Christian, Jewish and Zoroastrian Writings* (Princeton, 1997).

Ismail, O. S. A., 'Mutaṣim and the Turks', *BSOAS*, 29 (1966), 11–36.
Jabbur, J. S., *The Bedouins and the Desert*, trans. L. I. Conrad (Albany, 1995).
Jandora, J. W., 'Developments in Islamic Warfare: The Early Conquests', *SI*, 66 (1986), 101–13.
Jones, A. H. M., *The Later Roman Empire 284–602*, 3 vols (Oxford, 1964).
Kaabi, M., 'Les origines ṭāhirides dans la da'wa 'abbāside', *Arabica*, 19 (1972), 145–64.
Kaegi, W. E., 'The Contribution of Archery to the Turkish Conquest of Anatolia', *Speculum*, 39 (1964), 96–108, repr. in W. E. Kaegi, *Army, Society and Religion in Byzantium* (London, 1982a).
——'The First Arab Expedition against Amorium', *Byzantine and Modern Greek Studies*, 3 (1977), 19–22, repr. in W. E. Kaegi, *Army, Society and Religion in Byzantium* (London, 1982b).
——*Byzantium and the Early Islamic Conquests* (Cambridge, 1992).
——'Egypt on the Eve of the Muslim Conquest', in C. F. Petry (ed.), *The Cambridge History of Egypt*, vol. i (Cambridge, 1998), 34–61.
Kennedy, H., 'Central Government and Provincial Elites in the Early 'Abbasid Caliphate', *BSOAS*, 44 (1981a), 26–38 .
——*The Early 'Abbasid Caliphate: A Political History* (London, 1981b).
——*The Prophet and the Age of the Caliphates: The Islamic Near East from the Sixth to the Eleventh Century* (London, 1986).
——*Muslim Spain and Portugal: A Political History of al-Andalus* (London, 1996).
——'Egypt as a Province in the Islamic Caliphate', in C. F. Petry (ed.), *The Cambridge History of Egypt*, vol. i (Cambridge, 1998), 62–85.
——'Medieval Merv: An Historical Overview', in G. Herrmann, *Monuments of Merv: Traditional Buildings of the Karkam* (London, 1999), 27–44.
——'The sources of élite and military incomes in the early Islamic state' in J. Haldon (ed.) *Élites Old and New in the Byzantine and Early Islamic Near East* (Princeton 2001), 12–27.
——'Caliphs and their Chroniclers in the Early 'Abbasid period', in C. Robinson (ed.), *Essays in Honour of D. S. Richards* (forthcoming).
Kennet, D., 'Military Cantonments at Samarra', in C. F. Robinson (ed.), *Multidisciplinary Approaches to Samarra: A Ninth-Century Islamic City* (Oxford, 2000).
al-Khalaf, M., 'Die 'abbāsidische Stadtmauer von ar-Raqqa/ar-Rāfiqa', *Damaszener Mitteilungen*, 2 (1985), 123–31.
Khalidi, T., *Arabic Historical Thought in the Classical Period* (Cambridge, 1994).
Khoury, R., *Chrestomathie de papyrologie arabe* (Leiden, 1993).
Kolias, T., *Byzantinische Waffen* (Vienna, 1988).
Kraemer, C. J., *Excavations at Nessana, vol. 3, Non-Literary Papyri* (Princeton, 1958).
Kubiak, W., *Al-Fusṭāṭ: Its Foundation and Early Urban Development* (Warsaw, 1982, Cairo, 1987).
Lambton, A. K. S., 'Reflections on the Iqta'', in G. Makdisi (ed.), *Arabic and Islamic Studies in Honor of Hamilton A. R. Gibb* (Cambridge, Mass., 1965), 358–76.
Lancaster, W., *The Rwala Bedouin Today* (Cambridge, 1981).
Lane, E. W., *Arabic-English Lexicon* (London, 1886, repr., Cambridge, 1986).
Landau-Tasseron, E., 'Features of the Pre-Conquest Muslim Army in the Time of Muḥammad', *LAEI*, iii (1995), 299–336.
Lassner, J., *The Topography of Baghdad in the Early Middle Ages* (Detroit, 1970).
Le Strange, G., *Lands of the Eastern Caliphate* (London, 1905, repr., 1966).

Lev, Y., *War and Society in the Eastern Mediterranean* (Leiden, 1997).
Lokkegaard, F., *Islamic Taxation in the Classical Period* (Copenhagen, 1953).
MacMullen, R., 'How big was the Roman Imperial Army?', *Klio*, 62 (1980), 462–88.
Margoliouth, D. S., *Catalogue of Arabic Papyri in the John Rylands Library* (Manchester, 1933).
Masia, K., 'The Evolution of Swords and Daggers in the Sasanian Empire', *Iranica Antiqua*, 35 (2000), 185–289.
Matheson, S., *Persia: An Archaeological Guide* (London, 1972).
Meinecke, M., *Patterns of Stylistic Changes in Islamic Architecture* (New York, 1996), 5–30.
Melikian-Chirvani, A. S., 'Notes sur la terminologie de la métallurgie et des armes dans l'Iran musulman', *JESHO*, 24 (1981), 310–16.
Morimoto, K., *The Fiscal Administration of Egypt in the Early Islamic Period* (Dohosa, 1981).
——'The Dīwāns as Registers of the Arabic Stipendiaries in Early Islamic Egypt', in R. Curiel and R. Gyselen (eds), *Itinéraires d'Orient: Hommages à Claude Cahen* (Bures-sur-Yvette, 1994), 353–65.
Morony, M., *Iraq after the Muslim Conquest* (Princeton, 1984).
Morrisson, C., 'Le monnayage omayyade et l'histoire administrative et économique de la Syrie', in P. Canivet and J.-P. Rey-Coquais (eds), *La Syrie de Byzance a l'Islam* (Damascus, 1992), 309–17.
Murphey, R., *Ottoman Warfare, 1500–1700* (London, 1999).
Musil, A., *Palmyrena* (New York, 1928a).
——*The Manners and Customs of the Rwala Bedouin* (New York, 1928b).
Negmatov, N. N., *Srednevekovyi Shakhristan* (Dushanbe, 1966).
——'O Zhipovisi Dvortsa Afshinov Ustrushani (De la Peinture du Palais Royal d'Oustrouchana; Communication Preliminaire)', *Sovetskaya Arkeologiya,* 1973, 183–202.
Nicolle, D., 'Arms and Warfare in Classical Islam', in R. Elgood (ed.), *Islamic Arms and Armour* (London, 1979), 162–86.
——*The armies of Islam 7th–11th Centuries* (London, 1982).
——*Armies of the Muslim Conquest* (London, 1993).
——'Arms of the Umayyad Era', in Y. Lev (ed.), *War and Society in the Eastern Mediterranean* (Leiden, 1997), 9–100.
Northedge, A., *Samarra: Residenz der 'Abbāsidenkalifen* (Tübingen, 1990).
——*Studies on Roman and Islamic 'Amman* (Oxford, 1992).
Northedge, A. and Falkner R., 'The 1986 Survey Season at Samarra', *Iraq*, 49 (1987), 143–73.
Noth, A. and Conrad, L. I., *The Early Arabic Historical Tradition: A Source Critical Study*, trans. M. Bonner (Princeton, 1994).
Overlaet, B. J., 'Contribution to Sasanian Armament in Connection with a Decorated Helmet', *Iranica Antiqua*, 17 (1982), 189–206.
Overlaet, B. J. (ed.), *Hofkunst van de Sassanieden* (Brussels, 1993).
Palmer, A., *The Seventh Century in West-Syrian Chronicles* (Liverpool, 1993).
Petersen, E. L., *'Alī and Mu'āwiya in the Early Arabic Tradition* (Copenhagen, 1964).
Petry, C. F. (ed.) *The Cambridge History of Egypt*, vol. i (Cambridge, 1998).
Pipes, D., *Slave Soldiers and Islam: The Genesis of a Military System* (New Haven, 1981).
Popovic, A., *La révolte des esclaves en Iraq au IIIe/IXe siècle* (Paris, 1976).

Pourshariati, P., 'Local Histories of Khurāsān and the Pattern of Arab Settlement', *Studia Iranica*, 27 (1998), 41–81.

Puin, G.-R., *Der Dīwān von 'Umar Ibn al-Haṭṭāb* (Bonn, 1970).

Raghib, Y., 'La fabrication des lames damassées en Orient', *JESHO*, 40 (1997), 30–70.

Robinson, C. F., 'The Conquest of Khuzistan: A Historiographical Reassessment', in L. I. Conrad. (ed.), *History and Historiography in Early Islamic Times* (Princeton, 1998), 1–44.

Rogers, J. M., 'Samarra, A Study in Medieval Town-Planning' in A. Hourani and S. M. Stern (eds), *The Islamic City* (Oxford, 1970).

Rotter, G., *Die Umayyaden und der zweite Bürgerkrieg* (Wiesbaden, 1982).

Sayed, R., *Die revolte des Ibn al-Asat und die Koranleser* (Freiburg, 1977).

Schlumberger, D., *Qasr El-Heir El Gharbi* (Paris, 1986).

Schmidt, E. F., *Flights over the Ancient Cities of Iran* (Chicago, 1940).

Schwarzlose, F. W., *Die Waffen der alten Araber aus ihren Dichtern dargestellt* (Leipzig, 1886, repr. New York, 1982).

Sezgin, U., *Abū Mihnaf... ein betrag zu Historiographie der umaiyadischen Zeit* (Leiden, 1971).

Shaban, M. A., *'Abbasid Revolution* (Cambridge, 1970).

——*Islamic History,* AD *600–750*, vol. i (Cambridge, 1971).

——*Islamic History: A New Interpretation*, vol. ii (Cambridge, 1976).

Sharon, M., *Black Banners from the East* (Jerusalem, 1983).

——'The Military Reforms of Abu Muslim', in M. Sharon (ed.), *Studies in Islamic Civilisation in Honour of Professor David Ayalon* (Jerusalem, 1986), 105–44.

——*The Social and Military Aspects of the 'Abbasid Revolution* (Jerusalem, 1990).

Shatzmiller, M., 'The Crusades and Islamic Warfare – A Re-Evaluation', *Der Islam*, 69 (1992), 247–88.

Silvi Antonini, C., 'The Painting in the Palace of Afrosiyab (Samarkand)', *Rivista degli Studi Orientali*, 63 (1989).

Simonsen, J. K., *Studies in the Genesis and Development of the Early Caliphal Taxation System* (Copenhagen, 1988).

Sinclair, T. A., *Eastern Turkey: An Architectural and Archaeological Survey*, 4 vols, (London, 1987–90).

Sourdel, D., *Le Vizirat 'Abbāside*, 2 vols, (Damascus, 1959–60).

Southern, P. and Dixon, K. R., *The Late Roman Army* (London, 1996).

Taha, A. D., *The Muslim Conquest and Settlement of North Africa and Spain* (London, 1989).

Thackston, W. H. (trans.), *The Baburnama* (Oxford, 1996).

Töllner, E., *Die türkischen Garden am Kalifenhof von Samarra, ihre Entstehung und Machtergreifung bis zum Kalifat al-Mu'taḍids* (Bonn, 1971).

Treadgold, W. T., *The Byzantine Revival* (Stanford, 1988).

——*Byzantium and its Army* (Stanford, 1995).

Ullmann, M., *Worterbuch der klassischen arabischen Sprache* (Wiesbaden, 1957).

Urice, S. K., *Qasr Kharana in the Transjordan* (Durham, 1987).

Vasiliev, A. A., *Byzance et les Arabes*, 2 vols (Brussels, 1950–68).

Vogliano , A. (ed.), *Papiri della R. Università di Milano*, vol. i (Milan, 1937).

Walker, J., *A Catalogue of the Muḥammadan Coins in the British Museum*, vol. i, *The Arab–Sassanian Coins* (London, 1941), vol. ii, *The Arab–Byzantine and Post-Reform Umaiyad Coins* (London, 1956).

Wellhausen, J., *The Arab Kingdom and its Fall*, trans. M. Wier (Calcutta, 1927, repr., Beirut, 1963).

Whitby, M., 'Recruitment in Roman Armies from Justinian to Heraclius (*ca*. 565–615)', *LAEI*, iii, 61–124.

White, L., *Medieval Technology and Social Change* (Oxford, 1962).

Whittow, M., *The Making of Orthodox Byzantium, 600–1025* (London, 1996).

Wood, J., 'The Fortifications', in A. Northedge, *Studies on Roman and Islamic 'Amman* (Oxford, 1992), 105–27.

Zakeri, M., *Sasanid Soldiers in Early Muslim Society: The Origins of 'Ayyaran and Futuwwa* (Wiesbaden, 1995).

Zaky, A. R., 'Medieval Arab Arms', in. R. Elgood (ed.), *Islamic Arms and Armour* (London, 1979), 202–12.

Index